About the author

Matthew Hugh Erdelyi is professor of psychology at Brooklyn College and the Graduate Center of the City University of New York. He began
his researches on psychoanalysis and cognitive
psychology at Yale University, where he received
his Ph.D., and has since published numerous
theoretical and experimental articles on defense
processes, subliminal perception, and hypermnesia, the recovery of unconscious memories. He is also Research Scholar at the Unit
for Experimental Psychiatry of the Institute of
the Pennsylvania Hospital and the University
of Pennsylvania.

PSYCHOANALYSIS

A Series of Books in Psychology

Editors

Richard C. Atkinson
Gardner Lindzey
Richard F. Thompson

PSYCHOANALYSIS:
Freud's Cognitive Psychology

♦

Matthew Hugh Erdelyi

*Brooklyn College, City University of New York
and Unit for Experimental Psychiatry of the Institute of
Pennsylvania Hospital and University of Pennsylvania*

W. H. FREEMAN AND COMPANY
New York

The following publishers have given permission to use extended quotations from copyrighted works: From *The Discovery of the UnConscious* by Henri F. Ellenberger. © 1970 by Henri F. Ellenberger. Reprinted by the permission of Basic Books, Inc., Publishers. From *Studies on Hysteria* by Josef Breuer and Sigmund Freud, translated from the German and edited by James Strachey, published in the United States by Basic Books, Inc., New York by arrangement with The Hogarth Press, Ltd., London. From *Collected Papers,* Volumes 3, 4, and 5 by Sigmund Freud. © 1959 by Basic Books, Inc., Publishers. Reprinted by the permission of the publisher. From *The Psychopathology of Everyday Life,* Volume 6 by Sigmund Freud. Reprinted with the permission of Ernest Benn Ltd., London. From *The Standard Edition of the Complete Psychological Works of Sigmund Freud,* translated and edited by James Strachey. Reprinted by the permission of the Sigmund Freud Copyrights Ltd., The Institute of Psycho-Analysis, Ltd., and The Hogarth Press, Ltd. From *A General Introduction to Psychoanalysis* by Sigmund Freud, translated by J. Riviere. Reprinted by the permission of Sigmund Freud Copyrights Ltd.

Library of Congress Cataloging in Publication Data

Erdelyi, Matthew.
   Psychoanalysis: Freud's cognitive psychology.

   (A Series of books in psychology)
   Bibliography: p.
   Includes index.
   1. Psychoanalysis. 2. Psychotherapy. 3. Freud,
Sigmund, 1856–1939. I. Title. II. Series.
BF173.E646 1984   150.19'52   84-6056
ISBN 0-7167-1616-X
ISBN 0-7167-1617-8 (pbk.)

Printed in the United States of America
1 2 3 4 5 6 7 8 9 0   MP   3 2 1 0 8 9 8 7 6 5

MIKLÓSNAK

and to my living parents

VERONICA FÖLDES FRAME AND JOHN D. FRAME

CONTENTS

PREFACE

Despite perennial tensions and misunderstandings, there has existed a long tradition within both academic experimental psychology and psychoanalysis to find common ground and build toward integration. It is one of the paradoxes of the history of psychology that this integrative impulse reached its high point during a period when it could not possibly succeed and waned abruptly at the very juncture when it could no longer fail.

Whatever the reason, it is a fact that the bridge-building efforts between experimental psychology and psychoanalysis flourished during the era of behaviorism, when psychology was wedded to a scientific world view that in both substance and style was as antithetical to psychoanalysis as one could imagine. To behaviorism, the basic reality (and, therefore, subject matter) of psychology was surface phenomena, behaviors and stimuli that were palpably manifest and, therefore, "publicly observable"; to psychoanalysis, psychological phenomena were semantically multilayered, and it was not their brute, *manifest* features but their *latent* (deep) contents that constituted psychology's essential subject matter. Behaviorism eschewed theoretical models; psychoanalysis produced them in unchecked luxuriance. Behaviorism excluded consciousness from its purview; psychoanalysis made consciousness its therapeutic goal. Unconscious processes played no role in classic behaviorism; unconscious processes were the "fundamental premise" of psychoanalysis. Nevertheless, integrative efforts were pursued within both camps for several decades, reaching their culminating point in 1950 with Dollard and Miller's remarkable transposition of psychoanalytic concepts into neobehavioristic terms, *Personality and Psychotherapy*.

Although the book was a work of brilliance, the psychoanalytic ideas that Dollard and Miller addressed were—of necessity—circumscribed. For example, the "twilight phenomena" that are such an integral focus of psychoanalysis (and of the present book)—dreams, fantasy, art, jokes, psychotic thinking, religion—were by and large not dealt with, or only superficially. Then, also, the "neobehaviorism" of Dollard and Miller was already a far cry from classic behaviorism, constituting, terminology aside, an inchoate cognitivism, teeming with hypothetical mental entities and processes which it had been the objective—indeed, the *raison d'etre*—of behaviorism to circumvent. The work, in any event, was soon overtaken by an upheaval within experimental psychology which saw, in the 1960s, the collapse of behaviorism and the triumph of the "cognitive revolution." Psychoanalysis had been translated into a dying language.

Yet, the prospects for the integration of psychoanalysis and experimental psychology seemed brighter than ever. The cognitive psychology that was emerging from the dual soils of generative linguistics and information science shared not only the epistemological assumptions of psychoanalysis—as against behaviorism—but also many of its substantive concerns. The notion that manifest phenomena were the surface realization of transformations of deep, inaccessible structures was a cornerstone of Freud's work of 1900, *The Interpretation of Dreams*. The distinction between conscious and unconscious mentation—which made its appearance in psychology under a variety of guises—had already, in 1895, become the guiding premise of Breuer and Freud's *Studies on Hysteria*. The issue of mental representations, especially of the psychological significance of the differences between imagistic and verbal codes was another key topic delved into in the *Studies*, as was the issue of physiognomic codes (body language and memory). The question of the organization and structure of memory, and the problem of the recovery of inaccessible memories (hypermnesia), either in spontaneous dreamlike states and symptoms, or through hypnosis and other therapeutic techniques, were all key themes of the *Studies*. Similarly, the questions of attention, selectivity, capacity limits, the function and multiplicity of memory buffers, and even of flow-diagram models of information processing, were all central concerns of *The Interpretation of Dreams*.

The significance of these facts did not dawn upon me until my reading of Ulric Neisser's *Cognitive Psychology*, in the late 1960s. The cognitive revolution, it suddenly became clear (to me), had started in 1895 with the *Studies on Hysteria*. Psychology was coming full circle. Two vast continents had drifted in darkness and had suddenly touched.

But it is one thing to share a continent and another to know your neighbor. The psychologists creating the cognitive revolution, with only a few notable exceptions such as Neisser, knew little of psychoanalysis, and the second cognitive revolution developed in isolation from the first. Still, with the shift of focus toward increasingly complex stimuli (pictures, sentences, narrative texts), the trend of the modern cognitive psychology has been toward rather than away from psychoanalysis' center of gravity. Some of the signs: the semantization of psycholinguistics; the attendant emphasis of deep semantic contents ("information processing between the lines," "pragmatics") and, therefore, upon the unavoidability of interpretation; the triumph of constructivism; the contextualization of cognition; the formal incorporation, through mathematical decision theory, of motivation in the conception of perceptual and memory reports; the new focus upon irrational thinking and decision making; the mushrooming interest in metaphor; and, not the least, the immense new research interest in unconscious processes. Finally, and of tremendous significance for this history, clinical psychology, which had been lingering in its own behaviorist phase, has shown unmistakable signs of undergoing its cognitive transformation. The clinical psychology of today is closer to psychoanalysis than it was a decade ago and—as I have no doubt the future will bear out—rapidly converging upon it. Psychology, as a whole, seems poised on the brink of rediscovering psychoanalysis—or of reinventing major portions of it.

A long time has passed, however, and a massive forgetting of psychoanalysis has taken place. When, some decades ago, psychologists read psychoanalysis seriously, they did not have the cognitive schemas with which to assimilate it; now that they do, they no longer read psychoanalysis. In general, there is a poor understanding of Freud's thinking, inside and outside of psychology.

I, therefore, set out, some seven years ago, to reintroduce psychoanalysis to psychologists and students of psychology (in the broad sense of both terms). The present book is the result. The work is a modern exegesis of psychoanalysis that brings it into play with developments in psychology and the neurosciences since Freud. No comparable scientific exposition of psychoanalysis has appeared since Dollard and Miller's *Personality and Psychotherapy* some thirty-five years ago. The book covers the entire sweep of Freud's cognitive psychology—and, therefore, virtually all of psychoanalysis. The one major topic not dealt with systematically, by virtue of its falling outside the domain of cognition, is Freud's theory of psychosexual development; though by this is not meant the exclusion of the drives—especially of sex and aggression—but, rather, Freud's formal theory of their nature and development. As even the most casual reader will gather, the pervasive intrusiveness of passion—of sex, aggression, fear—into the functioning of thought is one of the bedrock themes of this book. Indeed, psychoanalysis' psychodynamic perspective, which stresses the ultimate inseparability of motives and thought in real-life contexts, and, thus, a conception of cognition that welds passion and intellect, is one of the fundamental contributions that psychoanalysis has to offer to the laboratory cognitive psychology of today.

Although it is a comprehensive exposition of Freud's psychology, the ultimate thrust of this book is not historical. Scientific psychology is maturing and the era of psychological "schools" is drawing to a rapid close. Psychoanalysis, which Freud emphatically conceived of as a branch of psychology, will not long survive—as it should not—as an independent, dissociated entity. Psychoanalysis needs to become part of modern psychology—as modern psychology needs psychoanalysis to become part of it. My basic purpose in writing this book, therefore, was to present psychoanalysis, at this point of conjunction, in a form that could be clearly understood, related to current experimental and theoretical developments, and selectively assimilated.

Throughout, I have been guided by a rough image, which may be flawed as history of science, but which for me had great power: Contrary to textbook tradition, the nineteenth century gave birth not to one but to two psychologies, one at Leipzig, the other, at Vienna. For a hundred years each struggled to develop into a viable science of mind but each, perversely complementing the other, remained incomplete, fated not to become whole until they became one.

August 31, 1984   Matthew Hugh Erdelyi

ACKNOWLEDGMENTS

I have labored long on this project and have accumulated many debts of gratitude.

I wish to thank my wife, Mireya, for her sustaining support throughout this undertaking. I am especially indebted to her for her willingness, at a time when she too was embarked upon a book and teaching full-time and our children were still very young, to agree to have a weekend husband for a year. Thus it was that while on sabbatical leave from Brooklyn College I sojourned, from Mondays through Fridays, at the Unit for Experimental Psychiatry in Philadelphia, completing a major portion of this work. Without her help and encouragement this book would not have been written. I also thank my daughters, Karina and Maya, who, during this time, have caused me much joy and no regrets.

I owe an immense debt to Martin T. Orne and Emily Carota Orne for inviting me to spend my sabbatical year, 1981–1982, at the Unit for Experimental Psychiatry, The Institute of Pennsylvania Hospital, to work on my book, which my teaching and other academic duties had been frustrating me from completing. At the Unit, I had numerous and valuable interactions with scholars of psychoanalysis, hypnosis, and sleep. I wish especially to acknowledge the contributions of Martin Orne and Emily Orne, David Dinges, David Soskis, Wayne Whitehouse, and Lester Luborsky—and to (the ghost of) Ulric Neisser. (It was a special honor and inspiration to be working on Freud's cognitive psychology at the very place where *Cognitive Psychology* was written.) I must thank the Ornes not only for inviting me to the Unit but also for making it possible for me to accept. This was made possible in part by Grant # MH-19156 from the National Institute of Mental Health and Grant # 2-S07-RR05590 from the National Institutes of Health. I wish also to express my gratitude to the Psychology Department of the University of Pennsylvania for its hospitality during my stay in Philadelphia, and my special thanks for exciting intellectual stimulation to Henry Gleitman, Paul Rozin, John Sabini and Marty Seligman.

I do not know the positive version in English of the expression, "It never rains but it pours." Whatever the words, I had the good fortune of it happening to me. Around the time I was invited to the Unit, I received another invitation, this time to be a Fellow at the Center for Advanced Study in the Behavioral Sciences at Stanford, California, the following year. My only formal duty so far as I could tell, and not even this was contractual, was to have lunch with the other Fellows. This extra year (during which I gained 20 pounds) proved crucial for the book since I needed more time to complete it. The book benefitted immensely from my associations at the Center. I wish to thank Gardner Lindzey, Director of the Center, for his assistance with the manuscript. For the rich and varied contributions of my fellow Fellows I thank especially Alison Clarke-Stewart, Gus Craik, Bob Crowder, Jim Fernandez, Bobby Klatzky, David Leary, Salvador Luria, Ellen Markman, Carol Ryff, Howard Spiro, and Tom Trabasso. I wish also to thank the members of the Stanford Department of Psychology and other visiting scholars for their interest in the project and their many valuable comments; I am especially grateful to Jim Geiwitz, Ernest Hilgard, Len Horowitz, Walter Mischel, Karl Pribram, David Rosenhan, Lee Ross, and Phil Zimbardo. Finally, I wish to thank the librarian of the Center, Margaret Amara, for her extraordinary helpfulness.

My year at the Center was supported in part by the John D. and Catherine T. MacArthur Foundation. I acknowledge this support with gratitude. Also I wish to thank the City University of New York for a Faculty Development Award for this period. Finally, I thank Alvaro and Vivian Perez for their special assistance at a special time.

I have thus far mentioned only my formal comings and goings. I must, however, acknowledge three extraordinarily fruitful summers during which, as a self-imposed visiting scholar, I managed to give shape and substance to the present book. I thank the Department of Psychology of the University of Massachusetts at Amherst for putting me up, on no notice, several summers ago. My thinking was tremendously enriched by my interactions with Jim Averill, Chuck Clifton, Sy Epstein, and Ervin Staub. Likewise, I am grateful to the members of the Harvard Department of Psychology and Social Relations for twice finding room for me in a very full inn. I am particularly indebted to Shep White for his contributions of space, time, and ideas. I also thank Bob Krauss, of the Columbia University Department of Psychology, for intellectual stimulation, and for making the school's library facilities available to me over the past years.

It is especially meaningful for me to acknowledge my indebtedness to two former teachers and advisors at Yale, now also friends, Ralph Haber and Bob Crowder. I thank them for their enduring gifts of knowledge, criticism, and support. I also acknowledge my immense debt to my current teachers—my students—who have suffered through many of my developing ideas and who have helped me incalculably in shaping and formulating my thinking.

A recent visitor at our home informed us that he had written a book. Our worldly eight-year-old, Karina, shot back: "But do you have a publisher?" I am happy to acknowledge that I have a publisher which, in the words of a fellow author, is "a class act." I thank the editors and staff of W. H. Freeman and Company for being that, with special thanks to Buck Rogers, Robin Carter, Heather Wiley, Laura McCormick, and Betsy Feist.

Finally, I wish to thank my colleagues at the Department of Psychology of Brooklyn College for having me, keeping me, and helping me over the past decade. For their direct and indirect contributions to my project, I wish to give special thanks to Issy Abramov, Bob Buckhout, Louise Hainline, Harry Jagoda, the late Ivan London, Neil Macmillan, Gloria Marmor, Ray Montemayor, Arthur Reber, Bernie Seidenberg, Norm Weissberg, and Carl Zuckerman. Also, I wish to thank the President of Brooklyn College, Robert Hess, for his support.

In concluding these acknowledgments, I cannot fail to note that I have had many things for which to be grateful. For this, itself, I am grateful.

CHAPTER ONE

PSYCHOANALYTIC PSYCHOTHERAPY: PREHISTORY AND DEVELOPMENT

◆

NEUROLOGY AND NEUROSIS

When financial necessity finally compelled a reluctant Sigmund Freud to give up a career in scientific research for medical practice, he soon discovered that his background in neuroanatomy had in no way prepared him to deal with the problems of his patients. At the University of Vienna, from which he obtained his medical degree in 1881 at the age of twenty-five and subsequently as a resident at the Vienna General Hospital and director of neurology at the Kussowitz Institute for Children, Freud had pursued extensive researches into a variety of neurological problems. These ranged from such exotic topics as the spinal cord of the primitive fish *Ammocoetes Petromyzon* and the then little-known drug cocaine to such mainstream concerns as cerebral paralyses of children and the neurophysiology of *aphasia* and *agnosia* (Freud's term), respectively, the inability to name or to recognize common objects.

With such a formidable neurological background, it was not surprising that Freud's private practice attracted individuals suffering from a variety of "nervous disorders." These "nervous" people exhibited symptoms that superficially resembled the effects of organic nerve damage, such as paralyses, analgesias, tremors, tics, and memory disorders. Yet, the similarities in symptoms, as well as the designation *nervous,* proved to be deceptive. In almost no case could any organic pathology be found to account for these patients' ailments, which, in any case, more often than not suggested neurological absurdities when they were carefully scrutinized. Thus, for example, a chronically bedridden patient, ostensibly paralyzed in both legs, might be discovered to sleepwalk on occasion. Or another patient, suffering from a paralysis of the left arm, might unexpectedly displace the paralysis to the right arm, regaining full use of the left one. Also, it often could be shown that the boundaries of affected regions corresponded more to psychological than to neurological realities, being "demarcated according to popular ideas of their limits rather than according to anatomical facts" (Freud, 1925b, p. 14). (See, for example, Figure 1.1.) From a strictly neurological standpoint, then, these patients with "bad nerves" were neurological frauds, "nervous" or "neurotic" in name, but not in fact. Indeed, many a physician was inclined to dismiss them as malingerers, undeserving of respect or medical treatment.

Although Freud's attitude was more sympathetic, he was nevertheless confronted with the fact that his neurological expertise was of little relevance in these cases; his formal medical studies had simply not prepared him for dealing with pseudoneurological ailments. In his own words: "There were, at that time, few specialists in that branch of medi-

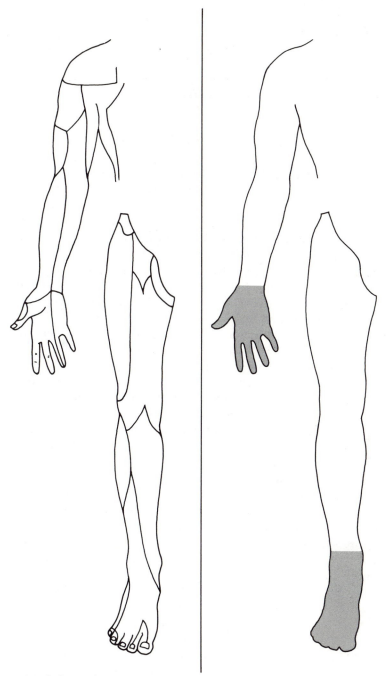

Figure 1.1. *Left panel:* true neurological boundaries (adapted from Gray, 1973, pp. 967 and 988). *Right panel:* two psychological boundaries (hysterical "glove" and "sock" anesthesia).

cine in Vienna, the material for its study was distributed over a number of different departments . . . there was no satisfactory opportunity of learning the subject, and one was forced to be one's own teacher" (Freud, 1925b, p. 11).

But what was there to be learned in those days about the treatment of neurotics? As it turns out, remarkably little.

REST, MASSAGE, BATHS, AND ELECTRICITY

Of the handful of available medical procedures, one of the most popular was, simply, to prescribe a prolonged vacation, preferably at a sanitarium, where the most minute cares of everyday life could be taken over by the staff. While such "rest cures" were by no means ineffective and, in some cases, could even precipitate major psychological changes (see, for example, Thomas Mann's *The Magic Mountain*), no profound medical training was required to dispense such a prescription.

Another class of treatments, which goes back to ancient Greek and Roman times, involved a variety of massage or hot bath (*hydrotherapy*) techniques. These survive today under a number of guises, including steam baths, saunas, mineral springs, and chiropractic. Their curative effects continue to be subjects of controversy.

Still another approach to nervous disorders, extremely popular in its time, was *faradic treatment* or *electrotherapy,* a mild variant of today's still-employed electroconvulsive shock treatment. Although the technique, consisting of the application of low-voltage currents to affected areas, has pretty much vanished from modern clinical practice, versions of it still survive in some isolated regions of the world. For example, this author's first direct exposure to electrotherapy was not in graduate school, but in an outdoor café in a remote village in the Colombian Andes, known by its Indian name, Fusagasuga. A simply clad young man, carrying what may have been at one time a shoe-shine box—now impressively fitted with an array of batteries and with two conspicuous wires protruding from it—went from table to table offering the treatment for a mere 2 pesos (a little less than a dime). He claimed a general benefit for any problems involving "the nerves" and made much of the fact that his cure, based as it was on electricity, was genuinely scientific, unlike the superstitious melange of leeches, herbs, cure-all potions, and religion of the local medicine men. He must have had some past successes for there were many takers, some obviously regular clients.

Freud himself made great efforts to master the techniques of electrotherapy, but in the end was distinctly unimpressed with its effects:

My knowledge of electrotherapy was derived from W. Erb's textbook, which provided detailed instructions for the treatment of all symptoms of nervous diseases. Unluckily I was soon driven to see that following these instructions was of no help whatever and that what I had taken for an epitome of exact observations was merely the construction of phantasy. The realization that the work of the greatest name in German neuropathology had no more relation to reality than some "Egyptian" dream-book, such as is sold in cheap book-shops, was painful, but it helped to rid me of another shred of the innocent faith in authority from which I was not yet free. So I put my electrical apparatus aside, even before Möbius had solved the problem by explaining that the successes of electric treatment in nervous disorders (in so far as there were any) were the effect of suggestion on the part of the physician. (Freud, 1925b, p. 16)

It would appear, then, that late nineteenth-century medical science had little to offer for the treatment of nervous ailments and that what it had was of questionable value. There was, however, one major development around this time that promised a decisive breakthrough. The technique was extremely avant-garde, and only the most up-to-date physicians were conversant with it. To be properly instructed in its use and to learn its range of applications required a training visit to one of France's two leading psychiatric institutes. The technique was hypnosis.

HYPNOSIS AND HYSTERIA

One of the two great centers of research in this area was the Salpêtrière Clinic in Paris headed by Jean Martin Charcot, at that time the world's most renowned figure in neuropathology. While still at the Vienna General Hospital, Freud applied for a traveling fellowship to study Charcot's work. Winning out over fierce competition, he was finally awarded a modest grant and traveled to Paris in the fall of 1885 for a four months' postdoctoral study.

Charcot's major research program at this time concerned the problem of *hysteria* which, because of its past association with superstition and charlatanism—and, it should be added, sex—had been expunged, until Charcot's revival of it, from the roster of scientific medicine. *Hysteria,* a term derived from the Greek word, *hystera,* meaning uterus, had been regarded since the Greeks as an affliction peculiar to women, arising from unsatisfied sexual or maternal cravings. Its manifestations, which should strike a familiar ring, included paralyses, fainting spells, analgesias, and so forth. In *The Timaeus,* Plato explains such affliction in the following manner:

In men the organ of generation—becoming rebellious and masterful, like an animal disobedient to reason, and maddened with the sting of lust—seeks to gain absolute sway; and the same is the case with the ... womb ... of women; the animal within them is desirous of procreating children, and when remaining unfruitful long beyond its proper time, gets discontented and angry, and wandering in every direction through the body, closes up the passages of the breath, and by obstructing respiration, drives them to extremity, causing all varieties of diseases. (P. 514)

Charcot, however, had observed some quite similar symptoms in a class of male patients. At the behest of an insurance company, he had concerned himself with the rehabilitation of railroad workers who had suffered "physical traumas," that is, accidents, in their line of work. He noticed that despite the apparently complete healing of the physical wounds, a configuration of symptoms, resembling those of hysteria, frequently persisted in these male patients. He was thus led to the suspicion that hysteria might not, after all, be exclusive to the domain of female pathology. In a still classic program of demonstrations (which, however, would probably not survive modern methodological standards), he proved his hypothesis by showing that he could induce hysterical symptoms in male subjects by means of hypnotic suggestion.

Beyond the obvious scientific import of these demonstrations, there was a potentially startling therapeutic dimension to this research: If hysterical symptoms could be induced through hypnosis, might they not also be eliminated through the same means? Although Charcot did experiment along these lines, he was severely limited by a theoretical preconception. As a self-conscious scientist, he had forced himself to assume that all these phenomena had to have a specific neurological basis. Thus, the traumatic hysterias (today they would be called traumatic neuroses or post-traumatic stress disorders) reflected, despite all appearances of healing, some permanent neurological impairment. From this followed an implausible physicalist explanation of hypnotically induced hysterias: Hypnosis merely served to activate already latent neurological degeneration caused by past traumas or hereditary defects. Indeed, Charcot assumed that *in order to be hypnotized* one already had to be latently "degenerate." Such a viewpoint, not surprisingly, dampened clinical applications of hypnosis since susceptibility in itself was now seen as a sign of disease.

Such theoretical encumbrances by no means afflicted the other major center of hypnotic research in Nancy, France, headed by Hippolyte Bernheim and Auguste Ambroise Liébeault. To the Nancy school the proper framework for understanding hypnosis was not neurology but psychology. Hypnosis was conceptualized as a state of heightened suggestibility whose effects, while altogether genuine, were psychologically rooted. Contrary to Charcot's views, hypnotizability was not a mark of neurological degeneration but a psychological aptitude more or less shared by the majority of normal people. The focus of the Nancy program was the exploration of the psychological possibilities of hypnosis, particularly its therapeutic potential. From this evolved Liébeault's and Bernheim's hypnotic suggestion technique for curing a wide range of ailments. The procedure was extremely simple. The patient was hypnotized and then instructed that his particular ailment—whether paralyses, headaches, constipation, stuttering, warts, or whatever—would go away. Remarkable cures were often achieved, sometimes in a single session. Interestingly, Bernheim gradually came to realize that he could dispense with the hypnotic part of the treatment and produce equivalent effects just with suggestion (a procedure he termed *psychotherapeutics*). We shall have occasion to return to this curious fact at a later point.

Freud was highly impressed with the Nancy program and made extensive use of the hypnotic suggestion technique for several years. For once he was enthusiastic: ". . . there was something positively seductive in working with hypnotism. For the first time there was a sense of having overcome one's helplessness; and it was highly flattering to enjoy the reputation of being a miracle-worker. It was not until later that I was to discover the drawbacks of the procedure" (Freud, 1925b, p. 17).

For the purpose of perfecting his hypnotic technique, Freud visited the Nancy clinic for a few weeks in 1889. There he had extensive conversations with Bernheim (whose books he agreed to translate into German, just as he had Charcot's a few years earlier). It is doubtful that Freud learned much about hypnotic induction techniques, per se; but he was deeply influenced by some of Bernheim's "astonishing" psychological demonstrations, especially those involving posthypnotic suggestion. In his voluminous writings he was frequently to cite one in particular.

In front of a group of students, Bernheim hypnotized a subject and instructed him as follows: Five minutes after awakening from the trance he was to interrupt whatever he might be doing, walk over to a corner of the room where there lay a folded umbrella, pick up the umbrella, and open it; he was not to remember that he had been thus instructed, but he would nevertheless carry out the command. Sure enough, five minutes after awakening, the subject did exactly as he had been told. When asked by Bernheim why he had acted as he had, the subject replied, bewildered and embarrassed, that he had not the slightest idea.

To Freud, such a demonstration gave experimental weight to the notion that one might not be aware of the true causes of one's own behavior—"that there could be powerful mental processes which nevertheless remained hidden from the consciousness of men" (Freud, 1925b, p. 17).

FREUD'S USE OF HYPNOTIC SUGGESTION THERAPY

One of Freud's earliest psychological articles dealt with hypnotic therapy: "A Case of Successful Treatment by Hypnotism: With Some Remarks on the Origin of Hysterical Symptoms Through 'Counter-Will'" (Freud, 1892–1893). Since it very nicely captures the flavor of the hypnotic suggestion technique and, moreover, advances some ideas that distinctly foreshadow psychoanalytic theory, it is worth excerpting some portions here.

> It was a case . . . of a mother who was unable to feed her newborn baby till hypnotic suggestion intervened, and whose experience with an earlier and a later child provided controls of the therapeutic success such as are seldom obtainable . . . . When the time approached for the birth of her first child of her marriage (which was a happy one) the patient intended to feed the infant herself. . . . Nevertheless, though her bodily build seemed favorable, she did not succeed in feeding the infant satisfactorily. There was a poor flow of milk, pains were brought on when the baby was put to the breast, the mother lost appetite and showed an alarming unwillingness to take nourishment, her nights were agitated and sleepless. At last, after a fortnight . . . the attempt was abandoned and the child was transferred to a wet nurse. Thereupon all the mother's troubles immediately cleared up. (Pp. 117–118)

Three years later another child was born and the mother once again made a determined effort to breast-feed her child. She was even less successful this time. In addition to her past symptoms, she now vomited up whatever little food she was able to take and seemed unable to sleep at all. Freud, who was personally acquainted with the patient, was called in as a last resort:

> I found her lying in bed with flushed cheeks and furious at her inability to feed the baby—an inability which increased at every attempt but against which she struggled with all her strength. In order to avoid the vomiting, she had taken no nourishment the whole day. . . .
> I at once attempted to induce hypnosis by ocular fixation, at the same time making constant suggestions of the symptoms of sleep. After three minutes the patient was lying back with the peaceful expression of a person in profound sleep. I cannot

recollect whether I made any tests for catalepsy and other symptoms of pliancy. I made use of suggestion to contradict all her fears and the feelings on which these fears were based: "Do not be afraid. You will make an excellent nurse and the baby will thrive. Your stomach is perfectly quiet, your appetite is excellent, you are looking forward to your next meal, etc." The patient went on sleeping while I left her for a few minutes, and when I had woken her up, showed amnesia for what had occurred. Before I left the house I was also under the necessity of contradicting a worried remark by the patient's husband to the effect that his wife's nerves might be ruined by hypnosis. (P. 119)

The hypnotic intervention had apparently produced an effect, for that same evening she ate a normal meal and slept peacefully, and the next morning she took breakfast and then successfully breast-fed her baby. However, the cure was short lived. When lunch was brought to her, she vomited at the first sight of the food and could not bring herself to eat anything, nor to breast-feed the child. That evening, Freud subjected her to a second hypnotic session,

... which led to a state of somnambulism as quickly as the first ... I acted with greater energy and confidence. I told the patient that five minutes after my departure she would break out against her family with some acrimony: what had happened to her dinner? did they mean to let her starve? how could she feed the baby if she had nothing to eat herself? and so on.

When I returned on the third evening the patient refused to have any further treatment. There was nothing more wrong with her, she said: she had an excellent appetite and plenty of milk for the baby, there was not the slightest difficulty when it was put to her breast, and so on. Her husband thought it rather queer, however, that after my departure the evening before she had clamoured violently for food and had remonstrated with her mother in a way quite unlike herself. But since then, he added, everything had gone all right.

There was nothing more for me to do. The mother fed her child for eight months; and I had many opportunities of satisfying myself in a friendly way that they were both doing well. I found it hard to understand, however, as well as annoying, that no reference was ever made to my remarkable achievement.

But my time came a year later, when a third child made the same demands on the mother and she was unable to meet them as on the previous occasions. I found the patient in the same condition as the year before and positively embittered against herself because her will could do nothing against her disinclination for food and her other symptoms.... Once again after the second hypnosis the symptoms were so completely cut short that a third was not required. This child too, which is now eighteen months old, was fed without any trouble and has enjoyed uninterrupted good health.

In the face of this renewed success the patient and her husband unbent and admitted the motive that had governed their behavior towards me. "I felt ashamed," the woman said to me, "that a thing like hypnosis should be successful where I myself, with all my will-power, was helpless." Nevertheless, I do not think either she or her husband have overcome their distaste of hypnosis. (Pp. 120–121)

FREUD'S THEORY OF HYPNOSIS AND HYSTERIA: EARLY PSYCHODYNAMICS

What was Freud's theory of the cause of the hysterical symptoms, and how did he account for the success of hypnosis in overcoming them?

Briefly, it was Freud's opinion that such patients suffered from a basic ambivalence (although he did not use the term at this point); essentially they were of two minds. On the one hand the patient *wished* to breast-feed her child, but on the other—without being aware of it—she did *not wish* to. Because awareness of her reluctance would have been painful to her, she "inhibited the antithetic idea" (the reluctance) and "dissociated" it from her conscious train of thought. The antithetic idea, according to Freud, is not thereby abolished (it can often be uncovered in hypnosis, for example); rather it "establishes itself, so to speak, as a *'counter-will,'* while the patient is aware with astonishment of having a will which is resolute but powerless (p. 122)." When the conscious "will" and the unconscious "counter-will" are roughly of equal strength, a kind of protracted internal civil war ensues, in which neither intention is fully satisfied. This conflict takes its toll in the form of hysterical symptoms. The effects can be conceived, as Freud often did, in terms of clashing force vectors, in line with nineteenth-century physics' fascination with dynamics. Thus, as illustrated below, one force is counteracted by a roughly equivalent counterforce, with the effect that each nullifies the other, resulting in either "weakness of will" (a), or "perversion of will" (b).

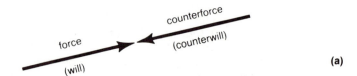

(a)

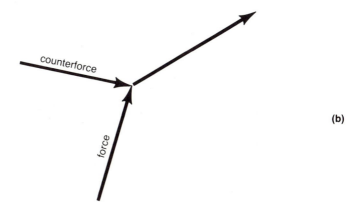

This conceptualization, later to be formulated in terms of *cathexes* (directed quanta of psychic energy) versus *anticathexes*, is a clear anticipation of the theory of repression, one of the seminal ideas of psychoanalytic psychology.

Hypnosis, in Freud's thinking, achieved its effects by reinforcing the conscious wish (will, force, idea), which now in concert with the hypnotic suggestion overpowered the counterwish:

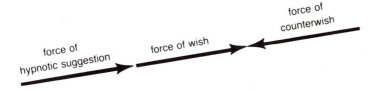

The fact that the counterwish was forcibly subjugated (but not eliminated) through the hypnotic alliance might account for the patient's restiveness toward hypnosis evidenced in this case. The phenomenon foreshadows the analogous "resistance" encountered in the "psychoanalytic alliance."

Clearly then, Freud's theory of hysteria is a theory of conflict—of will versus counterwill, idea versus antithetic idea—often expressed in the analogic garb of force dynamics and known later within psychoanalysis as *psychodynamics*.

THE NATURE AND HISTORY OF HYPNOSIS

Up to this point we have focused on the psychological possibilities of hypnosis without saying much about what precisely hypnosis might be. The answer to the question is actually not an easy one, for scholars of hypnosis are themselves at great odds over the issue (e.g., Barber, 1969; Barber and Ham, 1974; Bowers, 1976; Hilgard, 1965; 1977; Shor and Orne, 1965) or simply confess their ignorance on the point. Nevertheless, the question is of great significance to psychoanalysis since hypnosis, as we shall presently see, is the foundation upon which psychoanalysis was built and may be correctly viewed as the missing link between applied prepsychologies of antiquity, such as faith healing, exorcism, and astrology on the one hand, and psychoanalysis on the other. Moreover, contemporary developments since the founding of psychoanalysis, including placebo therapy, natural childbirth techniques such as the Lamaze method, and even components of behavior therapies (for example, Wolpe's "desensitization" therapy through "reciprocal inhibition") are unwitting or unacknowledged revivals of hypnotic techniques.

Although hypnosis in the late nineteenth century was, as already suggested, an avant-garde instrument, it was not actually a new one. On the contrary, the then-current interest in hypnosis was merely a revival within scientific circles of what had once been an active field of research, which had been relegated, after increasingly embittered debate, to the realm of superstition and quackery by the weight of professional opinion.

It is impossible to say who discovered hypnosis, for it has become increasingly clear that all civilizations, old and modern, had known and used it under one guise or another (see Ellenberger's [1970] monumental work, *The Discovery of the Unconscious*). In Western history, however, credit for the discovery of hypnosis is usually given to Franz Anton Mesmer (1734–1815) who, like Freud, was a Viennese physician. In retrospect it is safe to say that Mesmer's contribution was not so much a new *discovery* as a new *pretension*. What had hitherto been claimed for demons, gods, and spirits, Mesmer now claimed for science.

There were great healers in the days of Mesmer. One of the greatest—some say the greatest exorcist of all times—was a humble Austrian priest, Father Johann Joseph Gassner (1727–1779). Gassner distinguished between two different types of diseases, the "natural" ones, over which he claimed no authority and saw as the domain of medical doctors, and those he called the "preternatural" ones, caused by diabolical possession or sorcery. Over the latter he claimed power, though not in his own name; the absolutely essential prerequisite for a cure, Gassner made clear, was the patient's *own faith* in Jesus Christ.

Gassner traveled extensively over German-speaking lands, drawing crowds to even the tiniest village he visited. These crowds, which swelled to thousands as his fame spread, included not only the sick and the curious but also the skeptics. The latter, comprising the irreligious as well as doubters within the Protestant and Catholic churches, subjected his cures to critical scrutiny, and many firsthand accounts of Gassner's remarkable work survive. We shall have occasion to quote a lengthy segment from one such eyewitness account once we are in a position to contrast it meaningfully with Mesmer's and his followers' procedures.

Although Mesmer was taken with Gassner's achievements, he nevertheless rejected the idea of exorcism with contempt. As a self-conscious man of science, he knew—with the sure knowledge of faith—that there were no such things as spirits, demons, or witches, and he set out to create a bona fide *scientific* medical technique that would overshadow superstition-based "miracles," such as Gassner's. As was so often to be the case with self-anointed instruments of scientific enlightenment in psychiatry and psychology, Mesmer molded his thinking into the framework of the then-dominant epitomes of scientific progress. In his days these areas were electricity, magnetism, and astronomy. It was Mesmer's theory that a subtle fluid inhered in all material things, animate or inanimate, in the universe, accounting for the ubiquitous forces of attraction and repulsion existing between them. These forces, which had different observable manifestations and included electricity and magnetism, applied not only to the interactions between inanimate objects such as planetary bodies (gravity), but also to those between inanimate and sentient bodies (astrological influences) as well as those between one living being and another (for which he borrowed the term *rapport* from the then-current experimental research on electric rapport, showing that an electrically stimulated person could transmit the electric "fluid" to another person through touch).

Mesmer's medical principles drew heavily from the era's fascination with astrology, which had been stimulated by breakthroughs in gravity—if a planetary body could be influenced by another planetary body, then why not a human being?—as well as by earlier works on astrology such as the influential book, *Diseases That Deprive Men of their Reason,* by the incomparably named, Theophrastus Bombastus von Hohenheim (Paracelsus), who argued that heavenly bodies (and also sex, interestingly) had the power to subvert sanity. Vestiges of such astrological ideas still survive in everyday language; thus, a *lunatic* was thought to be a person unduly swayed by the power of the moon (*luna*).

It was Mesmer's thesis that diseases arose from an imbalance of the universal fluid in the body, from which idea followed the corollary idea that the task of medicine was to restore harmony in the body's distribution of the fluid. Allowing for differences in metaphors, the notion does not seem that remote from Freud's early thinking: In Mesmer's case we have a theory of fluid dynamics, in Freud's, a theory of psychodynamics.

Stimulated by some intriguing reports from England suggesting that cures might be produced for certain afflictions by the application of magnets to affected parts of the body, it occurred to Mesmer that magnets might be the instrument through which bodily fluid imbalances might be returned to harmony. He obtained some magnets from a friend, a Jesuit astronomer at the court of the Austrian empress, a Father Hell (who later was bitterly to complain that Mesmer had not only borrowed his magnets, but had stolen his ideas as well, claiming credit for Mesmer's discoveries), and proceeded to do experiments on the medical possibilities of magnetism. Success—and fame—came to him with the cure of a certain Fräulein Österlin, who had been afflicted with an extravagance of purportedly severe symptoms, including paralyses, headaches, vomiting, and paroxysms of rage. Mesmer had noticed that her condition exhibited a certain periodic quality, to the point that he could predict its ebb and flow. From this he drew confirmation for his presupposition that planetary motions, with their mathematical periodicities, underlay her conditions. He set about correcting the inferred fluid imbalances of her body by inducing, by means of his magnets, a restorative "artificial tide." He attached three magnets to her body; one to her stomach and one to each of her legs. Then, to maximize his magnets' effectiveness, he had her swallow a preparation containing iron. As Mesmer made "passes" over her with a magnet, Fräulein Österlin began experiencing strange bodily perturbations. Streams of fluid, she felt, radiated downward through her body. Her breathing got heavier; she started moaning; her body began trembling and then convulsing uncontrollably, reaching a grand crescendo of spasms and gasps— followed by unaccustomed peace. The high point of excitement, which Mesmer called the *crisis*, was construed by him as the final dramatic phase of fluidic readjustment. He did not apparently explore, at least not publicly, an alternative hypothesis.

After several such treatments, Fräulein Österlin was declared cured, proof for which was offered the fact that she was now able to marry—as it turns out, Mesmer's stepson—and be a sturdy wife and mother.

As Mesmer continued his magnetic treatments, he came to realize that it was not essential to utilize magnets to produce effective cures. For a while he employed a "magic wand," which, having been stored with real magnets, was assumed to have taken on magnetic properties (just as a regular piece of iron becomes magnetized when placed in contact with a magnet). Mesmer gradually abandoned this device, assuming that his extensive contact with magnets had made his own person brim with "animal magnetism" (after the demonstration by Volta of *animal electricity* in the frog). Eventually, he was to posit that all humans possess a greater or lesser degree of natural magne-

tism, which contact with real magnets helped to amplify. He was finally able to explain Gassner's achievements to his own satisfaction by claiming for Gassner an exceptionally high degree of natural magnetism, even greater than his own (which, however, Mesmer made sure he extended beyond Gassner's by constantly wearing several magnets about his body, and even sleeping with them).

After many successes, but also increasing opposition from his medical colleagues, Mesmer finally left Vienna for Paris. There, in the shortest time, he gained spectacular renown and a personal fortune. His practice was so huge that he simply could not see individually the majority of patients clamoring for his cure. Finally, he devised an instrument for group therapy, called a *baquet,* patterned after the recently invented Leyden jar (for storing electricity), designed in this case to hold and distribute magnetism. A visiting physician, cited by Ellenberger (1970, p. 64) described Mesmer's collective technique as follows:

> I was in his home the other day and was witness to his method of operating. In the middle of the room is placed a vessel of about a foot and a half high which is called here a *baquet.* It is so large that twenty people can easily sit around it; near the edge of the lid which covers it, there are holes pierced corresponding to the number of persons who are to surround it, into these holes are introduced iron rods, bent at right angles outwards, and of different heights, so as to answer to the part of the body to which they are to be applied. Besides these rods, there is a rope which communicates between the *baquet* and one of the patients, and from him is carried to another, and so on the whole round. The most sensible effects are produced on the approach of Mesmer, who is said to convey the fluid by certain motions of his hands or eyes, without touching the person. I have talked with several who have witnessed these effects, who have convulsions occasioned and removed by a movement of the hand. . . .

Mesmer thus seems to have been something of a pioneer in group therapy. Indeed, he might be also considered a precursor of community psychology, for in his desire to extend his cure to patients who could not afford his staggering fees, he magnanimously magnetized several trees, which poor peasants, clamoring to be cured of every manner of disease, lined up to touch. Mesmer's techniques began to create a sensational controversy in France. One party viewed them in millenial terms as the potential cure for all illnesses; another, as the rankest and most perfidious type of quackery. The king of France, Louis XVI, finally convened a royal commission consisting of some of the world's preeminent scientists, among them Lavoisier, Dr. Guillotin (by whose contraption Louis XVI was shortly to lose his head), and Benjamin Franklin (then the American ambassador to France) to study and pass judgment on "mesmerism."

Before we deal with the commission's conclusions, it may be instructive to describe an unusual split that was developing within the ranks of Mesmer's own followers around this time. The split arose over the issue of fluid dynamics. The orthodox "scientific" view, the proponents of which were termed the *fluidists,* came under the challenge of the so-called *animists,* who claimed that the effects of mesmerism, of which they were no less convinced than the fluidists, had nothing to do with fluids, magnetic or otherwise, but rather with the psychological powers of faith and belief—"the power of positive thinking," to borrow a contemporary expression from Dr. Norman Vincent Peale. The argument appears to be a clear preview of the debate to rage a century later between Charcot's physicalist position on hypnosis and Bernheim's and Liébeault's psychological one.

The leader of the animists was an illustrious French nobleman, the Marquis de Puységur, who when working with a male subject, a peasant from his estate named Victor Race, discovered a paradoxical crisis. Instead of the usual convulsions, Race exhibited something quite the opposite—a tranquil sleeplike state. It was not real sleep, however, since he could converse with Puységur. During this sleeplike state—to be known soon as *artificial somnambulism* and later as *hypnotism* or *hypnosis* from the Greek word *hypnos,* meaning sleep—the subject exhibited an unusual "lucidity." He was, for example, able to recall memories long since forgotten (a phenomenon later to be called *hypnotic hypermnesia,* which will figure in the discussion of the unconscious in the next chapter), foretell the future course of his symptoms, and even prescribe effective treatment for his ailments. He would snap out of the somnambulistic state, remembering nothing of what had transpired (a phenomenon now known as *hypnotic amnesia*), but decidedly improved. Since Puységur could replicate the effects on other subjects, it gradually dawned on him that the classic crisis, which Mesmer had held up as the motoric manifestation of the body's fluidic readjustment, was simply not a factor in the cure. His own, decidedly psychological position, was finally summarized as follows (cited in Ellenberger, 1970, p. 72): "The entire doctrine of Animal Magnetism is contained in the two words: *Believe* and *want.*" This theory of hypnosis, which was to shape Bernheim's approach, seems to have been rediscovered in contemporary times—but now, peculiarly, as a criticism of hypnosis—by T. X. Barber (1969).

But what was the royal commission's conclusion? Did it confirm or disprove the effects of mesmerism? Interestingly, its report did not challenge the *effects* of mesmerism but rather its *theory.* Just as the animists had independently disavowed the fluid theory, the royal commission was led, after a program of carefully controlled experiments, to essentially the same conclusion: There was no evidence for the operation of "magnetic fluids," and cures could only be ascribed to subjects' "imagination."

When we combine Puységur's motivational theory with the royal commission's "imagination" hypothesis, we have the substance of what is now, two centuries later, advanced as a new theory of hypnosis, the so-called *cognitive-behavioral viewpoint:*

> This approach proposes that a high level of response to suggestions, a hypnoticlike appearance, a change in body feelings, and other phenomena are produced in the hypnotic situation because specific factors within the hypnotic-induction procedure give rise to positive attitudes, motivations, and expectancies, and a willingness to engage in specific kinds of cognitive processes (a willingness to become involved in thinking and imagining that is relevant to the suggestions).
>
> If these basic assumptions are correct, we could predict that the performance of a subject in a hypnotic situation is related to his attitudes, motivations, and expectancies, and to his willingness to imagine and think with the themes that are suggested. (Barber and Ham, 1974, pp. 5–6)

There was one interesting historical footnote to the royal commission's conclusion. A secret report, secret out of deference to moral sensibilities, was appended to the main report to the king. It was suggested here that an extra dimension might operate in producing the effects of mesmerism, namely, the sexual attraction of the subject (usually female) to the mesmerist (usually male). This undercurrent of sexuality seems to be a recurring theme, sometimes explicit, sometimes implicit, from Plato to Freud. It makes its appearance in psychoanalytic therapy under the concept of the *positive transference,* which will be briefly touched on at the end of the chapter.

But to conclude our examination of hypnosis, the question must finally be asked: If the phenomenon, whatever it is to be called, reduces in the end to the power of belief, want, and imagination, then what finally is the difference, if any, between mesmerism (magnetism, somnambulism, hypnotism) and faith healing (exorcism, shamanism, voodoo, and so forth)? Perhaps the best way to answer the question is to quote two eyewitness reports of the effects produced by Mesmer and by Gassner (both taken from Ellenberger, 1970, pp. 59–60 and p. 54).

Cited first are the observations of an initially skeptical family tutor of a Hungarian baron whose castle Mesmer visited.

Shortly after Mesmer's arrival several of the castle's inhabitants began to feel pains or peculiar sensations in their bodies as soon as they came near him. Even the sceptical Seyfret [the tutor] noticed that he was seized with an invincible sleepiness when Mesmer played music. It was not long before he became thoroughly convinced of Mesmer's extraordinary powers. He saw how Mesmer could elicit morbid symptoms in people around him, particularly in those whom he had magnetized. A lady who was singing lost her voice as soon as Mesmer touched her hand and recovered it when he made a gesture with his finger. . . .

On the sixth evening, Mesmer announced that the Baron would have a crisis on the following morning—which actually happened. The crisis was unusually violent, and it was reported that the fever increased or decreased according to whether Mesmer came closer to the patient or drew away from him. A second, less violent crisis occurred a few days later, but the Baron found the treatment too drastic and Mesmer left Rohow, though not without healing, at the last minute, a peasant who had suddenly lost his hearing six weeks before.

Compare this now with a certain Abbé Bourgeois' eyewitness report of Gassner at work:

The first patients were two nuns who had been forced to leave their community on account of convulsive fits. Gassner told the first one to kneel before him, asked her briefly about her name, her illness, and whether she agreed that anything he would order should happen. She agreed. Gassner then pronounced solemnly in Latin: "If there be anything preternatural about this disease, I order in the name of Jesus that it manifest itself immediately." The patient started at once to have convulsions. According to Gassner, this was proof that the convulsions were caused by an evil spirit and not by a natural illness, and he now proceeded to demonstrate that he had power over the demon, whom he ordered in Latin to produce convulsions in various parts of the patient's body; he called forth in turn the exterior manifestations of grief, silliness, scrupulosity, anger, and so on, and even the appearance of death. All his orders were punctually executed. It now seemed logical that, once a demon had been tamed to that point, it should be relatively easy to expel him, which Gassner did. He then proceeded in the same manner with the second nun. After the séance had ended, Abbé Bourgeois asked her whether it had been very painful; she answered that she had only a vague memory of what had happened and that she had not suffered much. Gassner then treated a third patient, a high-born lady who had previously been afflicted with melancholia. Gassner called forth the melancholia and explained to the lady what she was to do in order to overcome it in case she was troubled by it again.

The conclusion is hard to escape: There is no fundamental difference between hypnotism and faith healing except for the theoretical metaphors employed in explaining their effects. Indeed, it can be safely surmised that a host of other curative instruments, from leeches, electrotherapy, placebos, and acupuncture, to the Shrine of Lourdes, draw their power from nothing other than *faith, want,* and *imagination.*

One cannot help but wonder how the high-powered young scientist, Sigmund Freud, always an ardent enemy of religion, might have reacted to the suggestion that his proud 1893 report of a successful hypnotic cure was, in fact, a case of successful exorcism! He might well have surprised us, however. In an article published in the same year he wrote:

> Let no one object that the theory of dissociation of consciousness as a solution of the enigma of hysteria is too far-fetched to suggest itself to the untrained and unprejudiced observer. In fact the Middle Ages had chosen this very solution, in declaring possession by a demon to be the cause of hysterical manifestations; all that would have been required was to replace the religious terminology of those dark and superstitious times by the scientific one of to-day. (Freud, 1893, p. 22)

There is one profound moral to this story, which is impossible to overestimate: Many of the virulent controversies which rent applied psychology in its unfolding history, especially those arising from an overweening sense of what is proper science, turned out in retrospect to have been wars of terminology and metaphor. It is hard not to suspect that some of the more modern cleavages in psychology, particularly those to be found in today's clinical psychology, might not be variations on the same theme. Coming immediately to mind is the self-conscious scientism of radical behaviorism (e.g., Skinner, 1953; Watson, 1930) which, like the fluidist and physicalist position of old, insists upon a theoretical framework that entails tangibles, things that are material rather than psychological—in this instance, behavior rather than cognition.

THE CATHARTIC TECHNIQUE: BREUER AND ANNA O.

The case of successful hypnotic suggestion therapy reported by Freud in 1893, which as we have seen is not clearly distinguishable from therapies of antiquity, was to undergo an explosively rapid sequence of evolutionary transformations, culminating, well before the turn of the century, in psychoanalysis.

Interestingly, the most critical development was not Freud's doing but rather of Joseph Breuer, an eminent Viennese physician and friend of Freud's. Indeed, Freud was frequently to credit Breuer and not himself with the discovery of psychoanalysis. It is worth noting that Breuer in turn attributed the discovery to another person, in this case his famous patient Anna O., who more or less foisted the procedure upon him. If we took Freud and Breuer at their word, it would follow that the discovery of psychoanalysis was neither Freud's nor Breuer's doing but that of the beautiful and gifted—and sumptuously neurotic—young woman, Anna O. In her own right, as Bertha Pappenheim, she was later to distinguish herself as a feminist leader and as a founder of social work in Germany.

Anna O. became Breuer's patient in 1880 at the age of 21 when, under the pressure of nursing her dying father, she suffered a nervous collapse. She developed a veritable museum of symptoms which included a labile pattern of incapacitating paralyses of the limbs; depression and listlessness; terrifying hallucinations of snakes, which transmogrified into death's heads and skeletons; painful coughing fits, especially in reaction to music; a period of severe hydrophobia, during which she could not bring herself to drink water; amnesias (blackouts) for recent events; severe paraphrasia (loss of language ability); a blinding squint; anorexia (unwillingness to take food); and several other serious dysfunctions.

Breuer proceeded to treat her by means of hypnotic suggestion. Gradually, after a systematic program of "suggesting away" specific symptoms, Anna began improving. When her father finally died, however, Anna relapsed with a vengeance, not only reacquiring her old symptoms but also developing some new ones. It was this fragility of the hypnotic cure, its propensity to unravel in the face of new crisis, which Freud alludes to as the "drawback" he was to discover later (see p. 7), and which eventually played a part in his abandoning hypnosis altogether.

At this point, Breuer could think only of picking up where he had begun, and he proceeded to readminister a regime of suggestive therapy. True, it had produced only a transitory effect before, but it had at least produced an effect. The therapeutic program, however, began to undergo a subtle transformation about this time. After several months of almost daily interaction, under the most taxing emotional conditions, a certain personal closeness began supplanting the conventional impersonality of the patient-physician relationship. Increasingly, Anna intruded conversations about her private mental life into the otherwise mechanical suggestive regime. To Breuer's credit, he did not discourage what might have been considered by someone more single-minded as an unwelcome interruption of the therapeutic program, even though Anna began to occupy more and more of their time together chitchatting about an assortment of trivia, from reminiscences of the past to daydreams of the present. These talking sessions, however, began to produce an unexpected psychological impact; not only did Anna emerge from them in a generally improved mood, but a remarkable fact soon came to light: When Anna's meandering conversations turned to the specific incidents from the past that had been connected with the outbreak of a particular symptom, the symptom disappeared. Let us take her hydrophobia as an example.

Around this period, in the middle of a scorching summer, Anna unaccountably developed an aversion to drinking water. Though she was tormented by thirst, she could not bring herself to imbibe water and was obliged to sustain herself on melons and other fruits. During one of their therapy sessions, after she had been placed under hypnosis, she began to talk about her governess, an English lady whom she apparently despised. This governess owned a lapdog that Anna detested with no less asperity. One day Anna entered the governess' room and surprised "the horrid creature"—the dog—drinking water out of a glass. The scene provoked a violent fury in Anna; how could a disgusting animal be allowed to drink water from one of their glasses! Anna, however, was a well-brought-up girl, and out of politeness said nothing to her lady companion.

After recalling this memory in all its details and giving full vent to the anger she had originally held back, Anna's hydrophobic symptom suddenly disappeared; right there and then "she asked for something to drink, drank a large quantity of water without any difficulty and woke from her hypnosis with the glass at her lips; and thereupon the disturbance vanished, never to return" (Breuer and Freud, 1895, pp. 34–35).

Anna's squint was eliminated in a similar manner. During another hypnotic session she began to ruminate about a particularly painful evening with her dying father. She had been sitting by his bedside, crushed with grief, trying to keep from crying, when he asked her the time. Tears suddenly came to her eyes. She contrived to hide them from her father by bringing her watch close to her face; the maneuver, which masked her tears, obliged her to squint in order to read the time. The revival and verbal expression of this painful memory brought an end to the hysterical squint.

Anna's nervous cough, which tended to be triggered by music, was disposed of in a similar manner. The critical memory once again involved her father. She was sitting by his bedside one evening when she heard some music from next door. A party was in full swing. She caught herself thinking how nice it would be if she could be there dancing instead of sitting in the dark by her father's bedside. She was immediately gripped by a terrible guilt: What kind of monster was she to be thinking of having fun at parties when her poor father lay dying right next to her? She began coughing violently. The recollection of the incident with all its painful emotion put an end to the recurrence of the symptom.

As the therapeutic power of the procedure became increasingly evident—Anna called it the "talking cure" or "chimney sweeping"—Breuer progressively abandoned hypnotic suggestion in favor of the new approach, which he formally named the *cathartic technique,* after the medical term, *catharsis,* meaning purgation. Actually, the concept as well as the term *catharsis* had ancient historical roots. It had been a major tenet of the classic Greek theater that purging one's soul of deep, pent-up emotions produced beneficial psychological effects. And, of course, we would need only substitute "demons" (spirits, spells, and so forth) for "emotions" (or memories, impulses) to find ourselves once again within the realm of exorcism.

The initial emphasis of the cathartic technique was, as its name suggests, the discharge or *abreaction* ("reacting-away") of pent-up emotions. While this remained its ultimate goal, it soon became evident that it was not a simple matter of giving expression to well-known emotional feelings; the more significant emotional memories, it turned out, were not as a rule readily accessible to the patient's recollection. Sometimes weeks or months of cognitive effort were required for the recovery of the significant materials. Thus, an increasingly emphasized aspect of the technique was the recovery of inaccessible (unconscious) memories.

One such intractable memory complex, for example, was connected with the paralysis of Anna's arm. Only after extensive effort over periods of months was the precipitating incident recovered in all its significant details. In this particular case, it turned out to be not an objective event but a terrifying fantasy (possibly a hallucination or a dream), which Anna experienced while sitting by her father's bedside. She had begun to doze off when she suddenly became aware of a monstrous black snake slithering toward her sleeping father. Terrified, she tried to ward off the snake with her hand, but she could not because her arm "had gone to sleep." She stared at her useless hand only to discover that her fingers had turned into little writhing snakes while her nails had become "death heads" (skulls). The final recollection of this horrifying fantasy, with all its attendant terror, put an end to the paralysis of her arm.

To summarize then, the cathartic technique, as finally worked out by Breuer, was fundamentally a hypermnesic instrument, that is, a counteramnesic technique for reviving inhibited or otherwise inaccessible memories for the purpose of discharging the pathogenic emotions attached to them. The patient was placed under hypnosis, which was assumed to widen his sphere of consciousness, and then urged to retrieve from memory the complex of events (and emotions) originally associated with the outbreak of a particular symptom. As has been repeatedly intimated, this was not merely a cold, intellectual exercise in memory retrieval; for the procedure to work, the patient had to recollect—relive might be the apter term—the incident in all its emotional intensity as well as detail, giving the material uninhibited verbal expression, and thereby abreacting the pent-up emotions sustaining the symptom.

The cathartic procedure was at once similar and fundamentally different from the technique of hypnotic suggestion from which it evolved. While both employed hypnosis and suggestion as basic tools, the object of the suggestions was quite different. In the earlier technique the therapist suggested away the symptoms, while in catharsis, he suggested that the patient recall the events (and thereby discharge the pathogenic emotions) that brought about the symptoms. Catharsis, therefore, is a more indirect approach; rather than attacking the symptom itself, it attacks the presumed cause of the symptom on the simple premise that eliminating the *cause* (the pathogenic emotions) must lead to the elimination of the *effect* (the symptom). Thus, hypnotic suggestion may be viewed as a cosmetic device, directed at the overt symptomatic manifestation of the neurosis, while the cathartic technique resembles more closely a surgical procedure, designed to eliminate the underlying pathology, and thereby (presumably) lead to a permanent cure.

Beyond their superficial similarities, then, hypnotic suggestion and catharsis involved fundamentally different therapeutic strategies. Catharsis, ultimately, may be viewed as an early, crude prototype of psychoanalysis, already embodying two of psychoanalysis' essential features: (1) its being a talking cure, based on the patient's verbalizations, and (2) its "uncovering" or consciousness-raising objective.

Despite the apparent success of Breuer's experiment, there was something vague and even mysterious about the case. Although Anna was reported to have been cured of her symptoms after about two years of treatment (about a year of it through the cathartic technique), Breuer never employed the technique again and let more than a decade elapse before publishing the unusual results, and then only after the most persistent importunations and, finally, collaboration of his younger colleague and friend, Sigmund Freud. The full case was first published in 1895 under the joint authorship of Breuer and Freud, in their classic book, *Studies on Hysteria*. In his later publications, Freud was to allude enigmatically to a certain "untoward event" which put a premature end to Anna's treatment; but the mystery was not explained until the psychoanalyst Ernest Jones (1953), Freud's biographer, finally gave a detailed accounting of the matter. We shall return to this little mystery presently.

THEORY OF CATHARSIS AND HYSTERIA: BREUER AND FREUD

In their joint report of the case of Anna O., Breuer and Freud set forth a psychological theory of both the therapy (catharsis) and the disease (hysteria). Their theoretical effort was to lay the conceptual foundation for much of psychoanalytic psychology. Their view of hysteria is succinctly expressed in their famous formula: "hysterics suffer mainly from reminiscences" (Breuer and Freud, 1895, p. 7). This summary statement conveys two complementary ideas. The most obvious, from the point of view of our discussion of Anna O.'s case, is that hysterics suffer from pathogenic traumatic memories which they have expunged from consciousness for the purpose of escaping unbearable pain. These emotional memories are not thereby eliminated, however; they are merely driven "underground"—into the unconscious—where they find new channels for expression through the somatic system and are "converted" into symptoms. From this idea follows the second meaning of Breuer and Freud's formula: The symptoms (paralyses, coughs, phobias, and so forth) of "conversion hysteria" are nothing other than reminiscences, that is, recollections, *expressed in body language,* a recondite dialect that the person himself as a rule fails to understand. (Thus Freud's insistence that despite their superficial senselessness "symptoms have meaning.") This rechanneling notion is essentially a recapitulation of Freud's (1893) conflict model of hysteria in terms of clashing force vectors (see pp. 10–11). The tendency to remember is opposed by a defensive countertendency *not* to remember so as to avoid pain, yielding a resultant "compromise formation" (see Figure 1.2) in which simultaneously the *memory is not remembered* (consciously) *but is remembered* (somatically).

The conversion metaphor is another product of nineteenth-century physics, in this case the famous first law of thermodynamics, the conservation of energy principle, which holds that energy cannot either be created or destroyed; it can only be transformed (converted) from one form to another. Thus, an emotionally charged memory cannot be destroyed; it can only be converted from one form (conscious psychological representation) to another (somatic representation). The symptom, then, is the transformed physical manifestation of the original, inhibited memory complex.

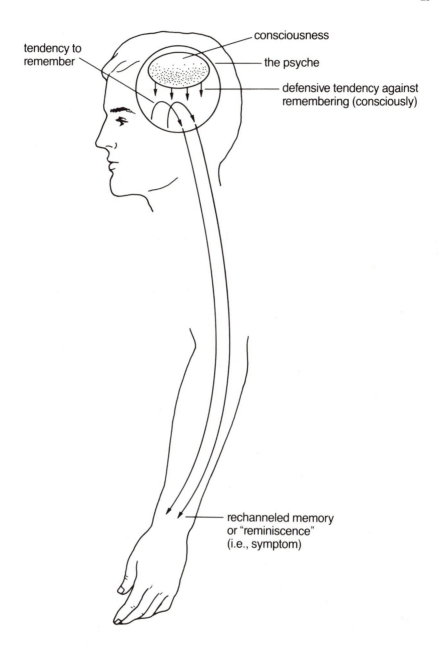

Figure 1.2. Schematic representation of the clash of opposing tendencies (to remember and not to remember) and the resultant "compromise," the somatic reminiscence (the symptom).

In a more modern cognitive framework this notion could be reformulated as follows: The original psychological representation is "recoded" into a somatic representation, in much the same way a verbal representation may be recoded into an imagistic representation, or vice versa, with important cognitive consequences (e.g., Atwood, 1971; Erdelyi, Finkelstein, Herrell, Miller, and Thomas, 1976; Erdelyi and Kleinbard, 1978; Paivio, 1971; Sperling, 1960). Actually, Freud himself, some seventy-five years before multicode conceptions became popular in cognitive psychology (e.g., Paivio, 1971) proposed, in effect, a multicode explanation of the hysterical symptom. Hysterics, according to him, were individuals with an undue propensity for recoding verbal thoughts—the adult cognitive modality—into the more primitive modalities of images or somatic codes (symptoms):

> Many other hysterical patients have reported to us that they have memories . . . in vivid visual pictures and that this applied especially to their pathogenic memories. [Breuer and Freud, 1895, p. 53] . . . Frau Cäcilie M. passed through a period during which she transformed every thought she had into a hallucination. . . .[p. 181] We . . . had often compared the symptomatology of hysteria with a pictographic script which has become intelligible after the discovery of a few bilingual inscriptions. [p. 129] . . . In all this, strictly speaking, the hysterical symptom is not behaving in any way differently from the memory-picture or the reproduced [verbal] thought which we conjure up [in therapy]. . . . There is an uninterrupted series, extending from the unmodified *mnemic residues* of affective experiences and acts of thought to the hysterical symptoms, which are *mnemic symbols* of those experiences and thoughts. [p. 297]

The implication, not clearly worked out in the absence of a computer analogy (see Chapter 3), is that the hysterical symptom is a form of miscoded memory. A corollary, which we shall return to later, is that one task of therapy is the recoding of thought into an appropriately manipulable programming code, so that a psychological reprogramming, the ultimate goal of therapy, can take place.

The conservation-of-energy analogy, when pushed to its logical limits, proves misleading. The problem is that a rigorous application of it leads one to expect that the symptom would gradually dissipate the pathogenic memory, just as a running motor eventually exhausts its source of fuel. Yet this precisely is what *does not* happen to unconscious memories, which unlike their conscious counterparts, are "eternal" as long as they remain unconscious (hence the need to recover them into consciousness).

An apter, but still not fully satisfactory, analogy might be a medical one (e.g., Breuer and Freud, 1895, p. 290). A chronically infected tonsil, for example, would be expected to continue to produce a set of symptoms (sore throat, sniffles, fever, and so forth) until the tonsil is surgically removed. The counterpart procedure in cathartic therapy is the recovery into consciousness of the emotionally charged memory (corresponding to the surgical unveiling of the affected region) and the consequent discharge (the extirpation) of the pathogenic affect. But what accounts for the abreaction of pathogenic affect once the emotional memory is recalled into consciousness—what is the psychological counterpart of the actual excision of the pathogenic mass? This is, in effect, asking for a psychological explanation of abreaction.

Breuer and Freud proposed that there were two mechanisms for abreacting pathogenic emotions, both requiring awareness of the emotion in question: *motoric* "reaction" (crying, screaming, attacking, and the like) or the more gradual *verbal* "wearing away" or "extinguishing" through "associative correction" (for example, "a memory of . . . a trauma, even if it has not been [motorically] abreacted, enters the great complex of associations, it comes alongside other experiences, which may contradict it, and is subjected to rectifications by other ideas. After an accident, for instance, the memory of the danger and the (mitigated) repetition of the fright becomes associated with the memory of what happened afterwards—rescue and the consciousness of present safety" [p. 9]).

CLASSICAL CONDITIONING AND EXTINCTION IN ABREACTION

The second mechanism, of obvious importance to any "talking cure," turns out surprisingly to be nothing other than the classical conditioning form of the extinction process: An emotionally toned memory complex, that is, a memory of an incident associated with fright, is cognitively emitted (recalled, imaged) in a nonfrightful, or relaxed context, until the memory of the incident stops eliciting the fright reaction.

Since extinction involves the substitution of one response for another (even if the "response" is the absence of a response), it is possible to conceptualize extinction as simply a special case of conditioning (or deconditioning, counterconditioning, reconditioning, and so forth) wherein a current response to a stimulus, such as fright, is supplanted by another response, nonfright (relaxation). This conceptualization yields the typical classical (Pavlovian) conditioning paradigm, involving in this case the pairing of a *conditioned stimulus* (CS), which elicits at the outset a previous *conditioned response* (CR), fright, with an *un-*

conditioned stimulus (UCS), which elicits the *unconditioned response* (UCR), relaxation:

$$CS_{(Scene\ a)} \rightarrow previous\ CR_{(fright)}$$
$$|$$
$$UCS_{(Scene\ b)} \rightarrow UCR_{(relaxation)}$$

The goal (loosely speaking) is to replace the previous CR (fright) with a new CR, the UCR (relaxation), as the dominant response to CS:

$$CS_{(Scene\ a)} \rightarrow CR_{(relaxation)}$$

It directly follows from this paradigm (see Dollard and Miller [1950] for a more extensive discussion), that no extinction or conditioning can take place without the actual production, overt or cognitive, of the conditioned stimulus, CS. This explains in classical conditioning terms why the emotionally charged memory must be produced in consciousness for extinction—associative correction—of the fright to take place. (The experimental literature has tended to corroborate theory: In humans, at least, there seems to be no conditioning without awareness [see Eriksen, 1962].)

The fact that the mechanism of verbal abreaction, namely associative correction, corresponds to the extinction process of classical conditioning is of considerable theoretical interest in view of the fundamental role played by extinction (deconditioning, etc.) in some major behavior-modification techniques, for example, Wolpe's (1958; 1961; 1973) "systematic desensitization" through "reciprocal inhibition."[1] This point seems to be insufficiently appreciated in the modern clinical literature, perhaps because of the polemic nature of most debates between proponents of behavior modification and psychoanalysis (but

---

[1] In the interest of brevity many points have been compressed, some of which may be controversial. For example, not every scholar of classical conditioning will accept the view that extinction is a special case of conditioning (or deconditioning, reconditioning, counterconditioning, and so forth). The logic of this equation is as follows: The casual prescription for producing extinction is repeatedly to present the conditioned stimulus (CS) by itself until the conditioned response (CR) gradually drops out. This shorthand formulation, however, leaves unexpressed the fact that no CS can be presented in a stimulus vacuum. Thus, the stimulus context in which the CS is produced in the extinction phase, that is, in the absence of the previous effective UCS, is now the *new* UCS, the new UCR being a null response (relative to the previous UCR). This conceptualization cuts through the controversies as to whether the Wolpean desensitization phenomenon is due to reciprocal inhibition (Wolpe, 1958; 1961; 1973), counterconditioning (Bandura, 1969; Davison and Wilson, 1973), or extinction (Crowder and Thornton, 1970; D'Zurilla, Wilson, and Nelson, 1973). At bottom, it is argued here, they represent the very same process.

A startling recent perspective, which *is* distinct, is that desensitization is a suggestion effect (Kazdin and Wilcoxon, 1976).

see Wachtel, 1977). Yet it is difficult not to come to the conclusion that we are once again dealing with a war of terminology and metaphor. Although it is true that terms such as *abreaction, discharge,* and *catharsis* convey different analogic nuances than *extinction, counterconditioning,* or *desensitization,* operationally they come to pretty much the same thing. There is little doubt that Freud would have viewed behavior-modification therapies as throwbacks to early psychoanalytic techniques, such as catharsis, prior to psychoanalysis' becoming a truly cognitive therapy, concerned with structure and meaning.

Consider some of the basic features of Wolpean therapy. Before the treatment can get properly under way, the patient is given extensive "relaxation training" along the lines outlined by Jacobson (1938). It turns out, however, that Jacobson's relaxation-training procedure shares features in common with standard hypnotic-induction techniques, which typically involve a variety of relaxation suggestions (e.g., Hilgard, 1965); indeed, it used to be common for Wolpe to supplement relaxation with hypnosis. Thus, the hypnotic induction associated with the cathartic technique (also, more generally, the couch, the permissive ambiance of the therapy situation, the rapport between patient and therapist, and other factors) seems to accomplish the same relaxing function as formal relaxation training in Wolpean therapy, although perhaps in a less explicit or systematic fashion.

Another characteristic aspect of Wolpean therapy is the production of emotional images by the patient (which are then juxtaposed with relaxation). Imagery production, however, is also an important feature of the techniques described by Breuer and Freud in *Studies on Hysteria,* which involve imagery suggestions to an unsuspected extent. Breuer and Freud speak repeatedly not just of memories but of "picture ideas" (p. 270), "memory pictures" (p. 297), "memory images" (p. 299), and so on. When instructing a patient to recover emotional memories, the patient is urged to "bring out pictures and ideas" (p. 153); if nothing comes to mind he is reassured that he will eventually "see" before him "a recollection in the form of a picture" (p. 270). A patient's recall is prodded by the query: "Do you see this scene clearly before your eyes?" (p. 114) and then further encouraged, "Go on looking at the [mental] picture; it will develop and become more specialized. . . . Be patient, just keep looking at the picture" (p. 119). Of his patient Elizabeth von R., Freud remarks: "It was as though she were reading a lengthy book of pictures, whose pages were being turned over before her eyes" (p. 153).

The juxtaposition in cathartic therapy of emotional imagery with relaxation (brought about by hypnosis, lying on the couch, trust in the therapist, and so forth) should produce extinction of the conditioned emotional response attached to the imagery, whether the therapist calls it *desensitization* or *abreaction.*

Finally, Wolpean therapy requires from the subject an ordered list of frightful items, from least frightful to most frightful—a "hierarchy"—so that desensitization can proceed in an orderly fashion (lest the emotional response overwhelm the relaxation response, instead of the reverse). Although no formal hierarchy is worked out in advance by the patient in cathartic or psychoanalytic therapy, the same result is achieved, for in the course of recalling or free associating, the subject, as a rule, covers the least frightful materials before advancing to the more frightful ones. (The therapist, in fact, must be on guard against pressing the patient to cover more ground than he is prepared to; when this happens, as it did in Freud's case of Dora [Freud, 1905d], anxiety overwhelms the therapy and the patient escapes from it by breaking off treatment—as did Dora.) From the beginning it was clear to Freud that the patient brought his own built-in hierarchy to the treatment:

> We must not expect to meet with a *single* traumatic memory and a *single* pathogenic idea as its nucleus; we must be prepared for *successions of partial* traumas and *concatenations* of pathogenic trains of thought.... The psychic material ... presents itself as a structure in several dimensions. ... To begin with there is a nucleus consisting in memories of events or trains of thought in which the traumatic factor has culminated or the pathogenic idea has found its purest manifestation. Round this nucleus we find what is often an incredibly profuse amount of other mnemic material which has to be worked through in the analysis. ... It was as though we were examining a dossier that had been kept in good order. ... Each [theme] is—I cannot express it any other way—stratified concentrically around the psychological nucleus. ... Resistance ... increases in proportion as the strata are nearer to the nucleus. ... The most peripheral strata contain the memories (or files) which ... are easily remembered and have always been clearly conscious. The deeper we go the more difficult it becomes for the emerging memories to be recognized, till near the nucleus we come upon memories which the patient disavows even in reproducing them. It is this peculiarity of the concentric stratification of the pathogenic material which ... lends to the course of these analyses their characteristic features. (Breuer and Freud, 1895, pp. 287–289)

In the end we have in one case a formal list "hierarchy" and in the other an implicit "concentric stratification" (see Figure 1.3). The difference seems ultimately to be one of detail, not substance. (For a similar analysis, see Wachtel, 1977.)

There are, of course, some differences. Wolpe's therapy is unquestionably more "systematic" and explicit, at least as far as classical condi-

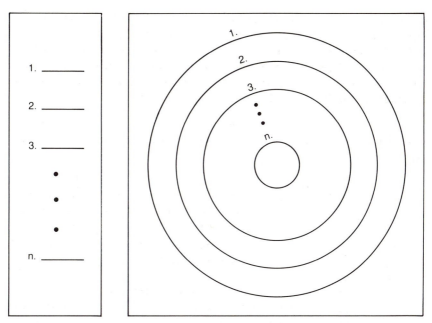

Figure 1.3. Organization of emotional material: Wolpe's explicit linear "hierarchy" (left) versus Freud's implicit "concentric stratification" (right).

tioning principles are concerned (though by now there is controversy among behavioral therapists themselves as to which set of specific mechanisms are in fact involved [see Kazdin and Wilcoxon, 1976]). The cathartic technique, on the other hand, is already a "deeper" therapy than Wolpe's since it is based on the assumption, originating with Breuer's experiences with Anna O. (see pp. 22–23), that the most significant emotional memories lie below the initial reach of the patient's recollections and must consequently be subjected to extensive retrieval work in order to be accessible for abreaction. Thus, Wolpe's therapy is in no way a hypermnesic instrument, being concerned solely with the patient's conscious hierarchy of fears generated at the outset of the treatment. From the psychoanalytic or cathartic standpoints—indeed from the standpoint of learning theory itself (e.g., Dollard and Miller, 1950)—such a hierarchy must necessarily be incomplete and even superficial.

Despite the existence of these nontrivial differences, it nevertheless remains significant that classical conditioning processes lie at the heart of both therapies. Although psychoanalysis evolved considerably beyond the cathartic technique, as we shall now see, there can be no question that extinction of painful affect is a paradigmatic component

of all members of the family of "talking cures," which involve the juxtaposition of painful cognitions with a relaxed, permissive atmosphere.
Indeed, after carefully reviewing the three supposedly "crucial"
ingredients of desensitization, Wilkins (1971) has concluded that imagination of fearful scenes is the only necessary component of successful
desensitization. The wheel seems to have turned full circle.

THE ABANDONMENT OF HYPNOSIS AND THE ADOPTION OF FREE ASSOCIATION

Studies on Hysteria consists of five case histories. The first is Breuer's
case of Anna O.; the remaining four are Freud's. Beyond their individual merit, the cases as a group make fascinating reading, for between
the two covers of the *Studies* one can witness firsthand the step-by-step
transformation of hypnotic-suggestion therapy into psychoanalysis
proper.

Freud's first case in the *Studies,* that of Frau Emmy von N., whom
he treated between 1888 and 1889, features a remarkable melange of
therapeutic efforts, suggesting a therapist in an acute experimental
phase, tinkering with every manner and combination of techniques in
search for the best procedure. With Frau Emmy von N., Freud made use
of virtually every historical technique discussed in this chapter, including warm baths, massage, faradic treatment, hypnotic suggestion, and
catharsis. By his last case in the *Studies,* however, that of Fräulein
Elizabeth von R., treated by Freud some three years later, Freud was
generally bypassing hypnosis, instituting free association as a basic
technique (although at this early stage it was more of a free-imaging
procedure), beginning to interpret the patient's productions for underlying meaning to encourage insight, and explicitly recognizing the
operation of resistance on the part of the patient against the uncovering
trend of the therapy. In short, Freud was using psychoanalysis, albeit in
a somewhat crude and as yet incomplete form.

One of the most important developments was the abandonment of
hypnosis, which began with the case of Miss Lucy R. in 1892. The im-
petus came from the prosaic fact that Freud had difficulty in hypnotizing many of his patients:

> I was accordingly faced with the choice of abandoning the
> cathartic method . . . or of venturing on the experiment of
> employing that method without somnambulism. . . . Further-
> more, I soon began to tire of issuing assurances and commands
> such as: "You are going to sleep! . . . sleep!" and of hearing the
> patient . . . remonstrate with me: "But, doctor, I'm *not* asleep."
> (Breuer and Freud, 1895, p. 108)

The major problem was that hypnosis was thought to "widen the field of consciousness" (see the work of Puységur, p. 16) and was therefore assumed to be the indispensable tool for engendering hypermnesias (recoveries of lost memories) required by the cathartic technique for the abreaction of unconscious emotional memories. Freud found a provisional solution in a concentration or pressure technique which he had learned from Bernheim during his visit to the Nancy Clinic:

> I was saved from this new embarrassment by remembering that I had myself seen Bernheim producing evidence that the memories of events during somnambulism are only *apparently forgotten in the waking state* [hypnotic amnesia] and can be revived by a mild word of command and a pressure of the hand intended to indicate a different state of consciousness. He had, for instance, given a woman in a state of som-nambulism a negative hallucination to the effect that he was no longer present, and had then endeavored to draw her attention to himself in a great variety of ways, including some of the decidedly aggressive type. After she had been woken up he asked her to tell him what he had done to her while she thought he was not there. She replied in surprise that she knew nothing of it. But he did not accept this. He insisted that she could remember everything and laid his hand on her forehead to help her recall it. And lo and behold! she ended by describing everything that she had ostensibly not perceived during her somnambulism and ostensibly not remembered in her waking state.
>
> This astonishing and instructive experiment served as my model. I decided to start from the assumption that my patients knew everything that was of pathogenic significance and that it was only a question of obliging them to communicate it. (Breuer and Freud, 1895, pp. 109–110)

The feasibility of recovering lost memories without formal hypnotic induction has been recently substantiated in a series of controlled laboratory experiments by the author and his colleagues (e.g., Erdelyi and Becker, 1974; Erdelyi and Kleinbard, 1978; Shapiro and Erdelyi, 1974). It has been shown that through concentration and repeated recall efforts, subjects can recover substantial amounts of initially inaccessible memories. Testing subjects over a period of a full week, for example, Erdelyi and Kleinbard (1978) were able to raise the average subject's recall for a list of stimuli by over 50 percent, producing memory functions (see Figure 1.4) which resemble upside-down versions of the classic Ebbinghaus (1885) curve of forgetting. Thus, instead of the usually observed forgetting (amnesia) over time, this laboratory program has produced the reverse of forgetting (hypermnesia) over time. An impor-

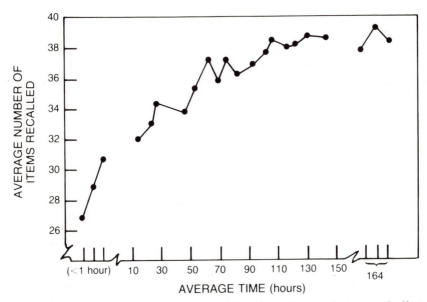

Figure 1.4. The recovery of lost memories (hypermnesia) with time and effort. Note that the recovered materials were pictorial. (Erdelyi & Kleinbard, J. Exp. Psych: Hum. Learn. & Mem., 4. Copyright 1978 by the American Psychological Assoc. Reprinted by permission.)

tant feature of these experiments is that they control for a potentially fatal confound in Bernheim's informal clinical demonstration, namely, the possibility that the subject is not really *remembering* more but merely *reporting* more in subsequent recall efforts. This *report criterion* problem, as it is technically termed (e.g., Egan, 1958; Erdelyi, 1970; Swets, Tanner, and Birdsall, 1961), can be extremely treacherous, as will be seen in subsequent discussions of topics such as the unconscious and Freud's infantile-seduction theory of the etiology of hysteria.

One intriguing discovery to emerge from this experimental work is an apparent link between hypermnesia and imagery processes. (For a recent critical discussion, see Erdelyi, 1982; Roediger, 1982; Roediger, Payne, Gillespie, and Lean, 1982.) Experiments involving *picture* stimuli yield powerful hypermnesias; memory lists consisting of words, on the other hand, usually produce amnesic or inert recall functions over time. If the subject, however, actively recodes the verbal input into "mental pictures," hypermnesias are obtained comparable to those with pictures (Erdelyi, Finkelstein, Herrell, Miller, and Thomas, 1976). The connection between imaginal processing and hypermnesia may help explain the prominent role played by imagery in the hypermnesia-oriented *Studies on Hysteria*. This emphasis on imagery disappears in Freud's later case histories when insight gradually replaces hypermnesia as the primary consciousness-raising objective of psychoanalytic therapy. Nevertheless, the problem of imagistic versus verbal thinking remains an important theoretical issue of psychoanalytic psychology, as we shall see, especially in connection with Freud's distinction between *primary* and *secondary* process functioning, and Freud's theory of dreams.

Freud's concentration-pressure technique for inducing hypermnesias without hypnosis was, then, a systematic application of the procedure he observed Bernheim employ for lifting hypnotic amnesias: When he could not hypnotize a patient, or perhaps did not care to, Freud would simply insist to the patient that he could remember, even if that did not seem possible.

In effect, Freud kept testing and retesting recall over a period of time, in the manner of recent laboratory procedures for producing hypermnesia. Also, Freud would often lay his hand on the patient's head and urge him onto even further effort under the (literal) pressure of his hand, a practice often seen in faith healing and other religious ceremonies.

The technique seemed to work for Freud, just as it had for Bernheim, but Freud soon tired of it. It was just as boring to keep up a litany of concentration harangues, of "yes you cans," as repetitively intoning, "You are falling asleep, you are falling asleep." In fact, starting with Emmy von N., his first patient in the *Studies,* Freud began to see problems in this "pushy" approach. The patient herself, a lady of strong will and uninhibited tongue, blew up at Freud during one of his mnemonic badgerings, complaining that he was actually ruining her concentration with his incessant harangues, and demanded that he allow her to recollect in her own good way and in her own good time.

Freud soon began to give the patient increasing leeway in the manner and tempo of the "work of recollection." Within a short while, in fact, he went from one extreme to the other. From the initial pressure technique—think harder, concentrate, you can recall, yes you can, try harder, concentrate—he moved to the exact opposite, a completely nondirective, unguided format, the free-association technique, in which the patient was told simply to lie back on the couch, relax, and say anything—but anything—that came to mind, without self-censorship. These free-association instructions were to become the "basic rule" of psychoanalysis. Actually, in the *Studies on Hysteria,* as already indicated, the free associations were slightly guided, at least with respect to the cognitive modality emphasized, since the patient was usually asked to call out any *image* or *scene* crossing his mind; later, the instructions were to become even less specific: Just call out *anything* that crosses your mind, withholding nothing. (Imagery, however, still played a role later, since free associations were often extracted in response to dreams, the imagistic cognitive medium par excellence, and in Freud's estimate, "the royal road to the unconscious.")

Thus, Freud shifted from an overbearingly pushy cognitive approach for recovering lost memories to a totally permissive one. Without realizing it, Freud had stumbled upon a subtle strategy of ancient oriental thinking, most directly expressed in Taoism: the paradoxical notion of *wei-wu-wei*, of doing without doing. The Taoists repeatedly emphasize that by trying too hard, by being pushy in seeking a goal, by huffing and puffing, one inevitably loses the goal. The best way to achieve is not to strain to achieve, to be loose, to let go, to let things come naturally:

> The secret waits for the insight
> of eyes unclouded by longing;
> those who are bound by desire
> see only the outward container. *(Tao Tê-Ching)*

Free associating is a cognitive form of doing without doing. The person lies back passively and tries not to force past structures or constraints upon his thinking and verbalizations. Ultimately, however, in Freud's estimate, it is a far more potent device for consciousness raising than either hypnosis or pressure, for with free association the patient gains access not only to lost memories (hypermnesia) but to inaccessible meanings as well (insight). Freud, who unlike Jung, had little contact with Eastern thinking, actually got his first idea for the free-association technique from an article by Ludwig Börne entitled "The Art of Becoming an Original Writer in Three Days," which Freud had read as a boy of fourteen but then apparently had forgotten. Freud's "discovery" of the free-association technique was, then, a form of unconscious plagiarism, or "cryptomnesia" (Freud, 1920a). Börne's formula, incidentally, for becoming an original writer in three days goes as follows:

> Take a few sheets of paper and for three days on end write down without fabrication or hypocrisy, everything that comes into your head. Write down what you think of yourself, of your wife, of the Turkish War, of Goethe, of Fonk's trial, of the Last Judgement, of your superiors—and when three days have passed you will be quite out of your senses with astonishment at the new and unheard-of thoughts you have had. This is the art of becoming an original writer in three days. (Cited in Freud, 1920a, p. 265)

As simple as the free-association procedure appears to be—what could be easier than saying aloud whatever crosses one's mind?—it is extremely hard. Indeed, it is psychologically impossible. Freud discovered that the patient, no matter how well-intentioned, inevitably cheats on the basic rule, selectively censoring his associations. Some thoughts are simply too painful. Free associations, it thus turned out, are never really free; there is always a profound "resistance" opposing the uninhibited flow of mental contents. Interestingly, this is not just a form of outward dishonesty, but reflects a pervasive internal tendency toward's self-deception in one's own private thinking. This inward dishonesty was to be known in its multiple manifestations as the *mechanisms of defense* (see Chapter 5). Their exploration and analysis was to be one of Freud's major contributions to the psychology of cognition, though the general notion has long been known to the artist:

> Every man has reminiscences which he would not tell to everyone but only to his friends. He has other matters in his mind which he would not reveal even to his friends, but only to himself, and that in secret. But there are other things which a man is afraid to tell even to himself, and every decent man has a number of such things stored away in his mind. (Fyodor Dostoyevsky, *Notes from Underground,* p. 57)

INSIGHT, INTERPRETATION, AND ANALYSIS OF RESISTANCES

Never underestimate small signs. (Sigmund Freud)

You know my method; it is founded upon the observation of trifles. (Sherlock Holmes, *The Bascomb Valley Mystery*)

It is a well-known phenomenon in science that the development of a new instrument can have far-reaching consequences for a field. The free-association technique was to be such a development, it being regarded within psychoanalysis as something akin to the microscrope in biology—a revolutionary instrument for bringing to light what is not visible superficially.

The objective of hypnosis and the pressure technique, which free association was meant to replace, was to yield a pinpoint hypermnesia of the traumatic incident that had originally given rise to the neurotic symptom. Free association, which now freed the patient to range over an unlimited psychological terrain, revealed, however, that it was a mistake to assume the existence of merely a *single* causal event; instead, it became clear that there was actually a confluence of events, widely dispersed over time and specific situations, which were nevertheless "linked" thematically around some underlying frustration, fear, or conflict. Thus, there was no single trauma that led to the symptoms; rather, symptoms were "overdetermined" by a vast subterranean network of causative factors. This submerged network was the underlying structure upon which the neurosis rested, and it was the indispensable role of free association to reveal this structure.

The consciousness-raising goal of psychoanalytic psychotherapy now underwent a subtle but profound transformation. The patient was to gain consciousness not just for isolated emotional events (hypermnesia) but, more importantly, for the pervasive psychological structure of which the events were merely components. This structure constituted not just a constellation of fear-evoking impulses and experiences, but also the configuration of defensive mechanisms by which they were excluded from consciousness and inhibited. Thus, to apprehend the structure in its completeness, it was also necessary to gain consciousness for the defensive components of the structure, that is, to *analyze the resistances* (or defenses), which in any event had to be mastered if they were to be penetrated and bypassed.

The patient's ability, then, to see beyond the superficial manifestations into the deep structure of which they are a part is what has come to be known as *insight*; it constitutes *seeing into* the underlying structure—the meaning—of superficially unrelated and, therefore, superficially meaningless events. The process for extracting underlying meaning from surface cues, such as symptoms, dreams, slips of the tongue, rituals, and even jokes, is what is called in psychoanalysis *interpretation*. The psychoanalyst, who unlike his patient, is unencumbered by the patient's specific resistances against insight, assists him in the process by sharing (in carefully measured doses, lest he make the patient too anxious [cf. Freud, 1940]) his own interpretations of the materials the patient brings forth.

Ultimately, it is exceedingly difficult, if not impossible, to speak meaningfully about insight and interpretation in the abstract. One gains a much more concrete grasp of the process through actual clinical examples, and for this reason we now turn to one such case. Out of practical necessity we can deal only with a very simple example, involving minimal resistances and requiring very little in the way of background and free-associative materials.

The example chosen is an incident described and analyzed by Freud in *The Psychopathology of Everyday Life* (1901b). It is a rather insignificant, even trivial event, involving an unpleasant secret. Nevertheless, Freud's treatment of it nicely illustrates the manner in which free association can uncover latent materials.

The incident involves what has come to be translated in English as a *parapraxis*, basically any trifling cognitive failure such as a slip of the tongue, a mishearing, a forgetting of an obvious thing, and similar occurrences. It was Freud's theory that a parapraxis was essentially a fleeting neurotic disturbance. Consequently, he thought it appropriate to apply the same tools of analysis to parapraxes as he applied to full-fledged neurotic symptoms.

Here then is the parapraxis and its analysis: Freud was taking—or rather trying to take—a vacation when he fell into a conversation with a young academician who was familiar with some of his theories. The young man was exceedingly dispirited about the state of the world in general and was embittered in particular about his own bleak prospects in academe. Not only were there few opportunities, but his Jewish background virtually guaranteed professional failure in the endemic anti-Semitism of the Austro-Hungarian Empire of those times. He sought to punctuate his outrage at the injustice by quoting a line from Virgil's *Aeneid,* in which the wronged Dido prays for revenge:

Exoriar aliquis nostris ex ossibus ultor.
(Let someone arise from my bones as an avenger.)

However, the young man had made a mistake; he had omitted the word *aliquis* (someone), saying: "*Exoriar . . . ex nostris ossibus ultor.*" Immediately aware of the error, he tried to correct it, but he just could not remember the fugitive word, and finally had to ask Freud to supply it. Rather put out by his failure, the young man tried to turn the table on Freud. He reminded Freud of his curious theory that such senseless miscues had meaning—"that one never forgets a thing without some reason"—and now challenged Freud to prove his theory.

Freud promptly took up the challenge, but on the condition that the young man follow the basic rule of psychoanalysis, "to tell me, *candidly* and *uncritically,* whatever comes into your mind if you direct your attention to the forgotten word without any definite aim" (Freud, 1901b, p. 9). The young man accepted and began his free associations:

"There springs to mind the ridiculous notion of dividing the word *aliquis* like this: *a* and *liquis.*" The next word to come to mind was "*reliquiem*" (relic); then: "liquefying," "fluidity," "fluid" (p. 9). Then a somewhat strange association arose:

"I am now thinking of *Simon of Trent,* whose relics I saw two years ago in a church at Trent. I am thinking of the accusation of ritual blood-sacrifice which is being brought against the Jews again just now . . ." (pp. 9–10). (The original event took place in the fifteenth century. Simon had been a two-and-a-half-year-old child whom the Jews had been accused of killing for the purpose of blood ritual. As a result, Simon was declared a martyr and a saint. Only centuries later did the Catholic Church exonerate the Jews, since confessions of the crime had been extracted under torture.)

The young man's next association was that he had recently read an article in an Italian newspaper entitled "What St. Augustine Thinks of Women." Then: "I am thinking of a fine old gentleman I met on my travels last week. He was a real *original,* with all the appearance of a huge bird of prey. His name was Benedict . . ." (p. 10).

At this point Freud broke into the subject's free associations: "Here are a row of saints and Fathers of the Church: St. *Simon,* St. *Augustine,* St. *Benedict,* [and] the Church Father . . . *Origen*" (p. 10).

The next free association was, "St. *Januarius* and the miracle of his blood" (p. 10).

Freud again interposed a comment: "Just a moment: St. *Januarius* and St. *Augustine* both have to do with the calendar. But won't you remind me about the miracle of his blood?"

The young man then explained:

"They keep the blood of St. Januarius in a phial inside the Church of Naples, and on a particular holiday it miraculously *liquefies.* The people attach great importance to this miracle and get very excited if it is delayed as happened once at a time when the French were occupying the town. So the general in command—or have I got it wrong? Was it Garibaldi?—took the reverend gentleman aside [the priest in charge of the church] and gave him to understand with an unmistakeable gesture towards the soldiers posted outside that he *hoped* that the miracle would take place very soon. And in fact it did take place. . . ." (P. 10)

And then something interesting happened. The free associations stopped and a look of consternation came over the face of the young academician. "Why do you pause?" asked Freud. The young man replied: "Well, something has come into my mind . . . but it's too intimate to pass on. . . . Besides, I don't see any connection, or any necessity for saying it" (p. 11).

Now Freud knew that he had him: "You can leave the connections to me. Of course I can't force you to talk about something that you find distasteful; but then you mustn't insist on learning from me how you came to forget your *aliquis*" (p. 11).

Finally, the young man reluctantly continued: "I have suddenly thought of a lady from whom I might easily hear a piece of news that would be very awkward for both of us" (p. 11).

At this point Freud delivered his interpretation, in the form of a question: "That her periods have stopped?" The young man was startled. "How could you guess that?" (p. 11).

Freud replied:

"That's not difficult any longer; you've prepared the way sufficiently. Think of *the calendar saints, the blood that starts to flow on a particular day; the disturbance when the event fails to take place;* the open threats that the *miracle must be vouchsafed or else....* In fact you have made use of the miracle of St. Januarius to manufacture a brilliant allusion to women's periods." (P. 11)

The young man's muted reaction was, "I certainly was not aware of it."

Freud then elaborated on his interpretation: The prefix *a* often means no; *liquis* means liquid. The young man was trying to reject from consciousness the frightening idea *"a-liquis,"* no-liquid, that is, no menstruation—she's pregnant! Also the young man might already have begun to feel guilty over a possible solution to the problem other than marriage, namely abortion, alluded to by St. *Simon,* who had been *sacrificed as a child,* and so on.

The young man asked Freud to stop: "I hope you don't take these thoughts of mine too seriously, if indeed I really had them. In return I will confess to you that the lady is Italian and that I went to Naples with her. But mayn't all this just be a matter of chance?" (p. 11).

This small psychoanalytic episode illustrates most of the features of the free-association procedure: The subject initially feels he is associating randomly, but in fact the material is structured; the psychoanalyst intervenes with interpretative hints to speed up insight; there is resistance (the pause in free associations; the tendency to censor "irrelevant" materials despite a commitment to the basic rule; the discomfiture at the uncovered insight; attempts at denying it through unreasonable skepticism; and so forth); the frequent involvement of sexual themes in repressed or otherwise inhibited materials; also, the artistic nature of the symptom, in this case "the brilliant allusion to a woman's period," foreshadowing Freud's future theory of art.

The analysis of this minor parapraxis, then, is the model for Freud's uncovering approach, through free association, to all significant cognitive phenomena, from dreams, delusions, art, and neuroses, to religion.

TRANSFERENCE

We finally come to the small mystery surrounding Breuer's case of Anna O., the "untoward event" that put a premature end to Anna's therapy. It terrified Breuer enough to make him abandon the cathartic technique altogether and to suppress from the case history what turned out in retrospect to have been a major discovery, the phenomenon of *transference.*

Transference, a technical term subsequently coined by Freud, refers to the tendency of patients, regardless of sex, to develop passionate feelings of love ("positive transference") and hate ("negative transference") toward their therapist. The reverse tendency on the therapist's part, *countertransference*, may also be observed, though it is less frequent and generally less intense. In Anna O.'s case, however, all variations of the transference phenomenon erupted, particularly of the positive erotic type, eventually wrecking the treatment. This aspect of the case, which Breuer completely censored from his account, was revealed some half a century later by Ernest Jones (1953, pp. 246ff.), to whom Freud had earlier confided the story.

The emotional rapport, which perhaps accounted for Breuer's initial tolerance for Anna's meandering chitchats during hypnotic suggestion sessions and from which arose the cathartic talking cure, apparently escalated into an intense emotional attachment. Breuer became progressively consumed with his star patient. Not only did he spend hours with her every day, but at home, to Mrs. Breuer's growing consternation, he spoke incessantly about the marvels of the new therapy —and of the patient. At some point, well into the second year of the therapy, Breuer began to gain insight (perhaps with some interpretative assistance from his wife) into the nonscientific dimension of his involvement with Anna. He was extremely disturbed by his new understanding and resolved to put a swift end to the therapy. This was a time when Anna was making exceptional progress and had virtually shed the last of her symptoms with the hypermnesia and abreaction of the terrifying "black snake" memory.

Breuer abruptly announced to Anna that he would see her no more. He told her that she was basically cured and had no further need of him. That night, however, Breuer received a frantic message from Anna's mother. Anna was very ill; could he please come immediately.

The scene that confronted Breuer at Anna's home was simultaneously bizarre and terrifying to the somewhat straight-laced physician. Thrashing about in her bed, a wild look on her face, Anna was in the throes of childbirth. Between gasps and screams she identified Breuer as the father of her child. In fact, however, there was neither a child nor a pregnancy; Anna was apparently playing out a fantasy—Freud would say a wish—substituting a hysterical pregnancy for the real thing. Breuer managed to keep his head. He approached Anna, placed her under hypnosis, and commanded her to calm down and to go to sleep. He was back to hypnotic suggestion. Breuer succeeded after some effort, but he was a shaken man. He hurried home, ordered his wife to pack her bags, and the next morning was off to Venice for a second honeymoon.

Anna suffered a relapse and was finally placed in a sanitarium. It is reported (Edinger, 1963; Freeman, 1972) that a number of physicians fell in love with her there and that she turned down several proposals for marriage. She improved considerably and finally left the sanitarium, moving with her family to Germany. There, as Bertha Pappenheim, she became a founder of social work and a radical feminist. She never married. One of her most quoted statements touched on childbirth: "If there is any justice in the next life women will make the laws there and men will bear the children" (Jones, 1953, p. 224).

As to Breuer, it may be said that he never recovered from the experience. It put an end to his experimentation with the cathartic technique and explains his reluctance to publish the case. After his joint publication with Freud, the friendship between the two men gradually unraveled, ostensibly because Breuer could not stomach Freud's increasing emphasis of the sexual etiology of the neuroses. Freud assumed that the whole issue was too painful for Breuer to come to terms with.

In fairness to Breuer, however, whose credibility is severely challenged by this later version of events, it should be said that no independent substantiation exists for Jones' revelations, which, in fact, contain a number of serious internal contradictions (see Edinger, 1963; Ellenberger, 1970; 1972).

The really important point regarding transference, however, is not the historical wrinkles associated with its discovery, but its psychological status. In his early practice Freud soon came to realize that Anna's reaction to Breuer (if we follow Jones' version) was more the rule than the exception, for Freud found that most of his patients (usually females at this juncture) developed overtender feelings toward him in the course of treatment. One dramatic example, which Freud cites in several of his writings, involved a patient in cathartic therapy. Freud was bending over her, commanding her to awake from her trance, when suddenly she not only awoke but put her arms around him in a passionate embrace. At this very moment one of Freud's maids accidentally walked into the room, putting an end to the interesting tableau.

As awkward as these passionate attachments could be for the therapist, Freud refused to be scared off by them. At first he viewed them philosophically as simply an unpleasant feature of his therapeutic technique, a kind of professional hazard, such as exists in every medical specialty, which had to be handled with care. He even managed to find a positive function for it: A deeply attached patient could be more easily persuaded to proceed with the painful "work of recollection" (Freud, 1914c) than the disinterested one. On the whole, however, Freud originally viewed transference as an impediment to therapy. Beyond the social embarrassment it might bring to the therapist—or the psychological problem of countertransference—the transference could also function as a form of resistance, since the patient inevitably tended to become more engrossed in her therapist than in her therapy. Another problem—and this is a paradoxical point—is that the patient may lose all her symptoms, a phenomenon termed a *transference cure*. The difficulty with such remissions of symptoms is that they are transitory, just as in the case of hypnotic suggestion, tending to mislead the patient into believing that a real cure has been achieved and that further effort, or even therapy, might be superfluous. Freud was specifically to assume that the transference cure was essentially another manifestation, this time in psychoanalysis, of suggestion, the ubiquitous active agent not only in Bernheim's hypnotic-suggestion technique, but also, as we have seen, in magnetism, faith healing, and exorcism (and even perhaps systematic desensitization): "What [Bernheim] called suggestibility is nothing else but the tendency to transference. . . . We have to admit that we have only abandoned hypnosis in our method in order to discover suggestion again in the shape of transference" (Freud, 1917, pp. 387–388).

A more profound psychological understanding of transference, however, eventually led to the conclusion that there was much more to the phenomenon than mere suggestion, and that, in fact, far from being an impediment, transference was an outright necessity for a successful therapy. Indeed, Freud was to argue that pathologically narcissistic patients (schizophrenics, for example) who were too wrapped up in themselves emotionally to develop meaningful relationships with other persons could not be successfully treated by psychoanalysis.

The new perspective arose from Freud's growing realization of the extent to which transference reactions were irrational. The passions evoked by the therapist, whether of love or hate, were simply not justified by the character or actions of the therapist. From this Freud surmised that the emotions thus unchained were not at bottom related to the therapist, whom in fact the patient, for the most part, did not even see—since the therapist sat, as was Freud's custom, behind the couch and thus constituted something of a "plastic field" in the style of a Rorschach inkblot. Rather, the therapy was rekindling long-buried emotions and interpersonal patterns from childhood which were now being "displaced" or *transferred* (hence the term) upon the person of the therapist. Thus, the *real* loves and hatreds involved significant persons from the patient's past—mother, father, siblings. In Freud's words, the transference represents a "new edition of the old disease" (Freud, 1917, p. 386). From this vantage point, transference could be viewed as an essential medium for hypermnesia and insight. The subject is not merely recalling but *reliving* long-lost conflicts responsible for the illness:

> The patient does not *remember* anything of what he has forgotten and repressed, but *acts* it out. He reproduces it not as a memory but as an action; he *repeats* it, without, of course, knowing that he is repeating it.
>
> For instance, the patient does not say that he remembers

that he used to be defiant and critical toward his parents' authority; instead, he behaves in that way to the doctor.[2] (Freud, 1914c, p. 150)

Through the vehicle of free association and the therapist's interpretative interventions, the subject can now hope to achieve truly profound insights into the structure and genesis of his problems. Moreover, and this is a critical point, the subject may transcend mere intellectual insight and achieve what might be called emotional insight—an understanding of the guts, not just of the brain. Freud called this dimension of emotional comprehension and mastery, *working through*. It is an essential ingredient of a successful psychoanalysis, representing the element of abreaction in it (Freud, 1914c).

The transference, in Freud's later view, recreated the genesis and subsequent elaborations of the illness, laying bare the emotional and cognitive structures in which the neurosis was rooted. In fact, it becomes a new, artificial reenactment of the neurosis—for this reason, called the *transference neurosis*. Since it is now replayed in a professional therapeutic context rather than in the hurly-burly of disturbed family settings (which presumably led to the neurosis), it becomes possible to restructure the original neurotic resolution into a new, healthier one. The psycho*analysis,* once it has analyzed the neurosis into its constituent structural elements, can now yield a new and healthier *psychosynthesis* (Freud, 1919), or in alternate terms, produce a "re-education" of psychological structure (Freud, 1905a). Freud might well have called it a *reprogramming* or *debugging* if the computer metaphor had been available to him (see Chapter 3).

The transference, then—which modern psychoanalysts conceptualize more broadly as the "relationship" between patient and therapist (e.g., Luborsky, 1984)—is a powerful hypermnesic medium, yielding not just recollection of distant events, but an actual reliving of lost conflictual memories, thus precipitating profound insights—cognitive and emotive—of the underlying structure of the patient's problem. The illness, in its recreated version, could now be resolved. In Freud's colorful language:

It is undeniable that the subjugation of transference-manifestations provides the greatest difficulties for the psychoanalyst;

[2]A rapidly growing experimental literature on "remembering without awareness" (Jacoby and Witherspoon, 1982) is demonstrating that both normal subjects as well as amnesics can evidence by their behavior the learning of complex skills (for example, mirror-image writing, solving puzzles and mathematical problems, specific fear reactions) without any awareness of having learned the knowledge in question (e.g., Cermak, 1982; Graf, Squire, and Mandler, 1984; Moscovitch, 1982; Tulving, Schachter, and Stark, 1982).

but it must not be forgotten that they, and they only, render the invaluable service of making the patient's buried and forgotten love-emotions actual and manifest; for in the last resort no one can be slain *in absentia* or in *effigie*. (Freud, 1912a, pp. 114–115)

SUMMARY

Psychoanalytic psychotherapy, as we have seen in this chapter, was no sudden discovery. It evolved only gradually, often serendipitously, and sometimes painfully. A brief recapitulation of what psychoanalytic therapy came to be is thus in order.

The patient lies down on a couch (a vestige of its hypnotic origin) and proceeds according to the basic rule to free associate without inhibition or censorship. These free associations are, however, never really free. The patient inevitably cheats on the basic rule since certain ideas are just too painful to utter—or even think. Moreover, the therapist himself subtly affects the content and direction of the free associations through his interpretations, and through his requests for associations to specific materials such as dreams, parapraxes, symptoms, transference manifestations, resistances, and so forth.

The object of free association is to uncover inaccessible memories (hypermnesia) and cognitive structures (insight), including defensive structures (resistances).

The patient's eventual transference reactions, positive and negative, are vital media for revealing complex maladaptive patterns encrusted in the patient's interpersonal repertory (that is, his neurosis); the emotional nature of transference, moreover, makes it a particularly appropriate medium for the working through—discharging and mastering—of the emotional component of the neurotic structure.

Despite almost continuous changes in theory and technique, psychoanalysis, from catharsis on, has abided by one constant guiding theme: the necessity for consciousness raising (making the unconscious, conscious). In earlier versions of psychoanalysis, the focus rested on hypermnesia, the recovery of lost (traumatic) memories for the purpose of abreaction. Later, the focus shifted to insight, the uncovering of—or *seeing into*—the deep structure of one's psychological makeup. In the end, the objective of psychoanalysis is nothing other than the ancient Socratic imperative, "know thyself." Its therapeutic rationale is straightforward: Knowing the true (deep) causes of one's behavior gives one power over these causes—and therefore over one's behavior.

In Freud's simple reckoning: "Knowledge is power."

CHAPTER TWO

THE
UNCONSCIOUS

♦

> The division of the psychical into what is conscious and what is unconscious is the fundamental premise of psychoanalysis. (Freud, 1923, p. 13)

A certain middle-aged woman, whose case is reported by Deutsch (1965), lost a pet dog she had recently acquired. Her reaction to the loss was puzzling: She sank into a profound depression that eventually required her hospitalization and developed the frightening delusion that, for well-deserved but unaccounted reasons, she would be thrown naked into the street and left there to suffer a terrible death.

How could such a strange reaction be explained? The question is not an idle academic one, for most clinical cases involve some form or other of pathological overreaction or "misreaction." It is instructive to contrast the behavioristic and psychoanalytic approaches to such baffling overreactions, which may be schematized as a small stimulus producing an over-large response:

The behavioristic explanation is typically framed in terms of classical conditioning (e.g., Dollard and Miller, 1950; Eysenck, 1960; Watson, 1924; Wolpe, 1973). Overreactions, such as phobias, result from the past pairing of a neutral stimulus (the conditioned stimulus, CS) with another stimulus (the unconditioned stimulus, UCS) that produces an intense response (the unconditioned response, UCR). In line with our schematization:

After one or more pairings, the initially ineffective (small) stimulus now elicits, on its own, a response similar to the UCR, called the conditioned response (CR):

Thus, overreactions and misreactions are learned in the same way that Pavlov's dogs learned to salivate to a bell.

A major advantage of the behavioristic conception, in addition to its compelling simplicity, is that overreactions of clinical interest, such as phobias, are readily produced in the laboratory. One widely cited experiment in psychology, for example, is Watson and Rayner's (1920) induction of a phobia to white rats in an infant, Little Albert, through the pairing of an initially innocuous white rat (the CS) with a frightening noise (the UCS). The rat, which had initially been an object of pleasure, thereafter produced crying and avoidance on the part of Little Albert.

Unfortunately for the classical conditioning formulation (which, as we have seen in Chapter 1, was actually implicit in early versions of psychoanalytic clinical theory), the picture tends to become murky in real life. Although it is not difficult to find naturally occurring examples that fit the classical conditioning model, the typical case fails to turn up any past traumatic experience (traumatic UCS) in connection with the currently feared but realistically harmless stimulus. Worse still, in most instances of misreactions it is not even clear how the classical conditioning paradigm might be sensibly applied. The baffling depression and delusion of Deutsch's patient is a case in point.

The psychoanalytic approach to such puzzling overreactions introduces a striking new perspective. It holds that, when properly examined, there is no such thing as an overreaction (e.g., Freud, 1909); what appears to be an overreaction arises from an illusion, namely, that the mild stimulus that appears to produce the overblown response is in fact the direct cause of the reaction. Psychoanalysis proposes instead that the direct cause of the response is fully commensurate with the response and the only reason it is not immediately obvious is that it exists at a level inaccessible to both the subject and the observer. The real cause, in short, is unconscious. The innocuous stimulus is assumed only to trigger or symbolically stand for the true cause of the overreaction. Thus the psychological situation in apparent overreactions is not:

but:

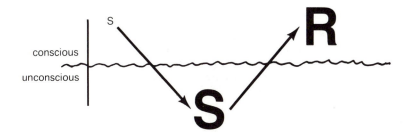

Note that the alternative conceptualization of the problem yields quite different strategies for therapy. The difference resides not in whether the response to the stimulus requires desensitization, reconditioning, abreaction, working through, and so forth—for these various techniques, as suggested in Chapter 1, are not substantively different from one another—but in identifying *what* stimulus it is that requires therapeutic attention. If the patient's problem is in fact one having to do with dogs, or the loss of dogs, then that should be the focus of the therapy. If, on the other hand, that stimulus is only a screen or trigger for an unconscious constellation of disturbing stimuli, then it is the unconscious problem that requires attention, and therapeutic excursions into the issue of dogs and their loss would constitute a woeful diversion. The fundamental difference between behavioristic and psychoanalytic approaches, therefore, is not so much what to do about the problem, but identifying what the problem is; and it is psychoanalysis' distinctive position that the structure of most real-life problems is predominantly unconscious, requiring protracted and difficult analysis—that is, *psychoanalysis.*

To put the issue into concrete form, we may now consider a few more details about Deutsch's patient. The patient had obtained her pet dog soon after her sister, with whom she had lived all her adult life, unexpectedly married and moved to a foreign land. The patient's overt reaction to the event, despite a twenty-five-year living partnership, had been remarkably generous; she seemed happy for her sister and wished her only the best. Yet, this sister had been the object of unusually stormy feelings during the patient's childhood and adolescence. The birth of the sister, who was eight years younger than the patient, had provoked an intense jealousy, and the patient had frequently expressed the wish that the sister should die. Instead, it was their mother who died a few years later, an event that resulted in a radical transformation in the patient's attitude toward the sister, whom she now regaled with extraordinary love and tenderness. Thereafter, the patient's life became immersed in the well-being of her sister. The patient also developed a peculiar compulsion in connection with her sister: She had to repeat her acts a certain number of times so that, through some magical property of the repetitions, her sister would be kept safe from harm. When the patient was twenty-one her father died, leaving the orphaned sisters destitute. The patient had hoped to embark on a writing career but now sacrificed her plans by taking a menial job to support her younger sister. The sister eventually developed literary ambitions of her own, and the patient continued to support her until her unexpected marriage.

These details do not, of course, prove anything. It is possible that the patient was unduly attached to her pet dog and that her reaction to the dog's loss was somehow commensurate with the event. Yet, it is difficult to escape the hunch that the patient's reaction had more to do with the loss of her sister than with the loss of her dog. The patient's therapy tended to confirm this surmise. The initial conscious feelings of love and dignified understanding gave way to a savage, recriminating hatred for the ungrateful sister who, the patient eventually insisted, deserved to be thrown out into the street, as indeed she would have been, had not the patient taken mercy on her.

PSYCHIC DETERMINISM AND THE UNCONSCIOUS

The foregoing case, although certainly not conclusive in any sense, illustrates the type of psychological riddle, encountered in endless variations in the clinic and in everyday life, that impelled Freud to adopt the theory of unconscious mentation. Although a variety of phenomena, both clinical and experimental in nature, tend to prove formally the existence of unconscious processes (these will be critically examined in later parts of this chapter), Freud's espousal of the unconscious was ultimately dictated not by any specific empirical fact but by scientific necessity; for without the assumption of an unconscious dimension of mind, psychological activity dissolves into a senseless unfolding of disconnected, haphazard, and even bizarre events. Such a view of intrinsically random mentation was, as Freud clearly saw, incompatible with the basic tenet of science that, underlying the surface appearances of chaos is harmony, structure, order. As a self-conscious scientist, Freud insisted that the psychological universe was also ruleful and coherent; the reason that it often appeared otherwise was, simply, because the harmonizing elements or links between psychological events were unconscious.

When developing this point formally Freud, like most serious scientists of the nineteenth and early twentieth centuries, articulated it in terms of the doctrine of determinism, which holds that all events are strictly determined by an unbroken sequence of causes and that, therefore, nothing occurs by chance or accident. Freud was altogether peremptory about his extension of the physical sciences' dogma of determinism to the psychological realm (hence, "psychic determinism") and used it as a justification for many of his guiding psychological assumptions. For example, in response to the often voiced objection that slips of the tongue and other trifling errors were not worthy of scientific interest because they were intrinsically meaningless events, "little accidents," Freud replied:

> What does the man [advancing such a criticism] mean by this? Does he mean to maintain that there are occurrences so small that they fail to come within the causal sequence of things, that they might as well be other than they are? Anyone thus break-

ing away from the determination of natural phenomena, at any single point, has thrown over the whole scientific outlook on the world (*Weltanschauung*). (Freud, 1917, p. 27)

The deterministic thread running through so much of psycho-analysis is emphasized here because there are at least two problems with it that should be confronted and that most contemporary treatments of psychoanalysis have either perpetuated or evaded.

The first and most obvious of these problems is that modern physics has broken away from strict determinism and, in so doing, has in fact "thrown over the whole scientific outlook on the world" as conceived by science up to the early twentieth century (Capra, 1975; d'Espagnat, 1979; Heisenberg, 1971; Hook, 1959; Koestler, 1967; von Bertalanffy, 1968). Quantum mechanics and Heisenberg's derivative principle of indeterminacy have resulted in a probabilistic conception of natural law. Events, at least at certain levels of systems, are no longer regarded as inexorably and absolutely determined; their occurrence is simply a matter of high or low probability.

The overthrow of strict determinism was a shattering development in modern science. Some of the giants of the field who had themselves contributed to its demise could not abide it. Albert Einstein, in an oft-quoted plaint, insisted that "God does not play dice with the world" (Clark, 1971, p. 414). But in this he was mistaken. God does indeed play at dice, though—and this might be a consolation of sorts—the dice are loaded.

The implication for psychoanalysis of the collapse of strict determinism has not been adequately explored, though it is clear from Freud's writings that he would have been no less disturbed by the development than Einstein. One tack that could be taken is to note that, logically, the breakdown of determinism in physics need not apply to the psychological realm. This stance would not be very convincing, however, since it was primarily from the physical sciences that psychoanalysis (and no less so, behaviorism) borrowed the doctrine in the first place.

A more pragmatic approach (e.g., Salmon, 1959; Sherwood, 1969) is to treat determinism as a useful heuristic rather than as an immutable principle of science and leave it to empirical research to uncover deterministic relations when and where they might apply:

There is nothing logically peculiar in looking for something even though we cannot be given iron-bound assurance that it exists. We merely need to know that it would be worth finding if it did exist. . . . Furthermore, even if it were not true that every event is subject to complete causal determinism, it might still be true that some very interesting causal relations exist. (Salmon, 1959, p. 274)

Finally, even if strict determinism failed in certain psychological domains, this would not mean that psychological events are therefore haphazard or lacking structure. The older, absolutistic determinism would simply give way to a "soft determinism" in which the structure and coherence of mental life assumed a probabilistic rather than absolute character (e.g., Rubinstein, 1973; 1975). Freud's extreme position, as reflected in the quotation on pages 51–52, would have to be moderated, but the basic thrust of his argument would still apply.

We may now consider the second problem resulting from psychoanalysis' espousal of determinism. It will be recalled that the basic notion that mental events had an underlying coherence or structure (which necessitated the assumption of unconscious mentation) tended to find formal expression in the guise of determinism. The problem here is that determinism, as usually understood, stipulates not just that events have a determinate structure (order, pattern, coherence, meaning, etc.) but that this structure is one of cause and effect. In espousing the doctrine of determinism, psychoanalysis unwittingly embraced a limiting formulation of the orderliness of natural events, one resting on the mistaken belief that determination is necessarily causal. The problem is a variant of the propensity to confuse correlation with causation. B may be perfectly correlated with A without being caused by A; yet, if the two variables are perfectly correlated, the value of B is completely determined once we know the value of A. The issue is also akin to the distinction between mechanistic and field theories in physics (Capra, 1975; Koestler, 1964; 1967; von Bertalanffy, 1968).

The cause-effect conception rests on a billiard-ball analogy. A particular entity or event (billiard ball A) has a specific, determining impact on another entity or event (billiard ball B). The broader notion of structural determination or determinateness (of which cause and effect is a special case) is conveyed by the analogy of a puzzle. The value or nature of a missing component is determined by the other elements of the puzzle. Suppose that through a printing error a letter was inadvertently omitted from the word *Lond_n*. The identity of the missing letter is obviously not haphazard but strictly (though perhaps not absolutely) determined by the available structure or "field" of letters. It would make little sense, however, to suggest that any one or the whole pattern of letters was "causing" the second *o* in *London*. Yet it is precisely such an unsatisfying formulation that the doctrine of determinism gratuitously foists upon psychoanalysis.

The implicit equation of structure in general (coherence, order, configuration, pattern, meaning, and so on) with a specific type of structure, cause and effect, has introduced much confusion into psychoanalytic thinking and has had a great deal to do with the obscuring of the essential cognitive nature of psychoanalysis. The point is not that psychoanalysis is not concerned with causes—that cause is a critical issue in psychoanalytic therapy has been underscored by the clinical samples we have examined, including that of Deutsch's depressed patient—but that the meanings with which psychoanalysis deals often have a wider scope.

Consider, for example, a rather basic question. Why do free associations lead to the uncovery of latent psychological meanings? The answer is not necessarily that each associate is inexorably linked, cause-effect style, to some original psychic cause which is agitating for expression; rather, free associations may yield deep meanings because they provide the necessary context (structure, field), crossword puzzle style, from which the missing meanings may be determined. The point is illustrated by the case of the young academician who forgot the word *aliquis* (Chapter 1, pages 39–41). His free associations unveiled the secret fear that his lady friend might be pregnant. The parapraxis fit into a coherent mental scheme, which could be apprehended once a sufficient number of elements were assembled (in the form of free associations and historical information). Freud's interpretation, which the subject confirmed, demonstrated that the subject's free associations were obviously not haphazard or accidental; they were determinate, part of an overall structure, just like the entries in a crossword puzzle. To say this, however, is not the same as to say that they were "caused." Freud implies (see page 41) that the subject's wish to repress the unpleasant thought caused the repression of the related *aliquis*. This, however, is a speculation that is not demanded by the data, nor by the successful demonstration that the parapraxis had meaning.

The confusion of meaning with cause underlies a remarkable range of controversies within and about psychoanalysis, including the question of the nature of interpretation and explanation in psychoanalysis (e.g., Hartmann, 1927; Rubinstein, 1973; 1976; M. Sherwood, 1969; Shope, 1973), the viability of psychoanalysis' formal psychological theory (e.g., Apfelbaum, 1965; Gill and Holzman, 1976; Holt, 1965; 1972; 1976; G. S. Klein, 1973; 1975; Peters, 1958; Ricoeur, 1970; Schafer, 1976), and the scientific status of psychoanalysis (e.g., Guntrip, 1961; Hook, 1959; MacIntyre, 1958; M. Sherwood, 1969; Wittgenstein, 1930–1932; 1942–1946). It is noteworthy that so many of the criticisms of psychoanalysis represent contrary tendencies with respect to the cause-effect issue. A major contemporary school of psychoanalytic thinking, for example, has gone as far as to reject the formal psychological theory of psychoanalysis (often termed *metapsychology*) because its mechanistic (cause-effect) formulations conceptually channel the field into outmoded physicalist notions such as "force," "energy," "etiology," and "hydraulics," which derail it from its true cognitive-psychological domain, semantics and intentions (see especially, Gill and Holzman, 1976; Holt, 1965; 1976; G. S. Klein, 1973; 1975; Schafer, 1976). On the other hand, the scientific status of psychoanalysis has been questioned precisely because it does not offer a true causal approach to psychological phenomena (e.g., Pap, 1959; Wittgenstein, 1930–1932; 1942–1946). The former criticism essentially objects to psychoanalysis' not being sufficiently psychological and cognitive, but fails to take into account Freud's use of multiple metaphor premises (see Chapter 3), and the likelihood that each, including the mechanistic framework, may complement the other. The latter criticism seems to hold it against psychoanalysis that it is too cognitive and psychological, that it is not truly deterministic (despite Freud's pretensions). This criticism reflects an outmoded conception of science, which increasingly is conceived of as dealing not with concrete physical forces or entities but relations, coherences, and dynamic structures (Capra, 1975). The "physical" sciences are less and less physical, and indeed, at times, give the striking impression of becoming "cognitive":

> Today there is a wide measure of agreement, which on the physical side of science approaches almost to unanimity, that the stream of knowledge is heading towards a non-mechanical reality; the universe begins to look more like a great thought than like a great machine. (Sir James Jeans, 1937; cited by Koestler, 1972, p. 58)

The present section has attempted to compress and simplify an extraordinarily complex—and controversial—set of issues in psychoanalysis, philosophy, and science. A brief recapitulation is in order. It was observed that considerations of coherence (structure, order, and so forth) compelled Freud to adopt the hypothesis of unconscious mentation, since only through the assumption of unconscious mental activity could the superficial haphazardness of mental events be resolved into a larger coherent order. This basic approach remains valid, though its articulation in terms of determinism requires two qualifications. Firstly, determinateness in the psychological realm, as in the physical realm, may be probabilistic. Secondly, the determinateness of psychological events need not imply (even if it often does) a cause-effect structure; the inference of unconscious processes follows just as much from structural determinateness as from cause-effect determinism.

IS THE UNCONSCIOUS A DISCOVERY OF PSYCHOANALYSIS?

A speaker at the Third International Congress of Psychology, held in Munich in 1896, read a paper in which he declared that the unconscious was not a question but *the* question of psychology; the unconscious, he said, was the foundation of all psychological life and could be likened to a chain of undersea mountains in which only the peaks emerge, the latter corresponding to consciousness (Ellenberger, 1970, pp. 773–774). The speaker was not Sigmund Freud but the psychologist Theodor Lipps, best known for his work on empathy. Lipps' talk, delivered when Freud was still an obscure physician, serves to underscore the increasingly appreciated fact that the unconscious was by no means a discovery of psychoanalysis (e.g., Ellenberger, 1970; D. B. Klein, 1977; J. G. Miller, 1942; Whyte, 1960). The problem of the unconscious, in one guise or another, was in fact a major preoccupation of nineteenth century thinking, not only in psychology and psychiatry, but in the overall Romantic trend of philosophy (that of Nietzsche and Schopenhauer, for example) and literature (the works of Dostoyevsky, Gogol, Ibsen among others).

In psychiatry, Pierre Janet, Charcot's most prominent student, had developed a psychotherapeutic system that in many ways antedated the work of Breuer and Freud and which had as its central premise the notion that "subconscious fixed ideas" were responsible for psychopathology (cf. Ellenberger, 1970). (Recriminations eventually broke out between Freud and Janet over the latter's claim that much of psychoanalysis was only an embellishment of his own system of psychological analysis and synthesis. The bitterness resulting from these wrangles over priority was probably a major factor behind Freud's abandonment of Janet's term *subconscious* as a synonym for the *unconscious*.) Hermann Helmholtz, the great physicist and physiologist (and a major influence on Freud) advanced the hypothesis of *unconscious inference* to account for the phenomena of depth perception and constancy scaling. He reasoned that since perceivers are not aware of the optical and mathematical principles that they must nevertheless employ to achieve their perceptual judgments, the inferential processes of perception must necessarily be unconscious. Gustav Fechner, the founder of psychophysics, and another critical influence on Freud, introduced the concept of *negative sensations* to refer to perceptual registration below the limen (or threshold) of consciousness. Frederick Myers, borrowing from many sources, including Fechner's work, attempted a grand synthesis of abnormal and parapsychological phenomena through the concept of the *subliminal self*. Earlier, in 1868, E. Hartmann published his highly influential as well as controversial book, *Philosophy of the Unconscious*. Still earlier, C. G. Carus (1846), in his book *Psyche*, made the unconscious the central explanatory principle of psychology: *"The key to an understanding of the nature of the conscious life . . . lies in the sphere of the unconscious"* (p. 1). In the 1820s, Herbart, one of the founders of modern scientific psychology, developed a dynamic psychology of thought in which "ideas" were conceived of as continuously interacting, either enhancing or inhibiting each other in their attempt to gain representation in consciousness. According to Herbart, ideas that are inhibited are not destroyed; they are merely driven below the "limen of consciousness" where they continue to exist in a "state of tendency." In the words of Boring (1950), "Freud's early description of the unconscious might almost have come directly from Herbart, although it did not" (p. 257). The same would of course hold true for Freud's early psychodynamics (Chapter 1, pages 10–11).

Just as the unconscious was not the discovery of any single individual, neither was it the preoccupation of any single century or culture. The issue of unconscious mentation actually constitutes a ubiquitous theme in philosophical and religious thought, receiving greater or lesser attention in different historical epochs (Ellenberger, 1970). Plato, of whose philosophic system it is often said that Western philosophy is only an extended footnote, explicitly advanced a doctrine of unconscious knowledge, holding that we never truly learn anything new because all knowledge is already inherent in the psyche; experience merely cues this latent knowledge, allowing us to "reminisce" it. The existence of the unconscious, for example, of unconscious feelings and unconscious latent powers, is also a central premise of a variety of non-Western philosophical-religious traditions, such as Buddhism and Hinduism, whose ultimate prescriptive goal is one form or other of consciousness raising.

What then was Freud's contribution? Although he did not by any stretch of the imagination discover the unconscious, he more than any other figure made the unconscious a permanent part of modern scientific psychology, and in so doing transformed the very meaning of psychology, which up to that point had been conceived of as the science merely of consciousness. Freud's achievement was not the discovery of the unconscious as such but the discovery of what could be done with the concept. In the hands of Freud, the unconscious was no mere theoretical trinket but a conceptual tool through which he was able to effect the unifying synthesis of an astonishing sweep of problems—from trivia, such as slips of the tongue, to the psychology of symptoms, jokes, dreams, defense mechanisms, religion, and even civilization.

THE STATUS OF THE UNCONSCIOUS IN PSYCHOLOGY

The unconscious has led a difficult existence within psychology. Wilhelm Wundt, the "father of experimental psychology" had defined psychology as the science of conscious experience and had thereby excluded, through definitional fiat, the whole issue of unconscious mentation from the field at its inception. Since Wundt's founding of the world's first psychological laboratory at Leipzig in 1879, there has existed a perennial tendency within academic psychology to avoid the problem of the unconscious. In good part, this avoidance stems from the fear that the unconscious would taint or even subvert the scientific status of the fledgling discipline. Such fears were in ample evidence even before the emergence of psychoanalysis. William James, hardly the timid academician, excoriated the notion of unconscious mentation as "the sovereign means for believing what one likes in psychology, and of turning what might become a science into a tumbling-ground for whimsies" (James, 1890, p. 163). In a similar vein, E. B. Titchener, one of Wundt's students, and a major figure of early American experimental psychology, wrote, "when we invent an unconscious mind to give coherence and continuity to the conscious . . . we voluntarily leave the sphere of fact for the sphere of fiction (Titchener, 1917, p. 40).

The rejection of the unconscious was carried a step further by behaviorism, the dominant force in American experimental psychology between the 1920s and the late 1950s, which did away with not only the unconscious but also the conscious—in short, the mind—as a proper subject for scientific psychology. Psychoanalysis was dismissed out of hand as an intellectual aberration on the plane with phrenology (Watson, 1924, p. 297) whose constructs, including the unconscious, were to be regarded as a contemporary reversion to demonology. This attitude is still to be encountered in personality-clinical psychology. Bandura and Walters (1963), for example, echoing Watson's stance as well as terminology, characterize basic psychoanalytic concepts, including the notion of unconscious psychodynamic forces, as a form of "demonology" and "mystical thinking" harking back to "the dark ages" (p. 30).

The period following the Second World War saw a marked change in experimental psychology's dogmatic dismissal of the unconscious. A concerted experimental program arose in the late 1940s, usually known as "the New Look," to explore the problem of subliminal (unconscious) perception, and the interaction of motives, including defenses, with perception and memory. The resulting literature (see Chapter 5; also, Dixon, 1971; 1981; Erdelyi, 1974; Erdelyi and Goldberg, 1979) was riddled with controversy. By the late 1950s the general consensus emerged that the venture had been a failure and that no methodologically sound demonstration of unconscious perception—and more generally, of unconscious processes—had been achieved (Bandura, 1969; Brody, 1972; Eriksen, 1958; 1962). The failure of experimental methodology to corroborate the existence of unconscious processes was taken, as a matter of course, to reflect a failure of the concept rather than a failure of the extant methodology (cf. Erdelyi and Goldberg, 1979). The unconscious, having been given its chance in the laboratory, and having fumbled it, seemed doomed as a scientific concept.

At this very time, however, in the late 1950s and early 1960s, a new theoretical revolution was brewing within psychology that would soon uproot behaviorism from mainstream experimental psychology and render the just-concluded experimental rejection of unconscious processes ingenuous. This new perspective, usually known as the *information-processing approach* or the *cognitive revolution* (cf. Broadbent, 1958; Haber, 1968; Miller, Galanter, and Pribram, 1960; Neisser, 1967) may be best understood as a new analogic departure, involving the adoption of the computer as the model of human information processing. Although the cognitive revolution had essentially no contact with psychoanalytic theory—and perhaps all the more impressive on that account—the adoption of the computer metaphor generated a host of theoretical constructs that came close to constituting rediscoveries of basic Freudian notions. For example: "censorship" (filtering, selectivity); "ego" (executive control processes, central processor); "conflict" (decision nodes); "force," "cathexes," "energies" (weights, attention); "mental economics" (capacity); "mental topography," "depth" (depth of processing, up-down processing); the "conscious" (working memory); "psychic structure" (routines, programs, software), and so forth (cf. Erdelyi, 1974; Erdelyi and Goldberg, 1979; Foulkes, 1978; Kahneman, 1973; Peterfreund and Schwartz, 1971). Since these new concepts had direct counterparts in the computer, there was nothing remotely mystical about them. The concept of unconscious processes—if not the term itself—was not only *not* controversial but an obvious and fundamental feature of human information processing. Independent from each other, numerous experimental psychologists reintroduced into cognitive psychology, under new labels, Freud's own distinction between the unconscious on one hand and the conscious or preconscious on the other; for example: "unavailable" versus "available" memories (Haber and Erdelyi, 1967), "trace storage" versus "trace utilization" (Melton, 1963), "availability" versus "retrievability" (Bower, 1970), "availability" versus "accessibility" (Tulving and Pearlstone, 1966).

The introduction of new terms rather than the readoption of the older *unconscious* is probably symptomatic of a continued nervousness on the part of experimental psychology about making its peace with the unconscious. The modern literature is replete with synonyms such as *automatic, inaccessible,* and *preattentive,* but only rarely does the unconscious itself make an appearance. There is no explicit discussion of the reason for this avoidance, though informal querying usually turns up a disinclination on the part of authors to be associated with *Freud's* unconscious, not any misgivings about nonconscious mentation. The psychoanalytic unconscious, it is usually claimed, carries excess theoretical baggage to which the typical modern investigator does not wish to give the appearance of subscribing.

This kind of concern brings to light a curious aspect of the controversy regarding the unconscious in psychology. Careful consideration suggests that the past rejection of the unconscious, like the modern avoidance of it, had less to do with the concept as such than with the theoretical or philosophic implications associated with the term. For example, William James' scathing rejection of the unconscious (page 58) may have been more a rejection of the nomenclature than the concept itself. In 1902 he was to write:

> I cannot but think that the most important step forward that has occurred in psychology since I have been a student of that science is the discovery . . . that, in certain subjects at least, there is not only the consciousness of the ordinary field, with its usual centre and margin, but an addition thereto in the shape of a set of memories, thoughts, and feelings which are extra-marginal and outside of primary consciousness altogether. (James, 1902, p. 233)

Here, James was referring to Myers' work on the "subliminal self" and appears to have made a complete about-face from his 1890 stance. Yet, as is persuasively argued by D. B. Klein (1977), James had not really come over to accepting the "unconscious," which he continued to regard as "almost certainly a misnomer" (James, 1902, p. 207) that ought to be "replaced by the vaguer term 'subconscious' or 'subliminal'." James does not elucidate this peculiar position, all the more puzzling in view of Myers' routine use of the "unconscious" as a synonym for the "subliminal." Probably one factor behind James' paradoxical stance was his fear of being associated with the loose metaphysical treatment of the unconscious by philosophers such as Hartmann and Schopenhauer. Such fear had in fact impelled Helmholtz and, apparently, also Wundt (D. B. Klein, 1977) to recant their earlier belief in "unconscious inference." A similar dynamic, this time in connection with Freud, probably explains modern psychology's own paradoxical attitude toward the unconscious. Thus, Albert Bandura rejects the unconscious while simultaneously embracing it under alternate labels such as *implicit, inhibited, automatic,* and *covert* (Bandura, 1969, pp. 587–594).

The question ultimately arises whether the controversy surrounding the unconscious is only a wrangle over terminology or whether there is in fact a substantive theoretical issue. The question is not an easy one, bringing us to the complex problem of the meaning of the unconscious in psychoanalysis.

WHAT FREUD MEANT BY THE UNCONSCIOUS: THE DESCRIPTIVE, DYNAMIC, AND SYSTEMIC SENSES OF THE UNCONSCIOUS

Despite the fundamental role played by the unconscious in psycho-analysis, close examination reveals considerable confusion at the core of the concept. In part this confusion results from Freud's use of the term *unconscious (das Unbewusste)* in not one but at least three formally ac-knowledged senses—the "descriptive," "dynamic," and "systemic" (Freud, 1912b; 1915b; 1923; 1933). Such polysemous use of a technical term cannot but produce, as Freud himself acknowledged (e.g., Freud, 1915b) some disconcerting ambiguities, which we must here try to resolve if we are to address seriously the scientific status of *"the un-conscious."*

The first and simplest sense of the unconscious is the *descriptive,* by which Freud signifies all psychological materials that are not at any given moment in consciousness. The unconscious in the descriptive sense arises from a partitioning of all psychic contents and processes into two subsets, those that are in awareness at any given time (the con-scious) and those that are not (the unconscious). Schematically:

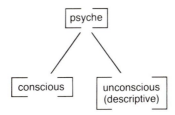

Since the span of consciousness is exceedingly limited (G. A. Mill-er, 1956), an iceberg model of the mind inevitably follows (see Chapter 3), in which virtually all mentation is submerged below awareness at any given time. In Freud's words:

> At any given moment consciousness includes only a small con-tent, so that the greater part of what we call conscious knowl-edge must in any case be for very considerable periods of time in a state of latency, that is to say, of being psychically uncon-scious. When all our latent memories are taken into consider-ation it becomes totally incomprehensible how the existence of the unconscious can be denied. (Freud, 1915b, p. 167)

Actually, the unconscious in *this* sense has ceased to be controver-sial in modern psychology and hardly requires empirical confirmation. The controversy originally surrounding it, in fact, never was empirical but philosophical, for the founders of psychology (Wundt, Titchener, James), in identifying the mind or psyche with consciousness, rendered the notion of unconscious mentation a contradiction of terms, treating "latent" memories and processes as *physical* dispositions or tendencies from which could arise bona fide *psychological* (that is conscious) experience. However, as Freud frequently noted, such an objection to the unconscious constitutes a *petitio principii,* a begging of the point, that gives rise not to a scientific controversy but to a war of words (Freud, 1915b).

Freud's second sense of the unconscious, the *dynamic* unconscious, also termed "the unconscious proper" or simply "the unconscious," results from a distinction that Freud makes between "two kinds of unconscious—one which is easily, under frequently occurring circumstances, transformed into something conscious, and another with which this transformation is difficult and takes place only subject to a considerable expenditure of effort or possibly never at all. . . . We call the unconscious which is only latent, and thus easily becomes conscious, the 'preconscious' and retain the term 'unconscious' for the other" (Freud, 1933, p. 71). We have here, then, a further partitioning of the psyche, in this case of the descriptive unconscious, into two complementary subsets, the *preconscious* and the *unconscious proper* (or *dynamic* unconscious):

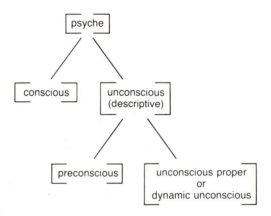

The unconscious (that is, the unconscious proper or dynamic unconscious) becomes the "inaccessible" (e.g., Freud, 1917, p. 93), and thus links up with contemporary psychological usage (e.g., Tulving and Pearlstone, 1966), the preconscious corresponding to "accessible" information and the unconscious to the "available but inaccessible."

As developed so far, matters are straightforward enough. Unfortunately, Freud's penchant for defining concepts in multiple ways introduces a jarring ambiguity at this point. The dynamic unconscious, it turns out, is defined by Freud not only as the (relatively) inaccessible but also as that which is repressed from consciousness:

> It is by no means impossible for the product of unconscious activity to pierce into consciousness, but a certain amount of exertion is needed for this task. When we try to do it in ourselves, we become aware of a distinct feeling of *repulsion* which must be overcome, and when we produce it in a patient we get the most unquestionable signs of what we call his *resistance* to it. So we learn that the unconscious idea is excluded from consciousness by living forces which oppose themselves to its reception, while they do not object to other ideas, the [pre]conscious ones. (Freud, 1912b, p. 264)

This twofold rendering of the unconscious (proper)—as (a) the inaccessible, and (b) the repressed—would pose no problems if the two definitions amounted to the same thing or if the one necessarily implied the other. But is this the case? Given that repression produces inaccessibility, does the converse follow that all inaccessible psychological contents and processes are inaccessible by virtue of being repressed? For example, are the optical rules for constancy scaling or the deep structure of syntax inaccessible as a result of repression? And if not, how should we designate such inaccessible psychic contents? They are not "preconscious," but if they are not unconscious in the sense of being repressed then in what sense are they unconscious? Does the demonstration of hypermnesia (pages 33–35) corroborate the existence of the unconscious proper? It does if by *unconscious* we mean the initially inaccessible but not if we also insist on the criterion of repression; for we have no proof that the inaccessible items were actually repressed or opposed by "living forces," nor did any subject ever report experiencing "a distinct feeling of repulsion" for any of the recovered items.

Textual analysis does not allow a clear choice between the weaker and the stronger definition of the unconscious (proper) since Freud never really confronts the issue. A case could be made that the problem does not arise practically in psychoanalysis because in Freud's system —rightly or wrongly—nothing escapes the purview of psychodynamic influences, and the inaccessible therefore is perforce the repressed. Unfortunately, Freud is not consistent on this score. For example, in his final sketch of the structural model of the psyche (see Figure 3.13) Freud includes a region of the unconscious that is not repressed but that is nevertheless deeper than the preconscious.

The position to be taken in this book—and a clear position must be taken if we are to know what it is that we are committing ourselves to when we commit ourselves to the existence of the unconscious—is that the question of the unconscious (the inaccessible) should not be entangled with any theory about *why* things are unconscious (such as repression). It is possible to believe in the existence of the unconscious, even of an active, intrusive and, therefore, "dynamic" unconscious, without necessarily espousing the proposition that repression accounts for all or even some of the unconscious. We shall, therefore, treat the problem of repression as a separate issue (Chapter 5) and adopt inaccessibility as the criterion of unconsciousness (proper).

As if these semantic convolutions were not enough, we must now turn to Freud's third acknowledged sense of the unconscious, the *systemic* sense, which even by Freud's lax standards was seen to overwhelm the term semantically, prompting him in 1923 to redesignate the *system Unconscious* as the *id*.

This last usage of the term *unconscious* has produced much confusion in psychoanalysis. Not only does it saddle the overburdened construct with a still further meaning, but it also regularly gives rise to a category error of the sort that one would make in confusing *justice* with Justice (the Department of) or *intelligence* with Intelligence (the CIA). For, the systemic Unconscious (*Ucs.* for short) refers not to a gradation of consciousness—though it is unconscious—but to a hypothesized *system* (structure, organization) of the mind that, in contrast to a conscious-preconscious system later designated the *ego,* is *exclusively hedonistic* ("it obeys the pleasure-unpleasure principle") and *primitive cognitively* (it operates according to "primary process functioning"). It is in this sense that "the laws of unconscious activity differ . . . from the conscious" (Freud, 1912b, p. 266). But since the systemic Unconscious is abolished by Freud in *The Ego and the Id* (1923) and incorporated into his "structural model" of the mind as the id (see pages 128–136), the formula must be revised to indicate that the laws of the id differ from those of the ego (the pleasure-unpleasure principle and primary process functioning versus the reality principle and secondary process functioning). This point is underscored because scholars of the unconscious, both advocates and critics, frequently make the mistake of assuming that for the "psychoanalytic" unconscious to be demonstrated, it must be shown that unconscious processes follow different rules than conscious ones. This latter question may be interesting in its own right but wholly subsidiary to the existence of unconscious mentation. In any case, the question is not likely to be too meaningful unless posed differently, since it is probable that different kinds of materials (such as, images as opposed to words) obey different psychological laws, irrespective of their relation to consciousness.

Before turning our attention to the scientific status of the unconscious, let us briefly review how matters stand: The problematical systemic Unconscious is abolished by Freud in 1923, becoming the id, and no longer figures as an issue for the unconscious (though it is an important feature of Freud's structural model of the mind, which will be discussed in Chapter 3). The weak sense of the descriptive unconscious, that is, the accessible but not accessed, is obvious, requiring no empirical proof, and is in any case distinguished from the unconscious proper by Freud's redesignation of it as the preconscious. What remains then is the unconscious proper (or "dynamic unconscious" or just "unconscious") which, in the present treatment is, simply, the inaccessible. Inaccessibility may or may not be due to repression, which is a different issue, though it should be emphasized that the inaccessible may be dynamic in the sense of being active or influential in shaping ongoing behavior.

THE SCIENTIFIC STATUS OF THE UNCONSCIOUS: PROOFS, PROBLEMS, AND PARADIGMS OF THE UNCONSCIOUS

The problem of the unconscious poses special challenges for scientific psychology. Not only are unconscious processes inaccessible to public observation, but they are also excluded, by definition, from private subjective experience as well. How then can the unconscious be known —if, indeed, there is such a thing as the unconscious?

The problem is difficult, but by no means unique. Much of twentieth-century physics, for example, deals with what might be termed *shadow phenomena*, entities or events (electrons, antimatter, quantum jumps, virtual particles) which may be known only from indirect evidence, from the shadows that these invisible phenomena cast. The unconscious is likewise a shadow phenomenon. It cannot be known directly, but only inferentially through, to use Freud's expression, a variety of indirect "proofs and signs" (Freud, 1912b, p. 260).

What are these proofs and signs? Psychoanalysts and psychologists have loosely treated a vast hodgepodge of clinical and laboratory phenomena—such as hysteria, dreams, neurotic symptoms, hypnosis, parapraxes, hypermnesia, defense mechanisms, subception, autonomic conditioning, automatic writing—as indicating the existence of unconscious processes. However, there has been little systematic effort to subject the logic of the evidence to scrutiny. Not all of these phenomena are persuasive "proofs" or "signs" of the unconscious, and in some cases they may not even be relevant. Fortunately, it will not be necessary to delve into this unmanageable sprawl of data, item by item, for careful analysis reveals that all the extant evidence falls under one of two classes of proofs or "paradigms" of the unconscious.

The Recovery or Hypermnesia Paradigm of the Unconscious: $\alpha_2 > \alpha_1$

Let us take up first the easier of the two paradigms, which we will designate the recovery or hypermnesia paradigm of the unconscious. Rather than attempt a formal definition at this point, let us instead start with some data from real life. Consider the following two excerpts from *The New York Times*, both involving the phenomenon of hypnotic hypermnesia (the recovery of inaccessible memories under hypnosis). The first excerpt is taken from a front-page article appearing on December 15, 1974:

Hypnosis Leads to a Hit-Run Suspect

LAKEWOOD, N. J., Dec. 14—The police have arrested a suspect in a hit-and-run accident after using hypnosis to help a policeman who witnessed the accident to recall part of the license-plate number of the car involved.

Sgt. Bernard Gindoff, police traffic-safety officer, said today that he had Patrolman Robert Maras hypnotized by a physician after the officer said that he could not recall the license number.

Frequently hypnotism helps persons recall things that they have subconsciously recorded in their memories but which they are unable to consciously recollect, said Sergeant Gindoff, who had been a fan of hypnotism since the department tried it here several years ago.

"It worked very well," Sergeant Gindoff continued. "He got four (of the six license-plate) numbers perfectly. With what he gave us and the other information we had we had no trouble locating the car. It was the hypnotism that was most responsible for it."

The second excerpt is also from *The New York Times* (Nov. 3, 1979, p. 24):

Man Identified by Hypnosis Convicted in Rape Upstate

SYRACUSE, Nov. 2—A jury in a rape trial here found the defendant guilty last night, in part on the basis of testimony drawn from the victim through hypnosis. . . .

The victim, married and 23 years old, was said to be so traumatized by the assault, in the spring of 1978, that for three months she could recall neither the circumstances of the rape nor the identity of her attacker.

> In a hypnotic state, however, she identified the assailant
> as Kirk Hughes, 21, her neighbor and a former baby sitter.

Setting methodological concerns aside for the moment, how would we make the argument for the unconscious from these data? We would say something along the following lines: The subject recovers into consciousness some information that he could not recall initially. This information had to come from somewhere—an available but inaccessible, that is, unconscious region of mind. The availability of the inaccessible material is revealed by its eventual recovery into consciousness.

Thus, the *recovery* or *hypermnesia* paradigm of the unconscious involves a consciousness-raising situation, which may be formalized as, $\alpha_2 > \alpha_1$, where α_1 is an indicator of information accessible to awareness at time one and α_2 is the same indicator of awareness at time two. To the extent that α is a faithful indicator of information accessible to consciousness or awareness, $\alpha_2 > \alpha_1$ implies the existence of an initially unconscious component of the mind from which the information is recovered.

Having established its simple logic, let us now turn to some methodological problems frequently associated with the paradigm. First, it should be emphasized that the scientific status of hypnosis is not a methodological issue. The essence of the paradigm is the recovery of inaccessible memories (hypermnesia), and the technique by which the recovery is effected is quite incidental. As long as it works, any hypermnesic procedure would do, including temporal lobe stimulation (Penfield, 1969; Penfield and Perot, 1963; Penfield and Roberts, 1959), pressure-concentration (which Freud substituted for hypnosis), free association (Freud's replacement for pressure-concentration), truth sera such as sodium pentothal, a rap on the head, the passage of time, and so forth.

There are actually two methodological problems that may arise with the recovery paradigm. The most obvious of these has long been recognized and is known under a variety of labels, including *confabulation, paramnesia, false memory,* and *false alarms.* The potential difficulty is evident in the second excerpt from *The Times:* The possibility cannot be discounted that the rape victim's presumptive hypermnesia was a paramnesia, a false, confabulatory recollection, instead. To the layman, unfamiliar with the vagaries of memory, in particular pressured memory, such a false recollection must appear highly unlikely. Yet, such confounds are not uncommon. In M. Bernstein's (1956) best seller, *The Search for Bridey Murphy,* for example, the hypnotically age-regressed subject, Ruth Simmons, manages to recover long-lost memories not only from early childhood, but from an earlier life as well! (Those not

inclined to dismiss reincarnation out of hand must contend with experiments showing that subjects under hypnosis are capable of not only
recovering long-lost memories from the past but also long-lost memories from the future [Kline, 1958; Rubenstein and Newman, 1954].)

Psychoanalysis itself almost shipwrecked on the problem of confabulation. Based on a handful of patients' painful recoveries of infantile seduction experiences, Freud jumped to the conclusion that
childhood sexual molestation was the etiological determinant of hysteria (Freud, 1896b). Soon confronted with the implausibility, and in
some cases impossibility, of some of these recollected incidents, Freud
was obliged to recant his hastily conceived seduction theory of hysteria
(Freud, 1906). There are intimations that Freud was so shocked by this
public blunder that he actually considered abandoning psychoanalysis.
Instead, Freud worked his way to the point of view that the patients
were recovering, if not true events, then true fantasies or wishes from
childhood, a position elaborated in his theory of the Oedipus complex
(Freud, 1906; 1917; 1924).

The confabulation problem may similarly undermine more modern
claims of dramatic hypermnesic effects; for example, Penfield's reports
of memory recoveries brought on by temporal lobe stimulation (cf.
Loftus and Loftus, 1980; Neisser, 1967).

Treacherous as it is, the methodological resolution of the confabulation problem is rather straightforward: The experimenter must
work with memory materials that can be verified or, better still, controlled. The laboratory provides the ideal setting for achieving the
desired control over target stimuli. Consider, for example, a study by
Haber and Erdelyi (1967) on the recoverability of subliminal stimuli
into consciousness through the medium of free-associative fantasy. Experimental subjects were tachistoscopically shown a complex stimulus
(see Figure 2.1) for one half second, after which they were required to
provide an exhaustive recall, in the form of a labelled drawing, of everything they had seen (α_1). Following the recall attempt, the subjects
reclined on a comfortable armchair and free associated for some forty
minutes. After their free associations, subjects were asked to attempt a
second recall (α_2) of the tachistoscopic stimulus. Unlike control subjects
(who, for example, threw darts for forty minutes instead of free associating), all experimental subjects recalled more stimulus items after fantasy
than before fantasy $(\alpha_2 > \alpha_1)$, even though the prefantasy recall attempt
(α_1) followed immediately upon the presentation of the stimulus. (For
examples of the types of recoveries obtained, see Figure 2.2.)

Confabulation cannot in this case account for the obtained hypermnesia effects since knowledge of the stimulus enabled the experi-
menters to distinguish between correct recalls ("hits") and false recalls
("false alarms").

Figure 2.1. The stimulus presented by Haber and Erdelyi (1967) for a half second. (J. Verb. Learning & Verb. Behavior, Vol. 6.)

70

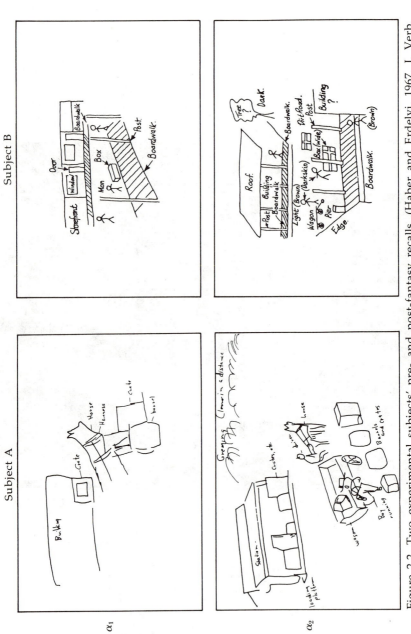

Figure 2.2. Two experimental subjects' pre- and post-fantasy recalls. (Haber and Erdelyi, 1967. J. Verb. Learning & Verb. Behavior, Vol. 6.)

But, there remains another, more subtle methodological problem. Even though some of the recovered information is veridical, the question may be raised whether this improved performance reflects enhanced memory or merely enhanced reporting. Are the subjects *remembering more* or only *reporting more* of what they remember? Consider the Haber and Erdelyi study: It is possible that free-associative fantasy makes contact with unconscious materials and enables subjects to recover some of this information in a postfantasy recall trial; it is also possible, however, that after forty minutes of essentially saying anything that comes to mind, the subject is more apt than before the free associations to hazard uncertain recollections, some of which may turn out to be correct.

The present issue turns out to be one of the fundamental problems of psychophysics: how to tell apart the subject's actual *sensitivity* to an uncertain stimulus from his *criterion for reporting* his sensitivity to the stimulus; for, in the end, the experimenter has only the subject's report of what he experiences, and a particular reporting strategy— which may differ over time or between subjects—may distort the actual experience. Modern application of mathematical decision theory (cf. Green and Swets, 1966; Swets, 1964) has resulted in a powerful statistical scheme, *signal detection theory* (SDT), for disentangling the two parameters that are confounded, the subject's *sensitivity* (or in memory terms, the accessibility of the information) from the subject's *criterion* for reporting what he has accessed, about which he may have considerable uncertainty. The former sensitivity parameter is usually designated as d' in the literature, and the latter report criterion factor, as β. In this framework, the second methodological problem of the recovery paradigm is whether improved performance actually constitutes enhancement of d' (sensitivity, accessibility, awareness) or merely a relaxation of β (a greater willingness to report uncertain recollections).[1]

In an effort to determine which of the two factors was responsible for the recovery outcome in the Haber and Erdelyi experiment, Erdelyi (1970) applied the tools of SDT to this type of study. One technique was to compare free-recall performance (in which the subject is asked simply to recall as much as he can, thus being free to set his own report criterion) to forced-recall performance (in which the experimenter obliges

[1]For the reader who is conversant with signal detection theory, it might be pointed out that both methodological problems of the recovery paradigm are actually consequences of shifting report criteria (β). Relaxation of β results, other things being equal, in an increase in both hits and false alarms. The criterion problem, as commonly understood, arises when the experimenter confuses an increase in hits with an increase in sensitivity/accessibility (d'). The grosser confabulation problem entails two errors, one built on the other: first, confusing false alarms with hits, and then, on top of this, confusing (what is thought to be) more hits with greater d'.

the subject to produce, guessing if necessary, a predetermined number of recalls, thereby controlling any shifts in β across trials and between subjects). The experimental outcome was straightforward. With the free-recall procedure, the Haber and Erdelyi recovery findings were easily replicated: postfantasy recall performance (α_2) was superior to prefantasy performance (α_1) while the corresponding performance of control subjects (that is, those who did not free associate between recall trials) showed no recall increments. However, with number of recall responses made constant through the forced-recall procedure, the difference between experimental and control subjects disappeared altogether. Thus, it was shown that free associations do not really produce the recovery of inaccessible memories (d') but only the recovery of unreported memories (β).

These findings were confirmed by more technical procedures, involving recognition memory, that actually permit the quantification of d' and β.

These various experiments, then, converge on the conclusion that the recoveries engendered by the free-associative fantasy constitute not true increases in memory (d') but only increases in the subject's willingness to report uncertain recollections (β). Such an outcome raises some troubling questions about the recoveries routinely reported in psychoanalytic therapy: Are they also, when not confabulations, merely report criterion effects? Clinical impression is not decisive here. The subjects in the Haber and Erdelyi study, for example, were adamant about having reported in α_1 all of the tachistoscopic input of which they were aware, and the experimenter's impression was no less certain that they had indeed exhausted whatever accessible information they had. The 1970 studies were to prove both the subjects and the experimenter wrong.

One potentially critical difference between the foregoing laboratory studies and clinical experience with hypermnesia is that the kinds of recoveries observed in therapy are not of fleeting tachistoscopic inputs but of substantive life events which have become, for whatever reason, inaccessible. This difference might bear on the generalizability of the laboratory outcomes. Thus, the problem of obtaining genuine recoveries of subliminal inputs might reside not in the recovery phenomenon itself but in perception; possibly not enough of the stimulus is registered and stored to be subsequently recovered. A better laboratory analog of hypermnesia might therefore be one which assures the original registration and storage of the target information to be recovered.

A simple expedient, pursued by Erdelyi and Becker (1974), is to move from a subliminal-perception design to a bona fide memory experiment. Erdelyi and Becker presented subjects eighty individual slides, each for five seconds. Half these slides were simple picture sketches (a snake, a hat, a sword, and the like); the other half were printed words (such as DUCK, TABLE, PIPE). At these slow, supraliminal presentation rates there could be no question about the initial registration and storage of the stimuli. To the extent that the subject could not subsequently access all the items—typically fewer than 50 percent of the items were initially recalled—the inaccessibility resulted from forgetting and not from failure to register them. The question was whether the forgotten could be "unforgotten," that is, recovered.

After the presentation of the eighty slides, a forced recall test (α_1) was adminstered to the subjects, which they had seven minutes to complete. At the end of the test period, the recall protocols were collected and the subjects were asked to free associate in writing ("automatic writing") for seven minutes. At this point, a second forced recall (α_2) was elicited from the subjects, followed by another free-association period and, finally, a third recall (α_3).

A control group of subjects attempted three successive recalls of the stimulus items with, however, no intervening free associations between them. This "no-interval group" was designed to assess the effect of the activity between recall trials upon recall performance.

A third group of subjects, instead of free associating between trials, was instructed to sit quietly, with closed eyes, and think about the stimulus items, concentrating on the items and nothing else throughout the interval. This "think-concentrate group" was designed to approximate Freud's pressure-concentration technique and was included to evaluate its efficacy in producing hypermnesia.

In summary: Three groups of subjects attempted to recall eighty stimuli, half pictures, half words, over three successive trials; one group free associated between trials, another silently thought about the stimuli between trials, and a third group had no interval between recall trials. Table 2.1 summarizes the experimental results.

Table 2.1 Average Number of Pictures and Words Recalled in Each Recall Trial (α_1, α_2, α_3) with Free-Association Intervals, Silent-Think Intervals, or No Intervals between Recall Trials

Group	Pictures			Words		
	α_1	α_2	α_3	α_1	α_2	α_3
Free association	16.65	18.30	18.59	14.00	14.17	14.23
Silent think	15.76	17.76	18.94	16.35	16.82	17.00
No interval	15.82	17.11	18.05	13.41	12.47	13.00
Average	16.08	17.72	18.53	14.59	14.49	14.74

One striking, and altogether unexpected, aspect of the outcome was the clear-cut difference in the recall patterns for words and pictures. Table 2.1 shows that none of the three groups of subjects improved in their recall of words over trials (at least not significantly) while, in every case, picture recall improved. The use of the two types of stimuli had been prompted by the suspicion that verbal free associations might lead to recovery of verbal but not of pictorial materials. As it turned out, not only was word recall inert over trials, but the free associations were ineffective in engendering hypermnesia. Although the subjects who free associated between recall trials did improve in their recall of pictures, their improvement was the smallest of the three groups. Silent think-concentration intervals, on the other hand, enhanced the hypermnesia effect. It appears from these data that free associations are not the effective factor in clinical recoveries of memories, though they might yet prove to be important instigators of insight.

The central finding of the study was the reliable hypermnesia effect with pictorial stimuli, with both the problem of confabulation and of shifting report criteria controlled. Subsequent research has corroborated these outcomes: Pictures, but usually not verbal materials, are hypermnesic over time with retrieval effort, whether in the form of overt recall trials or covert think-concentration periods. The effect, moreover, can be substantial. As has already been reported (pages 33–35), subjects attempting to recall pictures over a full week's interval improved, on the average, by more than 50 percent over initial recall (Erdelyi and Kleinbard, 1978).

Although verbal stimuli are usually inert, it has been shown that they can also be rendered hypermnesic by having subjects mentally recode the verbal input into images (Erdelyi, Finkelstein, Herrell, Miller, and Thomas, 1976). It appears, then, that imagery may play a key role in hypermnesia. (For a recent discussion of the imagery hypothesis, including some problems with it, see Erdelyi [1982] and Roediger, Payne, Gillespie, and Lean [1982].)

This program of laboratory research, then, demonstrates that initially inaccessible memories can be substantially recovered ($\alpha_2 > \alpha_1$), buttressing clinical claims of recoveries in therapy, and providing validation of the recovery paradigm of the unconscious, which has come under some question of late (e.g., Spence, 1982).

The role of repression (defense) has not been directly broached by these experiments, though it is easy to see how conscious or unconscious decisions on the part of the subject to think or avoid thinking about certain materials should have a decisive effect upon what is eventually accessible to the subject's awareness. Roediger et al. (1982, Study 3) have provided some preliminary experimental confirmation of this expectation. Thus, a biased allocation of the "work of recollection" (Freud, 1914) has, as one might suppose, an impact upon the mental contents accessible to the subject. This theme will be elaborated in the discussion of the mechanisms of defense (Chapter 5).

The Dissociation Paradigm of the Unconscious: $\epsilon > \alpha$

Although more difficult, the dissociation paradigm is also the more interesting of the two paradigms of the unconscious. As before, we shall begin with some real-life data, in this case, a protoclinical episode from everyday life involving a former graduate student, here given the name Elizabeth:

> Elizabeth, at this time a first year graduate student, was strikingly pretty. She had wavy blond hair, her eyes were deep blue, her skin was utterly free of blemishes. On a previous occasion, however, she had complained of a tendency to break out into a peculiar rash when intensely angry: First her neck and eventually her whole face would develop pink blotches that soon darkened into spots of red and scarlet.
>
> The event of interest transpired during one of our weekly research conferences. She had been making rather poor progress, and I had invited a more advanced graduate student (who happened to be male) to our meeting, in the vague hope that he might be induced to join our project. This graduate student, who had just returned from a year's leave of absence, had never before seen Elizabeth. As soon as he entered the room it was clear that he was very taken with her. Unfortunately, he did not know how to handle the situation and attempted to make an impression on Elizabeth by adopting a superior, overbearing manner. He criticized Elizabeth's proposed experiment in altogether abrasive terms: Her pilot studies were uninformative; she had control groups but had forgotten to include an experimental group; the control groups, in any case, controlled for the wrong variables; she did not understand the assumptions underlying analysis of variance; besides, analysis of variance was the inappropriate statistical plan for the study; and so forth. He interrupted most of her efforts to explain or defend her work, taking every opportunity to show off his expertise.
>
> Some twenty minutes into the meeting, during which he ignored several attempts on my part to defuse the atmosphere, I suddenly noticed Elizabeth's neck, and then her face, turning into a mottled mess of pink, red, and scarlet splotches. I decided to put an immediate end to the research conference, suggesting to the graduate student that he summarize his

major points in writing for future discussion. He had clearly noticed Elizabeth's dermal reaction, looked uncomfortable, and took his cue to leave eagerly.

But for Elizabeth's rash, it would have been impossible to deduce any untoward emotion; in every respect, in her overall demeanor, her expression, and her speech, she exuded a cheerful calm. I tried to smooth matters over and urged her not to be unduly angry at the graduate student. Elizabeth looked at me in surprise: "But I wasn't angry!"

I was unsure whether to drop the matter at this point or to pursue it further. Finally, curiosity compelled me to retort: "But Elizabeth, you have your famous rash all over your face and neck; you look like a pink leopard!"

"You are putting me on," she said. With a hint of annoyance, she reached into her pocketbook, took out her compact, and looked at herself. She started shaking her head and giggled in embarrassment. A normal blush lit up the pale rest of her face. "That's amazing," she said, "I was completely unaware of it!"

How might the existence of the unconscious be deduced from this episode? The argument would go something like this: Part of Elizabeth, the verbally reported conscious part, was unaware of her anger. At the same time, another part of Elizabeth, indicated by the dermal reaction, was in fact angry. This discrepancy or dissociation within Elizabeth between a conscious part and another (therefore, nonconscious) part, directly demonstrates the existence of unconscious mentation.

Let us recapitulate the paradigm more formally: Let α be an indicator of information accessible to awareness, and let ϵ be an event that indicates available (but not necessarily accessible) information. To the extent that $\epsilon > \alpha$, it follows that ϵ is indicating information that is available but inaccessible, thus, unconscious.

In the case of Elizabeth (see Figure 2.3), the indicator of information accessible to awareness is null ($\alpha : 0$, that is, no anger is indicated), while another indicator of mental content, ϵ, is positive ($\epsilon : +$, that is, there is anger). This discrepancy or dissociation between indicators ($\epsilon > \alpha$) implies a corresponding dissociation within the mind, in which one component in touch with anger is dissociated from, and therefore inaccessible to, another component, awareness.

The critical difference, it should be noted, between the recovery and dissociation paradigms of the unconscious is that the former involves a comparison of *a single indicator*, α, over *two successive occasions*, while the latter involves a *concurrent contrast* between *two different indicators*, ϵ and α. (This conceptualization owes much to Eriksen [1958].)

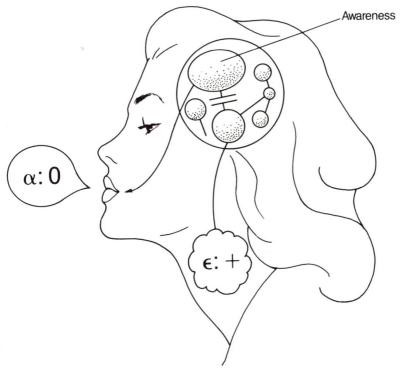

Figure 2.3. The dermal indicator (ϵ) registers anger; the verbal indicator of awareness (α) is null. This indicator discrepancy, $\epsilon > \alpha$, implies that the subject is angry but is unconscious of her anger.

Let us extend our analysis of the dissociation paradigm from the informal case of Elizabeth to the simple laboratory demonstration that Freud witnessed at Bernheim's clinic in Nancy, which we have already had the occasion to touch on in Chapter 1: Bernheim hypnotized a patient and instructed him that several minutes after awakening from the trance he was to get up, walk over to a part of the room where there lay a folded umbrella, pick up the umbrella and open it; the patient was to remember to carry out these instructions without, however, remembering that he had been thus instructed. At the appointed time the patient abruptly rose, walked over to the umbrella, picked it up and opened it. When asked why he had carried out this strange behavior, the patient replied, in confusion, that he didn't have the slightest idea. Commenting on this demonstration of posthypnotic suggestion, Freud writes: "This is the kind of occurrence we have in mind when we speak of the existence of *unconscious mental processes*; we may challenge anyone in the world to give a more correctly scientific explanation of this matter, and will then gladly withdraw our inference that unconscious mental processes exist" (Freud, 1917, p. 245).

Before we take up Freud's challenge, which it will be instructive to do, let us first review how Bernheim's demonstration fits into the dissociation paradigm. How do we know that the patient was not aware of the posthypnotic instruction? The answer, obviously, is that when he was queried about his behavior, the patient's response was that he did not know (α: 0). How do we know that the instructions were nevertheless available? Because the patient carried out the instructions (ϵ:+). The patient, then, had information (as indicated by ϵ) of which he was unaware (as indicated by the null α).

We may now turn to Freud's challenge. Our consideration of the methodological problems associated with the earlier, recovery paradigm supplies us with an alternative explanation of the outcome, one that does not require the assumption of unconscious mental processes. It is quite possible that what we have here is not an instance of unconscious mentation but of *report bias*. Since we cannot get into the subject's mind and directly assess what is and is not in awareness, we must rely on an *indicator* of information in awareness, α, in this case a verbal report. This verbal report might be biased, however; perhaps the patient is aware of the reason behind his behavior but to please Bernheim, or for any other reason, misrepresents the content of his awareness and claims ignorance (α: 0) of the relevant information. Now, if α misrepresents awareness—which it is supposed faithfully to indicate—then, $\epsilon > \alpha$ need not imply the operation of unconscious mental processes. Thus, a major methodological problem of the dissociation paradigm, not resolved by Bernheim's demonstration, is also the problem of report bias.

There is a second methodological problem associated with this paradigm, that of interpretation. It probably does not apply to the Bernheim demonstration but it might invalidate clinical evidence for the unconscious of the sort that the case of Elizabeth provides. It was assumed that Elizabeth's dermal reaction (ϵ) indicated underlying anger. But this is only an inference. She might have developed her blotches for any number of other reasons—embarrassment, sexual attraction, an allergic condition, or the like. If, in fact, she was not really angry, then her denial of anger would hardly constitute evidence for unconscious anger. Now, it is true, Elizabeth accepted her professor's interpretation. But this need not be decisive. She too might have erred in the interpretation or, alternately, she might have gone along with her professor for her own good reasons (report bias). The problem of interpretation may be seen as a variant of the confabulation problem. In the case of confabulation, the subject himself makes up a false memory (thought, emotion, and so forth); in the case of false interpretation, it is the *clinician/experimenter* who commits that error.

Up to now we have considered only informal evidence for the dissociation paradigm of the unconscious. There is actually a vast body of experimental research based on the paradigm, though there is doubt to what extent any of it succeeds in fully resolving both methodological problems.

Consider, for example, McGinnies' (1949) famous study of "perceptual defense." McGinnies presented subjects with tachistoscopically flashed words that were either neutral or "taboo" (for example, *house, apple* versus *Kotex, penis*), increasing exposure duration until the subject could correctly identify the flashed word. It was found that taboo words had higher identification thresholds than neutral words (that is, they required longer exposure durations for correct identification), presumably because the subjects were defending against perceiving the anxiety-provoking items. To demonstrate directly that the subjects were in fact subliminally registering the disturbing stimuli, McGinnies measured the subjects' galvanic skin response (GSR), an indicator of emotionality, throughout the threshold trials. The critical finding was the preidentification GSRs were significantly higher for the taboo words than for neutral words. Thus, it appeared that the subjects "knew" the emotional nature of the stimulus at some gut level before this information became accessible to awareness. In the formal terms of the dissociation paradigm, there was a prethreshold (t-1) discrepancy between two different concurrent indicators, one verbal (α) and one physiological (ϵ):

$$\alpha(\text{verbal})_{t-1}: 0$$
$$\epsilon(\text{GSR})_{t-1}: +$$

McGinnies' study generated immense interest as well as controversy. The most persistent criticism of it (e.g., Eriksen, 1958) was that it demonstrated not subliminal (unconscious) perception but a report bias effect: Subjects may have been equally sensitive to both the neutral and taboo words; but, out of embarrassment, put off verbally identifying the taboo words until further exposures removed any lingering uncertainties about the identity of these words. Thus, the elevated preidentification GSRs reflected awareness of the taboo stimuli which, however, the subject chose not to report until a later threshold trial.

The same report bias problem tends to undermine a fascinating study by Otto Pötzl (1917), which has become a small classic in the psychoanalytic literature. This work actually was presented to the Vienna Psychoanalytic Society in 1917 and prompted Freud to add an enthusiastic footnote about it in his 1919 revision of *The Interpretation of*

Dreams, one of the exceedingly rare occasions when Freud had anything positive to say about a laboratory experiment. Briefly, Pötzl had demonstrated that inaccessible subliminal components (α: 0) of a tachistoscopically presented stimulus tend to emerge in the contents of the subject's dreams (ϵ: +). Follow-up research was to show that such recoveries of subliminal stimuli could also be engendered in other disinhibited media such as daydreams, fantasy, free associations, and imagery (Allers and Teler, 1924; Eagle, Wolitzky, and Klein, 1966; Fisher, 1954; 1956; 1959; Fiss, Goldberg, and Klein, 1963; Haber and Erdelyi, 1967; Hilgard, 1962; Shevrin and Luborsky, 1958). It was subsequently demonstrated, however, that the effect probably results from a report criterion artifact (Erdelyi, 1972). Subjects, not surprisingly, adopt a laxer report criterion in reverie productions (ϵ) than in an intentional recall (α) of the tachistoscopic stimulus.

The report criterion problem continues to bedevil modern experimental work as well. Consider the following study by Hilgard ("Neodissociation Theory of Hypnotic Analgesia," 1973): The subject was first hypnotized (for a pictorial summary of the study see Figure 2.4); he was then instructed to place one of his hands in a container of ice-cold water and leave it there for several minutes; although the "cold-pressor test" can be extremely painful, the subject was instructed not to feel any pain; with his other hand, which was kept out of his view, the subject was asked to engage in "automatic writing"—to let the hand write anything without the subject's paying any particular attention to it. The outcome was striking. When asked how his immersed hand was feeling, the subject replied (α) that it was fine; at the same time, his other hand was complaining bitterly (ϵ) by writing things such as "it hurts!" "ouch!" and so forth. Hilgard theorizes that the hypnosis causes a dissociation within the psyche such that the conscious subsystem is unaware of the pain, while another part of the psyche—Freud would call it the unconscious, Hilgard calls it the "hidden observer"—is experiencing the pain and giving expression to it through the automatic writing. An alternative and more pedestrian explanation is that the subject is aware of the pain but biases his verbal report (α) to please the experimenter, while writing out his complaint (ϵ) in the ostensibly automatic task for which he need not take responsibility.

In a still more recent study, Nisbett and Wilson (1977) explored the interesting question of the extent to which conscious understanding guides consumers' behavior when making choices. Although the authors tend not to use the term "unconscious," the study is nevertheless a clear instance of the dissociation paradigm:

> We conducted two studies that . . . showed a position effect on evaluation of an array of consumer goods. . . . Under the guise

Figure 2.4. Pictorial summary of Hilgard's (1973) experiment on the neodissociationist theory of hypnotic analgesia. The discrepancy between the two indicators ($\epsilon > \alpha$) implies a corresponding dissociation within the psyche.

of a consumer survey, passersby were invited to evaluate articles of clothing. . . . [Subjects] were asked to say which article of clothing was [of] the best quality and, when they announced a choice, we asked why they had chosen the article they had. There was a pronounced left-to-right position effect, such that the right-most object in the array was heavily chosen. For stockings, the effect was quite large, with the right-most stockings being preferred over the left-most by a factor of almost four to one. When asked about the reasons for their choices, no subject ever mentioned spontaneously the position of the article in the array. And, when asked directly about a possible effect of the position of the article, virtually all subjects denied it, usually with a worried glance at the interviewer suggesting that they felt either that they had misunderstood the question or were dealing with a madman. (Pp. 243–244)

Unconscious mentation is implicated in the study by virtue of the discrepancy between two indicators. The behavioral indicator reveals a position strategy of consumer choice (ϵ: +) while the verbal denial of it (α: 0) implies that the adopted strategy is not accessible to the subject's awareness.

Although there is no overriding reason for the subjects' biasing their verbal response, we have already learned to be cautious about mere clinical impression in this connection (see pages 71–72). Actually, it would not be totally surprising if subjects were a trifle reluctant about acknowledging such a banal strategy in a task calling for sophistication in judging quality. (For an incisive discussion of criticisms of the Nisbett-Wilson type study, see Nisbett and Ross [1980].)

A recent experiment on subliminal perception appears for once to provide convincing control over the problem of report criteria. Based on previous findings that repeated exposure to a stimulus tends to enhance its attractiveness—in the laboratory, at least, familiarity apparently does not breed contempt—Kunst-Wilson and Zajonc (1980) repeatedly presented subjects with a series of geometric figures at subliminal levels. In a subsequent forced-choice recognition task, the subjects were shown a series of stimulus pairs, one of which in each case was a member of the former subliminal set and one of which was a new (distractor) item. The subjects were required to decide for each test pair, (a) which of the two had been a stimulus item and (b) which of the two they found more attractive. The subjects' recognition performance was at chance level (α: 0); distractor items were chosen as frequently as stimulus items, demonstrating a complete absence of conscious discriminability ($d' = 0$). At the same time, the former stimulus items, despite the fact that they could not be discriminated from the distractor items, were judged more attractive significantly more often than the new items (ϵ: +; $d' > 0$). It would appear, then, that judgments of attractiveness discriminate between old and new stimuli (ϵ: +) while actual attempts to recognize the old items from the new yield no discrimination (α: 0). This discrepancy in performance suggests that information that is inaccessible for conscious recognition (or is unconscious) is nevertheless available for attractiveness discrimination. Should the Kunst-Wilson and Zajonc study prove replicable, it will constitute one of the rare laboratory demonstrations of unconscious mentation based on the dissociation paradigm that controls for response bias effects. Unfortunately, recent, as yet unpublished work (Mandler and Shebo, 1981), suggests that when the experiment is properly done, the phenomenon may not replicate.

Similarly, questions arise in connection with two recent literatures on subliminal perception, associated with the work of Silverman and Marcel. Over the last decade Silverman and others have demonstrated that certain subliminal stimuli, such as the symbiotic message, MOMMY AND I ARE ONE, produce reductions in psychopathology or alterations in performance among certain classes of subjects, such as differentiated male schizophrenics. (For an overall review, see Silverman, 1983). A recent study by Ariam and Siller (1982) employing Silverman's technique on normal Israeli students showed that the symbiotic message, MOMMY AND I ARE ONE, presented in either of two Hebrew versions for several weeks, produced significant improvements in mathematics test performance. Although most studies to date—and there are several dozen, involving numerous variants on the technique—have tended to be positive, some failures of replication have begun appearing in print (e.g., Condon and Allen, 1980; Haspel and Harris, 1982; Heilbrun, 1980).

In a parallel literature, Marcel and others (Balota, 1983; McCauley, Parmelee, Sperber, and Carr, 1980; Marcel, 1980; Marcel, 1983a; 1983b; Marcel and Patterson, 1978) have shown that the meaning of subliminal stimuli can be available even when the stimuli cannot be identified at a better-than-chance level. One way of demonstrating this is through subliminal semantic "priming," in which it is shown that a subliminal word (HAND/TREE) nevertheless influences or "primes," the meaning given to a subsequent homograph (PALM) that is supraliminal. Although this type of demonstration appears to be readily replicable (Fowler, Wolford, Slade, and Tassinary, 1981), methodological questions have arisen (e.g., Merikle, 1982; Purcell, Stewart, and Stanovich, 1983), especially concerning the critical issue of the absolute subliminality of the priming stimuli. Thus, at this point, the status of these literatures, indeed of all the subliminal perception literatures, is far from resolved.

The dissociations that we have been considering thus far have in every instance been of a functional or psychological nature. However, considerable neurological literature has also accumulated on a very concrete form of mental dissociation, one actually brought about by the surgical separation of the two hemispheres (Bogen, 1969; Bogen, Fisher, and Vogel, 1965; Gazzaniga, 1970; Levy, Trevarthen, and Sperry, 1972; Sperry, 1968; Springer and Deutsch, 1981). Such "split-brain" operations are usually performed to mitigate uncontrollable epileptic seizures, which begin from an epicenter and spread to progressively wider areas of the brain. The purpose of the operation is to localize the spread of the seizure to only one hemisphere.

Such split-brain operations yield fascinating psychological data. What happens, for instance, if different information is presented to the two neurologically dissociated hemispheres? Will the subject be literally "of two minds"? The issue takes on added interest because of the specialization of the two hemispheres. The left hemisphere, for example, contains the various verbal control centers. What happens if the right hemisphere gets information and the left, verbal hemisphere is queried about it? Such questions have been pursued experimentally by a number of neurosurgeons and psychologists.

Consider the following case reported by Sperry (1968). The split-brain subject is presented two visual inputs (see Figure 2.5). The one in the left visual field is a dollar sign ($), the one in the right field a question mark (?). (The stimuli are flashed for only a fraction of a second so that the subject has no time to move his eyes and register the information in both hemispheres.) The information in the left visual field ($) falls on the right half of each eye's retina, and the information in the right visual field (?) on the left half of each retina. As a result of the neurological circuitry of the visual system, the information in the right half of the retinas ($) is projected onto the right hemisphere, and the information in the left half of the retinas (?) onto the left hemisphere. The subject is instructed to draw with his left hand what he has just seen—without looking at what he is drawing. The subject (note that the right hemisphere controls the left hand) confidently draws the dollar sign (ϵ: $). He then is asked, "What have you just drawn?" Reminiscent of Hilgard's subjects, "He tells us without hesitation that the figure he drew was the question mark [α: ?]. . . .In other words, one hemisphere does not know what the other hemisphere has been doing" (Sperry, 1968, p. 726).

The same procedure can be used to induce unconscious emotions in the split-brain subject. A *Playboy* pinup is flashed in the left visual field, and nothing in the right visual field. The subject, this time bringing to mind the case of Elizabeth, starts to blush and giggle (ϵ: +). When asked why, he responds in embarrassment that he does not know (α: 0).

Since the two hemispheres are literally dissociated, there can be, for once, no question about the subject's failing to report any information in consciousness. The physical dissociation between the two hemispheres ensures that the information in the right hemisphere never gets to the consciousness of the verbal left hemisphere, and so the claim by the subject that he does not know why he is giggling is consistent with neurological fact. Note that the information in the dissociated right hemisphere, unconscious to the left hemisphere, is "dynamic"—*dynamic* in the sense of not being inert but of producing powerful effects that are incomprehensible to the left hemisphere's consciousness.[2]

---

[2]It is not theoretically necessary for this analysis to address the long-standing issue in dissociationist theory of whether the two (or more) independent subsystems each have an individual consciousness. It is enough to demonstrate that the consciousness claimed by the verbal subsystem is genuinely unconscious of information in the other subsystem(s). If the latter subsystem has its own consciousness then it may be unconscious of information in the former.

85

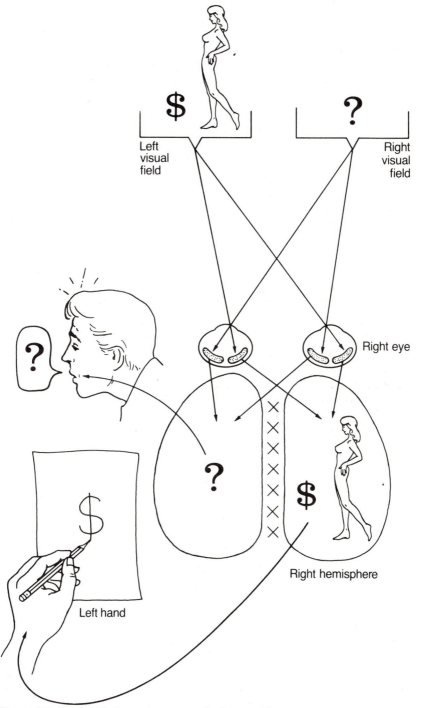

Figure 2.5. Flow of information in a split-brain subject.

Such cases, of course, are unnatural, dissociation being produced through the physical separation of the two hemispheres. Nevertheless, split brains provide an extreme (and unambiguous) neurological proto-type of the dissociation paradigm of the unconscious, which under more normal circumstances is brought about by *psychological* dissociation.

The Dissociation Paradigm with Complex Indicators: $[\epsilon] > \alpha$. Thus far, we have been dealing with indicators that, at least on first glance, appear to be discrete or unitary instruments for measuring information in the psyche. In the case of Elizabeth, for example, a single verbal state-ment (α: "I am not angry") is contrasted with a particular dermal reac-tion (ϵ). Similarly, in Hilgard's study on hypnotic analgesia, a verbal report (α: "I am fine") is shown to be contradicted by the subject's auto-matic writing (ϵ: "It hurts"). In both cases, we loosely treat our indica-tors, ϵ and α, as simple measuring instruments. This is an acceptable oversimplification for relatively limited situations, such as the laborato-ry. But in real life, and no less in the clinic, matters tend to be more complicated; the measuring instruments themselves tend to be complex rather than simple, by which is meant that the indicators, particularly of unconscious mentation, are made up of a combination of simple indi-cators. The dissociation paradigm, then, tends to assume the form, $[\epsilon] > \alpha$, where $[\epsilon]$ is a set of individual events, $\epsilon_1, \epsilon_2, \epsilon_3, \ldots \epsilon_n$, which as a group, but not individually, indicate psychological information that may not be accessible to consciousness. The situation is commonplace and understood by everyone. In the Dennis the Menace cartoon (Figure 2.6), for example, Margaret claims not to be angry,

$$\alpha: 0 \ (\text{"I'm } not \text{ burned up!)"},$$

but betrays her anger through a series of indicants, each of which by it-self would not be conclusive:

ϵ_1: gesticulates wildly
ϵ_2: face is all red
ϵ_3: breathing hard
ϵ_4: eyes "buggin'" out
ϵ_5: smashes umbrella
ϵ_6: walks off in a huff

The methodological problems remain as before: (1) report bias (does Margaret's verbal denial, α: 0, faithfully reflect the inaccessibility of her anger to awareness?) and (2) interpretation (does $[\epsilon]$ in fact in-dicate anger?—in this case, hardly in doubt). Although the problems remain the same, the more complex variants of the dissociation paradigm, as will soon become obvious, move beyond the ambit of

87

Figure 2.6. Illustration of the dissociation paradigm with a complex indicator. (DENNIS THE MENACE® used by permission of Hank Ketcham and © by News Group Chicago, Inc.)

precise methodological-experimental techniques, such as we have thus far attempted to apply to our material. It would be a dreadful mistake, however, to give up the scientific study of these more complex materials (as has been the wont of experimental psychology until recently), for it is these that bring us finally to some of the most fascinating phenomena of the human mind, including art, dreams, jokes, irony, poetry, religion, and symptoms. These topics, of course, lie at the core of the psychoanalytic enterprise, and it is their remarkable neglect by mainstream academic psychology that renders psychoanalysis, by default if nothing else, unique as a comprehensive psychology of the higher mental processes.

The Dissociation Paradigm with Hypercomplex Indicators: $\epsilon|[\epsilon] > \alpha$. We now turn to a complex form of complex indicators, hence "hypercomplex" indicators. Here we deal not just with the summation of a set of individual indicators, but with their interaction.

Hypercomplex indicators arise from the fact that the meaning of an isolated event, ϵ, is not necessarily the same as the meaning of the same event, ϵ, *given* a set of other events $\epsilon_1, \epsilon_2, \epsilon_3, \ldots \epsilon_n$, or $[\epsilon]$. Thus, $\epsilon \neq \epsilon|[\epsilon]$. A more familiar way of stating this is that an event, ϵ, in a *given context*, $[\epsilon]$, may mean something quite different from the event by itself (or in a different context). In human psychology, at least, a rose is not a rose is not a rose; psychological events tend to be polysemous, semantically multilayered. This is an absolutely seminal, if obvious, principle. Yet it is around this idea that the great divide between psychoanalysis and traditional scientific psychology may be said to form. For experimental psychologists, in the service of methodological expediency, restricted themselves to simplistic stimuli—nonsense syllables, isolated words—which had either no meaning or only a simple plane of meaning and lulled themselves into thinking that the psychological message inhered in the physical "stimulus," and that therefore a single meaningful stimulus conveyed a single meaning. Such artificial, uncontexted stimuli inevitably led to a "flat-world psychology" (Koestler, 1967), one lacking the dimension of semantic depth. For over half a century, the methodological tail wagged the theoretical dog. Only in recent times, with a growing interest in more complex stimuli (sentences, paragraphs, narrative texts) has experimental cognitive psychology begun to contend with the semantic multilayeredness of human communication (e.g., Bransford and Franks, 1971; Bransford and McCarrell, 1974; Dooling and Lachman, 1971; Franks, 1974; Harris and Monaco, 1978; Monaco and Harris, 1978). Psychoanalysis, operating as it did from a clinical matrix, and thus continually informed by real-life materials, began, in contrast, from the premise that below the surface presentations—the "manifest content" of events—lie the deeper meanings—the "latent content"—of events.[3] It is these latent contents that hypercomplex indicators indicate.

Let us turn to some concrete illustrations (it is no accident that our "stimuli" become real-life materials). Consider the figure below (Figure 2.7).

Figure 2.7.

What is it? Now consider Figure 2.8. It too depicts a bottle (ϵ = bottle).

[3]Latent contents are customarily treated in the psychoanalytic literature as unconscious. The reason for this is that they are almost invariably discussed in the context of dreams and symptoms, the underlying meanings of which are, in fact, typically unconscious. Since, however, the same semantic multilayeredness characterizes other psychological materials such as jokes (Freud, 1905a), the latent-manifest content distinction does not coincide with that of unconscious-conscious. Thus, latent contents, which are the deep meanings underlying manifest events, can be conscious as well as unconscious.

Figure 2.8. (Courtesy Hiram Walker & Sons, Ltd.)

But does it convey any additional content? Would there be any validity, for example, to perceiving a latent, albeit *physically* nonexistent, penis ($\epsilon | [\epsilon] = $ penis)? There would be little basis for such a perception in Figure 2.7, but perhaps a case could be made, admittedly not a decisive one, for the "penis" interpretation in Figure 2.8 (considering, for example that, ϵ_1: the tip of the bottle abuts the suggestive opening of the

Victrola speaker; ϵ_2: the speaker juts out from the midsection area of the young woman; ϵ_3: the two lovers are reclining in an intimate pose; ϵ_4: advertisers often inject sexual themes into their materials; and so forth). Consequently, some grounds exist for the notion that, whereas

$$\epsilon = \text{bottle}$$
$$\epsilon|[\epsilon] = \text{penis (?)}$$

It is important to note that the significant context is not restricted to the physical stimulus; some of it, often the most important, is the knowledge that the observer brings to the stimulus (ϵ_4, for example). This is reminiscent of the stance taken by modern physics (Heisenberg, 1971) that the separation between "phenomena" and the "observer" is artificial.

Each of the succeeding pictures (Figures 2.9 and 2.10) conveys, with

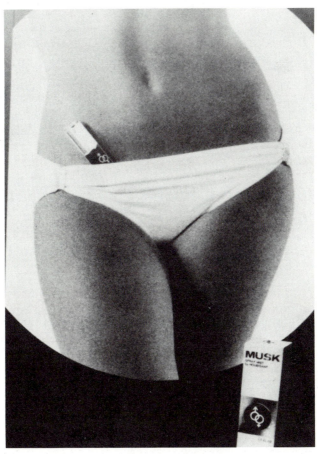

Figure 2.9. (Courtesy of Musk, by Houbigant.)

92

Figure 2.10. (Reproduced by Special Permission of PLAYBOY Magazine: Copyright © 1975 by PLAYBOY.)

increasing force, a latent penis as part of the message. It could be said that this is the "subliminal" message of the materials.[4] In the *Playboy* cover (Figure 2.10), there is little doubt that a double message is in-

---

[4]Theoretically, the term *subliminal* denotes a level of stimulus below the threshold (limen) of consciousness. In practice, however, the limen is a statistical rather than absolute value, defined in psychophysical tasks probabilistically as the level of stimulus at which the observer identifies the stimulus only a fraction (such as, 50 percent) of the time. Consequently, any stimulus, manifest or latent, that is only fractionally detectable in some sense, is "subliminal," whether the lack of stimulus "clarity" results from brief exposure, dim illumination, masking (in the case of manifest stimuli), or from contextual factors (in the case of latent contents).

tended. (It is easy enough to establish this empirically by asking a handful of subjects.) While the simple indicator, ϵ, conveys the surface information, bottle, the hypercomplex indicator, $\epsilon|[\epsilon]$, communicates "penis" as the message (where $[\epsilon]$ includes, ϵ_1: this is the cover of *Playboy* magazine; ϵ_2: *Playboy* deals with sex: ϵ_3: the young woman is holding the bottle between her thighs; ϵ_4: everything about the young woman, her seminudity, her provocative expression, the way she grasps the head of the "bottle" is sexually suggestive; and so forth).

It should be clear that there is nothing special about these bottles. The "objective," publicly observable stimulus, ϵ, is really quite secondary in importance, the crucial factor being the context, $[\epsilon]$, in which it occurs. Any reasonably adequate manifest stimulus will do, given the appropriate context. The painting (Figure 2.11) by Alan Aldridge (*The Beatles Illustrated Lyrics*, 1980) makes this clear. There is no need to assume, as Freud sometimes does (Freud, 1901a; 1917), the existence of "universal" symbols—"phallic symbols," for example—though it is easy to see that it helps (even if it is not absolutely essential) for the manifest stimulus roughly to resemble the object that is being latently conveyed.

Also, it should be clear that these effects are not restricted to visual materials. The following Groucho Marx joke has the same psychological structure as the preceding pictures:

Groucho Marx Joke

PREAMBLE

Groucho Marx is interviewing a man on his T.V. show. The program was cancelled soon after the exchange.

THE JOKE TEXT

Groucho: *"How are you?"*
Man: *"Fine."*
Groucho: *"Well, tell me, are you married?"*
Man: *"Yes; I've been married for nine years."*
Groucho: *"Gee, that's swell! Do you have any kids?"*
Man: *"Yes, nine already and the tenth is on the way."*
Groucho: *"Wait a minute! Ten kids in nine years?!"*
Man: (sheepishly) *"Well, I happen to love my wife very much."*
Groucho: *"Well, I love my cigar too, but I take it out of my mouth once in a while!"*

Obviously, one need not be a Freudian to believe in "Freudian symbols." One who gets the joke, and it is a rare person who doesn't, un-

Figure 2.11. (From Aldridge, *The Beatles Illustrated Lyrics*, 1969, p. 76. Dell.)

derstands that the significant content of the retort is not "cigar" and "mouth" but "penis" and "vagina." Thus,

$$\epsilon_i = \text{cigar, but } \epsilon_i|[\epsilon] = \text{penis}$$

and

$$\epsilon_j = \text{mouth, but } \epsilon_j|[\epsilon] = \text{vagina}$$

Not "getting" the joke means, precisely, not getting (interpreting) its latent content, of being stuck at the surface (manifest) level. Freud's classic work, *The Interpretation of Dreams* (1900), complex, sprawling, and rich as it is in ideas, makes essentially one basic point: We are not "getting" the dream if we stick to the surface, manifest content of the material.

The foregoing illustrations underscore some basic psychological facts. Most obviously, they demonstrate the perpetual play of latent meanings in complex human communications and, therefore, the absolute necessity of interpretation in making sense of these communications. Critics of psychoanalysis sometimes lapse into treating interpretation as an unacceptable tool in psychology on the grounds that it is unscientific. This, however, is nothing less than a denial of reality, no different than would be the banishment of perception from psychology because its rules of operation are not fully understood and because it too is sometimes untrustworthy, as in the case of illusions and hallucinations.

Although interpretations can go wrong and there is no fail-safe methodology for validating any particular interpretation, it would be incorrect to assume that interpretation is therefore arbitrary or haphazard. Our illustrative materials make this abundantly clear. Although the interpretation, penis, might be uncertain in some cases (e.g., Figure 2.8), there are materials for which interpretative consensus reaches virtual unanimity (e.g., the *Playboy* "bottle," Aldridge's "elephant trunk," Groucho Marx's "cigar"). This consensus is the crux of the matter. We might not consciously know the explicit rules by which we interpret latent meanings (just as we are not fully aware of the rules by which we generate grammatical speech or the rules by which we extract three dimensions from a two-dimensional retinal image), nevertheless we demonstrably apply ruleful processes to the extraction of deep meanings from deep stimuli—otherwise, there would be no consensus. Thus, the problem of interpretation is not that it is in principle unscientific (unruleful) but rather that we do not as yet have a science of interpretation that goes substantially beyond intuitive understanding.

Our illustrative materials nevertheless reveal the general basis of all latent meanings and their interpretation: *context*. Freud, although he did not elaborate it theoretically, was aware of this fact ("Symbols frequently have more than one or even several meanings, and, as with Chinese script, the correct interpretation can only be arrived at on each occasion from the context" [Freud, 1900, p. 353]).

As in visual depth perception (e.g., Gibson, 1950; Gregory, 1969), the contextual ecology of an event imparts depth to the event. Without appropriate context, there is no psychological depth, either of sight (Figure 2.12) or of insight. The "uncontexted" bottle in Figure 2.7 fails to yield the latent meaning of the contexted bottle in Figure 2.10; similarly, Groucho Marx's line, "I love my cigar too, but I take it out of my mouth once in a while," would hardly warrant the interpretation of a latent penis and vagina without the contextual backdrop of the preceding interchange.

Figure 2.12. The contextual ecology of an item gives depth to the item.

The central role of context helps explain why clinical interpretation often gives the appearance of arbitrariness. Without the vast contextual base to which the therapist has access—biographical detail, free associations, the ongoing events in the patient's life, dreams, gestures, and so forth—any interpretation, no matter how valid, must perforce appear shrouded in uncertainty. By the same token, incorrect, "reckless" interpretations (Freud, 1900, p. 353) are generated when there is insufficient contextual background to justify the interpretation, as when, for example, one attempts to analyze a single, isolated dream without the necessary background material (free associations, previous dreams, and the like). It is in part for this reason—the necessity for building context—that psychoanalysis is such a long-term, drawn-out process.

Our focus on the role of context provides us with an insight into at least one of the basic functions of free associations in the analysis of mental events. Free associations (as anticipated on page 36) provide the context that makes it possible for us to interpret the latent content underlying isolated manifest events. From this perspective, then, free association is context generation.

Finally, it must again be emphasized that a significant component of context resides in the observer and not just in what is observed. This actually is also the case in visual depth perception, wherein organismic cues (such as retinal disparity, ocular convergence) importantly supplement the depth cues of the external stimulus field. In *semantic* depth perception—insight—the interpreter must bring to bear to no less an extent his own internal knowledge of the world to the materials under analysis. The Groucho Marx joke, for example, would be undecipherable if one did not bring to it a rudimentary knowledge of anatomy and sex. Similarly, Freud could never have discovered the secret meaning of *aliquis* (pages 38–41) without applying his own extensive knowledge of culture, literature, and sex to the subject's associations. This helps explain why jokes often do not "translate" from one culture to another and why serious perturbations in interpretation occur when one attempts to understand the materials of an alien culture or even of a different social class. The violation of sociocultural expectations (the internal context that the culture-bound observer brings to his materials) can produce the selfsame "illusions" in interpretation that violations in visual expectations produce in visual illusions.

The materials we have been considering thus far have in every case featured latent contents that were conscious to the communicator. There can be little doubt, for example, that Groucho Marx was aware of the double meaning (ϵ and $\epsilon|[\epsilon]$) of his witty retort. Where, then, does the unconscious come into the picture? Actually, the linkage was deliberately postponed until the ground for it was fully prepared. The goal up to this point was only to establish the semantic multilayeredness of real-

life events and to demonstrate how context-driven hypercomplex in-
dicators, $\epsilon|[\epsilon]$, convey the latent content underlying surface, manifest
events, ϵ. Now the fact that latent contents exist and are conveyed by
hypercomplex indicators does not in itself mean that they need be unconscious. The dissociation paradigm of the unconscious is only
brought into play when it is demonstrated that there is a latent message
and also that the latent message is unconscious.

Unfortunately, it is far more difficult to provide illustrative proof of
unconscious latent contents than it is of merely latent contents. Latent
contents that are unconscious tend to be "deeper" than conscious ones
and typically require an inordinate amount of background context to be
interpreted convincingly. No simple picture or joke will do; the usual
materials necessary are outright case histories (which explains the general neglect of unconscious latent contents by experimental psychology). We shall here consider a brief protoclinical episode—a phone conversation. This material is the most complex that we will have examined
thus far; even so, it is probably still too abbreviated to provide the type
of convincing demonstration of unconscious latent contents that only a
full-fledged case report can offer.

The Case of J.[5]

PREAMBLE

A close friend, J. had recently completed his Ph.D. studies in
an abstruse field of science and won an appointment to one of
the country's top universities. After his first year, which was a
brilliant one, J. took a year's leave of absence to accept a postdoctoral fellowship at one of the leading laboratories in his
area of specialty. J. returned a changed person. Emaciated
physically, he was withdrawn and sullen. He drank heavily
and experimented with drugs. He appeared chronically anxious, suffered from a variety of tics, and had lost a great deal of
his social grace. He was singularly unsuccessful with women.
His performance in his department deteriorated rapidly, and
despite efforts by his colleagues to help him, he was not able to
complete his term of contract. Subsisting on his savings for
several months, he led a desultory, aimless existence. Eventually he found himself a job at a small bookstore, which he
managed to hold down despite some initial frictions with his
boss, Mrs. W., and the other clerk at the store. He seemed con-

[5]Certain facts of this case as well as of others reported in the book have been omitted or altered to protect the privacy of the individuals discussed.

tent with this simple existence, though he had horrendous long-distance arguments with his widowed mother, who was outraged at his having "squandered" his career in science. With his new job, J.'s drinking abated somewhat, and he gave up, for the most part, the drugs that he had been taking. Even so, he was unusually taciturn and became progressively more isolated socially; also, he stopped visiting his mother.

I feared greatly for my friend. It was around this time that I gave him a long-distance phone call to find out how he was managing.

TEXT OF PHONE CONVERSATION WITH J.

His answer to my conventional "How are you?" was melo-dramatic.

"I have finally done it! I have flipped!"

"What do you mean?" I asked him anxiously.

"Right in front of my apartment. The sidewalk was a sheet of ice [it was winter]. *I flipped full circle and broke my leg. The doctor said it was a classic skier's fracture. My whole leg is in a cast."*

I was astonished. Could he really have been missing the idiomatic sense of "flipped?" It was not impossible since he was an immigrant and spoke an accented English. But it seemed unlikely.

J. proceeded to tell me that after an initial tendency *"to minimize the whole incident—so many people break an ankle* [sic?], *big deal!"*—he was *"only now coming to realize how ill* [he] *truly was."*

I was again startled by his mode of expression. Was he alluding, after all, to a psychological crisis? Finally I suggested that he might be depressed, a common reaction.

J. replied that he had been depressed for a while but that his most notable psychological experience was an *"inexpressibly violent attack of guilt after the accident."*

At this point, J. shifted to another matter, the impending visit of his older brother from _____, his first to the United States. (This older brother, J.'s only sibling, was very different from J.: He was handsomer, married, and the father of two children; also he was internationally famous in his own specialty of science, the purpose of his visit being, in fact, to deliver a series of invited colloquia at American universities.) J. related how his mother had been pestering him day and night over the phone about going to _____ Airport to meet his brother, despite the fact that J. lived in another city and had no car. He now matter-of-factly pointed out that he would not be able to meet his brother. Thereupon, J. launched into a remarkable tirade. Screaming into the phone, he declared that *his brother was after all a grown-up man with a family; he had* *children; a wife; surely he would know how to find a taxi to the City; as far as he was concerned, his mother could rant and rave and he would not care in the slightest; his brother would surely not be the first person in the history of ___ Airport to arrive unmet; nor would he be the last; he could, like countless others, find the wit to find himself a taxi; and if his mother couldn't see this, well then she could just as well go fuck herself! And so could his brother! By God, he had a broken leg and he was in no condition to go meeting anybody at ____ Airport!*

I asked whether his mother was still nagging him about making the trip to the airport.

He barely replied (she wasn't) and launched into a new diatribe.

Eventually, I asked J. about the "excruciating guilt" he had previously mentioned.

He explained that he *so hated to overburden his poor associates at the bookstore who, with him out, would have to do all kinds of extra work; they were really very nice people, and he just didn't want to push his own work upon their shoulders.* Indeed, upon his return from the hospital, he had called up to say that he would come in to work despite his cast, but his boss, Mrs. W., had vetoed this, assuring him that she and the other clerk could manage at the bookstore, that he need have no concerns about his salary or his job, and that he should rest two weeks before returning to work. J. had protested, but she was firm.

Despite this, J. said, "*I felt incredibly guilty the whole day; it was unbearable, overwhelming! I felt so guilty about those two doing all my work.*"

I finally asked J. whether part of his guilt might not be connected to his incapacity with respect to the *other two people* of whom he was telling me—his *mother* and his *brother.*

To this I received a curt and vehement response: "*Most certainly not! I have suffered almost two nervous collapses from her nagging, and I'll be damned if I'll suffer another one! They have nothing to do with it.*"

After a brief new outburst of vituperation about his mother and brother we shifted to a few trivia and concluded the conversation.

Many questions arise about just what was being communicated by J. in his phone conversation. His very first utterance is strikingly ambiguous. At the manifest level,

$$\epsilon = \text{``I have finally done it! I have flipped!''}$$

but the context of the remark (our knowledge of the usual idiomaticness of "I flipped," J.'s various psychological and social problems, and so forth) tends to suggest a latent message,

$$\epsilon|[\epsilon] = \text{I am in a psychological crisis (or some such)}$$

Indeed, the remark could easily have constituted a verbal prank played on an overanxious psychologist friend, though in this case no joke was intended. Actually, if it had been a joke, matters would be simpler; no doubts would arise about the double meaning of the utterance. Taken seriously, however, the meaning of the remark is more problematic. Is there actually no latent content, or is the latent content unconscious? When queried several weeks later, J. flatly denied any latent message about psychological distress, claiming simply to have meant the literal act of flipping over. Was he not aware of the idiomatic sense of flipped? Yes, he was, but he had not intended it in this case. Why then had he prefaced his statement with "I have finally done it!"? Because the streets had been covered with ice for several days, and he had often worried about having an accident, which in fact he finally did. J.'s denial of the inferred latent content poses a dilemma. Is the denial a sign that the latent content was unconscious or that the author (who obviously was "set" to see a psychological unravelling in J.) had misinterpreted the remark and had read into it a nonexistent layer of meaning? Without further context there is no resolution to the dilemma.

There are a number of other remarks by J. which suggest latent contents consistent with the figurative sense of the earlier "flipped" comment. What does J. really mean when he says how excruciatingly guilty he felt toward "those two"? Could he actually have been feeling such an inordinate guilt toward his two associates at the bookstore, which, given the circumstances, would be nothing short of bizarre—bringing to mind the overreaction of Deutsch's patient to (ostensibly) the loss of her dog (pages 48–51). Would not the reaction, despite J.'s denial, make far more sense in connection with the *other two* persons, his mother and brother? J. was not only crossing his mother, which always caused him turmoil, but he must have also been burdened with feelings of jealousy and hostility—and, therefore, guilt—towards his successful brother who, by his arrival, would accent J.'s abject failure in the eyes of his mother. J., however, denied all this.

One may also entertain questions about J.'s "accident." Was it a purposeful (but not necessarily conscious) act designed to foil his mother and, at the same time, to punish himself for his unworthy feelings and behavior? (The possibility of there being more than one latent content, defined by different contextual considerations, is in no way an embarrassment. Such multilayered latent meanings are easy to demonstrate with artistic materials such as poems.)

Interestingly, despite his initial denials, J. was eventually to acknowledge the possibility that his "accident" may not have been altogether accidental. About a year later he raised the issue on his own: "You know, I have been thinking of this for a while. I am not really sure, but now I have this inkling that maybe I made myself have that fall so as not to have to meet my brother at the airport."

This was the only point on which J. was to reverse himself. What of the other inferred latent contents? Are they illusory, a product of faulty interpretation, or are they veridical but unconscious? These questions cannot be resolved without a great deal more context. And even with more context, there can be no *absolute certainty* about any interpretation. In fact, there is no absolute certainty about *any* latent content, even in such obvious cases as Groucho Marx's joke; at best, the latent content of an utterance is so highly probable (as in the latter case) as to be, for all practical purposes, incontrovertible. The absence of absolute determinateness does not, however, make latent contents and their interpretation "unscientific." The probabilistic nature of phenomena, as has been noted, is hardly a novel notion to twentieth century science, and even the strictest experimental psychologist accepts the statistical nature of laboratory outcomes, settling on some agreed upon criterion of plausibility (such as the .05 or .01 region of rejection of the null hypothesis). Similarly, latent contents are never certain, but only more or less probable; to be given credence only when reaching some relatively strict criterion of plausibility (which it might be the function of clinical training to establish in the trainee as a standard). Once a credible latent content is extracted, of which the subject has no awareness, it may be assumed that the latent content is unconscious.

Up to this point we have focused on the problem of interpretation exclusively from the standpoint of the experimenter or clinician. What about the subject/patient himself? Does he not also have to interpret his own communications and that of others? This is a remarkably neglected issue in psychology (but see Nisbett and Ross, 1980). If the experimenter makes an error of interpretation he has produced a methodological "artifact." If the subject himself makes such an error, however, it is not an artifact but a psychological fact of the utmost significance. The subject's own errors in interpretation fundamentally affect his perceptions and behavior toward the world and are therefore better viewed not as a problem but a problem area in psychology, constituting, as will be seen in Chapter 5, the cognitive foundation of psychodynamics. For, in real life, the potential context of an event is not clearly delimited but is, for all practical purposes, infinite. We are, therefore, obliged to *sample* a universe of potential contextual items to extract the latent content underlying manifest events. But we know about sampling bias from statistics. Since there are no explicit rules for sampling a contextual ecology, it becomes an easy matter to lie to ourselves for the purpose of defense by tendentiously choosing a context sample, $[\epsilon]_p$, which when applied to a manifest event, ϵ, will produce a desirable latent meaning, $\epsilon|[\epsilon]_p$.

When J. interpreted the meaning of his guilt toward "those two" in a way different from the author, J. was obviously bringing different contextual considerations to bear on the utterance—with a resultant difference in extracted meaning. Thus, by sampling a different context, $[\epsilon]_p$ versus $[\epsilon]_q$, the same manifest event, ϵ, takes on different latent meaning (that is, $\epsilon|[\epsilon]_p \neq \epsilon|[\epsilon]_q$).

We might reformulate this conceptualization slightly into one that is logically equivalent but which readily links up with Freud's approach to psychodynamics in terms of directed quanta of energies or forces (cf. Kahneman, 1973). The subject may be seen as selecting his context by assigning weights to all potential contextual items. The items that are ignored may be thought of as having been assigned zero weightings, while those that are selected are assigned weights commensurate with their judged importance. The relative weightings of contextual items may now be linked to the metaphor of "force," as when, for example, the author wrote on pages 91–92 that "each of the succeeding pictures conveys, with increasing force, a latent penis as part of the message." The term *force* is, of course, used metaphorically, but no less metaphorically than the concept of force in Newton's gravitational formula (see Chapters 3 and 5). What really counts is that directed "magnitudes" of some form are being manipulated; the gravitational formula would work just as well if one spoke not of the gravitational attraction, that is, force, between two masses, but their mutual "lust" for each other. Similarly, a computer program for interpreting latent contents would be equivalent regardless of whether one designated the magnitudes as "weights" or "forces."

By weighting (and thereby selecting) his contextual ecology, the subject substantially determines the meanings with which he is confronted. As an exercise, one can demonstrate the different latent contents that would arise in regard to J.'s "those two" as a result of differential context sampling/weighting. Table 2.2 lists a series of contextual items with their hypothetical weightings by J. and the author. To simplify matters, only 0 and 1 are used as weights, although in real life these would vary over a wide range of magnitudes. J.'s weightings of the contextual items is such that "those two" (ϵ) may be seen, in its selected context ($\epsilon_1, \epsilon_3, \epsilon_5, \epsilon_7, \epsilon_9, \epsilon_{11}$), to mean his associates at the bookstore ($\epsilon|[\epsilon]_{odd}$), while according to the author's selected context, his mother and brother ($\epsilon|[\epsilon]_{even}$).

To the extent that J.'s or the author's selection/weighting of the contextual ecology is tendentious, that is, biased for or against a particular semantic outcome, the interpretation constitutes a form of mo-

Table 2.2   Biased Weighting of Contextual Items from the Case of J.

	Hypothetical Weights	
	J.'s	Author's
ϵ_1: Two persons worked at the bookstore.	1	0
ϵ_2: Two persons were causing J. distress, his mother and his brother.	0	1
ϵ_3: One should not shirk one's own work by shifting it to others.	1	0
ϵ_4: Thou shalt honor thy father and thy mother.	0	1
ϵ_5: J.'s boss, Mrs. W., had been decent to J.	1	0
ϵ_6: One should love one's brother and rejoice in his successes. Jealousy and hatred are sins.	0	1
ϵ_7: J. had been raised a Calvinist and inculcated with the Calvinist work ethic.	1	0
ϵ_8: J.'s brother was immensely successful, but J. was a failure.	0	1
ϵ_9: J. could have been of some use at the bookstore despite his cast.	1	0
ϵ_{10}: Even in the best cases, sibling rivalry is a source of conflict; this was not the best of cases.	0	1
ϵ_{11}: J.'s mother had already caused him grief, and he was not about to let her add to it.	1	0
ϵ_{12}: J. found it disturbing to say "no" to his mother.	0	1

tivated cognition. At the level of hypercomplex indicators, which demand sampling of the contextual ecology, the issue of intent, for example, defense, is not easily detached from the function of interpretation itself—a fact that Freud probably grasped intuitively, causing his vagueness with respect to the "dynamic" unconscious (see pages 62–64). For, to the extent that we utilize "unconscious inference" in extracting latent contents (and we do) and our inferential processes are not disinterested with respect to the semantic products they generate (and they are not), cognition becomes psychodynamic cognition.

One may begin to understand why experimental psychology, in contrast to dynamic clinical psychology, has taken such a different stance on phenomena such as repression (Chapter 5). Experimental psychology, in the service of simplification and control, has studied *manifest* events, specific memory episodes or percepts (as in perceptual defense). It is not typical, however, for a normal college subject to resort in the laboratory to such drastic defenses as to block out a clear memory episode or perceptual experience. Consequently, experimental psychology has had great difficulty in demonstrating repression in the laboratory and has understandably taken a skeptical attitude toward this phenomenon. Clinicians, on the other hand, deal continually with latent contents, and in this realm the selective blocking or distortion of information through context manipulation is utterly commonplace. The clinician shakes his head in disbelief at the experimental psychologist, whose paltry methodology cannot even demonstrate a phenomenon as obvious and ubiquitous as repression. The experimentalist similarly shakes his head at the credulity of the psychodynamic clinician, who embraces notions unproven in the laboratory and that, moreover, rest on the presumed existence of nonconscious, indeed, physically nonexistent, latent contents.

CHAPTER THREE

MODELS OF
THE MIND
AND
THE LANGUAGE OF
THE MODELS

♦

THE LANGUAGE PROBLEM

Babel, n. [Heb. *bābel;* Assyr.-Babylonian *Bāb-ilu,* Babylon, lit.,
gate of God . . .], 1. in the *Bible,* a city in Shinar in which
Noah's descendants tried to build a tower intended to reach
to heaven: God punished its builders for this presumption
and prevented them from finishing by causing them all suddenly to speak in different languages so that they could not
understand one another. . . . (*Webster's New World Dictionary,* 1955)

Concretistic Thinking in Science: Literalization of Metaphor

A says to B: *You seem to be under a lot of pressure these days.*
B replies: *Not at all. I measured the pressure on me just
                this morning and it's* c *grams per square centi-
                meter, exactly the average at this altitude.*

What is wrong with B's response? The answer, of course, is that B
has misconstrued A's query (or wishes to give the impression of having
done so), confusing the surface, literal meaning of *pressure* with the
term's deeper figurative meaning. B has literalized a metaphor; he is
dealing with the same *word* but a different domain of *meaning.* In effect,
A and B are speaking different languages while using the same
vocabulary.

Although the problem in the present rudimentary case is plain
enough to us—if not necessarily to B—we nevertheless tend to make
the same type of error when dealing with only slightly more complex
communications. We have already seen from the historical survey of the
background and development of psychoanalysis the extent to which perennial controversies and confusions hinged on the mishandling of
metaphor (analog) systems. In turning to Freud's models of the mind,
we are now prepared to consider the more drastic claim that psychoanalysis (indeed, most modern psychology) is riddled with such errors,
and that fundamental confusions exist among both proponents and opponents of psychoanalysis about what constitute basic psychoanalytic
ideas and what constitute merely provisional metaphors for giving
expression to these underlying ideas. Nowhere is the problem more
acute than in general models of psychological structure such as we take
up in this chapter, where direct observation tends to lose its anchoring
function. Since the referents are often abstractions rather than observable objects or events, it is particularly easy to confuse the literal with the
figurative. To avoid this pitfall, we shall focus, before turning to Freud's
actual models, on the general problem of language in theory. This
problem has actually become a fundamental preoccupation of modern

psychoanalytic scholars (e.g., Edelson, 1975; Gill and Holzman, 1976; Holt, 1965; 1972; 1976; G. S. Klein, 1973; 1975; Peterfreund and Schwartz, 1971; Ricoeur, 1970; Schafer, 1976).

Language, Analogy, and Theory

The danger of literalizing metaphors is particularly obvious in psychoanalysis. This is so because of Freud's untrammelled propensity to analogize, to the point that most psychoanalytic ideas have gained articulation through a vast sprawl of more or less improvised analogies.

Freud has been criticized for his exuberant analogizing by his critics as well as his exponents. There is something inherently unscientific—or so we are led to believe—about "mere analogies." Nevertheless, this depreciation of analogies reflects a misconception; for ultimately all scientific theories are analogies of one form or another, the expression of similarity between two realms—usually some facet of nature on the one hand and an analog on the other. The significant difference between "respectable" analogies (as in physics) and casual analogies (as in psychology) lies in the sophistication of the analogic medium, not in the recourse to analogy.

Vernacular and Formal Analog Languages. In the advanced sciences, theories tend to be articulated in mathematical languages, specialized symbolic systems characterized by highly formal and explicit rules (grammars) for symbol manipulation. For example, the classic Newtonian equation for gravitational attraction, $f = c \cdot \dfrac{m_1 \cdot m_2}{d^2}$, precisely relates mass (m) and distance (d) to gravitational force (f). The Newtonian formula, like any other theory (or "law") of physics, is ultimately nothing but a precise analogy. It posits that the symbolic game expressed by the mathematical formula mimics (parallels, is "isomorphic" to) nature's game "out there." When the mimicry is successful, it is said that the theory has "a good fit," that is, the mathematical analogy tends to be consistent with reality.

In the less advanced sciences, such as psychology, the approach is not basically different; but the analogic systems employed are relatively more amorphous and implicit—in short, primitive. Ideas are typically conveyed through the medium of ready-made (as opposed to *tailormade*) analogs as in *similes,* such as "the mind is like a computer," and *metaphors,* such as "the mind is a computer." In both cases the meaning of the vernacular analog (the computer) is left vague and subject to interpretation (unlike the mathematically formulated analog, $"c \cdot \dfrac{m_1 \cdot m_2}{d^2}"$). This vagueness includes not just the generality intended but also the depth or literalness at which the analogy is to be taken. Not surprisingly, confusions arise. Because of the vagueness of the vernacular analog (the "computer"), the analogy ("the mind is like a computer") means different things to different people.

The greater differentiation and explicitness of formal analogs has another major consequence. Formal, unlike vernacular, analogs are relatively flexible. If it should turn out that a specific mathematical analogy such as $f = c \cdot \dfrac{m_1 \cdot m_2}{d^2}$ achieves a poor fit to reality, other analogies formulated in the same analog language may be tried out, for example, $f = c \cdot \dfrac{m_1 \cdot m_2}{d^{1.7}}$, or $f = c \cdot m_1 \cdot m_2 \cdot d^2$, or $f = c \cdot \dfrac{d^2}{m_1 \cdot m_2}$, and so forth. In contrast, vernacular analogies—ordinary similes and metaphors—are rigid; they cannot be easily adjusted in the face of new data to produce a better reality fit. A disconfirmed simile such as, "He is brave as a lion," cannot be meaningfully modified within the same analog language ("He is brave as a cowardly lion," for example). Because of their inflexibility, vernacular analogies more easily lose touch with the reality they are meant to model. The theorist must either shift to a new analog or try to qualify the original analog with results not usually more enlightening than the "cowardly lion" example. Psychoanalysis is replete with such qualified (*tortured* might be more descriptive) metaphors.

Flexibility, however, is not an all-or-none but a more-or-less property of analog languages. The modern physicist too is often forced to fracture his mode of expression, adopting different analog systems (different mathematics) to express different facets of the reality he is attempting to illuminate. This fact is widely appreciated in modern physics. Contemporary academic psychology, in contrast, has typically ignored the problem, treating the language of theory as a more or less incidental detail. In this respect modern psychology recapitulates the outmoded belief of classical physics that language—and therefore the language of theory—is a passive medium for communicating concepts, whose own effect upon the communicated concepts may be conveniently disregarded.

Yet, a good case can be made for the view that the major conceptual revolutions in twentieth-century psychology—Kuhnian "paradigm shifts" (Kuhn, 1962)—arose precisely from shifts in basic metaphor systems. Thus, behaviorism may be seen as a psychological system adopting the rat (or the pigeon, dog, or reflex arc) as the metaphor premise of psychology. Koestler (1967) has aptly termed the approach "ratomorphism." Information-processing cognitive psychology (e.g., Broadbent, 1958; Haber, 1968; Miller, Galanter, and Pribram, 1960; Neisser, 1967) rejects the rat metaphor in favor of the computer. Piagetian cognitive psychology, on the other hand, adopts formal logic as the fundamental metaphor of mind. Kelly's (1963) psychology of personal constructs posits science as the metaphor of psychological process, treating "mankind in its scientist-like aspects" (p. 21). The adoption of different metaphor systems at times merely yields differences in terminology and pointless controversy. At other times, however, a shift in metaphor premise produces a veritable transformation of a field, giving rise to radically new questions, theories, research, and even methodology and overall epistemology.

How does psychoanalysis fit into this scheme? Is psychoanalysis to be viewed as one more psychological system defined by a particular metaphor premise? Many scholars of psychoanalysis have suggested as much. Some have emphasized the medical metaphor ("the medical model") as the analogic foundation of psychoanalysis. Others have focused on its biological or neurological underpinnings (e.g., Pribram and Gill, 1976; Sulloway, 1979). Still others have placed the accent on the analogic role of nineteenth-century physics (determinism, hydraulics, force dynamics, conservation of energy, and so on). Others have underscored the importance of the archeology metaphor in Freud's thinking (e.g., Spence, 1982). Freud himself, in one of his later works (Freud, 1921), makes explicit a sociopolitical metaphor base that is implicit in much of his earlier writings (involving notions such as defense, agencies, repression, economics, compromise formation). It is possible to discover additional metaphor premises in psychoanalysis. For example, psychoanalysis tends to treat psychological phenomena as if they were artistic products (for example, symbolism, latent meaning, allusion, ellipsis, displacement of accent, condensation, censorship, plastic word representation). Freud's *psychoanalysis* of dreams, parapraxes, jokes, and myth is quite similar to *literary* analysis, a feature that will be elaborated in Chapter 4.

What then *is* the metaphor premise of psychoanalysis? The answer seems to be that psychoanalysis is unique; unlike major "schools" or "movements" in academic psychology, it adheres to no single analogic medium. Psychoanalysis is a mixed-metaphor system. Freud, unlike major academic theoreticians, was not willing to be fettered by any single metaphor premise. When one analogic medium failed to elucidate some facet of psychological reality, he was willing to try out new analogic tools rather than simply to ignore, as traditional academic psychology has typically done, the recalcitrant reality. In this respect psychoanalysis, despite its experimental provincialism, is much closer to the spirit of twentieth-century physics than contemporary academic psychology.

Analogic Domains: Representational and Misrepresentational. A *theory*, to recapitulate, is an *analogy* expressed in a particular *language,* the *analog* system. Regardless of whether the analog system is formal or vernacular, the objective of the analogy is the same: to represent or map some domain of reality by asserting an equality or similarity between the analog (such as, $c \cdot \dfrac{m_1 \cdot m_2}{d^2}$ or the computer) and reality (gravitational attraction, the mind).

Now, it is well known in science that any theory, whatever its language base, has a more or less limited generality. Every analogy has, to borrow an expression from George Kelly (1963), its "range and focus of convenience." Thus, the fit (isomorphism) between the analog and reality tends to break down beyond a certain domain of application. Newtonian mechanics, for example, fail in the realm of subatomic physics; they work only in "the zone of middle dimensions" (Capra, 1975, p. 53).

ANALOGIC "NOISE" AND ANALOGIC "WARP." When an analogy is pushed beyond its representational domain, its range or focus of convenience, it begins to misrepresent reality. In some cases the analogy becomes merely more "noisy," that is, a less and less accurate representation of reality; in other cases, however, the analogy becomes fundamentally misleading, warping reality altogether.

Consider, for example, the representation of a three-dimensional (3-D) object, a sphere, by a 2-D analog, a circle (see Figure 3.1). Let us first focus on the angles between the lines making up the squares on the surface of the 3-D "reality" and its 2-D analog. Note that for relatively

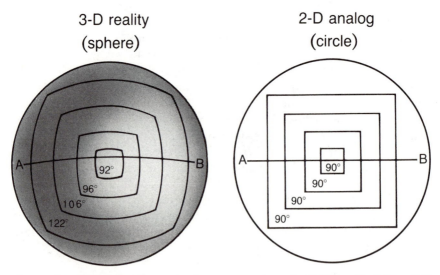

Figure 3.1. Representation and misrepresentation of a 3-D "reality" by a 2-D analog.

small squares the 2-D analog produces a reasonably accurate (noiseless, errorless) representation of the 3-D counterparts, although of course not a perfect one (90 degrees versus 92 degrees; 90 degrees versus 96 degrees, for example). The larger the squares, however, the more noisy the representation (90 degrees versus 106 degrees; 90 degrees versus 122 degrees). As the area represented increases, so does the error in the representation. Still, for not too large an area, the analog is serviceable, yielding at least a "ball park" if not perfect fit.

But now consider another feature of the analogy. Suppose we were to ask the question: What is the relationship between the length of line A-B and the distance between points A and B? From the standpoint of the 2-D *analog* the answer is self-evident; the longer the line A-B, the further the points A and B are from each other. In fact, the answer is so obvious that the question would probably never arise within the analogic framework, for the two notions—length of A-B, and distance between A and B—seem to be one and the same notion. This, however, is a delusion—a reality warp—introduced by the analogic system adopted, for, as "empirical research" on the 3-D "reality" would reveal, as line A-B gets longer the distance between points A and B gets at first longer, then shorter, and then again longer, and again shorter, ad infinitum. This is the type of mind-boggling paradox that has become the hallmark of twentieth-century physics. Here is one example:

> If we ask, for instance, whether the position of the electron remains the same, we must say "no"; if we ask whether the electron's position changes with time we must say "no"; if we ask whether the electron is at rest, we must say "no"; if we ask whether it is in motion, we must say "no." (Robert Oppenheimer, cited in Capra, 1975, p. 139).

Such paradoxes have forced modern physics to become acutely concerned with the problem of the analogic medium—the language—that is used to conceptualize reality, for such paradoxes obviously cannot reside in the reality—what is, is—but in the analog system through which, by way of analogy, we try to grasp reality. In the next section (pages 115–126), which takes up an information-processing model proposed by Freud in *The Interpretation of Dreams,* we shall have occasion to witness such a paradox in a psychoanalytic model.

For the present, let us turn to a case that has been already touched on. In Chapter 1 we saw how the metaphor of force dynamics helped to explain, or at least formulate, the phenomena of inhibition and perversion of will (pages 10–11). Such an analogic framework can be quite reasonably applied to a number of defense phenomena subsequently elaborated by Freud such as repression, censorship, displacement, and sublimation. Repression is simply a variant of inhibition (page 10), and displacement and sublimation of perversion (page 11). In displacement the subject retargets an impulse to a new and less anxiety-provoking object; in sublimation, which is a special version of displacement, the new target is not only more acceptable, and therefore less anxiety-provoking, but actually socially valued. The concept of censorship, involving the selective withholding of forbidden ideas or impulses from consciousness, can still be handled in force dynamics terms, but not as comfortably. Different ideas or impulses would now have to be represented as different force vectors; censorship would result from a select set of countervectors. The force analog is already becoming awkward (accounting, probably, for Freud's shift to the sociopolitical "censorship" metaphor). It becomes quite unwieldy, distorting, and perhaps even warping, when applied to other defensive phenomena such as, for example, *projection* (in which a taboo unconscious idea, such as the homosexual notion, "I love you" becomes defensively distorted into "You love me" on its way to consciousness through the transposition of the idea's subject and object). How could projection be articulated in the language of force dynamics? The task is almost hopeless. Other defense phenomena such as *reaction formation* (the defensive transformation of an idea's predicate into the opposite of the predicate; for example, "I love you" becomes "I hate you") seems completely beyond the ken of force dynamics language. Without a shift in analog language, the psychological phenomenon cannot be really conceptualized; attempts to retain the inadequate analog framework lead to absurdities such as the following sample of Freud's on conversion:

> We must suppose that there was present in the Ucs some love-impulse which demanded to be translated into the system Pcs; the preconscious cathexis, however, recoiled from it in the manner of an attempt at flight, and the unconscious libidinal cathexis of the rejected idea was discharged in the form of anxiety. (Freud, 1915b, p. 130)

BREADTH AND DEPTH WARPS. In the discussion of representational domains we have thus far focused on what might be termed "horizontal" domains, the breadth of reality which is reasonably represented by the adopted analog and beyond which the analog introduces severe noises or warps. To the extent, however, that the analog has more than one plane of meaning—that is, a range of meanings from relatively surface (literal) to relatively deep (figurative)—the "domain" question becomes pertinent to the analog itself. Since it may be possible for an analog to produce a good fit at one level of meaning but to distort or warp at another level, it becomes crucial to consider the "vertical" domain (the level of meaning) at which the analog is appropriate: How literally or figuratively are we to take the analog in the analogy?

The ubiquitous problem of the literalization of metaphor (as in the "pressure" example) may now be seen as a special case of the domain problem. Although psychologists tend to be sensitive to the horizontal (generalizability) constraints of their theories, they are almost universally unmindful of vertical domain constraints and, therefore, of the drastic noises and warps introduced when transgressing beyond them. This is a fundamental problem in psychology (whether psychoanalysis or experimental cognitive psychology), where many problems that on face value seem to be conceptual or methodological turn out in the end to be semantic (cf. Erdelyi, 1974; Erdelyi and Goldberg, 1979). Analogs explicitly intended as *figurative* are inexorably literalized by other researchers (and often by the original proponents themselves), until scientific variants of the "pressure" pseudodialogue ensue. In psychoanalytic terms, *manifest* content is confused with *latent* content. The problem is a most pernicious one because the commonality of vocabulary yields the illusory impression of shared meaning. The builders of the tower of Babel were comparatively fortunate; they at least knew that they were not understanding each other.

THE STRUCTURE OF THE PSYCHE

Do not mistake the scaffolding for the building. (Freud, 1900, p. 536)

Throughout his creative life Freud tinkered with a variety of models or analogies of the psyche. In most cases, these were informal, passing similes or metaphors as in "the mind is an arena, a sort of tumbling-ground for the struggle of antagonistic impulses" (Freud, 1917, p. 68); in other cases, these were elaborate schemes, such as the intricate Chapter VII of *The Interpretation of Dreams* (1900), *The Ego and the Id* (1923), and the monograph-length, "Psychology for Neurologists" (1895), which was abandoned by Freud as a failure, but has since been published posthumously as the *Project for a Scientific Psychology*.

We shall begin our examination of Freud's conception of psychological structure by analyzing in some detail the model he develops in the famous Chapter VII. This model is unusually instructive. It underlies a great deal of Freud's subsequent thinking, and is, moreover, remarkably prescient, anticipating by more than half a century the information-processing approaches that were to become the hallmark of the "cognitive revolution" in contemporary scientific psychology. Also, this model reveals a basic flaw—an analog warp—in Freud's premature information-processing theorizing.

The Chapter VII "Compound Instrument" ("ψ-Systems") Model: A Precomputer Information-Processing Scheme

One is hard put to decide upon the correct title for the Chapter VII model. In the space of a few pages Freud likens the "mental apparatus" to a "compound instrument"; a "photographic apparatus"; a "compound microscope"; a "telescope"; and "reflex apparatus" that is made up of component "agencies" or "systems" ("ψ-systems"), which are organized according to "psychical locality," "regions," "spatial relations," "temporal sequence," or "stages" (pp. 536–538). We shall adopt one of Freud's own terms, and refer to it as the "compound instrument" model.

Freud begins his discussion with a preliminary "schematic picture" of the "instrument" he envisions (Figure 3.2). At one end is the perceptual system (*Pcpt.*), which is responsible for the reception of stimuli. At the other end is the motor system (*M*), which is responsible for the generation of responses. The flow of "innervation" or "traces"—today we would usually say "information"—is normally from left to right, as indicated by the arrow in the bottom of the diagram. The vertical lines intervening between the systems *Pcpt.* and *M* are initially left undefined.

The model, in this preliminary form, resembles the classic stimulus-response formula of the behaviorists:

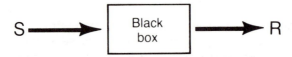

Even the underlying analog, the reflex arc (see Figure 3.3) is the same: "The psychical apparatus must be constructed like a reflex apparatus. Reflex processes remain the model of every psychical function" (p. 538).

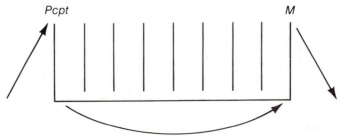

Figure 3.2. "The most general schematic picture of the psychical apparatus" (Freud, 1900, p. 537).

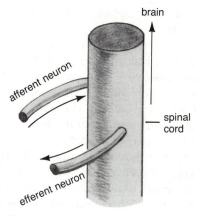

Figure 3.3. The reflex arc.

No sooner does Freud say this than he proceeds to contradict himself. He now turns his attention to the internal structure of the apparatus—the behaviorist's forbidden "black box"—and the reflex analog immediately proves oversimple. Freud's first concern is to make a distinction, on purely theoretical grounds, between the perceptual system, *Pcpt.*, and a system of memory subsystems, *Mnem. Mnem', Mnem''* behind it (see Figure 3.4): "We shall suppose that a system in the front of the apparatus receives the perceptual stimuli but retains no trace of them and thus has no memory, while behind it there lies a second system which transforms the momentary excitation of the first system into permanent traces" (p. 538).

Freud's reasoning, explicitly based on the analogous distinction between a camera's lens and its photographic plate or film, is that the perceptual system (like the lens) must be fresh for the reception of each succeeding new impression and therefore free of memory; otherwise, each new stimulus input would be hopelessly distorted by previous

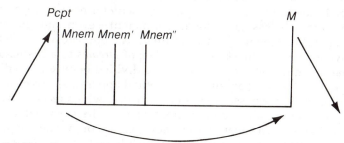

Figure 3.4. Freud's second, more elaborate, sketch of the compound instrument (Freud, 1900, p. 538).

(remembered) inputs, as happens when one takes multiple photographs on a single frame of film.

This playful bit of conceptual tinkering results in the anticipation
of one of the major empirical findings of modern information-processing psychology, the discovery by Averbach and Coriell (1961) and
Sperling (1960) of "iconic" storage (Neisser, 1967), a fleeting photographic form of memory, which everyone possesses, that, unlike
later-stage memories (short-term memory, long-term memory), loses its
rich information content within a small fraction of a second. Thus, the
Pcpt. system actually does have a memory, albeit a very fleeting one.
Freud was quite right, however, in supposing that such a memory
would produce perceptual distortions; research on visual "masking"
and "metacontrast" (e.g., Fehrer and Raab, 1962; Kahneman, 1968;
Raab, 1963; Turvey, 1973; Weisstein, 1966) reveals that different inputs
occurring within 0–100 msec of each other do in fact disrupt each other.

A quarter century after the publication of *The Interpretation of
Dreams*, there appeared a curious little article by Freud (1925a) under
the title, "A Note Upon the 'Mystic Writing-Pad.'" It is a rather trivial,
almost silly piece, which however reveals (as Freud taught us often to
expect of trivial events) an underlying problem—in this case, Freud's
inability to find an appropriate analog vehicle for his modeling, something already evident in his promiscuous characterization of the
psychic apparatus in *The Interpretation of Dreams*. Freud's paper on the
"mystic pad" suggests the desperation with which he was straining
toward the then unavailable computer analog. Freud begins by recapitulating the original argument for the necessity of distinguishing between a perceptual and a memory system:

> All the forms of auxiliary apparatus which we have invented
> for the improvement or intensification of our sensory func-
> tions are built on the same model as the sense organs them-
> selves or portions of them: for instance, spectacles, pho-
> tographic cameras, ear-trumpets. Measured by this standard,
> devices to aid our memory seem particularly imperfect, since
> our mental apparatus accomplishes precisely what they can-
> not: it has an unlimited receptive capacity for new perceptions
> and nevertheless lays down permanent—even though not
> unalterable—memory traces of them. As long ago as in 1900 I
> gave expression in *The Interpretation of Dreams* to a suspicion
> that this unusual capacity was to be divided between two dif-
> ferent systems (or organs of the mental apparatus). According
> to this view, we possess a system *Pcpt.-Cs.*, which receives per-
> ceptions but retains no permanent traces of them, so that it can
> react like a clean sheet to every new perception; while the per-
> manent traces of the excitations which have been received are

preserved in "mnemic systems" lying behind the perceptual system. (P. 228)

Freud's recapitulation is a faithful one except for a small inconsistency: What had been termed the *Pcpt.* system in *The Interpretation of Dreams* is now labeled the system *"Pcpt.-Cs."* We shall return to this discrepancy later. Freud now proceeds to describe the "Mystic Writing-Pad," which he conscripts to serve as an analog for the distinction between the perceptual system and the memory system:

> Some time ago there came upon the market, under the name of the Mystic Writing-Pad, a small contrivance that promises to perform more than the sheet of paper or the slate. It claims to be nothing more than a writing-tablet from which notes can be erased by an easy movement of the hand. But if it is examined more closely it will be found that its construction shows a remarkable agreement with my hypothetical structure of our perceptual apparatus and that it can in fact provide both an ever-ready receptive surface and permanent traces of the notes that have been made upon it.
>
> The Mystic Pad is a slab of dark brown resin or wax with a paper edging; over the slab is laid a thin transparent sheet [see Figure 3.5], the top end of which is firmly secured to the slab while its bottom end rests upon it without being fixed to it. This transparent sheet is the more interesting part of the little device. It itself consists of two layers, which can be detached from each other except at their two ends. The upper layer is a transparent piece of celluloid; the lower layer is made of thin translucent waxed paper. When the apparatus is not in use, the lower surface of the waxed paper adheres lightly to the upper surface of the wax slab.
>
> To make use of the Mystic Pad, one writes upon the celluloid portion of the covering-sheet which rests upon the

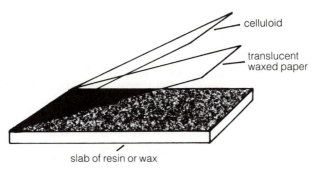

Figure 3.5. The Mystic Writing-Pad.

wax slab. For this purpose no pencil or chalk is necessary, since the writing does not depend on material being deposited upon the receptive surface. . . . At the points which the stilus touches, it presses the lower surface of the waxed paper on to the waxed slab, and the grooves are visible as dark writing upon the otherwise smooth whitish-grey surface of the celluloid. If one wishes to destroy what has been written, all that is necessary is to raise the double covering-sheet from the wax slab by a light pull, starting from the free lower end. . . . The Mystic Pad is now clear of writing and ready to re-ceive fresh notes.

The analogy would not be of much value if it could not be pursued further than this. If we lift the entire covering-sheet—both the celluloid and the waxed paper—of the wax slab, the writing vanishes and, as I have already remarked, does not re-appear again. . . . But it is easy to discover that the permanent trace of what was written is retained upon the wax slab itself and is legible in suitable lights. Thus the Pad provides not only a receptive surface that can be used over and over again, like the slate, but also permanent traces of what has been written, like an ordinary paper pad: it solves the problem of combining the two functions *by dividing them between two separate but interrelated component parts or systems.* . . . I do not think it is too far-fetched to compare the celluloid and waxed paper cover with the system *Pcpt.-Cs.* and its protective shield, the wax slab with the unconscious behind them, and the ap-pearance and disappearance of the writing with the flickering-up and passing away of consciousness in the process of per-ception. . . . (Pp. 228–231)

We need not be disturbed by the fact that in the Mystic Pad no use is made of the permanent traces of the notes that have been received; it is enough that they are present. There must come a point at which the analogy between an auxiliary apparatus of this kind and the organ which is its prototype will cease to apply. (P. 230)

Freud's last remark touches on the problem of analogic domains. In reading these passages on the Mystic Writing Pad it is difficult to refrain from wondering about the impact that the computer analog would have had upon Freud's theorizing, had it been available. Actu-ally, Freud appears at times to be making a direct, almost plaintive plea for the computer analog: "It is true too, that, once the writing has been erased, the Mystic Pad cannot reproduce it from within; it would be a mystic pad indeed if, like our memory, it could accomplish that" (p. 230).

That, of course, is precisely what even the simpler, hand-held "mystic pads" of our computer age can accomplish (see Figure 3.6, for

Figure 3.6. A modern Mystic Pad: the Hewlett-Packard (HP-25) programmable scientific calculator.

example). The contents of the display panel (corresponding to *Cs.*) can be stored (by pushing the command button, STO) in any of several memory buffers (1, 2, 3, . . .) and left there ready for later recall (RCL), long after the original display data have been erased or operated upon. Moreover, in mimicry of "unconscious processes," direct operations upon the contents of the memory buffers can be performed (for example, add the contents of Memory 1 to that of Memory 2, and if this addition results in a certain value, store in Memory 3; otherwise store in Memory 4, erasing the content of Memory 1) without ever involving the display buffer (*Cs.*).

Freud's mystic pad, unfortunately, was not mystical enough, as were not his various compound instruments in *The Interpretation of Dreams*. Not only do they prove incapable of communicating crucial features of Freud's thinking, but they introduce, as we shall presently see, an invalidating analog warp.

Upon distinguishing the perceptual and memory systems, Freud proceeds in his Chapter VII to elaborate the memory system into an unspecified number of component subsystems (*Mnem, Mnem', Mnem''*): "Closer consideration will show the necessity for supposing the existence not of one but of several such *Mnem* elements, in which one and the same excitation . . . leaves a variety of permanent records" (p. 539).

In this respect, Freud anticipates contemporary multitrace conceptions of memory (e.g., Paivio, 1971) and the practice of subdividing memory into subsystems (short, intermediate, long, and so on [cf. Baddeley, 1976; Crowder, 1976; Neisser, 1967]) or processing levels (Craik and Lockhart, 1972).

At this point, Freud turns to psychodynamic considerations. He posits, on the basis of his studies of dreams, the existence of what he variously terms, a "screen" (p. 540), a "critical agency" (p. 540), or "censorship" (pp. 542, 617)—the contemporary metaphors would be "filter," "gate," or "decision node"—that stands between the unconscious contents of the mnemic systems and consciousness. This censorship is identified with a new system, "the preconscious," which is located at the motor end of the apparatus, just before consciousness (see Figure 3.7). Freud's third and last diagram, his most elaborate sketch of the hypothesized compound instrument, does not fully incorporate his verbal descriptions of the apparatus. He fails to sketch in, for example, the last component of his instrument at the motor end—consciousness—or to indicate in the diagram the existence of a second "censorship" (pp. 542, 617) intervening between the preconscious and consciousness that functions on the principle of selective allocation of "attention." Freud's final sketch will therefore be supplemented with a fourth one (Figure 3.8), which faithfully incorporates

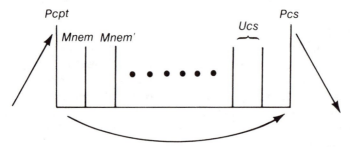

Figure 3.7. Freud's third and final sketch of the compound instrument. Note the inclusion of *Ucs.* (unconscious) and *Pcs.* (preconscious) at the motor end of the apparatus.

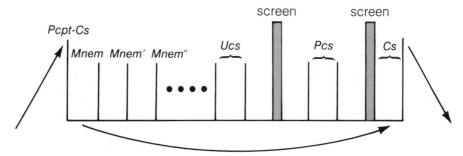

Figure 3.8. A sketch of the compound instrument that incorporates Freud's verbal elaborations.

Freud's various verbal elaborations. Also, the *Pcpt.* component will be designated as *Pcpt.-Cs.* in accord with Freud's own linkage of perception with consciousness in the "Note on the 'Mystic Writing-Pad'" as well as in other of his writings (e.g., Freud, 1923, p. 24; 1933, p. 78) and also, implicitly, in his Chapter VII (where Freud explains the perceptual, hallucinatory quality of dream-consciousness by positing a "regressive," or backward flow of excitation in dreams, from the motor to the perceptual end).

But there is something amiss here, as examination of Figure 3.8 will reveal. The problem is underscored by a footnote added by Freud to this section of Chapter VII in 1919:

> If we attempt to proceed further with this schematic picture, in which the systems are set out in linear succession, we should have to reckon with the fact that the system next beyond the *Pcs.* is the one to which consciousness must be ascribed—in other words, that *Pcpt.* = *Cs.* (P. 541)

We are in some kind of muddle. Where actually *is* the locus of *Cs.*? At the perceptual or motor end of the apparatus? Freud has placed it at both ends! Either the model collapses internally or we must infer that Freud is proposing the existence of *two* consciousnesses—which he is not. We have here a concrete illustration of an analog warp. By dint of committing himself to a miscroscope/telescope analog, the elements of which are "set out in linear succession," Freud is doomed to express something he never intended to express. Freud wants to link consciousness to perceptual experience and at the same time to make consciousness the terminus of a series of psychological processes, including preceding censorships; but the analog medium of the linear compound instrument cannot realize Freud's message. Forced beyond its domain, the medium warps the message, giving rise, quite against Freud's intent, to two consciousnesses (something which Freud conveniently does not discuss, leaving the quandary to the hapless reader).

Enterprising students of the author have on occasion suggested a simple solution: Why not "bend" the linear instrument into a circle, so that the Cs. at the perceptual end and the Cs. at the motor end overlap happily into a single Cs.? This tack would indeed resolve the problem of the analog, but at the cost of defeating its original purpose; for then the analog would cease to be itself—a microscope/telescope—and might as well be dispensed with altogether (as in the case of "cowardly lions"). The problem is not one of message but of medium, as becomes obvious if we supply Freud with the analog he seemed to be groping for but did not have, the computer. It becomes a trivial matter now to have different systems (*Pcpt., Pcs.*) feed information into a single system (*Cs.*), which then in turn controls motor activity (see Figure 3.9). The transposition of Freud's model into the analogic framework of the computer yields the, by now, ubiquitous information-processing type of model of cognition (e.g., Broadbent's classic 1958 flow diagram, shown in Figure 3.10).

There is another crucial dividend to shifting to the computer analog, one having to do with the "censors" ("critical agencies," "screens") in the model. Although a modern microscope/telescope could be made to mimic Freud's instrument (Figure 3.9) through semiopaque mirrors, there is no way that it could model a semantically tuned "censor" (cf. Erdelyi, 1974). To handle this problem, Freud is obliged to graft on a new metaphor:

> A rough but not inadequate analogy to this supposed relation of conscious to unconscious activity might be drawn from the field of ordinary photography. The first stage of the photograph is the "negative"; every photographic picture has to pass through the "negative process," and some of these nega-

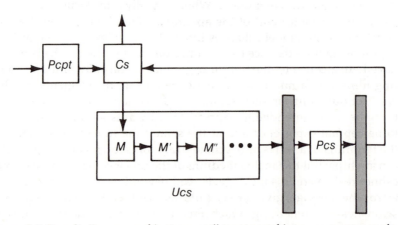

Figure 3.9. Freud's "compound instrument" transposed into a computer analog.

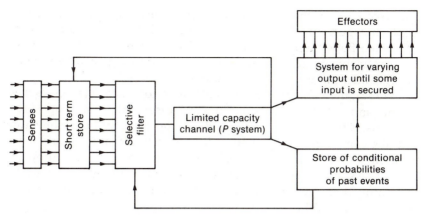

Figure 3.10. Broadbent's information-processing "flow diagram for the organism." (Reprinted with permission from D. E. Broadbent: Perception and Communication, Copyright 1958, Pergamon Press Ltd.)

tives which have held good in examination are admitted to the "positive process," ending in the picture. (Freud, 1912b, p. 264)

Freud here introduces an external intelligence, a human decision maker, to examine and admit (or reject) "negatives" for the "positive process." When such a human executive is internalized, it leads to the much criticized *homunculus*—little man in the head—notion. The computer analog easily resolves the problem (cf. Erdelyi, 1974): The censor—critical agency, screen, filter, or the like—is conceived of as a computer decision routine which passes on each piece of information. There is nothing fanciful about such decision routines; they can be a trivial programming exercise. (In Chapter 5, which deals with the mechanisms of defense, it will be shown that the variegated defenses posited by Freud and other theorists can be unified in the computer framework as constituting different decision programs for tendentious information processing.)

A final point: The transposition of Freud's compound instrument into the computer format yields both new insights as well as theoretical flexibility. Examination of Figure 3.9 shows, for example, perceptual information gaining direct access to consciousness without any selectivity or censorship, something that is inconsistent with the overall dynamic thrust of psychoanalytic thinking. Thus, the model in its present form could not encompass the phenomenon of "perceptual defense," the perceiver's tendency to defend against anxiety-producing perceptual inputs (see Chapter 5). The problem, however, is readily resolved within the computer framework, either through the introduction of new censorships or by the rearrangement of the existing ones—as, for example, in Figure 3.11. The point here is not the ultimate adequacy of the elaborated flow diagram of Figure 3.11 (see Erdelyi, 1974, for a more comprehensive model), but the powerful flexibility gained by the new analogic medium for conveying desired meanings.

We see, then, that the adoption of a superior analog system resolves various and, what appear to be in some cases, intractable conceptual problems. Although Freud never had the opportunity of experimenting with the computer analog, there is little question that he would have; for, as he himself reminds us, "we must always be prepared to drop our conceptual scaffolding if we feel that we are in a position to replace it by something that approximates more closely to the unknown reality" (Freud, 1900, p. 610).

The Iceberg Model

We now take up briefly one of the models of the mind for which Freud is best known, the famous "iceberg" model. As the name suggests, the mind is conceived of as an iceberg (Figure 3.12), the vast bulk of which is almost entirely hidden from view (the unconscious), with only an insignificant tip jutting above the surface (the conscious); a small, intermediate region just below the surface (the preconscious) can sometimes be glimpsed, but, in any event, virtually all of the structure remains hid-

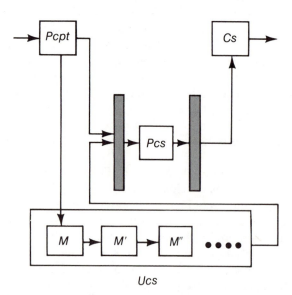

Figure 3.11. Incorporation of perceptual censorship into the model shown in Figure 3.9.

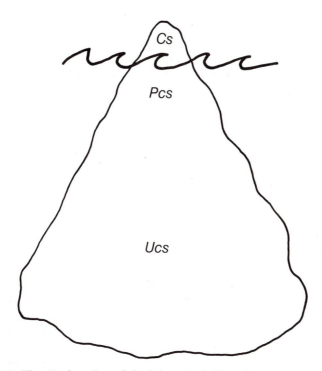

Figure 3.12. The "iceberg" model of the mind (Cs = the conscious; Pcs = the preconscious; Ucs = the unconscious).

den. To confuse the puny, visible tip for the whole, that is, to disregard the undersea monolith below, is drastically to misjudge the object, a serious error for sea captain or psychologist.

This "depth psychology" model, as far as it goes, accords well with the modern cognitive viewpoint: Although the span of long-term memory is vast, the capacity of short-term memory—the "span of consciousness"—is miniscule, a mere 7 ± 2 chunks of information (cf. G. A. Miller, 1956).

The model, however, if it can be dignified as such, is little more than a passing simile, the sole theoretical thrust of which is to underscore the unconscious depth of the psyche. Perhaps its most intriguing aspect is a historical quirk: Although it may be described accurately as "one for which Freud is best known," it actually was never explicitly advanced by Freud himself; it is not Freud's model. The analogy actually goes back to Theodor Lipps (page 56), who in turn probably borrowed it from Fechner. Nevertheless, the model is fully consistent with Freud's descriptive distinction between conscious and unconscious (see Chapter 2, pages 61–62), although this distinction for Freud was merely the first step toward a dynamic and structural conceptualization of the mind. Freud's "structural model," to which we now turn (see Figure 3.13), may in fact be conceived of as a superimposition of structural and dynamic properties upon the inert iceberg model. Because the shape of his elaborated "iceberg" is unmistakably that of an eyeball (an atavistic allusion to his preoccupation with perception in *The Interpretation of Dreams* [1900]), it could be thought of syncretically as the "eyesberg" model.

The Structural Model

The structural model was first proposed by Freud in *The Ego and the Id* (1923) and was later recapitulated, with only minor modifications, in the *New Introductory Lectures on Psychoanalysis* (1933). Our discussion will be based on Freud's 1933 diagram of the model (Figure 3.13), which differs only slightly from the 1923 version.

It should be evident that what we have here, at least in some sense, is a peculiar version of the iceberg model: The psyche is like an iceberg—albeit a strange-looking, eyeball-shaped iceberg—which, except for a tiny surface area associated with perception (*Pcpt.-Cs.*), is unconscious. A relatively superficial region, the preconscious, is unconscious but is capable of being conscious. The deeper we go, however, the more deeply unconscious (less accessible to consciousness) the psyche becomes, the vast expanse of the psyche being permanently shrouded in unconsciousness. (The area of the unconscious appears smaller here than in the iceberg model; this does not reflect a theoretical shift on Freud's part but, merely, laziness about redrawing his diagram: "It is certainly hard to say to-day how far the drawing is correct. In one

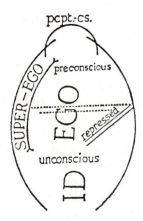

Figure 3.13. The structural model of the psyche (Freud, 1933, p. 78).

respect it is undoubtably not. The space occupied by the unconscious id ought to have been incomparably greater than that of the ego or the preconscious. I must ask you to correct it in your thoughts" [Freud, 1933, p. 79].)

Up to this point the model, except for its quixotic shape, is identical to the iceberg notion. It begins to be something different, however, with the introduction of a dynamic factor, something necessarily alien to the iceberg metaphor: A deep region of the psyche is not merely unconscious, but repressed, or unconscious because of repression (see Figure 3.13). This portion of the psyche corresponds to the strong (repression) version of the "dynamic unconscious" (pages 62–65). It will be noted, further, that some new entities make an appearance—the id, ego, and super-ego. At this point the iceberg analogy of the mind becomes totally inapplicable, for we now are dealing no longer with topographies of awareness, but with "structures"—systems, organizations—of the psyche which, in fact, do not neatly coincide with the conscious, preconscious, and unconscious. The three systems are defined not through their status with respect to consciousness or unconsciousness, but according to their characteristic (1) *goals and functions* and (2) *cognitive style*.

The id (*das Es*), a term Freud took over from Nietzsche, which literally means "the it," supplants Freud's earlier "system Unconscious." This system is conceived of as being unconscious, but the fact of its being unconscious is not its critical feature; rather, its defining criteria, which distinguish it from the ego, are its peremptory hedonism, that is, "it obeys the pleasure-unpleasure principle," and its primitive cognitive style, "primary-process thinking." The id is the primitive, bestial aspect of the psyche; it is, according to Freud, the only structure extant at birth, and is thus the mind, as we might suppose it to be, of the infant, "a chaos, a cauldron of seething excitations" (Freud, 1933, p. 73). It exclusively obeys the pleasure-unpleasure principle, namely, to obtain pleasure and avoid pain (unpleasure) at all costs and without delay. Its cognitive style, primary-process thinking, is crude and primitive: It is not logical; there is no negation, no contradiction; opposite thoughts and impulses exist side by side; there is no concept of linear time; there is no morality; there is no benefit from experience; no doubt; reality and fantasy are not distinguished; it is undiscriminating (in the energy metaphor, "cathexes are mobile"); it employs imagistic (rather than abstract) representation. In short, it is the thinking we associate with psychosis and dreams, states which, according to Freud, represent profound regressions to infantile—"idish"—thinking.

The id cannot long remain the sole structure of the psyche; from the standpoint of the real world it is unsustainable, entailing a fundamental contradiction between its hedonistic goal and its primitive, ineffective cognitive style. If pleasure is to be achieved and pain avoided, a more effective cognitive orientation must be put into operation, one that is logical, attuned to reality, and capable of benefiting from past experience. Reality knocks, and the id must give way. A portion of the id begins to differentiate and, over the course of years, develops into a major new subsystem or structure, the ego.

The *ego* (*das Ich,* or "the I") is the executive component of the psyche. It arises because of reality and is primarily concerned with reality; in Freud's terminology, it obeys or is under the sway of the "reality principle." Its cognitive style is the opposite of the id's, operating according to "secondary-process thinking": It is logical, discriminating, attuned to past experience, and realistic. It differentiates time and utilizes abstract forms of representation (such as words). Unlike the id, the ego is part unconscious and part preconscious (and therefore part conscious). It also harbors a paradoxical nature, for the ego, which obeys the reality principle, is also the seat of the defense mechanisms, sophisticated psychological strategies for avoiding or distorting reality (see Chapter 5). In the real world, it would appear, one must be realistic, even about reality.

The growing child, starting especially around the age of two or three (which Freud associates with the period of toilet training), begins to be aware of a special subclass of reality, a reality not necessarily connected with physical fact, logic, or good sense. The child is confronted with social reality: It is disgusting to play with one's feces; one does not masturbate, it's naughty, sinful, dangerous; you must say "please" and "thank you"; you must show respect to your elders; you must say your prayers; you must not taunt your little sister; you must not soil your pants. And so forth. None of this revealed truth is logically or empirically evident to the child, but it is, nevertheless, a "reality" that he or she may not ignore on pain of punishment. Starting around two or three, and culminating around six or seven, a new structure, the *super-ego* (*das Über-Ich*), differentiates from the ego to specialize in this particular domain of reality management. The super-ego, part unconscious, part conscious, is the internalization of social mores as transmitted (primarily) by the child's parents. It is the internalized system of dos and don'ts and of punishment for transgressions. Although Freud never uses the formula, the super-ego could be said to obey the "morality principle." Its cognitive style is more problematical: Although it is supposed to differentiate from the ego, and in some sense be above (*über*) it, the super-ego actually fuses secondary- and primary-process thinking. Freud's diagram (Figure 3.13) implies as much. A great deal of religion and morality is illogical, irrational, and concretistic (characteristics associated with primary-process thinking); yet religion can also be practical, subtle, and abstract (even beyond words).

In summary, then, three often conflicting realities are at play: selfish, biological reality—the reality of the passions (the id's); social or moral reality (the super-ego's); and physical reality. The executive ego's task is the impossible one of reconciling all three.

When the ego cannot satisfy one of its "three masters" (Freud, 1933), it experiences anxiety—"reality anxiety" (with respect to external reality), "moral anxiety" or guilt (with respect to the super-ego), or "neurotic anxiety" (with respect to the id). The anxiety, whatever its nature, serves as a "signal" of danger (Freud, 1926) and also as a prod to action. To escape the distress of anxiety, which can easily become unbearable, the ego undertakes whatever measures it can, reasonable if possible, unreasonable when there is no other recourse (defensive distortions of reality, for example). Also, of course, the ego may fail, in which case the personality begins to unravel, possibly to the point of psychological collapse (for example, psychosis), and even of physical extinction (as in suicide, often brought on by intolerable moral anxiety, such as guilt, feelings of worthlessness, depression). Since the ego's balancing task is inherently impossible, it is bound to fail at least to some extent, its success being ultimately measured negatively, by the mildness of its failure. In "normal" people the "collapse" of personality is not absent but only less severe or more subtle. The person doesn't commit suicide but is "accident prone"; or he (unconsciously) attenuates his guilt by baffling failures in professional endeavors or personal relations. At the point of greatest success, he becomes inexplicably depressed. Or he avoids entire gamuts of reality with which the ego cannot cope; he avoids, for example, meaningful connections with members of the opposite sex (or of the same sex) or clings pathologically to destructive relations or jobs out of fear of the new, and leads a pathetic, embittered life. Freud's psychology, not surprisingly, is often viewed as severely pessimistic. Freud, however, saw himself not as pessimistic but as realistic: It's not a pretty picture, but it is reality; just look around you, he would challenge.

The structural model is not easily accommodated to modern information-processing models of cognition, which typically (as one would expect of models based on the computer metaphor) avoid the problem of emotions and morality. The structural model could, of course, be simulated by a complex computer program, but that would be a post hoc exercise (though perhaps not an unuseful one). The best extant analogy for Freud's dynamic structural model is sociopolitical; social systems, such as bureaucracies or nations become the natural model, though Freud never went beyond some preliminary adumbrations of the analogy (Freud, 1921). Some modern trends in this direction are only now becoming discernible (e.g., Greenwald, 1980).

The notion of an embattled executive attempting to satisfy the peremptory demands of conflicting interest groups, and doing so by makeshift stratagems that are often shoddy, illogical, and even self-destructive from the long-range standpoint, is the essence of the political process. It, like the ego's task, is the "art of the possible."

Before concluding our examination of Freud's structural model, we should confront, even if schematically, the question of its scientific status. The question has various facets. For example: Do the id, ego, and super-ego actually exist? Are the posited developmental sequences accurate? Is the model internally consistent?

We might start by noting that problems exist with the developmental features of the model. Consider one of the cruder ones, which impinges also on the internal consistency issue. Freud claims that the id is the sole psychic structure at birth. He also claims that the id is all unconscious. Are we then to conclude that wakeful infants are not conscious? Also, development aside, why should the entire id be unconscious? Are we not aware of at least some of our sexual and aggressive impulses? Or if not these, how about biological drives such as hunger and thirst? Since the ego and the super-ego are not defined through the criterion of consciousness-unconsciousness, it is not clear why the id, except for force of habit (it having been the system Unconscious for more than two decades), should be totally consigned to unconsciousness. These theoretical embarrassments are really superficial and rather easy to resolve: All that needs to be done is to shift the boundaries of the preconscious (the parallel dashed lines in Figure 3.13) downward so as to include at least a portion of the id (or, alternately, expand the scope of the id upward).

Another developmental question that arises is whether infants are as cognitively chaotic as Freud suggests. Are they completely undiscriminating? Do they totally fail to benefit from experience? Not only common observation, but also extensive experimental research over the past decades (e.g., Clarke-Stewart, 1983; Flavell, 1977; E. J. Gibson, 1969; Stone, Smith, and Murphy, 1973) suggests that the neonate is far more sophisticated cognitively than it was the fashion to suppose (Freud having merely given expression to the prevalent point of view). Not only the neonate but even apparently the fetus can benefit from experience, as some studies of fetal conditioning suggest (Spelt, 1948).

The developmental inadequacies of the structural model soon became apparent to psychoanalytic scholars, and an influential tradition, one already foreshadowed in Freud's late writings (e.g., Freud, 1937; 1940), and more explicitly in Anna Freud's (1936), gradually emerged under the label of "ego psychology," holding that the ego is a structure on its own right, not merely a derivative of the id and that both id and ego develop out of an early undifferentiated phase of psychological organization (Hartmann, 1939; Hartmann, Kris, and Loewenstein, 1945–1962). The emergence of the super-ego has also been shifted backward in time by some psychoanalytic scholars (e.g., M. Klein, 1932) to the child's first year of life, though this position is far less accepted than the ego psychology perspective. Developmental research, furthermore (e.g., Kohlberg, 1981; Piaget, 1932), suggests that the development of morality is a more drawn out process than conceived by Freud, being tied to long-range cognitive development rather than—or merely—to pressured social learning periods such as toilet training. (It is worth noting, for example, that the two-to-three-year-old child is mastering not only toilet training but also language.)

Beyond the developmental issues, the more fundamental question arises whether the structures of the structural model (whatever their developmental characteristics) are real—do the id, ego, and super-ego actually exist? In many ways the question itself is more problematical than the answer, for it must be wondered just how literally the constructs are to be taken. Should we seek to determine whether actual brain structures exist corresponding to the hypothesized systems of the mind, or would this be an exercise in fatuity because the "structures" posited are mere figures of speech, convenient abstractions for summarizing a body of psychological observations? Would searching for the physiological homologue of the id, for example, amount to the measuring of air pressure impinging upon the person claimed to be "under pressure"? The problem, thus, is not merely empirical but linguistic as well: How literally are Freud's metaphors to be taken in this context?

We might start by noting that the structural model, perhaps more than any other Freudian concept, is articulated through a vast tangle of similes and metaphors:

> We approach the id with analogies: we call it a chaos, a cauldron of seething excitations. (Freud, 1933, p. 73)

> The super-ego, the ego and the id—these, then, are the three realms, regions, provinces, into which we divide the individual's mental apparatus. (Freud, 1933, p. 72)

> Let me give you an analogy; analogies, it is true, decide nothing but they can make one feel more at home. I am imagining a country with a landscape of varying configuration—hill-country, plains, and chains of lakes—, and with a mixed population: it is inhabited by Germans, Magyars, and Slovaks, who carry on different activities. Now things might be partitioned in such a way that the Germans, who breed cattle, live in the hill-country, the Magyars, who grow cereals and wine, live in the plains, and the Slovaks, who catch fish and plait reeds, live by the lakes. If the partitioning could be neat and clear-cut like this, a Woodrow Wilson would be delighted by it; it would also be convenient for a lecture in a geography

lesson. The probability is, however, that you will find less orderliness and more mixing, if you travel through the region.
Germans, Magyars, and Slovaks live interspersed all over it; in
the hill-country there is agricultural land as well, cattle are bred
in the plains too. A few things are naturally as you expected,
for fish cannot be caught in the mountains and wine does not
grow in the water. Indeed, the picture of the region that you
brought with you may on the whole fit the facts; but you will
have to put up with deviations in the details. (Freud, 1933, pp.
72–73)

The ego is after all only a portion of the id, a portion that has
been expediently modified by the proximity of the external
world with its threat of danger. From a dynamic point of view
it is weak, it has borrowed its energies from the id. (Freud,
1933, p. 76)

The functional importance of the ego is manifested in the fact
that normally control over the approaches to motility devolves
upon it. Thus in its relation to the id it is like a man on horse-
back, who has to hold in check the superior strength of the
horse; with this difference, that the rider tries to do so with his
own strength while the ego uses borrowed forces. The analogy
may be carried a little further. Often a rider, if he is not to be
parted from his horse, is obliged to guide it where it wants to
go; so in the same way the ego is in the habit of transforming
the id's will into action as if it were its own. (Freud, 1923, p.
25).

The nucleus of the *Ucs.* [the id] consists of instinctual representatives which seek to discharge their cathexis; that is to say,
it consists of wishful impulses. These instinctual impulses are
[not] co-ordinate with one another, exist side by side without
being influenced by one another, and are exempt from mutual
contradiction . . . The cathectic intensities are much more
mobile. (Freud, 1915b, p. 186)

However, the following, last quotation from Freud, is especially
telling:

Research has given irrefutable proof that mental activity is
bound up with the function of the brain as it is with no other
organ. We are taken a step further—we do not know how
much—by the discovery of the unequal importance of the different parts of the brain and their special relations to particular
parts of the body and to particular mental activities. But every
attempt to go on from there to discover a localization of mental
processes, every endeavour to think of ideas as stored up in
nerve-cells and of excitations as travelling along nerve-fibres,
has miscarried completely. The same fate would await any

theory which attempted to recognize, let us say, the anatomical position of the system Cs.—conscious mental activity—as being in the cortex, and to localize the unconscious processes in the subcortical parts of the brain. There is an hiatus here which at present cannot be filled, nor is it one of the tasks of psychology to fill it. Our psychical topography has *for the present* nothing to do with anatomy; it has reference not to anatomical localities, but to regions in the mental apparatus, wherever they may be situated in the body.

In this respect, then, our work is untrammelled and may proceed according to its own requirements. It will, however, be useful to remind ourselves that as things stand our hypotheses set out to be no more than graphic illustrations. (Freud, 1915b, pp. 174–175)

The last quotation suggests that it might indeed be a mistake to attempt linking components of Freud's structural model to anatomy. Yet, this would be an extreme stance, one that would belie Freud's own ambivalence over this issue throughout his writings.

To escape the trap of extreme literalism, it was emphasized at the outset that the problem was "not merely empirical but linguistic as well" (see page 133). To avoid the contrary extreme, it might now be emphasized that the problem is not merely linguistic but empirical as well. Freud, after all, had attempted a grand synthesis of his psychological notions with physiology (his "Psychology for Neurologists" [*Project for a Scientific Psychology*, 1895]), an attempt which, as has been noted, turned out a failure in Freud's judgment. Freud, however, never altogether gave up the expectation—or hope—that such an integration might become possible at some point in the future. What was not possible around the turn of the century may no longer be as out of reach today; indeed, some of the "completely miscarried" efforts of the past that Freud alludes to have by now borne fruit. That which in Freud's time was a "hiatus which at present cannot be filled" may in *today's* present hold possibilities. It would be foolhardy literally to search in the brain for "a cauldron of seething excitations" (though it would appear otherwise if we were actually to find one), or for a horse and its rider, or for Germans, Magyars, and Slovaks, or cathexes (mobile or otherwise), or even for specific localities corresponding to the id, ego, or super-ego; but it is a legitimate empirical question whether brain structures or functions exist that correspond in some significant way to those stipulated by the structural model. For, even if the latter were claimed to be "no more than graphic illustrations," it is important—indeed necessary from the standpoint of science—to determine how good and how general the illustrations are of reality, and to modify the model to bring it into correspondence with new knowledge.

We have seen that the id and ego are distinguished in terms of two functional criteria: (1) the pleasure-unpleasure principle versus the reality principle and (2) primary- versus secondary-process thinking. Important physiological work exists bearing on both.

Pleasure-Unpleasure Brain Centers. In 1954, Olds and Milner reported a remarkable discovery. They had been investigating the functions of the reticular formation (see Figure 3.14) by implanting electrodes in various sections of this structure in the brains of rats. One of the implants was apparently misplaced, for the rat in question behaved in a most peculiar fashion: When stimulated, the rat gave every sign of pleasure and foraged around as if seeking more of the stimulus. The rat could be made to move into any desired spot in the cage simply by selectively stimulating him for moving toward the chosen spot and not stimulating him when moving elsewhere. Olds and Milner pursued this serendipitous finding with a systematic follow-up: Electrodes were implanted in the same "wrong" brain area of a number of fresh rats, and they were placed in a modified Skinner box in which the pressing of a lever resulted not in the delivery of food or water, as in the usual case, but in a mild electric stimulus in the area of the implant (see Figure 3.15 for a sketch of the arrangement and an X-ray of the implanted brain).

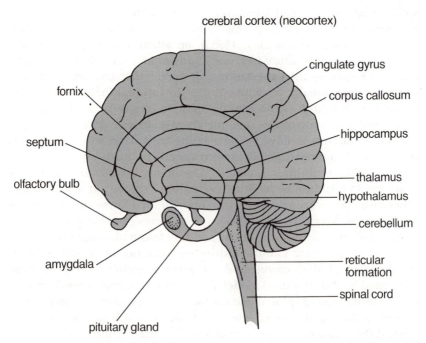

Figure 3.14. Orienting sketch of several anatomical structures under discussion (drawn out of proportion).

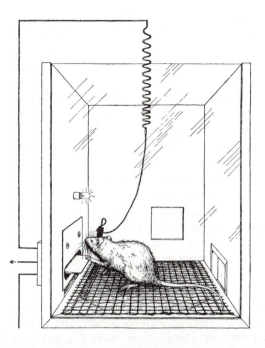

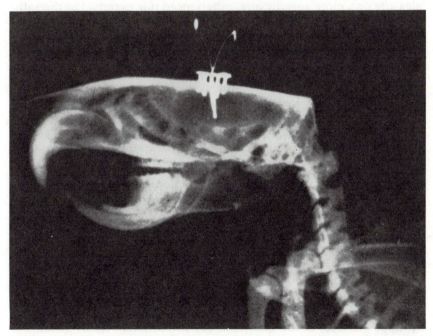

Figure 3.15. *Top panel:* Modified Skinner box arrangement. Pressing the bar was reinforced by central stimulation of the implanted region. *Bottom* X-ray of electrodes implanted in the rat's brain. (From Olds, 1956, pp. 108 and 105.)

The findings were consistent: The rats pressed the bar for central stimulation with a vigor and persistence never previously observed, pressing for hours on end, to the point, in some cases, of physical collapse. Other animals were soon investigated for the behavior, with similar results.

These "reinforcement" or "pleasure" centers are distributed widely in the brain, especially in structures of the limbic system such as the lateral hypothalamus, amygdala, septum, cingulate gyrus, hippocampus, and also in adjoining areas such as the thalamus and, at least in some species, the olfactory bulb (see Figure 3.14). The phenomenon has now been demonstrated in a wide variety of animals, including rats, pigeons, cats, goldfish, monkeys, dolphins—and humans.

Just prior to Olds and Milner's (1954) finding, there appeared a converse discovery by Delgado, Roberts, and Miller (1954) of the existence of *negative* reinforcement or "pain" centers in the brain (though the latter description is a misnomer, since the experience is not painful but, rather, the opposite of pleasurable—let us call it "unpleasurable"). The unpleasure centers are also widely distributed in the brain, being found in the thalamus, the fornix, the hypothalamus, and other areas.

One (of several) early questions concerning pleasure centers was whether the effect of stimulation was a general undifferentiated pleasure or a more specific one, experienced (for example) as the satisfaction of some alimentary or sexual drive. With animals, of course, such questions are difficult to resolve. It is now known, however, from human reports obtained from volunteers undergoing open-brain surgery that the experience is a general one. The patient will smile with pleasure, report a general "feeling of well-being," even of "extreme euphoria"—and ask for more stimulation from the surgeon (cf. Heath and Mickle, 1960; Sem-Jacobson and Torkildsen, 1960).

The physiological work on pleasure-unpleasure centers has several implications for Freud's pleasure-unpleasure principle. In part, it is an exciting physiological corroboration of the fundamental role played by pleasure-unpleasure in psychological functioning. The brain appears to be extensively programmed neurologically for the experience of pleasure and unpleasure. But there are also problems. For example, Freud assumed, as did learning theorists (e.g., Dollard and Miller, 1950; Hull, 1943), that pleasure/positive-reinforcement resulted from tension/drive reduction—that, in short, pleasure was the cessation of pain or drive tension (this point being sometimes dubbed by Freud, the *nirvana principle*). The physiological facts suggest otherwise, pointing to a "motivational dualism" (Olds, 1958): Pleasure and unpleasure appear to be not the opposite sides of the same coin but two different coins; pleasure is not the absence of unpleasure nor is unpleasure the absence of pleasure.

More importantly for psychoanalysis, however, is the fact that the "pleasure" arising from stimulation of the pleasure centers is general in nature, *not* sexual, as a great deal of psychoanalytic writing suggests (e.g., Freud, 1905c).

Left Versus Right Hemisphere. Another major body of psychophysiological research bearing on the structural model is the asymmetry (both neurological and functional) of the cerebral hemispheres in humans. It has long been known (Broca, 1861; Jackson, 1874; Wernicke, 1874) that, at least for most persons, the left hemisphere controls verbal-propositional functioning (speech comprehension and production, reading, and writing). More generally, it has been proposed that the two hemispheres specialize in distinct forms of cognitive functioning, the left hemisphere being verbal, analytic, and linear and the right hemisphere, imagistic, spatial, and holistic (e.g., Bogen, 1969; Levy, 1969). More recent work suggests (though it is not uncontroversial) that lateralization, or "hemisphericity," extends to emotional functioning as well. The right hemisphere appears to be crucially implicated in both the understanding (e.g., A. F. Wechsler, 1973) and the expression (e.g., Sackeim, Gur, and Saucy, 1978) of emotions, with the possible—and notable—exception of anxiety, which has been linked with the left hemisphere (Tucker, 1981). The right hemisphere appears to be more intuitive, spontaneous, and impulsive, while the left hemisphere is (excepting anxiety) nonemotional (Schwartz, Davidson, and Maer, 1975) and self-inhibitory or censoring (Bakan, 1969; Hall, Hall, and Lavoie, 1968). There is also developing evidence for a correlation between hemisphericity and personality. Hysterics and, more generally, emotionally labile but thought-repressing individuals tend to be right-hemisphere dominant (Gur and Gur, 1975); hysterical conversion reactions, moreover, occur significantly more often in the left side of the body, which is controlled by the right hemisphere (Galin, Diamond, and Braff, 1977; Stern, 1977). On the other hand, obsessive-compulsive types and, more generally, people prone to intellectualizing, vigilant, and ruminative cognitive styles, tend to be left-hemisphere dominant (Smokler and Shevrin, 1979).

Not surprisingly, the possibility of linking primary-process functioning with the right hemisphere and secondary-process functioning with the left hemisphere has not escaped the attention of some scholars (e.g., Galin, 1974). As in the case of pleasure-unpleasure centers, however, the psychophysiological data cut both ways. In part, the data are strikingly corroborative, particularly in regard to the imagistic versus verbal/propositional distinction and the (less well established) association of anxiety and self-inhibition with the left hemisphere. However, some other features of Freud's model do not fit as well. It would be wrong, for example, to maintain that the right hemisphere is undiscriminating and incapable of learning from experience since on the contrary it, and not the left hemisphere, discriminates pictorial-imagistic as well as emotional information (except anxiety). Moreover, the differences between the hemispheres are not absolute but only relative and statistical. Not every individual conforms to the majority pattern, and even for those who do, the hemisphere differences are relative, the right hemisphere having *some,* if lower-level, verbal capacities, and the left hemisphere, likewise, being not without *some* capacity for imagistic-spatial processing. It should also be noted that the right hemisphere is not "primary" developmentally, at least not in the gross anatomical sense, for we are born with two hemispheres.

So far nothing has been said about the super-ego. The reason, in part, is that the super-ego is supposed to constitute an outcropping from the ego, and so it seemed more central to attempt uncovering the existence, if any, of correlates of the more basic id-ego distinction. Further, the super-ego is not so clearly defined, it being distinguished from the other agencies only in terms of goal (to be moral) and not in terms of cognitive style (in the super-ego's case, an amalgam of primary and secondary-process functioning). It is not clear, therefore, what we might wish to search for physiologically, especially if we take into account the amorphous sweep of the concept of morality, the functioning of which would encompass phenomena from inhibition, anxiety, guilt, aversive learning, and rote learning of rules and regulations to philosophical reasoning and profound metaphysical contemplation. We will restrict ourselves here merely to noting that the frontal lobes, especially the right-frontal lobe, have for a long time been linked with self-inhibition and responsible behavior (e.g., Flor-Henry, 1977; Hecaen, 1964; Luria and Homskaya, 1970).

Limbic System and Cortex.   In this final psychophysiological section we take up briefly another possible neurological correlate of the id-ego distinction, one which, in a cruder form (cortex versus subcortical regions) was rejected by Freud in 1915 (see pages 134–135). Research developments since then, especially the delineation of the (mostly subcortical) limbic system and of its pervasive role in the mediation of drives and emotions have rekindled interest in the more specific modern variant— cortex versus limbic system—of this earlier contraposition (Koestler, 1967; MacLean, 1958).

The cortex, the convoluted surface region of the brain of humans and other high mammals (see Figure 3.14) is phylogenetically the newest brain system, having differentiated from the older subcortical regions. Fish have no cortex; amphibians only a rudimentary adumbration of the cortex; in humans, of the roughly 12 billion brain cells, 9 billion are cortical. The cortex in humans controls the major "reality" functions such as perception and motility, and is, without doubt, the "organ" of the higher mental functions—speech, poetry, music, abstract reasoning, and so forth. The cortex modulates as well as inhibits the activities of the subcortical systems, although the nature of this interaction is complex as well as reciprocal.

The limbic system (MacLean, 1949; Papez, 1937) is the center—if it makes any sense at all to think in terms of brain centers—of drives and emotions. If there is anything in the brain analogous to a "cauldron of seething excitations," it is the limbic system. Its constituent subsystems—the hypothalamus, amygdala, septum, fornix, hippocampus, and cingulate gyrus (see Figure 3.14)—all are involved in major aspects of motivational and emotional functioning.

It may be instructive to focus on some of these subsystems. Perhaps the most remarkable of these, because of the incredible range of its involvements, is the hypothalamus. Roughly half the size of a finger in humans, it is a crucial control post for vegetative functions (such as breathing, temperature regulation, blood pressure, heart rate) as well as drives (hunger, thirst, sex, aggression, fear, curiosity). The ventral-anterior region contains two sex centers. Electrical stimulation of the more anterior of these produces prodigious hypersexuality. In one study on rats (Vaughan and Fisher, 1962 [in Milner, 1970]), stimulated male rats maintained continuous erections and mounted females at rates of up to twenty times per hour. Ablation of this nucleus results in irreversible loss of sexual functioning. The more posterior sex nucleus appears to control sexual functioning through the endocrine system by means of its control of the pituitary gland, the master gland, which in turn controls the sex glands or gonads; destruction of this nucleus results in the atrophy of the gonads which can, however, be arrested or reversed by appropriate sex hormone injections.

The hypothalamus also contains two aggression centers. Stimulation of the medial region produces rage reactions, while stimulation of the lateral areas results in predatory attacks: A cat stimulated in the lateral hypothalamus will attack a mouse in its cage; stimulated in the medial region, it will attack not the mouse but the experimenter (or another cat or a dog). The anterior region of the hypothalamus also contains a fear center as well as a placidity (or rage-inhibition) center. Interestingly, the posterior region of the hypothalamus houses what might be termed a "curiosity center": When stimulated in this region, the animal will sniff around and explore its environment.

The amygdala excites aggression and fear, and inhibits sexuality. This pattern of functions was first proposed by Klüver and Bucy (1939), who reported that ablation of the amygdala in monkeys produced, (a) hypersexuality, (b) docility, and (c) loss of fear. The Klüver-Bucy syndrome—as the three consequences of this ablation have come to be known—has been extensively investigated, in part because of the mystery surrounding the fact that while 80 percent of the replication studies (usually of cats) corroborate Klüver and Bucy's findings, some 20 percent produce contrary effects (such as hyperaggressiveness). The effort to explain the inconsistency of results has yielded an important theoretical insight (e.g., Delgado, 1967; Rosvold, Mirsky, and Pribram, 1954): Not only is it a mistake to overcompartmentalize brain functions, since different physiological structures interact to produce unique effects, but personality and sociological factors must be taken into account as well. Thus, stimulation may produce violent aggressiveness toward *social inferiors* but cowering fear toward *social superiors*. Apparently, physiology interacts with sociology. Moreover, not all social inferiors are attacked; a dominant male might not aggress against his socially inferior friend, nor will he attack females.

The septum may be thought of as the "dove" of the limbic system, inhibiting rage and other forms of emotionality. Removal of the septum results in a nervous as well as savage animal, although the animal becomes calmer with the passage of time, which suggests that other brain centers may take over some of the septum's functions.

One of the more crucial lessons to emerge from even this cursory sketch of physiological functioning is the remarkable interactiveness of brain centers—in Freudian parlance, the psychodynamic character of brain functions. For example, it has now been established that the aggression-inciting function of the amygdala is effected through the amygdala's stimulation of the hypothalamus' rage center; if the neural pathways between the amygdala and the hypothalamus are severed, stimulation of the amygdala will not, as usually, produce increased aggression (Hilton and Zbrozyna, 1963 [in Milner, 1970]). The septum, on the other hand, works at cross-purposes with the amygdala, sending inhibitory commands to the hypothalamus. One can begin to think in force-vector terms (pages 10–11), with one system pushing for aggression and the other against aggression. The pattern of "forces" is actually far more complex; any behavior of the animal being, in Freud's terminology, "overdetermined." The hippocampus, for example, tends to inhibit sexuality but to excite aggression. The cerebral cortex contributes its own influences, tending to inhibit the outbreak of aggression but promoting its expression once it has been set in motion. There is also, as we have already noted, the play of personality and sociological forces. The picture becomes so complex that, just as in modern physics (see Chapter 5), it makes more sense to speak not of "forces" but of "fields of forces." Apart from issues of detail, Freud's overall premise that the mind is based on a psychodynamic model—of conflict, push and pull, excitation-inhibition, a play of forces—is ubiquitously corroborated by psychophysiological fact.

At the same time, the finer-grained features of limbic system functioning tend to call into question some of Freud's more specific hypotheses. The existence of several distinct drive centers, one even for curiosity, once again undermines Freud's propensity to universalize the sex drive, or to categorize all drives as either sexual or aggressive.

Also, the wide distribution of inhibitory regions in the limbic system casts doubt on the notion that self-restraint is a late-appearing function associated with ego and super-ego development. Inhibition of self-destructive as well as of selfish aggressive and sexual drives is a basic neurological fact of the phylogenetically primitive limbic system. Ethological research (e.g., Lorenz, 1966) amply substantiates that animals with little or no cortex—fish, lizards, birds—exhibit highly refined moral-type behaviors, such as inhibition against biting females ("chivalry"?), self-sacrifice for offsprings or other members of the species ("heroism," "altruism"?), and stereotyped courting patterns ("ceremony," "ritual"?). This is not to say that, especially in humans, learning plays no role in moral development, but that moral proclivities may already be neurologically programmed or primed (just as phobias may be genetically "prepared" [Garcia, McGowan, Ervin, and Koelling, 1968; Milner, 1970; Seligman, 1971]). Moses' Ten Commandments may have been writ, at least in part, upon tablets of genes. Actually, Freud himself vacillated on this score, suggesting, especially in his earlier, prestructural writings, that some forms of primitive morality ("an eye for an eye," for example) might be inborn.

Finally, it ought to be emphasized that while the limbic system is a sort of "cauldron of seething excitations," it is most definitely *not* also "a chaos," being far more rigidly programmed neurologically than the more plastic cerebral cortex. Freud's disavowal of any crude equation of ego with cortex, and id with subcortical areas was, it seems, wise.

CONCLUSION

In this chapter on psychological structure we have seen the need to emphasize, often with the help of admonitory quotations from Freud himself, the danger of taking Freud's proposed analogies or models too literally. In some cases the temptation did not arise; for example, we never felt inclined to search for icebergs in the brain for corroboration of the "iceberg model." In other cases, however, the issue was not as clear-cut, for the semantic domain of an analogy is not always self-evident but often—strictly speaking, always—an empirical question. Had we, for example, discovered a structure in the brain that answered in every detail to the psychological characteristics attributed to the id, we would have unhesitatingly disregarded Freud's warning against anatomizing the construct and would have considered the discovery a revolutionary breakthrough. The real physiological picture turns out, as might have been expected, to be mixed. There are striking physiological counterparts to certain postulated id-ego characteristics, but there are also notable discrepancies.

We saw that the brain—just like the psyche posited by Freud—is a dynamic system, functioning on the principle of conflict, of interaction and counteraction among its constituent parts. We also discovered that the brain is extensively programmed for the mediation of pleasure and unpleasure, and that left and right hemispheres do exhibit some (but not all) of the posited differences between primary and secondary process functioning. We also gained some negative insights. It is quite clear, as common sense always suggested and now physiology confirms, that pleasure is by no means exclusively sexual in nature, nor is it merely the absence of unpleasure. Specific "centers" of drives and emotions further argue against the universalization of sex—or sex and aggression—as the primary drive(s).

Although physiological knowledge holds important lessons for us, we must be careful not to overestimate it at this juncture, an error perhaps as serious as disregarding it altogether. (Freud, probably because of his disappointment with his "Psychology for Neurologists," swung from one extreme to another in this connection, although it is not without significance that he qualifies his physiological disclaimers with *"for the present"*—see pages 134–135). Many of the physiological "facts" discussed here (such as the lateralization of cognition and emotion) are still controversial and might, in retrospect, prove chimerical or oversimple. Notions as basic as brain centers are for the most part problematical, certainly crude, because of the extreme interactiveness of brain systems. There is no question, for example, that destruction of the anterior sexual center of the hypothalamus results in the abolition of sexual behavior and that, therefore, the hypothalamus is in some sense a center of sexuality. And yet, other systems, subcortical as well as cortical, are necessary for sexual behavior in mammals, so that the hypothalamus can hardly be *the* sex center. Since the brain is pervasively interactive, a living, unified system, the notion of physiological structure is ultimately best understood not in terms of anatomic topography but in terms of programs of interaction among anatomical parts. Thus, even if there should exist some physiological structure corresponding to the id—or ego or super-ego—it is not likely to be a simple physiological locality but an organization of functioning structures—a structure of structures.

CHAPTER FOUR

TWILIGHT PHENOMENA

♦

Dreams, Daydreams, and Fantasy
• The Dream-Work
• The Dream-Work as Nonwork
• Dream Interpretation
• Problematical Issues in Psychoanalytic Dream Theory
• Daydreams and Fantasy
Jokes
Art
Symptoms
Religion

146/Psychoanalysis: Freud's Cognitive Psychology

It is a magnificent feeling to recognize the unity of a complex of phenomena which appear to be things quite apart from the direct visible truth. (Albert Einstein, 1901; cited in Clark, 1971, p. 77)

In this chapter we take up a far-flung family of phenomena, among them, dreams, daydreams, fantasy, jokes, art, symptoms, and religion. The juxtaposition of such startlingly diverse topics within a single chapter is not an arbitrary organizational scheme but a consequence of one of Freud's seminal theoretical contributions to psychology: his discovery of an underlying unity, or at least connectedness, among these superficially uncorrelated phenomena.

The designation *twilight* (not Freud's) is used to underscore the peculiar "in-betweenness" that characterizes these phenomena—an intermediateness or compromise between light (conscious) and darkness (unconscious), the primitive and the advanced, the rational and the irrational, the real and the unreal. Freud occasionally refers to these as "psychological hybrids" or "half-breeds."

As a guiding framework for the discussion to follow it might be helpful to list briefly the common threads, beyond the one just mentioned, that tend to interlink these phenomena:

1. Twilight phenomena are regressive. They involve psychological contents and styles that are infantile in character.

2. Twilight phenomena are semantically multilayered, having *manifest* (surface) as well as *latent* (deep) semantic content (see pages 88–105). The extraction of the latent content (or contents) requires *interpretation*, success at which results in *insight*—sight into the deep semantic content of a stimulus. Insight may be conceived of as the semantic counterpart of visual depth perception, in which a three-dimensional percept is extracted from a two-dimensional display. Latent contents may be unconscious (as in dreams and symptoms) or conscious (as in jokes and art).

3. Latent contents are frequently taboo (sexual or aggressive in character) and, therefore, anxiety-provoking when explicit and conscious.

4. A psychodynamic "transformational grammar" (to borrow Chomsky's expression) is postulated, which transforms latent into manifest content. Freud's general term for this is *translation* or *transduction*, though he tends to use specialized vocabulary—*dream-work, joke-work, conversion*—when dealing with specific phenomena. The transformational grammar in Freud's system (unlike Chomsky's) is psychodynamic; the translation from one level to the other tends to be biased in the service of motives, in particular, defense. Thus, the transformation of the latent content into the manifest content involves not just translation but also mistransla-

tion: The underlying "text" is tampered with so as to eliminate or at least diminish its threat value.

We may now turn to a more detailed examination of how these common factors operate in different twilight phenomena. We will begin with dreams and, since they are conceived of by Freud as wakeful conterparts of dreams, daydreams and fantasy.

DREAMS, DAYDREAMS, AND FANTASY

In Freud's estimate, his *Interpretation of Dreams* (which was completed in 1899 but withheld from publication until 1900 so that it might be counted a work of the twentieth century) was his greatest achievement. He was obviously reluctant to tamper with its content for, although he repeatedly returned to the problem over the next several decades, he never seriously revised his original formulations. Even so, despite some theoretical anachronisms, Freud's theory of dreams remains the prototype of much of his psychological theory and, as Freud himself periodically emphasized, to understand his theory of dreams is to understand psychoanalysis.

The theory, which actually has many precedents (cf. Ellenberger, 1970; Van de Castle, 1971), may be thought of as a vast elaboration of Plato's notion, voiced in *The Republic:* "In all of us, even in good men, there is a lawless wild beast nature which peers out in sleep." "Reasoning" and "shame" become suspended and the "beast within us . . . goes forth to satisfy his desires; and there is no conceivable folly or crime— not excepting incest or any other unnatural union, or parricide—which . . . [he] may not be ready to commit" (Book IX, pp. 281, 280). Roughly speaking, Plato's "reason" corresponds to Freud's ego, "shame" to the super-ego, and the "wild beast" to the id. As with Plato, Freud's wild beast is thought to peer out in sleep because of the dormant state of the ego (and its mechanisms of defense). The "beast," apparently, sleeps neither in Plato's nor in Freud's system. There is, however, one difference in nuance that is important theoretically. In Freud's scheme, the ego is not altogether "suspended" but merely weakened; we might say it is groggy but not completely asleep. Consequently, sleep consciousness—dreams—are substantially "idish," but not completely so. They are a good part id but still part ego; they are, quintessentially, twilight phenomena.

Freud's theory of dreams rests upon a fundamental distinction, that between the dream's manifest content and its latent content. Since the general principle has been examined in some detail already (Chapter 2), no lengthy exposition of it is required here. The manifest content is the dream at face value, the dream as it is consciously experienced and reported by the dreamer. It tends towards the nonsensical, and at times it is sheer gibberish. Yet, according to Freud, dreams have meaning. When properly interpreted it is possible to uncover a coherent, underlying meaning, the latent content. The dreamer, typically, is unconscious of the latent content of his own dream and is thus prone to assume, with the majority of people, that the manifest content of the dream is the whole dream. To concretize the issues, let us examine an actual dream, one taken from a case history by Lindner (1955):

Preamble

The subject, Mac, was a Communist agitator who had out-maneuvered Lindner at a political function. Despite Mac's open contempt for Lindner's "Social Democratic" politics and for psychoanalysis ("a bourgeois science") Mac subsequently sought Lindner out for therapy: his wife had left him, he felt empty, depersonalized, and suffered from impotence. Although Mac seemed to make progress in the early, "honeymoon" phase of therapy, he made no headway with his problem of impotence. Also, a conflict festered in the background concerning the "basic rule" of psychoanalysis, for Mac vowed never to reveal Party secrets to his therapist, and thus circumscribed the freedom of his "free" associations. These events transpired in Baltimore, Maryland.

Mac's Dream

I am walking along Charles Street (in Baltimore) toward Mount Vernon Place. There is no traffic on the street and I seem to be alone. There is no one behind me but I hear footsteps. This scares me and I open my mouth to scream, but when I do, my tongue falls out on the ground. This doesn't surprise me: I just pick it up and put it in my pocket and go on walking.

Ahead of me I see the monument (The George Washington Monument at Mount Vernon Place in Baltimore). Now I notice that the side of the street I'm on is in very bright sunlight, but the other side is dark, pitch-black almost. Then I see the man who is behind me but he is on the other side of the street, the black side. He seems to be paying no attention to me but I somehow feel that he is really watching me very carefully. I walk on a little way—begin to feel very tired. It gets so I can hardly lift my legs and Mount Vernon Place seems miles away. I become worried that I'll never make it to the monument, I'm so tired. I try to call the man to help me but I have no tongue and can't make a sound. I reach into my pocket to get it but it's gone. I search for it frantically and awake in terror with the blankets all tangled up. (Pp. 67–68)

The material, as reported, is the manifest content of Mac's dream. Although reasonable in some respects it is also absurd in others: Mac opens his mouth and his tongue falls out; this does not surprise him; there is no one behind him, but there is someone behind him. All in all, the dream—at this level—is hardly edifying. If this were all there were to dreams it would make sense for scientists to ignore them, as they in fact did before Freud.

The trick to approaching dreams properly, according to Freud, is not to take them literally but to uncover, through interpretation, the meaningful substratum of the material, the latent content. Freud's exploration of dreams from this perspective led him to one of his major contributions to dream theory, the articulation of the (inferred) psychological operations by which the underlying latent content is translated into the manifest content. This class of transforming operations Freud called the *dream-work*. Interpretation may be thought of as the reversal of the original dream-work: The dream-work translates the latent content into the manifest content, whereas interpretation translates the manifest content back to the latent content. An explicit understanding of dream-work operations is therefore a powerful conceptual tool of interpretation. We now turn to these processes.

The Dream-Work

Censorship. A major component of the dream-work is the censorship of threatening latent content. This psychological censorship, as in the case with political censorship (Freud's analog for this aspect of the dream-work), constitutes not one but a class of operations, some crude and some quite subtle. Freud tended to group the various forms of censorship into three rough categories:

1. OMISSION-ATTENUATION. This is the simplest, most obvious type of censorship. Problematical material is simply excised (like the missing $18^1/_2$ minutes of the Watergate tape) or in some way rendered "fainter, more indefinite, or more dubious" (Freud, 1917, p. 125)—as when one lowers one's voice or mumbles when saying something one does not wish to say.

2. MODIFICATIONS, HINTS, ALLUSIONS, ELLIPSES. These rather amorphously demarcated censorship techniques are, essentially, more subtle psychological variants of attenuation. An example may be observed in Mac's dream, when he refers to *a man who is behind him who seems to be paying no attention to him but who is really watching him very carefully.* This seems to be a rather transparent allusion to his therapist, Lindner, who, in the fashion of a classic psychoanalytic therapist, does actually sit behind him, in some sense not paying attention to him (the

technique is called "hovering attention") but in fact paying very close attention to him. The therapist is presumably "listening with the third ear" (or, as Yogis put it, "seeing with the third eye") and is, to Mac's growing anxiety, beginning to penetrate into the "dark, pitch-black" side of things, while Mac wishes to stay in the safe "bright sunlight." This interpretation of the manifest content is buttressed by Mac's understandable contradictoriness toward the man behind him: In the context of not being able to lift his legs and Mount Vernon Place seeming to be miles away (what could this allude to?), he calls to the man for help—the very man whose footsteps caused him such dumbfounding fright.

Examples of this type of censorship abound in everyday life. Consider this advertisement for Vantage cigarettes in *The New York Times* (June 14, 1977, p. C9):

VANTAGE IS SOLVING
A LOT OF MY PROBLEMS
ABOUT SMOKING.

You see, I really enjoy smoking. To me it's a pleasure. But it was no pleasure hearing all the things being said against high-tar cigarettes. . . .

What is the advertisement alluding to with the expression "all the things being said against high-tar cigarettes"? Displaced to a corner of the full-page advertisement, in small type (attenuation?), is the statement: "Warning: The Surgeon General Has Determined that Cigarette Smoking is Dangerous to Your Health."

Figure 4.1 gives another example, a type of politically motivated press censorship with which Freud, as a citizen of the autocratic Austro-Hungarian Empire, was only too familiar.

3. DISPLACEMENT OF ACCENT. This censorship technique employs the device of displacing (hence, misplacing) emphasis from the crucial to the trivial, and vice versa. Something that is important but disturbing in the latent content emerges in the manifest content as unimportant, trivial, a mere afterthought. The Chinese press again provides an excellent example of the technique. The news of the historic arrival of Richard Nixon to the People's Republic of China in 1971 was consigned to a laconic sentence, set in small type, stating that the United States president had arrived on a state visit and had been met at the airport.

LIU SHAO-CHI'S DEATH REPORTED BY PEKING

Once Mao's Heir, Former Chief of State Was Disgraced During the Cultural Revolution

By WOLFGANG SAXON

Liu Shao-chi, the former Chinese head of state who became the principal victim of the Cultural Revolution, was reported dead yesterday by Peking's official press agency in the roundabout fashion that it often uses to report on delicate matters.

The agency, Hsinhua, did not say when or where Mr. Liu had died. Instead, it reported in a dispatch from Peking that Wang Kuang-mei, "widow of Liu Shao-chi," was present at a party celebrating the Chinese new year attended by Hua Kuo-feng, the Chairman of the Chinese Communist Party.

...

Figure 4.1. The Chinese press' indirect announcement of the death of Liu Shao-Chi. (Saxon, W. *The New York Times*, January 29, 1979, p. A9. Copyright © 1979 by The New York Times Co.)

The full-page headline that day announced the determination of a certain commune to boost its productivity the following year.

The report of Liu Shao-chi's death (Figure 4.1) also exemplifies the technique of displacement of accent, since the emphasis is shifted away from the controversial political figure onto his widow.

The following excerpt from the *Times* remarks on the curious information-processing style of the Chinese press, which manages to share with the dream-work even the common feature of being an outpouring of the night:

In some ways journalists stationed in Peking still depend on the routine tools of the trade that made China-watching in Hong Kong (before the U.S.-Chinese rapprochement) somewhat akin to Talmudic scholarship. First there is the daily outpouring of the Chinese press agency, Hsinhua—more precisely a nightly outpouring, since Peking favors the middle of the night for important news. In addition, the agency often "buries" news in otherwise mundane items. For example, Hsinhua's recent disclosure that the Chinese Communist Party had appointed its first Secretary-General in over a decade was lodged in the middle of a story about a soirée for artists and writers. That is the equivalent of an American newspaper reporting, say, that President Carter had replaced Zbigniew Brzezinski, in the middle of an article on a Washington restaurant where they were having dinner. (Fox Butterfield, *The New York Times,* January 21, 1979, p. E3)

Before leaving the topic of censorship, it should be emphasized that the various specific techniques that have been discussed are not clearly demarcated from one another but occur in various overlapping shadings and combinations. The examples we have examined may have already underscored this point. The Vantage cigarette advertisement, for instance, *alludes* to the danger of cancer and other ailments, *attenuates* the warning of the surgeon general, *displaces* the warning to a peripheral region of the advertisement, *displaces the accent* onto high-tar cigarettes from cigarettes in general, and *omits* the fact that "the things being said" are being said about low-tar as well as high-tar cigarettes. Actually, as will become evident, not only specific variants of censorship but also other operations of the dream-work tend to overlap functionally, and are distinguished more in exposition than in fact.

Symbolization. Symbolization is one of the more fascinating operations of the dream-work. Elements of the latent content are expressed not directly but symbolically in the dream's manifest content. To say this, however, is not to say too much—at least not more than that dreams have meaning—since all human communicative acts, from religious rituals to algebraic proofs, are symbolic in character. The distinguishing feature of dream symbols is their primitive nature: Unlike abstract symbols, the symbols in dreams (and, we might add, jokes, art, religion, and symptoms) tend to be concretistic; they resemble physically or in some concrete functional way the objects they symbolize. The penis, for example, tends to be symbolized by objects that have the single or composite characteristic of being elongated, intrusive, a frontal appendage, capable of engorgement, able to defy gravity, and so forth. Common phallic symbols, therefore, include objects such as *umbrellas, poles, knives, swords, guns, airplanes, blimps, serpents.* Similarly, the vagina is rendered symbolically by items such as *boxes, caves, pockets, pouches,* the *mouth, jewel cases.* Sexual intercourse is expressed by activities such as *climbing, swimming,* and *flying* (e.g., Erica Jong's *Fear of Flying*). Parents appear in dreams as *king, queen, emperor, empress*; siblings as *little animals, vermin*. Death is rendered as *traveling* or a *journey*.

The claimed "universality" (Freud, 1900; 1917) of such symbols may be understood to arise from the physical or functional similarity between the symbols and the (in fact, universal) objects. Nevertheless, it is the *context* that ultimately determines the meaning of a symbol—and whether an item is, actually, a symbol in the first place. A cigar, after all, is sometimes only a cigar (as Freud occasionally observed between puffs). In the Groucho Marx joke (page 93), however, the symbolic function of *cigar* and *mouth* is beyond doubt, and it is the context that makes it so. In more complex situations, as in dreams or poems, considerably more context (and interpretational experience) is required, and even then a certain indeterminateness necessarily attaches to the symbols. Mac's dream is unusually transparent in this regard—it was chosen for this reason—and we can readily detect (or is this not the case?) several clear symbolic elements, such as "the Monument," "my tongue falls out," "I can hardly lift my legs," "Mount Vernon Place seems miles away," and "I'll never make it to the monument."

It should be apparent how readily symbolism overlaps and merges with censorship. It seems, for example, altogether arbitrary whether we designate Mac's statement, "Mount Vernon Place seems miles away" a symbolic utterance or a hint or allusion. (Perhaps all symbols are ultimately nothing but more or less explicit hints and allusions.) Moreover, to the extent that the dreamer himself is unaware of the meaning of his dream symbols, the device becomes an effective censorship technique, a defensive compromise in which the underlying idea is (a) communicated, but (b) in a language inaccessible to the dreamer's consciousness. Interestingly, symbolism has defensive properties even when used consciously, as in *euphemisms* ("Excuse me, I want to powder my nose," versus, "Excuse me, I want to defecate," for example).

Plastic Word Representation.   This operation of the dream-work has already been largely anticipated by our discussion of the primitive character of dream symbolism. *Plastic word representation* (sometimes called *dramatization* by Freud) refers to the fact that dreams are generally experienced not in the language of abstractions but in concrete sensory-motor images, in pictures, sounds, smells, bodily sensations, actions. Dreams, like certain psychotic experiences, tend to be hallucinatory. This fact may be understood as a consequence of the disinhibition in dreams (and psychosis) of primitive, primary-process functioning, a notable feature of which is imagistic representation (see pages 129–130).

Religious prohibitions against "graven images" suggest a tacit understanding of the primitive, idish character of plastic representation. The struggle against such regressive tendencies is, for example, a perennial theme in the Old Testament. When Moses descends from the mountain to discover that, in his absence, God has been represented in the plastic form of a golden calf, he puts those responsible for the regressive act to death—a rather brutal punishment for the all too common sin of literalizing an abstraction. (And, it might be noted, the rendition of Moses' own experience of God, including the burning bush and the thundering voice, is not itself much less concretistic.) In the same vein, many puritanical Christian and Moslem sects prohibit any form of "graven images" (statues, pictorial symbols) in their places of worship, and, in some cases, even forbid the viewing of pictorial art and, especially, movies. Not only the impulses, but the very language of the id is taboo.

Even words can be overconcrete. The major Taoist text, the *Tao Tê-Ching* (Watts, 1957), starts with the admonition:

> The Tao that can be named
> Is not the eternal Tao.

Orthodox Jews will not utter or write the name of God (Yahweh), but only *allude* to it by its Hebrew consonants, YWH, or, when writing in English, G_d, in both cases using standard censorship techniques.

Dreams have no such compunctions. Note the concretistic, almost cinematic character of Mac's dream: *he is walking; he hears footsteps; he is scared and opens his mouth to scream; his tongue falls out; he picks it up and puts it into his pocket; he sees the monument; he sees the man behind him—on the black side; he can hardly lift his legs; he reaches into his pocket;* and so on. It is as if Mac, the dreamer, had improvised a brilliant "charade" representation of the latent ideas (assuming the interpretation to be correct): *My therapy is approaching a crisis; it is getting too close to my repressed impulses; I wish to free associate, as I must if I am to improve, but I can't anymore; I am terrified I shall be punished with castration; I am tired and afraid; I can't have an erection; I will never be able to regain my potency; I need my therapist's help, but I can't be helped since I can no longer free associate; if I free associate I'll lose my penis.* Probably most of the interpreted latent content is obvious to the reader, with the possible exception of the castration theme. This facet of the interpretation, which Mac eventually corroborates in his therapy, may be clarified by the next aspect of the dream-work, condensation (which, of necessity, presupposes the operation of displacement, not just of accent but of physical elements as well).

Condensation and Displacement. Condensation involves the compression of several ideas or objects into one. It is also known in developmental and anthropological literatures as *syncretism*. Obvious examples abound in mythology. A *centaur,* for example, is a literal fusion of man and horse; the *Minotaur* of man and bull; the *Sphynx* of a woman, lion, and serpent. Condensation implies the operation of displacement in that some aspect of an object—the hindquarters of a horse, for example—is displaced onto another object—the upper body of a man.

Again, condensation and displacement may be understood to result from the disinhibition of primary-process modes of thinking, in this case its indiscriminateness and its primitive propensity to equate by juxtaposition (as in "guilt by association"). As suggested earlier, the id is not actually without logic, as Freud tends to put it hyperbolically, but rather primitive or crude in its logic.

This logic, faulty though it might be, is crucial for interpretation. A subject reports this brief dream fragment: "I dreamt of my older brother but he had Hitler's moustache." We are not satisfied merely to identify the displacement of Hitler's moustache onto the brother's face, and therefore the condensation of Hitler and the brother; but we wish to be alert for the possible latent message, crudely put as it is, that "my brother is in some respect like Hitler" or "my feelings for my brother are those I have for Hitler."

Note that this type of juxtapositional logic is all that might actually be possible with plastic representations. How could one, for example, render a complex thought such as, "My speaking has some intimate connection with my penis in that by talking I might not only be cured of my impotence but also, I fear, suffer the risk of castration." How about: "This scares me and I open my mouth to scream, but when I do, my tongue falls out. . . . I just pick it up and put it in my pocket"? Note the physical displacement of the tongue, which often symbolizes the penis, to the area of the penis, and therefore the virtual condensation of tongue and penis. Crude as it might be, it is about as much as we might expect from a pictographic language. We suddenly find ourselves confronting again, though from a different vantage point, the issue of language effects (Chapter 3): The linguistic medium controls the logic of the message.

Secondary Revision (or Elaboration).   This last aspect of the dream-work constitutes an attempt to package or normalize the end product of the previous dream-work operations. The distorted, gap-filled material is worked over and elaborated into a more sensible form. The process can subserve defensive functions since it tends to hide the tampering to which the latent content had been subjected, and can thus serve as a "cover-up of the cover-up."

One can informally glimpse the operation of secondary revision by comparing dream recalls recorded immediately upon awakening to those recorded after the lapse of some time. The latter inevitably lose some of the wild, fantastic, paraverbal twistings of the former, becoming more mundanely realistic versions of them. Classic experimental work on this revisionary or "constructive" aspect of memory has been done by Bartlett (1932). His memory materials were not actual dreams but dreamlike stories, which subjects attempted to recall over extended periods of time. The types of memory changes observed in the successive recall samples are the kinds of normalizing elaborations and revisions posited by Freud. Here is one of the stories, an adaption of an American Indian folktale (originally translated by the anthropological linguist, Franz Boas):

The War of the Ghosts

One night two young men from Egulac went down to the river to hunt seals, and while they were there it became foggy and calm. Then they heard war-cries, and they thought: "Maybe this is a war-party." They escaped to the shore, and hid behind a log. Now canoes came up, and they heard the noise of paddles, and saw one canoe coming up to them. There were five men in the canoe, and they said:

"What do you think? We wish to take you along. We are going up the river to make war on the people."

One of the young men said: "I have no arrows."

"Arrows are in the canoe," they said.

"I will not go along. I might be killed. My relatives do not know where I have gone. But you," he said, turning to the other, "may go with them."

So one of the young men went, but the other returned home.

And the warriors went on up the river to a town on the other side of Kalama. The people came down to the water, and they began to fight, and many were killed. But presently the young man heard one of the warriors say: "Quick, let us go home: that Indian has been hit." Now he thought: "Oh, they are ghosts." He did not feel sick, but they said he had been shot.

So the canoes went back to Egulac, and the young man went ashore to his house, and made a fire. And he told everybody and said: "Behold I accompanied the ghosts, and we went to fight. Many of our fellows were killed, and many of those who attacked us were killed. They said I was hit, and I did not feel sick."

He told it all, and then he became quiet. When the sun rose he fell down. Something black came out of his mouth. His face became contorted. The people jumped up and cried.

He was dead. (Bartlett, 1932, p. 65)

The folktale has an eerie, otherworldly character that is, as several subjects noted, dreamlike.

Here is the first recall reproduction by one of the subjects (P):

The War of the Ghosts

Two youths were standing by a river about to start seal-catching, when a boat appeared with five men in it. They were all armed for war.

The youths were at first frightened, but they were asked by the men to come and help them fight some enemies on the other bank. One youth said he could not come as his relations would be anxious about him; the other said he would go, and entered the boat.

· · · · ·

In the evening he returned to his hut, and told his friends that he had been in a battle. A great many had been slain, and he had been wounded by an arrow; he had not felt any pain, he said. They told him that he must have been fighting in a battle of ghosts. Then he remembered that it had been queer and he was very excited.

In the morning, however, he became ill, and his friends gathered round; he fell down and his face became very pale. Then he writhed and shrieked and his friends were filled with terror. At last he became calm. Something hard and black came out of his mouth, and he lay contorted and dead. (P. 72)

The reproduction, as Bartlett emphasizes, contains a variety of omissions, simplifications, elaborations, and logical "rationalizations." Note, for example, the normalization of the logically baffling conclusion, "Oh, they are ghosts." The reproduction loses not just details but, perhaps more importantly, a great deal of the haunting, evocative power of the original. It is, somehow, less dreamlike.

Here is P's third reproduction, some six weeks after his original exposure to the story:

The War of the Ghosts

Two youths went down to the river to fish for seals. They perceived, soon, coming down the river, a canoe with five warriors in it, and they were alarmed. But the warriors said: "We are friends. Come with us, for we are going to fight a battle".

The elder youth would not go, because he thought his

relations would be anxious about him. The younger, however, went.

. . . . .

In the evening he returned from the battle, and he said that he had been wounded, but that he had felt no pain.

There had been a great fight and many had been slain on either side. He lit a fire and retired to rest in his hut. The next morning, when the neighbours came round to see how he was, they found him in a fever. And when he came out into the open at sunrise he fell down. The neighbours shrieked. He became livid and writhed upon the ground. Something black came out of his mouth, and he died. So the neighbours decided that he must have been to war with the ghosts. (Pp. 73–74)

Some three years later the subject, P, "not having seen or, according to his own statement, thought of the story in the meantime" (p. 75), agreed to attempt one more reproduction (his fifth):

Some warriors went to wage war against the ghosts. They fought all day and one of their number was wounded.

They returned home in the evening, bearing their sick comrade. As the day drew to a close, he became rapidly worse and the villagers came round him. At sunset he sighed: something black came out of his mouth. He was dead. (P. 75)

Some of the essential points remain but the magic of the story is gone. It is by now a rather domesticated ghost story. Even the time of the man's death has drifted toward the hackneyed; the man dies, as the literary cliché would have it, at sunset.

Bartlett's work provides experimental corroboration of the pervasive revisionistic tendency of memory: Over time and successive reproductions, memories are progressively worked over to fit the subject's preexisting cognitive *schemas*—his expectations, sense of logic, cultural biases, and personal experiences. This is precisely what Freud meant to convey by the notion of secondary elaboration or revision, although in the case of psychoanalysis, the motivational, and in particular the defensive, aspects of the subject's psychological structure receive special emphasis. In Freud's system, secondary revisions of personally salient materials—of dreams, for example—work in tandem with the requirements of defense (censorship), so that memories are rendered not only more reasonable but also more palatable. For purposes of exposition one may distinguish between censorship and secondary revision, but in practice the two (as well as other features of the dream-work, as has already been emphasized) are inextricably intertwined.

Trenchant examples from the real world of such defensive secondary revisions are provided by the Watergate transcripts made public by the Nixon White House. A unique feature of this particular source material is that we can, with the eventual recovery of the original tape recordings, directly produce, without interpretation, the true "text" upon which the revisions were foisted.

The present sample is excerpted from a news article that originally appeared in the *Washington Post* in mid-June of 1974, at the height of the Watergate crisis (which, it should not be forgotten, was a crisis of information processing—of break-ins into files, "leaks," "plumbers," "cover-ups," and "cover-ups of the cover-ups"):

WASHINGTON (WP)—A confidential House Judiciary Committee staff memo says that on an April 16, 1973, White House tape, President Nixon said he was "planning to assume some culpability" in the paying of hush-money to Watergate conspirator E. Howard Hunt, because he knew of the proposed transaction.

The memo, a copy of which has been obtained by the Washington Post, lists this phrase as one of the five instances in which the actual tape in the committee's hands differs from the transcript of the same taped conversation made public by the White House.

Taken together, the memo suggests, the five points make a stronger basis for argument that Nixon knew of such payments, for which his White House aides, H. R. Haldeman and John D. Ehrlichman, and others have been indicted. The question of his own culpability in the hush-money payments is also considered to have been a major consideration in the grand jury's naming of Nixon as an unindicted co-conspirator. . . .

The conversation was one between the President and then White House counsel John W. Dean 3rd on the morning of April 16, in which Dean retraced the March 21, 1973, meeting in which he had told Nixon about Hunt's request.

[The] memo gives the dialogue first as [heard] on the tape, and then as it appeared in the White House version:

P[resident]: "What was the situation, John? The only time I ever heard any discussion of, uh, this supporting of the defendants . . . [Note: White House transcripts say "support for the defense fund . . . "]

". . . was when you mentioned to me some, something about the, I mean, I think the last time we talked about Haluh, Hunt having a problem . . . " [Note: Transcripts say "something about hard-hitting problem"]

D[ean]. "Ehrlichman said at the time, 'Well, is that problem with Hunt straightened out?' He said it to me and I said, 'Well, ask the man who may know: Mitchell.' And Mitchell said, 'I think that problem is solved.'"

P. "That's all?"

D. "That's all he said."

P. "Right. That's good. In other words, that was done at the Mitchell level." [Note: "Right. That's good" does not appear in the transcripts.]

D. "That's right."

P. "But you had knowledge; Haldeman had a lot of knowledge and Ehrlichman had knowledge." [Note: Transcripts omit the words "a lot of."]

D. "That's right."

P. "And I suppose I did. I mean I am planning to assume some culpability on that." [Note: Transcripts say: "That assumes culpability on that, doesn't it?"]

In the White House transcript, the dialogue then continues with Dean disagreeing that such knowledge assumed culpability and Nixon responding: "Why not? I plan to be tough on myself so I can handle the other thing. I must say I did not even give it a thought at the time."

In the Watergate cover-up indictments, it is charged that after the March 21 meeting, Haldeman phoned former Attorney General John N. Mitchell, also indicted, who allegedly arranged for payment of approximately $75,000 to Hunt through his lawyer that night. (Jules Witcover, *The Washington Post*, June 18, 1974, pp. 1 and 7)

In the real world, clearly, censorship and secondary revision work hand in glove.

Ulric Neisser (1981), in a similar vein, provides an examination of the psychodynamic distortions that crept into John Dean's legendary memory during his testimony to the Watergate committee of the United States Senate in June 1973:

When Dean first testified, his "facility for recalling details" seemed so impressive that some writers called him "the human tape recorder." Ironically, a very real tape recorder had been tuned in to some of the same "details." Not long after its interrogation of Dean, the Senate Committee discovered that all conversations in Nixon's Oval Office were routinely (but secretly) recorded....

The testimony and the transcripts are now in the public domain. I propose to treat them as data, as if they had resulted from a deliberately conducted memory experiment. (P. 2)

...Comparison [of Dean's testimony about September 15] with the transcript shows that hardly a word of Dean's account is true. Nixon did not say *any* of the things attributed to him here: he didn't ask Dean to sit down, he didn't say Haldeman had kept him posted, he didn't say Dean had done a good job (at least not in that part of the conversation), he didn't say anything about Liddy or the indictments. Nor had Dean himself said the things he later describes himself as saying: that he couldn't take credit, that the matter might unravel some day, etc. (Indeed, he said just the opposite later on: "nothing is going to come crashing down.") His account is plausible, but entirely incorrect. In this early part of the conversation Nixon did not offer him any praise at all, unless "You had quite a day, didn't you," was intended as a compliment. (It is hard to tell from a written transcript.) Dean cannot be said to have reported the "gist" of the opening remarks; no count of idea units or comparison of structure would produce a score much above zero.

Was he simply lying to the Senators? I do not think so. The transcript makes it quite clear that Nixon *is* fully aware of the cover-up: Haldeman and Dean discuss it freely in front of him, and while he occasionally asks questions he never seems surprised. Later on he even praises Dean for "putting his fingers in the leaks." Because the real conversation is just as incriminating as the one Dean described, it seems unlikely that he was remembering one thing and saying another. His responses to Senator Baker during cross-examination . . . also indicate that he was doing his best to be honest. Mary McCarthy's assessment of Dean has stood the test of time: she wrote in 1973 of her overpowering impression " . . . not so much of a truthful person as of someone resolved to tell the truth about this particular set of events because his intelligence has warned him to do so." (Pp. 9–10)

. . . Comparison of his testimony with the actual transcripts shows systematic distortion at one level of analysis combined with basic accuracy at another. Many of the distortions reflected Dean's own self-image; he tended to recall his role as more central than it really was. (Abstract)

The Dream-Work as Nonwork

Dreaming is intrinsically the not-doing of sleep. (Carlos Castaneda, 1981, p. 28)

Two themes emerge from our overview of the dream-work process: First, that there is a primitive aspect to dreams; and second, that dreams are overlaid by defensive efforts.

This dual aspect of dreams follows readily from Freud's structural model (which, however, was not explicitly advanced until almost a quarter of a century after *The Interpretation of Dreams,* and is therefore not clearly reflected in it):

Dreams are disinhibited phenomena. The executive control system—the ego—is weakened in sleep and consequently fails to inhibit the primary-process functioning id to its usual extent and to carry out fully its own secondary-process tasks. Hence, dreams are idish; they are "the royal road to the knowledge of the [system] unconscious" (Freud, 1900, p. 608). The dream-"work" elements of plastic word representation, primitive symbolization, condensation, and displacement are primary-process features that emerge in dreams not from any unique work performed by the dream process but, on the contrary, from the failure of the ego to overlay the primitive mentation of the id with its own more advanced secondary-process functioning. Thus, the dream-work in large part constitutes "nonwork." The actual "work" part of the dream-work is the censorship (and, to the extent that it takes place during sleep, secondary revision), though even here the processes are not unique to dreaming but, actually, less effective in dreams, and therefore merely obvious in dreams.

Dream-work, then, is something of a misnomer (see Anna Freud, 1936, p. 192). Dreams can be understood simply as "compromise formations" between the ego and the id in which the id aspects are particularly prominent because of the weakness of the ego.

We have here not a contradiction of Freud's basic position but a logical simplification that is consistent with his subsequent theorizing. The point is not that psychological "work" is not involved (namely, primary-process functioning, and debilitated defensive and reconstructive cognition); rather, that such work is not peculiar to dreams but merely more evident in them as a result of the relative nonwork of the ego.

Dream Interpretation

Dream interpretation is often conceptualized as the reversal of the dream-work. The reformulation of the dream-work as nonwork does not alter this perspective; one need only interpolate that in those cases where nonwork rather than work (censorship, secondary revision) is involved, the task of the interpreter is to reverse the nonwork, for example, to translate primitive symbols and representations into abstract ones, superimpose order upon primitive displacements and condensations, and restore coherence to the temporal and logical discombobulations of primary-process thinking.

Although knowledge of the nature of primary-process and secondary-process functioning is helpful, the interpretation of dreams is hardly arcane, involving ultimately the same processes as the interpretation of, for example, jokes, sarcasm, poetry, allegory. Once again, the Freudian position, stripped of its complex metaphorical gyrations, turns out to be starkly simple—in this, and not in its superficial complexity, lies its genius.

How, then, is a dream interpreted? The first step, obviously, is to have a dream—or rather, since we all have dreams, to remember a dream. In recording (or reporting) the dream, no effort should be made to prettify or censor it (although the temptation to do so, even when recording the dream for one's private use, is surprisingly common). The next step, required only if the dream is to be interpreted by someone else, is the preparation of a preamble (e.g., pages 98–99 and 148), which provides some of the basic informational background relating to the people and places alluded to in the dream.

The next step is the crucial innovation in Freudian dream interpretation. The dream material is segmented by some more or less reasonable rule—such as, sentence by sentence—and each segment is free associated to. If the reader wishes to try the technique on a dream of his own—and this is a worthwhile exercise since the procedure, if faithfully implemented, quite frequently yields some telling psychological discovery—he might try proceeding sentence by sentence: Copy the first sentence of the recorded dream and below it write anything—but anything—that comes to mind, omitting nothing, censoring nothing. Keep free associating ("automatic writing") until there seems to be nothing more to say. Now proceed to the next sentence, free associating to it thoroughly, then to the third, all the way through the last. As the material is free associated to, some insights are likely to emerge which (since every thought must be produced) find their way into the associations. These rudimentary insights are gradually elaborated and correlated with other thoughts until, by the end of the sequence, they merge into a deeper, often unexpected, understanding of the dream.

For a detailed example, the reader is referred to Freud's analysis of his own "Irma dream" (1900, pp. 106–121). Unfortunately, the more one succeeds at the task, the more difficult it is to share one's insights. Freud obviously censors much of what he uncovered, and admits as much. However, enough is revealed, in part through hints and allusions, to make it an illuminating case, one worth comparing to one's own effort. A major limitation of an analysis of one's own dream (or better still, several dreams) is that the insights one may gain, even if at times unexpected, are perforce superficial. Our defenses ultimately preclude us from penetrating too deeply into our own unconscious.

Such limitations, of course, are not in force when a therapist analyzes the dreams of his patient, and it is in the therapeutic milieu that the profoundest dream analyses can take place. Unfortunately, case reports involving deep interpretations are not always convincing (e.g., Freud's analyses of several dreams of his patient, Dora [1905b]), because of the difficulty—irrespective of the validity of the interpretation—of conveying in any manageable length of text the enormous contextual background, some of it nonverbal, that gives rise to and justifies the interpretation. It is for this reason that for our example Mac's rather transparent dream, the latent content of which was substantially accessible to Mac even without Lindner's interpretation, was selected.

Before concluding this section on the psychoanalytic approach to dream interpretation, we might briefly address the question why free association should be conducive to the uncovering of latent contents. Actually, there may be no one reason.

Implicit in much of psychoanalysis is the notion that free association engenders a retracing of the original causal chain of mentation. Thus, if a particular manifest event, E, is the terminus of an associative chain,

$$A \rightarrow B \rightarrow C \rightarrow D \rightarrow E,$$

free association is thought to produce a "tracing in a backward direction ... of the same associative pathways" (Foulkes, 1978, p. 36), that is,

$$A \leftarrow B \leftarrow C \leftarrow D \leftarrow E,$$

with the result that the original, usually unconscious cause, A, is uncovered. There are obvious problems with this supposition, not the least of which is the asymmetry of associative relations. Thus, just because $A \rightarrow B$ with a high probability, it does not follow that $B \rightarrow A$ with the same high probability.

Another explanation, sometimes suggested by Freud and stressed in previous chapters (see also Foulkes, 1978) is that free associations provide the indispensable contextual ecology in which deep meanings can be realized. Thus, if a manifest event, ϵ, is accompanied by free-associative context, $[\epsilon]$, it becomes possible to extract the latent content, $\epsilon | [\epsilon]$.

A still further explanation could be that drawn-out free associations eventually produce the cues critical for triggering inaccessible target memories. (For a discussion of cueing effects in memory see, Baddeley, 1976; Crowder, 1976; Glass, Holyoak, and Santa, 1979; Klatzky, 1980; Tulving and Thomson, 1973.)

Finally, it is possible that because free-associative fantasy, like dreaming, involves uncritical or "loose" thinking (cf. Erdelyi, 1970; 1972), crucial but hitherto suppressed components of a psychological puzzle are generated, with the result that the solution to the psychological puzzle (the deep or latent meaning) suddenly jumps into place. This perspective is related to the often-emphasized role of regressive, loose thinking in creative problem solving (e.g., Kris, 1952). (For a formal analysis in terms of contemporary decision theory, see the author's article, "On the Transmutation of Base Bias $[\beta]$ into Informational Gold $[d']$" [Erdelyi, 1985].)

Even this cursory discussion suggests that there are many compel-

ling reasons for expecting that free association should produce the recovery of inaccessible memories or meanings. It is surprising, therefore,
that no experimental corroboration has appeared to date (cf. Erdelyi,
1970; 1972; 1984; Erdelyi and Becker, 1974).

Problematical Issues in Psychoanalytic Dream Theory

Dreams as Wish-Fulfillments. One of Freud's most obstinately held
views, despite repeated criticisms, was the notion that dreams are
wish-fulfillments (Freud, 1900; 1917; 1940). Freud maintained that we
try to satisfy in the hallucinatory world of dream fantasy what we cannot satisfy in reality, occasionally pointing to daydreams as the waking
analog of the process (e.g., Freud, 1917). He presumably arrived at this
conclusion empirically, from his experiences with the dreams of his patients, though the position follows readily from his structural model
(formalized only in 1923 but already implicit in *The Interpretation of
Dreams*). Since dreams are substantially idish, and the id is governed by
the pleasure-unpleasure principle, it is only natural that dreams should
be focally concerned with the satisfaction of pleasure (or the relief of
drive tensions producing unpleasure). This, simply, completes the idea
that dreams are the "royal road" to the knowledge of the id (the system
Unconscious): Dreams are idish not only in their primitive cognitive
style but also in their hedonistic goal orientation.

The problem with the wish-fulfillment conception of dreams is
readily apparent: What is to be made of dreams which have nothing to
do with pleasure or which, worse yet, are unpleasant (punishment
dreams and nightmares, for example)? Freud tried a variety of explanations over the years, but in the end they strike one as belabored,
reminiscent at times of the explanation of the damaged kettle he cites in
his *Jokes and Their Relation to the Unconscious*:

> A. borrowed a copper kettle from B. and after he had returned
> it was sued by B. because the kettle now had a big hole in it
> which made it unusable. His defense was: "First, I never bor-
> rowed a kettle from B. at all; secondly, the kettle had a hole in it
> already when I got it from him; and thirdly, I gave him back
> the kettle undamaged." (Freud, 1905b, p. 62)

Freud's most important defense of the wish-fulfillment hypothesis
of dreams is to emphasize the distinction between the manifest and latent content of dreams; a dream which appears not to fulfill a wish at the
manifest level may nevertheless be shown (through interpretation) to
do so at the latent level. Unfortunately, this possibility is not always
borne out by observation, and even Freud's examples often fail to support his claim (cf. Foulkes, 1978). Moreover, the meaning of a "wish" is

soon stretched to include unpleasant (nonhedonistic) events, with the justification that wishes may, after all, be masochistic; that is, the wish satisfied might be a wish to punish oneself (Freud, 1900; 1917). This latter position gains a certain legitimacy with the introduction of the super-ego (Freud, 1923), although one is inclined to wonder about the boundary conditions of the hypothesis if both hedonistic as well as masochistic events are subsumed under the term.

What of anxiety dreams or nightmares? Freud here takes another tack. Having emphasized that dreams are compromise formations (between the id and the weakened ego) he goes on to suggest that, at times, the compromise in the making may be too compromising; too much of the id content (of a wishful but forbidden nature) threatens to break through the defenses of the debilitated ego. The ego responds to this perceived danger with anxiety, which serves as a signal to awaken and fully mobilize the ego's defensive resources against the emerging id impulses. The dreamer awakens experiencing the ego's fright but remembering only a censored or distorted version of the wishful impulse which prompted it. The psychotic, in Freud's view, is someone whose fully mobilized waking ego is not strong enough for the task and who therefore actually experiences in wakefulness—and even acts out—the impulses that threaten most people only in sleep.

Freud's patchwork of explanations would appear to have introduced unlimited degrees of freedom into the hypothesis, which is now a wish-fulfillment theory of dreams that seems able to accommodate all varieties of dreams—palpably hedonistic dreams, indifferent dreams, punishment dreams, and nightmares. This is not altogether so, however. A class of dreams, observed in tragic abundance during World War I, finally undermined the wish-fulfillment hypothesis. These were the *repetition compulsion* dreams of war neurotics (traumatic neurotics) which remorselessly reenacted, night after night, the traumatic events from their combat experiences. How could a wish-fulfillment hypothesis of dreams possibly accommodate such repetitions of terrifying life experiences? Freud finally had to yield ground, though he did so grudgingly and covered his retreat with ambiguity. He came "to admit for the first time an exception to the proposition that dreams are fulfilments of wishes" (Freud, 1920b, p. 32). The repetitive nightmares of traumatic (or war) neurotics were not wish-fulfillments but the consequence of a new principle: the "compulsion to repeat." This class of dreams, however, is viewed as an exception, one that Freud tries to make light of: "I will not invoke the saying that the exception proves the rule: its wisdom seems to me most questionable. But no doubt the exception does not overturn the rule" (Freud, 1933, p. 29).

Freud finally tries to harmonize these observations by introducing one theoretical modification: Dreams are not—technically—wish-fulfillments; rather, they are *attempts* at wish-fulfillment (Freud, 1917, p. 29). The nightmares of war neurotics, therefore, represent *failures* in the attempt to satisfy a wish, specifically, the wish to master, in dream fantasy, what proved overwhelming in reality.

At this point it would be difficult to improve upon Freud's own commentary: "Now you will probably think that with all this there is very little of the famous wish-fulfilment left" (Freud, 1917, p. 195). Elsewhere he goes on to ask rhetorically:

> Admitting that every dream means something and that this meaning may be discovered by employing the technique of psychoanalysis, why must it always, in face of all the evidence to the contrary, be forced into the formula of wish-fulfilment? Why must our thoughts at night be any less many-sided than our thoughts by day; so that at one time a dream might be a fulfilment of some wish, at another time, as you say yourself, the opposite, the actualization of a dread; or, again, the expression of a resolution, a warning, a weighting of some problem with its pros and cons, or a reproof, some prick of conscience, or an attempt to prepare oneself for something which has to be done—and so forth? Why this perpetual insistence upon a wish or, at the most, its opposite. . . . Cannot we be satisfied with having discovered the meaning of dreams and the ways by which we can find their meaning? (Freud, 1917, pp. 197–198)

The question could not be put more trenchantly. Unfortunately, the answer never does justice to the question. Should the reader wish to witness firsthand how boggled Freud manages to get on the topic, he is encouraged to read Freud's chapter on wish-fulfillment in *A General Introduction to Psychoanalysis* (Freud, 1917, pp. 190–203).

Children's Dreams and the Wish-Fulfillment Hypothesis. According to Freud, the dreams of young children have a unique characteristic. Because of their psychological underdevelopment, children's dreams are relatively untrammelled by defensive distortions, and so the usual difference between manifest and latent content is not encountered or at least not to its usual extent (Freud, 1900; 1917). For this reason, Freud considered children's dreams to be particularly decisive for the wish-fulfillment hypothesis. He lists case after case of children's dreams, which almost invariably turn out to be the satisfaction of some wish, usually involving food. For example, a 19-month-old girl—Anna Freud by name—who had been kept from food for a day because of a stomach infection, was heard to call out excitedly in her sleep: "Anna Fweud, stwawbewwies, wild stwawbewwies, omblet, pudden!" (Freud, 1900, p. 130).

From a host of such examples, usually taken from actual dream reports of older children, Freud (1900) concludes that "the dreams of children are pure wish-fulfilments."

But is this so? Are, for example, the *wakeful* thoughts of children pure wish-fulfillments? Should they not be, given Freud's presupposition that the inhibitory structures of the psyche (the ego and super-ego) are absent or feeble in the first years of life? For dreams, at any rate, Freud modifies his assertion in his 1911 revision of *The Interpretation of Dreams* to read, "the dreams of children are frequently pure wish-fulfilments" (see Footnote 1, p. 127, of *The Standard Edition* of Freud, 1900). Freud explains that some dream distortion is to be expected in children as young as four to five, and so the wish fulfilled may already be disguised. Recent research, in fact, suggests that the majority of children's dreams are not manifestly wish-fulfilling (Foulkes, 1978).

The occurrence of nightmares in young children—and even in infants—are problems with which Freud does not attempt to grapple. Similarly, Freud altogether circumvents any serious discussion of dreaming—and nightmares—in animals, something that would seem to pose insuperable problems for the wish-fulfillment hypothesis.

Implication of Freud's Revision of His Drive Theory for the Wish-Fulfillment Hypothesis. Freud's difficulties with the wish-fulfillment hypothesis may ultimately be adduced to his failure to revise his dream theory and align it with subsequent theoretical developments in psychoanalysis. Thus, the wish-fulfillment hypothesis may be seen as one of the theoretical anachronisms in Freud's dream theory referred to earlier. It may be understood in terms of Freud's early conception of drives (roughly, between 1900 and 1920) as either self-preservative (like hunger and thirst) or sexual, or both. If the id is the psychological representative of basic drives, and the basic drives are sexual or self-preservative in nature—and if, further, dreams are idish—it follows that dreams should substantially deal with such drives, which, given their nature, manifest themselves as wishes (for sex, for food, for security, and so forth).

In his 1920 monograph, *Beyond the Pleasure Principle (Jenseits des Lustprinzips)*, Freud introduces a crucial reformulation of his drive theory. Drives are now conceived of as being essentially of two kinds, anabolic, life drives (including sex and self-preservation) and catabolic, death drives (destructive drives against oneself and others). Following our previous chain of reasoning, we would now expect dreams to reflect both categories of drives, the latter often unpleasant in nature. At this point, we would appear to be ready to abandon a wish-fulfillment hypothesis of dreams. Instead, Freud abandons the consensual meaning of *wish:* "*the aim of life is death*. ... organisms wish to die" (Freud, 1920b, p. 38).

Freud's speculation about the existence of biological self-termination programs may not be as fanciful as it appears on first blush (e.g., Schmeck, 1982); however, his calling such programs, "wishful," is. We may be once again witnessing an instance of linguistic warping: The implicit consequence of using the word *drive* versus *program* is different; the former tends to imply a wish, the latter does not.

Dreams as Guardians of Sleep.   We turn now to one more hypothesis about dreams on which Freud was almost certainly in error. This was the notion that dreams are guardians rather than disturbers of sleep (Freud, 1900; 1901a; 1917). The observation is more speculative than empirical. Freud argues (e.g., 1917, pp. 115–116) that the sleeper is continuously assailed by stimuli, external and internal, which threaten to awaken him. In response to these disturbing stimuli, particularly unavoidable internal stimuli (unfulfilled drives), the sleeper responds with a dream, in which the disturbing stimulus is dealt with and satisfied (wish-fulfillment). By dealing with the mental stimulus in a dream, sleep can continue. Thus, dreams are not disturbers of sleep but protectors of sleep.

Modern experimental research on dreams casts serious doubts on the tenability of Freud's hypothesis (cf. Foulkes, 1978). First, one would expect that an experimenter-produced disturbance (a noise, a strong smell, and so forth) would be incorporated in a dream so as to maintain sleep. Although there is some evidence for the occasional incorporation of external stimuli, this is hardly a regular occurrence; most disturbing external stimuli are not incorporated into dreams. Moreover, disturbing stimuli do not provoke a dream. Studies of REM sleep (when dreaming takes place) show that stimulus incorporation, when it happens, occurs only when dreaming is already in progress (Foulkes, 1978, p. 95). The cyclic regularity of REM sleep (Dement, 1976; Foulkes, 1978; Van de Castle, 1971) militates against any attempt to portray dreams as direct responses to external or internal disturbances threatening sleep (unless one wished to argue that such disturbances occur with precise regularity every 60 to 90 minutes, the typical interval between REM periods in adults).

Daydreams and Fantasy

Except for a glancing reference here and there we have not yet taken up the topic of daydreams and fantasy. And yet, we have fully dealt with the topic by virtue of having dealt with dreams. For, in Freud's thinking, dreams and daydreams (or fantasy) are essentially the same phenomenon but for degree: "day-dreams are the kernels and models of night-dreams; fundamentally the night-dream is nothing but a day-dream" (Freud, 1917, p. 325). The night dream is more extreme, however, since the ego is less in operation during dreams than in wakeful fantasy. Thus: Dreams are hallucinatory whereas daydreams are merely vividly imagistic (Freud, 1917, pp. 117, 325); the latent content of dreams is less censored, more revealing than of daydreams; dreams are essentially involuntary, whereas daydreams are substantially under our control; finally, according to Freud, "day-dreams are literally wish-fulfilments, fulfilments of ambitions or erotic wishes" (1917, p. 117). (This last point is logically surprising; we would expect the less-defended dream to be more transparently wish-fulfilling. The wish-fulfillment hypothesis seems to bring theoretic grief to whatever it touches.)

Not only are the hypotheses similar but so are the problems. Although daydreams, in common usage, do refer to wish-fulfilling fantasies, the fact is that many fantasies are disagreeable and anxiety provoking. Indeed, obsessive-compulsive neurotics and traumatic neurotics often suffer from repetitive ruminations about events, real or imagined, that are acutely disturbing. At other times, fantasy is emotionally neutral, involving intellectual problems rather than wishes. Here is a well-known example involving the young Einstein:

> As early as the age of sixteen, he had considered what he would see were he able to follow a beam of light at its own velocity through space. Here is a problem picture as graphic as any of the number with which he was to explain his ideas. What, in fact, would be seen by anyone who could travel as fast as the oscillating electromagnetic waves which by the turn of the century were known to cause the phenomenon of light? The answer, in Einstein's words, was "a spatially oscillatory electromagnetic field at rest." But this was a contradiction .... He abandoned many fruitless attempts "until at last it came to me that time was suspect." (Clark, 1971, pp. 114–115)

The point, it should be stressed, is not that dreams and fantasy are not often wish-fulfilling, but that they are not invariably wish-fulfilling.

We shall presently return to many of these issues as we turn to examine culturally valued forms of fantasy such as art, myth, and, to start with, jokes.

JOKES

What has been said about daydreams and fantasy applies substantially to jokes as well. Jokes are essentially like dreams. They are forms of psychic regression which, however, in the case of jokes, are voluntary and playful. Freud points out that there can be much pleasure in regression, in throwing off the stifling weight of socialization (Freud, 1905b).

Jokes are regressive in both cognitive style and in content. Let us take up first their cognitive style which, like that of dreams, is suffused with primary-process features.

To start with, jokes tend to be *imagistic,* in some cases literally so (e.g., Figure 2.11; Figure 4.2; Figure 4.3, left panels). The imagery is often auditory, as in the case of puns, in which the joke depends on two different meanings sharing the same sound. (Puns, therefore, also illustrate the operation of condensation.) Here is an example, the comment of an aspish socialite from a bygone era on the goings on at Yale after football games: "If all the girls at a Yale football game were laid from one goalpost to the other, I wouldn't be at all surprised."

The "joke-work" (the counterpart in jokes of the dream-work) often features clear cases of *condensation* and *displacement* (e.g., the joke just cited; Figure 2.11). There is, of course, primitive *symbolization* (e.g., Figure 2.11; Figure 4.3, bottom-left panel; the Groucho Marx joke on pages 93–95).

A prominent joke technique is regressive, *faulty logic* (such as coexistence of opposites, flawed reasoning, and so forth). Here is an example, probably from Abbott and Costello:

Q. *Why is a loaf of bread the mother of airplanes?*
A. *A loaf of bread is a necessity; airplanes are an invention; since necessity is the mother of invention, therefore, a loaf of bread is the mother of airplanes.*

Figure 4.2. Visual joke (graffitto from a café in Greenwich Village).

Figure 4.3. *Left panels:* Cartoons from *Sex to Sexty* #2 (1971), SRI Publishing Co., Inc., John W. Newbern. *Right panels:* Pseudo-cartoons.

We have here a breakdown in logic, a faulty syllogism which, nevertheless, succeeds in aping in everything but sense the formalism of an algebraic proof:

If:

a (bread) $= b$ (necessity),
b (necessity) $=$ mother of c (invention), and
d (airplanes) $= c$ (invention),

Therefore, by substitution,

$a =$ mother of d.
Q.E.D.

The logical flaw in this spoof of secondary-process thinking, interestingly enough, is the literalization of a metaphor, in this case, "mother of." As we have seen in Chapter 3, the problem often arises—unfortunately—outside of the domain of jokes.

Other jokes depend on the *abrogation of reality testing,* as is illustrated in this example offered by Freud:

> A man who had fallen on hard times borrowed 25 florins from a prosperous acquaintance, after much moaning and groaning about his calamitous circumstances. The very same day his benefactor met him again in a posh restaurant, eating salmon mayonnaise [a luxury dish]. The benefactor reproached him: "What? You borrow money from me and then order yourself salmon mayonnaise? Is that what you have used the money for?" "I don't understand you," replied the object of the attack; "if I haven't any money I *can't* eat salmon mayonnaise, and if I have some money I *mustn't* eat salmon mayonnaise. Well, then, when *am* I to eat salmon mayonnaise?" (Freud, 1905b, adapted from pp. 49–50)

There are, finally, the various versions of *censorship,* for example, *hints* and *allusions* (Figures 4.2, 4.3, etc.).

A fascinating point made by Freud in support of his contention that the joke-work (essentially, primary-process thinking and censorship) is crucial for the comical effect, is that the joke falls flat or misfires if the joke-work is undone—if the joke is translated into secondary-process language or is insufficiently censored. The remark about Yale would hardly be funny if the lady had said bluntly that after football games the girls visiting Yale had sexual intercourse with the Yale boys. Or it would hardly be amusing for someone to suggest that a cubist like Picasso has cubes for testicles. Nor would it be funny for an unwed mother to turn up at her lover's home to tell him, child in arms, that coitus interruptus had not been an effective birth-control technique.

A breakdown in censorship also undermines the comical effect. Apparently, not everyone was amused by Groucho Marx's witticism (page 93); the outcry, it is said, caused the network to suspend the program. In jokes, the line between insult and amusement can be very thin, and it is not always drawn in the same place at the same time by everyone (hence jokes that are in "poor taste").

Let us now turn to the content of jokes, though in a sense we have already been broaching the issue. A joke that is in *poor taste* is one that—for a particular person—does not sufficiently separate manifest from latent content. For those who took umbrage at the Groucho Marx joke, the latent meaning was too transparent; the outrage that it provoked in some viewers corresponds to the disturbance we all experience when some latent content—problematical for *us*—is broached too openly. For different people, of course, different contents are upsetting. The author has observed two cases in which a joke badly misfired. In one, a devout Christian stormed out from a reception where a slightly tipsy guest of honor told a crude religious joke (which, however, some of the listeners found amusing); in the other, a racial joke almost caused a violent altercation.

In a curious and, apparently, unrecognized departure from the dream model, Freud suggests that there are essentially two types of jokes: *innocent* jokes and *tendentious* jokes. Innocent jokes, as their name suggests, have latent contents (if in fact they have clearly defined latent contents) that are innocuous; their comical effect depends solely on form or style, that is, on the use of some primary-process element, not on content (e.g., Abbott and Costello's loaf of bread joke; Freud's joke about the damaged kettle [page 165]). When such a joke misfires it is not because it gives offense but rather because it is judged silly or infantile. Tendentious jokes (that is, those with a certain semantic "tendency" or bias), on the other hand, involve latent contents—usually sexual or aggressive in nature—that are taboo. The art of the joke is to express the forbidden content with just enough distortion to prevent anxiety, but with sufficient clarity to allow us to partake in the content. Put differently, the art of the tendentious joke is to permit us momentarily to suspend some of our repressions toward the forbidden material and enjoy it. Thus, according to Freud, humor has a "liberating" aspect (Freud, 1927b, p. 162). "Explosive" laughter, usually limited to tendentious jokes, is explained by Freud in terms of the energy metaphor: It corresponds to the momentary freeing of the energy that had been bound up in repression.

Jokes, at least tendentious jokes, unmistakably have both manifest and latent content, though in the case of jokes the latent content is conscious to the joker. As in the case of dreams, interpretation is necessary to get at the latent material; not "getting the joke" amounts to failing to interpret its latent content.

From an experimental standpoint, jokes present a tremendous methodological advantage over dreams. The existence and interpretation of latent contents can be reliably assessed. Thus, jokes escape the criticism, frequently leveled against psychoanalysis, that interpretation of dreams and symptoms represents flights of fancy on the part of the *interpreter*. With jokes, the latent contents extracted through interpretation can be readily validated.

Moreover, a great deal can be learned about the process of interpretation itself. Thus, it can be immediately shown that context, both what is provided in the joke itself and what is brought to it by the interpreter from his culturally shaped store of knowledge (what Tulving [1972] terms, "semantic memory") is crucial for the extraction of latent contents. The top-left cartoon in Figure 4.3 could never be interpreted correctly unless we knew about coitus interruptus. Most college-level students are sufficiently knowledgeable about such matters to be able to get this joke. Moreover, and this is critical, those who get the joke invariably get the *same* content (the reader can readily verify this). Clearly, interpretation is not haphazard; it is not a random "reading into" the material. This can be further verified by recourse to the nonsense jokes in the right panels of Figure 4.3. Most subjects do not "get" these "jokes," a reassuring fact since there is nothing to get. And those who claim to have gotten the jokes (the problem of response biases and paramnesias is never absent), produce discrepant latent contents. Thus, the fact that some materials are not readily interpretable, or produce different interpretations, is not proof that interpretation is suspect. Like memory and perception, it is merely fallible.

Because of the possibility of unambiguously verifying its latent content, the joke has a very serious role to play in the experimental corroboration of psychoanalytic concepts. It represents the stimulus version of the Golden Mean: It is neither oversimple like nonsense syllables, nor overcomplex like dreams and symptoms.

ART

> Shall we dare really to compare an imaginative writer with one
> "who dreams in broad daylight," and his creations with day-
> dreams? (Freud, 1907/1963, p.'39)

In having taken up the topic of jokes we have in effect taken up the topic of art. Jokes, after all, are only a special art form, one which often blends indistinguishably with more "serious" artistic creations. Alan Aldridge's painting of Figure 2.11 is surely a joke—most people on first seeing it laugh with gusto. Cervantes' *Don Quijote de la Mancha*, one of the great novels of all time, is a sublimely comical work. That it has its utterly serious aspect, that it grapples with the question with which all philosophy and science and indeed all great literature ultimately struggles—what is reality?—hardly contravenes this stance. Jokes too can have a serious intent; tragedy and comedy are not different breeds of art.

As in the case of jokes (and to some extent, daydreams and fantasy) the regressive aspect of art is voluntary and playful. And, as with all twilight phenomena, the regression can involve form (primary-process thinking) or content (primitive drives) or both. It hardly needs stressing that primitive-drive content, especially sex and aggression, is what a great deal of art—movies, novels, T.V. shows—are about; so much so, that society continually presses for *censorship* of the untrammelled expression of such materials. Of course, there is much art that deals with other matters. Freud might have made the distinction, though he did not, between "innocent" and "tendentious" art (*Jonathan Livingston Seagull* versus *Portnoy's Complaint*, for example). It is difficult, however, to think of many major novels or movies that do not deal, at least to some degree, with aggression and sexuality.

The artist, according to Freud, is a juggler of reality. His sleight of hand—his art—enables him to play with planes and modes of meaning, some of them taboo, that more mundane mortals either ignore or reject.

> How the writer accomplishes this is his innermost secret; the essential *ars poetica* lies in the technique by which our feeling of repulsion is overcome, and this has certainly to do with those barriers erected between every individual being and all others. We can guess at two methods used in this technique. The writer softens the egotistical character of the day-dream by changes and disguises, and he bribes us by the offer of a purely formal, that is, aesthetic, pleasure in the presentation of his phantasies. (Freud, 1907/1963, p. 43)

Of course, art can misfire too, just like jokes. *Lady Chatterley's Lover* may be a work of genius to some, but it is a mean and filthy tract to others—some of whom are even now agitating for its removal from our libraries.

The cognitive style of art is (in part) also regressive. This, if one thinks about it, is remarkable. It is precisely the artist who has the most rarified mastery over the secondary-process tools of his craft—over style, structure, form, lexicon. What distinguishes him from the lawyer, journalist, or illustrator, is not the crudeness or imperfection of his skill; rather, what he does, in contrast to his more sober nonartistic counterparts, is to intermix the headiest distillate of secondary-process functioning with primary-process elements. A Picasso is no slouch with the brush; a Kafka or a Gogol is hardly out of touch with reality—quite the contrary. The artist, like Carlos Castaneda's sorcerer, operates between worlds; the seer works in the twilight, in the crack between the two worlds (Castaneda, 1974; 1977; 1981).

Art tends to abrogate the reality principle (e.g., Figure 4.4). A novel, by definition, is fictional. ("This novel is a work of fiction. Names, characters, places and incidents are either the product of the author's imagination or are used fictitiously, and any resemblance to actual persons, living or dead, events or locales is entirely coincidental" [Harold Robbins, 1981]).

Figure 4.4. René Magritte's *Le Soir Qui Tombe*. (Private Collection.)

A standard story opening is some version of: "Once upon a time ..."

Once upon a time and a very good time it was there was a moocow coming down along the road and this moocow that was coming down along the road met a nicens little boy named baby tuckoo. . . .

His father told him that story: his father looked at him through a glass: he had a hairy face. (Joyce, 1916, p. 1)

The story is not true; it's fantasy; there are no such things as "moocows" (auditory imagery, condensation), only pedestrian cows that go "moo." And probably his father never told him that story, or not quite that way; it is Joyce who is making up a story about a story. Art is a lie—in a sense.

> As Gregor Samsa awoke one morning from uneasy dreams he found himself transformed in his bed into a gigantic insect. He was lying on his hard, as it were armor-plated, back and when he lifted his head a little he could see his dome-like brown belly divided into stiff arched segments on top on which the bed quilt could hardly keep in position and was about to slide off completely. His numerous legs, which were pitifully thin compared to the rest of his bulk, waved helplessly before his eyes.
>
> What has happened to me? he thought. It was no dream. His room, a regular human bedroom, only rather too small, lay quiet between the four familiar walls. (Kafka, 1915, p. 19)

Note the meshing of absolutely realistic details with outlandish fantasy, a dreamlike technique aptly termed *fantastic* or *magical* realism.

Figure 4.5. Jean Dubuffet's *Besognes et Moments* (1957). (Courtesy of Galleria D'Arte del Naviglio, Milan, Italy.)

The infantilism that more or less explicitly creeps into art—*child-ishness* when it misfires, *childlikeness* when it succeeds—is graphically illustrated by the painter, Dubuffet. His painting in Figure 4.5 is difficult to distinguish from an actual child's production (e.g., Figure 4.6). Unlike the child, however, the artist can move beyond the child's range without, at the same time, losing his childlike touch (e.g., Figure 4.7). The two worlds are comingled in the artist's creation.

Primitive or flawed logic is another frequent feature of art. A familiar example comes from *Alice in Wonderland,* a dreamlike story about a little girl's dream:

Tweedledee smiled gently, and began again:

"The sun was shining on the sea,
    Shining with all his might:
He did his very best to make
    The billows smooth and bright—
And this was odd, because it was
    The middle of the night.

The moon was shining sulkily,
    Because she thought the sun
Had got no business to be there
    After the day was done—
'It's very rude of him,' she said,
    'To come and spoil the fun!'

The sea was wet as wet could be,
    The sands were dry as dry.
You could not see a cloud, because
    No cloud was in the sky:
No birds were flying overhead—
    There were no birds to fly.

The Walrus and the Carpenter
    Were walking close at hand:
They wept like anything to see
    Such quantities of sand:
'If this were only cleared away,'
    They said, 'it *would* be grand! . . .

'The time has come,' the Walrus said,
    'To talk of many things:
Of shoes—and ships—and sealing-wax—
    Of cabbages—and kings—
And why the sea is boiling hot—
    And whether pigs have wings.'
        (Carroll, 1865, pp. 161–162, 164)

The abrogation of linear time is another frequent artistic device, especially in modern art. Buñuel and Dali's surrealistic movie, *Un Chien*

Figure 4.6. *Hello Kitty* (1982) by Karina (age 7).

Andalou (1929), features an orgy of time discombobulations (as well as other absurdities). This aspect is also blatant in Dali's painting, *The Persistence of Memory* (Figure 4.8).

James Joyce, in *Finnegans Wake* (1939, pp. 3, 628), bends time into a circle; the end flows into the beginning:

> riverrun, past Eve and Adam's, from swerve of shore to bend of bay, brings us by a commodius vicus of recirculation back to Howth Castle and Environs. . . .

> . . . End here. Us then. Finn, again! Take. Bussolftlhee, mememormee! Till thousendsthee. Lps. The keys to. Given! A way a lone a last a loved a long the

We associate the abrogation of time—of linear time—with primary-process functioning. Yet there is something perplexing here. Modern physics, that epitome of secondary-process thinking, seems to do it also. According to Einstein, his breakthrough began with the realization (page 170) "that time was suspect." In modern physics time not

Figure 4.7. Jean Dubuffet's *Cow* (1954). (The Museum of Modern Art, New York. The Joan and Lester Avnet Collection.)

only does not flow linearly but, at least according to some formulations, actually flows backwards (Capra, 1975; Zukav, 1979).

Plastic word representation is yet another prominent feature of art, and not just by virtue of its recourse, as in paintings, cinema, and music, to pictorial or auditory—plastic—forms; the accent falls also on *representation*. The Aldridge painting in Figure 4.9 is a pointed example. What is the painting "saying"? Is it not a polemic against the "system"—probably capitalism? (Poor innocent babies are ground up by a vicious, money-grubbing system that excretes them as gold/feces—note the fly.)

182

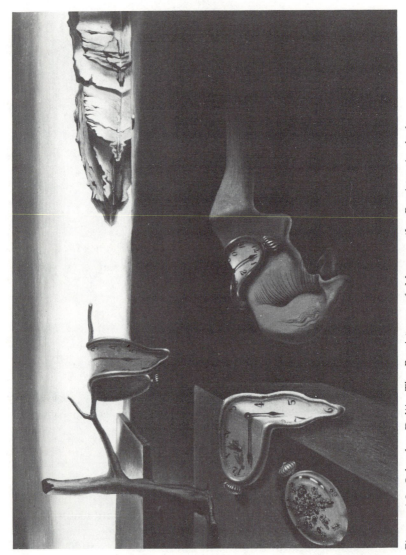

Figure 4.8. Salvador Dali's *The Persistence of Memory* (*La Persistencia de la Memoria*) (1931). (The Museum of Modern Art, New York. Given anonymously.)

Figure 4.9. (From Alan Aldridge, *The Beatles Illustrated Lyrics*, 1969, p. 69. Dell.)

Consider also the painting of the Colombian, Fernando Botero (Figure 4.10). Replete with the censorship techniques of hints and allusions, this painting, a frame of a triptych, is (probably) a blaspheming joke on the Catholic Church of Colombia. Note: A veil was used by Veronica to wipe the bloodied forehead of Christ on his way to Calvary; there is a tradition that holds that Christ's visage was miraculously impressed upon the assuaging veil; a nun is married—to Christ; marriage implies sex; sex brings to mind genitals; women, and therefore nuns, menstruate, a fact of female genitality; the apron is held in front of the nun's midsection; the miracle of the appearance of the visage of Christ (or of the Virgin) is a popular theme in Latin countries; in marriage a man and a woman become one; here, Christ's blood and the nun's blood become one; hence: Christ's visage is formed by the nun's menstrual flow.

In the same way that knowledge of one dream helps to unravel another, Botero's other paintings tend to substantiate the above interpretation. The three pillars of traditional Colombian society—the Church, the military, and the moneyed upper class—are pilloried

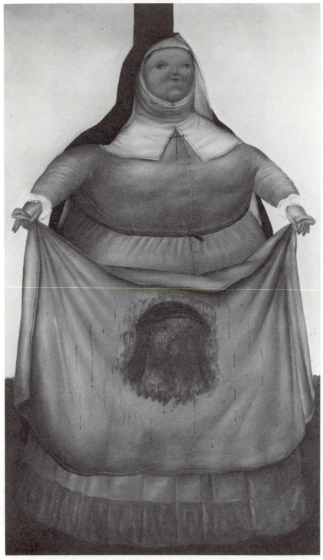

Figure 4.10. Fernando Botero's nun (left panel of *Triptico de la Pasión*, 1970). (Private Collection; photo courtesy Marlborough Gallery, N.Y. Photo by Otto E. Nelson.)

mercilessly. Observe the treatment of the soldier (allusion to the centurion at the crucifixion of Christ) which comprises another frame of the triptych (Figure 4.11). Note the plastic word insult to the soldier's manhood; in every respect he is elephantine except in the place where it counts (misplacement of accent). Note also the use to which the soldier

Figure 4.11. Fernando Botero's soldier (right panel of *Triptico de la Pasión*, 1970). (Private Collection; photo courtesy Marlborough Gallery, N.Y. Photo by Otto E. Nelson.)

puts his puny weapon (symbolism). He is no great warrior; he cuts flowers, deflowers beauty and innocence.

Probably every single dream-work process is featured, and with a vengeance, in the triptych by Hieronymous Bosch, *The Garden of Delights* (Figure 4.12). His tortured, bizarre concoction, presumably

Figure 4.12. Hieronymous Bosch's *The Garden of Delights* (right panel of triptych). (SCALA/Art Resource.)

Bosch's vision of Hell, is a comprehensive plastic word representation of the id, of primary-process thinking and primitive drives. It prefigures psychoanalysis by some four centuries. Note (Figure 4.12a) the primitively symbolized male genitalia (two ears and the knife). Next to it is a strange "organ" (the female reproductive organ?—vagina, womb, ovaries, fallopian tubes?). Gold is excrement (Figure 4.12b). Condensations and displacements are the rule rather than the exception. Perverse sexuality—oral, anal, genital—pervades these "delights"; so do sadism and masochism; birth is anal (Figure 4.12b); love is blasphemous, bestial (see the pig-nun cavorting with her human lover in the bottom right-hand corner of the main panel). To the artist, "Life is a dream" (Calderón, 1635)—often a nightmare.

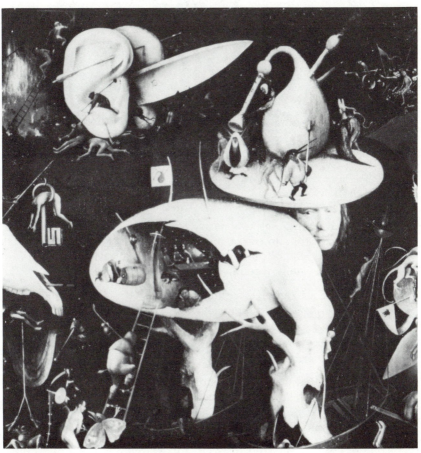

Figure 4.12a. Detail from *The Garden of Delights*. (SCALA/Art Resource.)

Figure 4.12b. Detail from *The Garden of Delights.* (SCALA/Art Resource.)

SYMPTOMS

> It might be maintained that a case of hysteria is a caricature of
> a work of art, that an obsessional neurosis is a caricature of a
> religion, and that a paranoiac delusion is a caricature of a
> philosophic system. (Freud, *Totem and Taboo,* 1913, p. 73)

Some of the art samples we have considered—Bosch's nightmare
canvas, for example—could themselves be viewed as manifestations of
insanity. We have repeatedly noted the subtle, even ambiguous, shad-
ing separating one twilight phenomenon from another. Symptoms of
psychopathology are no exception.

> He believed that he had a mission to redeem the world and to
> restore it to its lost state of bliss. This, however, he could only
> bring about if he were first transformed from a man into a
> woman. (Freud, 1911, p. 16)

The "he" being referred to is Dr. Jur. Daniel Paul Schreber, once
Senatspräsident (Presiding Judge of the Court of Appeals) in Dresden,

whose *Memoirs of My Nervous Illness* (written in an insane asylum and published in 1903) inspired Freud's classic case study, "Psychoanalytic Notes upon an Autobiographical Account of a Case of Paranoia (Dementia Paranoides)" (1911). There are some eerie affinities between Bosch's "Garden of Delights" and Schreber's "state of bliss" (quoted in Freud [1911]):

> "I should regard Professor Flechsig [Schreber's hospital psychiatrist] or his soul as my only true enemy—at a later date there was also the von W. soul, about which I shall have more to say presently—and that I should look upon God Almighty as my ally. I merely fancied that he was in great straits as regards Professor Flechsig, and consequently felt myself bound to support him by every conceivable means, even to the length of sacrificing myself. It was not until very much later that the idea forced itself upon my mind that God himself had played the part of accomplice, if not of instigator, in the plot whereby my soul was to be murdered and my body used like a strumpet. I may say, in fact, that this idea has in part become clearly conscious to me only in the course of my writing the present work."

> "Every attempt at murdering my soul, or at emasculating me for purposes *contrary to the order of things* (that is, for the gratification of the sexual appetites of a human individual), or later at destroying my understanding—every such attempt has come to nothing. From this apparently unequal struggle between one weak man and God himself, I have emerged triumphant—though not without undergoing much bitter suffering and privation—because the order of things stands upon my side." (Freud, 1911, p. 19)

Note the copious use of hints, allusions, and other censorship techniques. What specifically is meant by "purposes *contrary to the order of things*"? Who is the "human individual" for whose sexual appetites Schreber must suffer soul murder and emasculation? Note also the peculiar commingling of high-order secondary processes with crude primary-process thinking, including gross breakdowns in logic and reality testing, and hallucinatory plastic word representation.

> "Rays of God not infrequently thought themselves entitled to mock at me by calling me 'Miss Schreber,' in allusion to the emasculation which, it was alleged, I was about to undergo" (p. 127). Or they would say: "So *this* sets up to have been a Senatspräsident, this person who lets himself be f——d!" (p. 177). Or again: "Don't you feel ashamed in front of your wife?" (p. 177).... "Now, however,...I became clearly aware that the order of things imperatively demanded my

emasculation, whether I personally liked it or no, and that no *reasonable* course lay open to me but to reconcile myself to the thought of being transformed into a woman. The further consequence of my emasculation could, of course, only be my impregnation by divine rays to the end that a new race of men might be created" (p. 177). (Freud, 1911, p. 20)

It is not clear whether "f——d" constitutes censorship exercised by Schreber himself or by the *governmental* censors—important segments of Schreber's *Memoir* were expunged (e.g.: "The passage which follows is unsuitable for publication" [quoted by Freud, p. 39]).

"The *only thing* which could appear unreasonable in the eyes of other people is the fact, already touched upon in the expert's report, that I am sometimes to be found, standing before the mirror or elsewhere, with the upper portion of my body partly bared, and wearing sundry feminine adornments, such as ribbons, trumpery necklaces, and the like." (Freud, p. 21)

Later on, this transvestism becomes biological (in Schreber's delusion), and blatantly sexual:

"Something occurred in my own body similar to the conception of Jesus Christ in an immaculate virgin, that is, in a woman who had never had intercourse with a man. On two separate occasions (both while I was in Professor Flechsig's sanatorium) I have possessed female genitals, though somewhat imperfectly developed ones, and have felt a stirring in my body, such as would arise from the quickening of a human embryo. Nerves of God corresponding to male semen had, by a divine miracle, been projected into my body, and impregnation had thus taken place." (Freud, p. 32)

"... I am a woman luxuriating in voluptuous sensations (p. 281)....God demands a *constant state of enjoyment.*" (Freud, p. 34)

As in Bosch, the themes of emasculation, religion, bizarre sexuality, unnatural impregnation and birthing, and sadism course rampantly through the material, as does anal sexuality.

"Although it will necessitate my touching upon an unsavoury subject, I must devote a few more words to the question that I have just quoted ('Why don't you sh——?') on account of the typical character of the whole business. The need for evacuation, like all else that has to do with my body, is evoked miraculously. It is brought about by my faeces being forced forward (and sometimes back again) in my intestines; and if, owing to there having already been an evacuation, enough material is not present, then such small remains as there may still be of the contents of my intestines are smeared over my anal orifice. This occurrence is a miracle performed by the upper God, and it is repeated several dozens of times at the least every day. It is associated with an idea which is utterly incomprehensible to human beings and can only be accounted for by God's complete ignorance of man as a living organism. According to this idea 'sh——ing' is in a certain sense the final act; that is to say, when once the call to sh—— has been miracled up, the aim of destroying my understanding is achieved and a final withdrawal of the rays become possible. To get to the bottom of the origin of this idea, we must suppose, as it seems to me, that there is a misapprehension in connection with the symbolic meaning of the act of evacuation, a notion, in fact, that any one who has been in such a relation as I have with divine rays is to some extent entitled to sh—— upon the whole world.

"But now what follows reveals the full perfidy of the policy that has been pursued towards me. Almost every time the need for evacuation was miracled up in me, some other person in my vicinity was sent (by having his nerves stimulated for that purpose) to the lavatory, in order to prevent my evacuating. This is a phenomenon which I have observed for years and upon such countless occasions—thousands of them—and with such regularity, as to exclude any possibility of its being attributable to chance. And thereupon comes the question: 'Why don't you sh——?' to which this brilliant repartee is made on my behalf: 'Because I'm so stupid or something.' The pen well-nigh shrinks from recording so monumental a piece of absurdity as that God, blinded by his ignorance of human nature, can positively go to such lengths as to suppose that there can exist a man too stupid to do what every animal can do—too stupid to be able to sh——. When, upon the occasion of such a call, I actually succeed in evacuating—and as a rule, since I nearly always find the lavatory engaged, I use a pail for the purpose—the process is always accompanied by the generation of an exceedingly strong feeling of spiritual voluptuousness. For the relief from the pressure caused by the presence of the faeces in the intestines produces a sense of intense well-being in the nerves of voluptuousness; and the same is equally true of making water." (Freud, pp. 26–27)

A major interpretation that Freud makes of the material is that Schreber is attempting a desperate defense against the eruption of homosexual feelings. As the effort gradually unravels—at first the "order of things" stands against Schreber's emasculation and soul murder, eventually for it—this latent theme becomes progressively obvious, though never outrightly manifest. A secondary revision of the material, a "rationalization" of it (Freud, p. 49), renders the sexual events "miraculous" and, moreover, forced upon him—by Flechsig,

God, and others. Freud assumes that Schreber was in fact sexually attracted to his physician, Dr. Flechsig, but, unable to come to terms with
his own homosexuality, "projects" his sexual desires upon Flechsig.
(Freud extends this observation to paranoia in general, proposing that
the syndrome constitutes a defensive maneuver to ward off unacceptable homosexual desires.)

Freud also points out that in Schreber's mind "'Flechsig' and 'God'
were ideas belonging to the same class" (p. 49); sometimes they are literally condensed (as in, "God Flechsig"). Although the latent meaning
of "God" does not emerge clearly from the material, Freud ventures the
view that God stands for Schreber's own father, an observation that
adumbrates his conception of God in "mass delusions," that is, theistic
religions:

> We are perfectly familiar with the infantile attitude of boys
> towards their father; it is composed of the same mixture of rev-
> erent submission and mutinous insubordination that we have
> found in Schreber's relation with his God, and is the unmis-
> takable prototype of that relation, which is faithfully copied
> from it. But the circumstance that Schreber's father was a
> physician, and a most eminent physician, and one who was no
> doubt highly respected by his patients, is what explains the
> most striking characteristics of his God and those upon which
> he dwells in such a critical fashion. Could more bitter scorn be
> shown for a physician such as this than by declaring that he
> understands nothing about living men and only knows how to
> deal with corpses? No doubt it is an attribute of God to per-
> form miracles, but a physician performs miracles too, effects
> miraculous cures—or so his enthusiastic clients proclaim.
> (Freud, p. 52)

Material has since emerged that tends to corroborate Freud's inferred connection between Schreber's "God" and Schreber's father
(Niederland, 1959; 1974; Schatzman, 1963; 1973); so much so, that Freud
is taken to task (Schatzman, 1963; 1973) for resorting to interpretation
when the available data—the writings of Schreber's eminent father, Dr.
Daniel Gottlieb Moritz Schreber, founder of "therapeutic gymnastics"
in Germany—made the symbolic link, as well as the meaning of many
of Schreber's specific symptoms, obvious:

> These procedures and the following ones were part of the fa-
> ther's program to keep the bodies of children of all ages
> straight at all times: when they stood, sat, walked, played, lay
> down, or slept [e.g., Figure 4.13]. He thought that children must
> sleep in a straight position only, that on their backs; babies
> under four months must lie only on their backs when resting.
> It is important, he taught, to start with infants, since he

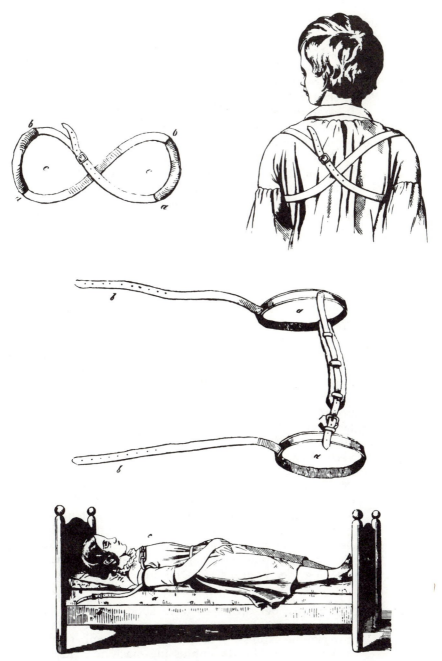

Figure 4.13. *Top panel:* A shoulder band to prevent "falling forward of the shoulders." Dr. Schreber thought it should be worn every day, all day, "until the bad habit is regulated." *Middle panel:* A belt for the sleeping child. *Bottom panel:* The belt in use. (From Schatzman, 1973, pp. 45 and 48.)

thought it harder to train older children. In his book *The Harm-ful Body Positions and Habits of Children, Including a Statement of Counteracting Measures* (1853), he presented as medical fact his false idea that if a child lies too long on one side his body on that side may be damaged, "the nutrition is impaired," the "flow of juices is impeded," the "blood stops and piles up in the vessels," and the vessels "lose a large part of their life tension" (1858, p. 12). This may lead later to paralysis of the arm and foot on that side, he said (*ibid.*, p. 54).

Son: "One of the most horrifying miracles was the so-called *compression-of-the-chest-miracle...*; it consisted in the *whole chest wall being compressed*, so that the state of oppression caused by the lack of breath was transmitted to my whole body." (*Memoirs*, p. 133)

Father: He invented a device called *Schrebersche Geradhalter* (Schreber's straight-holder) to force children to sit straight.... This was an iron crossbar fastened to the table at which the child sat to read or write. The bar pressed against the collar bones and the front of the shoulders to prevent forward movements or crooked posture. He says the child could not lean for long against the bar "because of the *pressure* of the hard object against the bones and the consequent discomfort; the child will return on his own to the straight position" (1858, p. 204). "I had a *Geradhalter* manufactured which proved its worth *time and again with my own children...*" (*ibid.*, p. 203). He says that the vertical bar which supported it was useful too since it prevented young children from crossing their legs. "Checks in blood flow and other delicate reasons" make sitting with legs crossed "particularly wrong for youthful persons" (p. 201)....He also fastened a belt with ring-shaped shoulder straps to the child's bed. It ran across *the child's chest* to ensure that the child's body remained supine and straight when sleeping [see Figure 4.13]. The aim was to prevent "turning and tossing to either side."

Son: "This was perhaps the most abominable of all miracles—next to the compression-of-the-chest-miracle; the expression used for it if I remember correctly was 'the head-compressing-machine.' [*Kopf-zusammenschnürungsmaschine*: literally, the head-together-tying machine]....The 'little devils'...*compressed my head as though in a vice* [sic] by turning a kind of screw, causing my head temporarily to assume an elongated almost pear-shaped form. It had an extremely threatening effect, particularly as it was accompanied by severe pain. The screws were loosened temporarily but only very gradually, so that the *compressed state usually continued for some time.*" (*Memoirs*, p. 138)

"I suffer from almost uninterrupted headaches of a kind certainly unknown to other human beings, and hardly comparable to ordinary headaches. They are *tearing* and pulling pains." (*Ibid.*, p. 201)

Father: He invented a *Kopfhalter* (head-holder) to prevent the child's head from falling forward or sideways. The *Kopfhalter* was a strap clamped at one end to the child's hair and at the other to his underwear so that it *pulled* his hair if he did not hold his head straight [see Figure 4.14]. It served as a "reminder" to keep the head straight: "The consciousness that the head cannot lean forward past a certain point soon becomes a habit." "This instrument can similarly be used against a sideways posture of the head." He admits it was apt to produce "*a certain stiffening effect* on the head" and should therefore be used only one or two hours a day (1858, pp. 198–199).

He also had a chin band made, which was held to the head by a helmetlike device [Figure 4.14]. This was to ensure proper growth of the jaw and teeth (*ibid.*, pp. 219–220).

Son: "Every word spoken near or with me, every human action however small which is combined with some noise, for instance opening the door-locks on my corridor, pressing the latch on the door of my room, ... etc., is accompanied by a painful blow directed at my head; the sensation of pain is like a sudden *pulling* inside my head which calls forth a very unpleasant feeling ... and may be combined with the tearing off of part of the bony substance of my skull—at least that is how it feels." (*Memoirs*, p. 164)

Possibly upon hearing a sound he turned his head toward its source and reexperienced or remembered the pulling of the *Kopfhalter* when he had turned his head as a child.

These comparisons show uncanny similarities. It is as if the father taught his son a language of sensory stimuli by which to experience parts of his own body.

Niederland wonders if Schreber's experiences of having

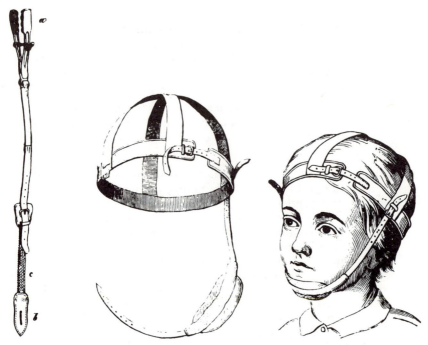

Figure 4.14. Dr. Schreber's *Kopfhalter* and chin band. (From Schatzman, 1973, p. 50.)

been tied and strapped by the father into orthopedic apparatus are the origin of the "divine miracles" of "being tied-to-earth" and "fastened-to-rays."

> God is inseparably tied to my person through my nerves' power of attraction which for some time past has been inescapable; there is no possibility of God freeing Himself from my nerves for the rest of my life—(*Ibid.*, p. 209)

The son thinks the "miracles" are enacted upon objective anatomical organs of his body. He does not see that he is reenacting his father's behavior toward his body.

Schreber suffers from reminiscences. His body embodies his past. He retains memories of what his father did to him as a child; although part of his mind knows they are memories, "he" does not. (Schatzman, 1973, pp. 44–52)

Schatzman takes Freud and others to task for ignoring the evidence: "Irony is everywhere. An eminent pedagogue has a psychotic son [his other son commits suicide]; it does not hurt his reputation. Freud, an avid reader, neglects books on child-rearing—as do his followers—by a man whose son's childhood experiences he tries to derive. German parents rear their children by the ideas of a man whom many people now would consider sadistic and mentally ill" (Schatzman, 1973, p. 11). Nevertheless, Schatzman ends up by rediscovering Freud's insight of 1895 in *Studies on Hysteria*: The patient "suffers from reminiscences." Symptoms are a form of "remembering without awareness" (Jacoby and Witherspoon, 1982; see footnote 2 of Chapter 1).

We have focused in this section upon a single case history so that we might achieve a modicum of depth in our coverage. It should be understood clearly, however, that the principles elaborated—the dream-work-like aspect of symptom formation—apply to other types of symptomatologies than paranoia, from the more moderate psychopathologies such as hysteria to the so-called psychopathologies of everyday life, the parapraxes (see Chapter 1). Because of the inevitable complexity of any psychopathological material, it is not possible to provide a wide sampling of such cases. It is left to the reader to discover for himself in other materials (for example, the case of the obsessive-compulsive "Rat Man" [Freud, 1909]) the pervasive play of dream-work techniques in the formation of symptoms.

RELIGION

> The whole thing is so patently infantile, so foreign to reality, that to anyone with a friendly attitude to humanity it is pitiful to think that the great majority of mortals will never be able to rise above this view of life. (Freud, 1930, p. 74)

The Schreber case history substantially foreshadows Freud's conception of religion (Freud, 1913; 1927a; 1930). For Freud, the difference between a paranoid delusion such as Schreber's and a religious system lies chiefly in the fact that one constitutes a private delusion, the other a "mass delusion" (Freud, 1930, p. 85). A critical feature of both is the fundamental breakdown of logic and reality testing.

Consider the Apostles' Creed, a basic confession of faith of Christians:

> I believe in God the Father Almighty, Maker of Heaven and earth; and in Jesus Christ His only Son, Our Lord; who was conceived by the Holy Ghost; born of the Virgin Mary; suffered under Pontius Pilate; was crucified; dead and buried; He descended into Hell; the third day He rose again from the dead; He ascended into Heaven; and sitteth on the right hand of God the Father Almighty; from thence He shall come to

judge the quick and the dead. I believe in the Holy Ghost; the Holy Catholic Church; the Communion of Saints; the forgiveness of sins; the resurrection of the Body; and the life everlasting.

Amen

The beliefs expressed may be altogether genuine, but the facts asserted, one after the other, fly in the face of common sense, logic, or verifiable reality. This, actually, is openly acknowledged. Tertullian, an early Church father, is known (and several times quoted by Freud) for his dictum, *Credo quia absurdum* (I believe because it is absurd): Religious faith transcends logic or pedestrian reality; it belongs to a higher plane. But, then, what makes Schreber's delusional system, hardly lacking in the element of the absurd, any less valid than that of the Christian (or of the Moslem, Jew, or Hindu)?

According to Freud, religious faiths constitute a broad-front regression to infantilism. This regression is neither playful nor voluntary as in the case of jokes and art, nor transitory as in dreams. It is, rather, a defensive retreat forced by the intolerability of one's helplessness in the world and, ultimately, by the unmastered terror of one's own death. To cope with his predicament, the believer redintegrates an analogous epoch of his own earlier life when, as a helpless child, he looked to his parents, especially to the powerful father (in patriarchal societies), for protection and sustenance. The believer thus recreates the protected but dependent stance of a child toward his father. The adult becomes a child (observe, for example, the person in prayer). The omnipotent father, however, is no longer the real father, who has long since been unmasked of his illusory omnipotence; the "father" now is truly omnipotent, the "Almighty, Maker of Heaven and earth." Yet the believer still treats him as a child might his father. In the Lord's Prayer we witness a well-known ploy—butter up the old man, then ask him for what you want:

Our Father who art in Heaven, hallowed be thy name; thy Kingdom come, thy will be done, on earth as it is in Heaven.
—Give us this day our daily bread. . . .

The Father is not only a provider but also a source of dread punishment. This is illustrated by the religious tract on Hell (Figure 4.15) which, though it denies it, demonstrates religion's tendency to coerce faith not only by promises but by threats.

Like jokes, art, and symptoms, religion is dreamlike. Censorship techniques are in abundant evidence. For many centuries the entire Bible was withheld by the Catholic Church from public access, sometimes on pain of death, lest it lead to faulty interpretation by the laity

Our Lord spoke of "hell ... the fire that never shall be quenched" (Mark 9:42–48) When He did so He was warning of stark and horrible reality. He was no waster of words; *hell is real!*

Neither Christ nor His ministers speak of hell in order to frighten people into religion. They speak of it because it is a fact. Just as a sensible father warns his child not to touch the stove because it will burn him, even so true preachers earnestly warn people to avoid hell because it burns—everlastingly. In each case the fear of harm is intelligently and reasonably used to encourage godly behavior.

Never did Christ, nor do His ministers, stoop to the use of any dishonest alarms to turn men to righteousness. When Jesus warned of hell we know He was not deceiving His hearers. He was speaking of reality . . . .

Figure 4.15. Tract on Hell distributed in a New York City subway. (Courtesy, Evangelical Tract Distributors, Edmonton, Alberta.)

(or, according to Protestants, to perception of the discrepancy between Church practices and Biblical teachings). On a less sweeping scale, we have in the doctrine of the Virgin Birth a blatant denial of Mary's sexuality (analogous to a child's disgust with and denial of the idea of his parent's sexuality). The extent of this denial varies somewhat among Christian sects. Most Protestants, for example, believe in the Virgin Birth of Christ but do not deny Mary's subsequent sexual activity, which resulted in the birth of Christ's two brothers, James and Jude. Catholics, on the other hand, deny Mary's sexuality altogether—she remains the Virgin Mary—and do not regard Jude and James to be the literal, that is, biological, brothers of Christ. The Bible's Song of Songs, a soaring poem of love, is sufficiently couched in hints and allusions to allow disagreements about its true (latent) theme—sexual passion or religious rapture.

Symbols, of course, pervade religious systems: the host in Christianity; the parables in the Old and New Testaments; the esoterica of the cabala in Judaism; the T'ai-chi T'u or yin-yang symbol—the "Diagram of the Supreme Ultimate"—of the Taoists and Buddhists (which embodies some of the elements of the Freudian id-ego contraposition, on a cosmic plane):

Plastic-word representation is also rife. Christ himself is often conceived of as the plastic realization—the living embodiment—of an overly abstract, unreachable God. Although there is tension about their propriety, in view of the commandment against graven images, many Christian sects—Catholic, Eastern Orthodox, High Episcopalian—are redolent with statues and icons. In the same vein, the often elaborate ceremonies of religions (which Freud compares to the rituals of obsessive-compulsive neurotics) are symbolic "dramatizations" of latent meanings.

Displacements and condensations are also abundant and obvious. Christ is man-God; God is a Father-Son-Holy Ghost trinity. The act of conception is displaced from Joseph onto the Holy Ghost. Our sins—and their punishments—are displaced upon Christ (as they had been by the ancient Jews upon the "scapegoat").

Finally, secondary revision can be found ubiquitously. Christ (the man-God) is crucified and dies, an impossible ending for an eternal God. His death, however, is revised to be only temporary: On the third day he arises from the dead, and so forth.

Similar defensive elaborations are to be found in the Old Testament. Ecclesiastes, a work of elemental despair, which runs against the grain of conventional religious attitudes, is overlaid by elaborations and revisions of later religious writers that tend to soften or distort the thrust of the original. Here is an extended excerpt (a shorter one might not provide sufficient context) portraying the original theme:

The words of the Preacher, the son of David, king in Jerusalem.

2 Vanity of vanities, saith the Preacher, vanity of vanities; all *is* vanity.

3 What profit hath a man of all his labour which he taketh under the sun?

4 *One* generation passeth away, and *another* generation cometh: but the earth abideth for ever.

5 The sun also ariseth, and the sun goeth down, and hasteth to his place where he arose.

6 The wind goeth toward the south, and turneth about unto the north; it whirleth about continually, and the wind returneth again according to his circuits.

7 All the rivers run into the sea; yet the sea *is* not full; unto the place from whence the rivers come, thither they return again.

8 All things *are* full of labour; man cannot utter *it*: the eye is not satisfied with seeing, nor the ear filled with hearing.

9 The thing that hath been, it *is that* which shall be; and that which is done *is* that which shall be done; and *there is* no new *thing* under the sun.

10 Is there *any* thing whereof it may be said, See, this *is* new? it hath been already of old time, which was before us.

11 *There is* no remembrance of former *things*; neither shall there be *any* remembrance of *things* that are to come with *those* that shall come after.

12 ¶I the Preacher was king over Israel in Jerusalem.

13 And I gave my heart to seek and search out by wisdom concerning all *things* that are done under heaven: this sore travail hath God given to the sons of man to be exercised therewith.

14 I have seen all the works that are done under the sun; and, behold, all *is* vanity and vexation of spirit.

15 *That which is* crooked cannot be made straight: and that which is wanting cannot be numbered.

16 I communed with mine own heart, saying, Lo, I am come to great estate, and have gotten more wisdom than all *they* that have been before me in Jerusalem:

> yea, my heart had great experience of wisdom and knowledge.
>
> 17 And I gave my heart to know wisdom, and to know madness and folly: I perceived that this also is vexation of spirit.
>
> 18 For in much wisdom *is* much grief: and he that increaseth knowledge increaseth sorrow. (Eccles. 1:1–18)

> 19 For that which befalleth the sons of men befalleth beasts; even one thing befalleth them: as the one dieth, so dieth the other; yea, they have all one breath; so that a man hath no preeminence above a beast: for all *is* vanity.
>
> 20 All go unto one place; all are of the dust, and all turn to dust again.
>
> 21 Who knoweth the spirit of man that goeth upward, and the spirit of the beast that goeth downward to the earth? (Eccles. 3:19–21)

> So I returned, and considered all the oppressions that are done under the sun: and behold the tears of *such as were* oppressed, and they had no comforter; and on the side of their oppressors *there was* power; but they had no comforter.
>
> 2 Wherefore I praised the dead which are already dead more than the living which are yet alive.
>
> 3 Yea, better is *he* than both they, which hath not yet been, who hath not seen the evil work that is done under the sun. (Eccles. 4:1–3)

But now consider the ending of Ecclesiastes, which is a revisionary graft. The theme is turned inside out; the style, even in translation, is discernably altered. From this concluding section, tacked on at a later period, one gains the impression that the preacher had been delivering some innocuous Poloniads which, moreover, one should not trouble oneself with unduly:

> 8 ¶Vanity of vanities, saith the preacher; all *is* vanity.
>
> 9 And moreover, because the preacher was wise, he still taught the people knowledge; yea, he gave good heed, and sought out, *and* set in order many proverbs.
>
> 10 The preacher sought to find out acceptable words: and *that which was* written *was* upright, *even* words of truth.
>
> 11 The words of the wise *are* as goads, and as nails fastened *by* the masters of assemblies, *which* are given from one shepherd.

12 And further, by these, my son, be admonished: of making many books *there is* no end; and much study *is* a
weariness of the flesh.

13 ¶Let us hear the conclusion of the whole matter: Fear
God, and keep his commandments: for this *is* the
whole *duty* of man.

14 For God shall bring every work into judgment, with
every secret thing, whether *it be* good, or whether *it be*
evil. (Eccles. 12:8–14)

The secondary revision, which brings to mind the altered Watergate transcripts (pages 159–160), works effectively. The average
reader does not realize that the text had been tampered with and carries
away a distorted understanding of the thrust of Ecclesiastes. Even so, Ecclesiastes came close to being expunged outright from the Bible:

Had it not been for these pious revisions, and the tradition that
Solomon had written the book, it is doubtful it would have
found its way into the Old Testament canon. In fact, Ecclesiastes was one of the three books [Song of Songs and Esther being
the other two] whose right to be included in the Bible was
seriously questioned by the rabbis at the Council of Jamnia in
about A.D. 90. A favorable decision was rendered at that time,
but a strong minority vote of disapproval was expressed. (Anderson, 1957, p. 478)

The book of Job provides another clear-cut example. It features
three spokesmen, Eliphaz, Bildad, and Zophar, for traditional religious
values: If you do good God will reward you; if you do bad He will
punish you. These three argue against Job's rebellion against God's justice. Job was decidedly *not* patient; that he is known for his patience
(e.g., James 5:11) is but one more example of the revisionistic tendency
of memory. Presumably Job *should have been* patient and should not
have dared to challenge God. But God does not agree. At the end God
chastises the spokesmen for orthodoxy and sides with Job: "The Lord
said to Eliphaz the Temanite, My wrath is kindled against thee, and
against thy two friends: for ye have not spoken of me the thing that is
right, as my servant Job hath" (Job 42:7).

Traditional elements later superimposed a fourth character, Elihu
(Chapters 32–37), "to speak on God's behalf" and against Job ("because
he justified himself rather than God"). Elihu, however, merely regurgi-
tates the stance of the three mouthpieces of conventional doctrine
whom God had discredited.

Every chapter of the Old Testament is overdetermined, the product
of political and theological conflict. Not surprisingly, it is a psychodynamic, dreamlike creation.

Religion is regressive and dreamlike not only in cognitive style but in content as well. Although it is moralistic (like the super-ego) about primitive drives, it also (like the super-ego) gives vent—in rationalized form—to the sanguinary propensities of human nature. Figures 4.16 and 4.17 provide two modern-day examples of Islamic justice, administered "In the name of Allah, the Beneficent, the Merciful."

In these punishments, the Koran is only echoing Old Testament commandments, for example, "And the man that committeth adultery with another man's wife, even he that committeth adultery with his neighbor's wife, the adulterer and the adulteress shall surely be put to death" (Lev. 20:10).

This reversion to practices from several thousands of years ago is not without conflict, as can be sensed from some of the hesitations and evasions mentioned in these reports; moreover, the regression is not untrammelled. Probably no modern-day Islamic, Jewish, or Christian religious body would enforce the following Mosaic precedent:

> 32 And while the children of Israel were in the wilderness, they found a man gathering sticks upon the sabbath day.
> 33 And they that found him gathering sticks brought him unto Moses and Aaron, and unto all the congregation.
> 34 And they put him in ward, because it was not declared what should be done to him.
> 35 And the Lord said unto Moses, The man shall be surely put to death: all the congregation shall stone him with stones without the camp.
> 36 And all the congregation brought him without the camp, and stoned him with stones, and he died; as the Lord commanded Moses. (Num. 15:32–36)

Thus far we have touched on only the three main branches of Western religion: Judaism, Christianity, Islam. What of the major Eastern religious systems, such as Hinduism, Buddhism, Taoism? Do they fit into the Freudian scheme? Freud does not say; except for a few glancing references to Yoga, he is silent on these religions.

Psychological common points, especially in vulgate versions of these systems, are not difficult to discern. The Hindu-Buddhist doctrine of reincarnation does away with the permanence of death; *karma,* as popularly understood, is the counterpart of the Orthodox Judaic view of God's justice: Good karma results in a better life after death (a beggar might be reborn a prince), bad karma in a worse life (he might return as a dog). In popular practice, Hindu, Buddhist, and Taoist precepts tend to degenerate into superstitious rituals and magic, designed to bring

Four in Iran Executed by Stoning

By Reuters

TEHERAN, Iran, July 3—Four Iranians convicted of sexual offenses were buried up to their chests today and stoned to death, with the presiding judge of a revolutionary court casting the first stone.

The executions, the first in memory to have been carried out in Iran under the old traditions of Islam, took place in the southern town of Kerman. A court official, reached by telephone, said it took the condemned prisoners—two men and two women—15 minutes to die.

7 Executed by Firing Squad

The official Pars press agency said the revolutionary court had convicted the women of prostitution and of deceiving young girls, one man of homosexuality and adultery and the other of raping a 10-year-old girl. Stones ranging in size from walnuts to apples had been gathered for the executions, and five people joined in hurling them at each of the condemned.

The court official said that the two women, both about 50 years old and married, had been involved in prostitution for 20 years with one of the men. According to the Teheran radio, he was a worker with six children. The other man was said to be a married farmer of about 22.

Meanwhile, seven more prisoners were sent to firing squads in various parts of Iran for drug trafficking, sex offenses and murder. Two people each received 80 lashes in the Caspian Sea port of Resht for the consumption and sale of alcohol.

These developments followed new calls by Ayatollah Rubollah Khomeini for the Iranian people to practice Islam. . . .

The revival of the ancient Islamic execution by stoning, a traditional punishment for adultery and gross sexual crimes that has fallen out of use, was described by the Kerman court official as not necessarily connected with Ayatollah Khomeini's demands for greater Islamization.

Following the Laws of Islam

But when asked why that form of execution had not previously been imposed by Iranian revolutionary courts, he said, "Perhaps it's because they haven't been following the proper laws of Islam."

Describing the preparations for what he called the "ceremony" of execution, the official said leading local Islamic clergymen were invited to visit the condemned yesterday, and the prisoners were washed and clothed in white garments that completely enveloped their bodies.

The prisoners were also masked in ceremonial "hoods of the dead," the official went on, before they were buried up to their chests and stoned. When they were dead, prayers were said, and they were buried.

Figure 4.16. (*The New York Times,* July 4, 1980, p. 1.)

good fortune, long life, enhanced sexual prowess, and so forth; sectarian disputes, as in Islam, Judaism, and Christianity, have not failed to materialize and lead to bloodshed.

Pakistan's Grim Islamic Law Is Not Just a Threat

Special to The New York Times

KARACHI, Pakistan—An 18-year-old high school student and the 24-year-old school bus driver with whom she eloped were ordered recently to be flogged and then stoned to death for adultery.

It was the first such sentence passed by a religious court here since Pakistan adopted traditional punishments for violations of Koranic law more than three years ago.

The ruling, announced here Sept. 1, is the most dramatic example of the Government-sponsored attempt to foster standards of probity and private behavior that are defined as Islamic.

Most of these efforts center on relations between men and women, and in the last month they have involved decisions to limit or ban female models on television and the cancellation of a foreign trip by a women's field hockey

United Press International

A Pakistani being lashed in public two years ago after he was found guilty of "committing immoral acts" in Rawalpindi. Floggings are now administered out of public view.

Figure 4.17. (*The New York Times*, September 17, 1981, p. A2. U.P.I. Photo Library.)

team on the ground that there would be male spectators watching the games. Meanwhile, Government organizations are considering a national standard of dress.

Punishment Still in Doubt

Whether the young couple here will actually undergo the punishment ordered by the sharia, or religious court, remains in doubt, and like so many of the rulings involving women's rights, the matter is likely to arouse some controversy.

Since the Islamic punishments gained Government sanction, none of the harsher penalties has yet been imposed. A few convicted thieves have been sentenced to have their hands cut off but no amputations have been carried out. In fact, as the sentence hangs over the convicts, Government-financed religious councils remain divided over such technical and sectarian issues as how much of the hand should be severed, should the operation be surgically administered and should the event be televised.

Floggings for such offenses as drinking alcoholic beverages, pimping or frequenting brothels are carried out routinely, however. After the outcry abroad that accompanied the imposition of the initial lashings, these are now administered out of public view in prison compounds....

Nevertheless, clear-cut differences are evident. The element of the "father complex," so much emphasized by Freud, tends to be absent in these religions; if anything, there is a propensity toward a "mother complex," for example:

Lazily, I drift
As though I had no home
All others have enough to spare;
I am the one left out.
I have the mind of a fool.
Muddled and confused!
When common people scintillate
I alone make shadows.
Vulgar folks are sharp and knowing:
Only I am melancholy.
Restless like the ocean,
Blown about, I cannot stop.
Other men can find employment,
But I am stubborn; I am mean.
Alone I am different
Because I prize and seek
My sustenance from the Mother! (*Tao Tê Ching*, Poem 20)

The point, however, is not the adoration of a mother figure but the exaltation of the feminine (yin) principle—the soft, intuitive, unobtrusive aspect of our psychological make-up:

The great land is the place
To which the streams descend;

It is the concourse and
The female of the world:
Quiescent, underneath
It overcomes the male. (*Tao Tê Ching*, Poem 61)

The passionate savagery of the male-oriented Old Testament ("God is a warrior") is markedly absent from these poems, and in this respect they diverge from Freud's model of religion. Nevertheless, primary-process thinking, sometimes of the most eccentric kind, abounds in these systems, particularly in Taoism and Zen Buddhism. (The presence of primary-process thinking in the absence of primitive drives brings to mind Freud's distinction between innocent and tendentious jokes.)

The Zen Master Mumon was said to have pondered for six years on the koan of Mu (Q. Does a dog have Buddha nature? A. Mu, that is, void, no-thing, nothing, nonexistence, no). Upon suddenly reaching enlightenment, he composed the following poem:

Mu! Mu! Mu! Mu! Mu!
Mu! Mu! Mu! Mu! Mu!
Mu! Mu! Mu! Mu! Mu!
Mu! Mu! Mu! Mu! Mu!

Is this a joke? Schizophrenic word salad? Religious enlightenment? Twelfth-century Chinese Dada? (cf. Schrafstein, 1975). Whatever it is, it is hardly atypical. Here is another sample of Zen "discourse":

A monk asked Kan (Chien), who lived in Haryo (Pa-ling), "Is there any difference between the teaching of the Patriarch and that of the Sūtras, or not?" Said the master, "When the cold weather comes, the fowl flies up in the trees, while the wild duck goes down into water." Ho-yen (Fa-yen) of Gosozan (Wu-tsu-shan) commented on this, saying: "The great teacher of Pa-ling has expressed only a half of the truth. I would not have it so. Mine is: When water is scooped in hands, the moon is reflected in them; when the flowers are handled, the scent soaks into the robe." (Suzuki, 1949, p. 117)

At a superficial (manifest) level, the material is sheer gibberish, as woolly as a dream or psychotic production might be. Nevertheless, it too has meaning; at a deeper (latent) level, it conveys an epistemological stance, an extremist attitude toward the language problem raised in Chapter 3: Words are crazy; words, logic, concepts, are not the stuff of enlightenment; the monk's question to Kan, with its subliminal presuppositions about the power of reason, are as absurd to the Master as the Master's answer is to the novice. Mumon's poem is understood in the same vein. Mumon is not replying to the question manifestly posed by the koan (*mu* can mean *no* or *nothing*, that is, a dog has no Buddha nature, nothing; or *mu* can mean *no-thing, void,* that is, the essence of Buddha nature). Rather, Mumon's egregious absurdism points to the absurdism—according to Zen—to which the armamentarium of rationality—words, symbols, images, logic, concepts—willy-nilly lead.

As eccentric and extreme as this religious stance appears, it does not fit the Freudian model of religion and tends, therefore, to delimit it. Wise or misguided, it does not constitute an involuntary regression, as in dreams and psychosis, but a voluntary regression, as in jokes and art—and psychoanalysis. Indeed, the Zen master brings to mind the oft-made claim of psychoanalysts that intellectual insight is paltry; that psychoanalysis as therapy can be comprehended only experientially, in the living medium of the transference relation; that, in short, psychoanalysis can truly be understood only in psychoanalysis.

In summary: Freud regards religion as an infantile mode of coping with the harshness of nature, especially the inevitability of death. It is not, in his view, voluntary or playful (like art) or transitory (like dreams) but a harmful, often brutalizing psychological "narcotic" (Freud, 1927a) by which the believer permanently denies aspects of reality (like the neurotic or psychotic) and, by so doing, relinquishes the possibility of confronting reality in an adult way. Religions, as conceived and practiced popularly, exhibit regressive cognitive functioning, especially the abrogation of the reality principle. However, many religious systems, notably those from the East, do not feature the "father complex" posited by Freud, and in some cases (such as Zen) enlist regression voluntarily and with sophisticated intent.

CHAPTER FIVE

PSYCHODYNAMICS AND DEFENSE

♦

Psychodynamics
Repression (Defense Processes)
• *Meaning and Evolution of the Repression/Defense Concept*
• *Repression (in the Narrow Sense): Suppression, Censorship,*
Denial, and Isolation
• *Theoretical Conceptualizations of Repression: Sociopolitical,*
Neobehavioristic, and Information-Processing
• *The Empirical Evidence for Repression*
• *Displacement and Sublimation*
• *Projection*
• *Reaction Formation*
• *Rationalization*
• *Symbolization*
• *Conclusion*

PSYCHODYNAMICS

Psychodynamics (or *dynamics*) is one of the most bandied-about terms in the psychoanalytic literature. Yet it is rarely defined. It bears an obvious relation to the concept of repression or defense (for example, "the dynamic unconscious") yet the precise nature of the link tends to be unspecified. Because of its association with notions such as drive, force, energy, conflict, it is often treated as a synonym for *motivation* and contraposed with *cognition*; yet the relationship between psychodynamics and modern cognitive psychology is uncharted.

In this section an attempt is made to address these issues.

To begin with, we should note that *psychodynamics* is the psychological counterpart of the notion of dynamics in the physical sciences (though what that notion has ultimately come to signify in modern physics is not a clear-cut matter, as will be seen).

Here is a textbook definition of dynamics from around the turn of the century, before the advent of relativity theory and quantum mechanics:

> Dynamics is the science which treats of the action of force on bodies.
>
> When a body is acted on by one or more forces, their effect is either (1) to compel rest or prevent motion, or (2) to produce or change motion.
>
> Dynamics is therefore conveniently divided into two portions, *statics* and *kinetics*.
>
> In statics the subject of the equilibrium, or balancing, of forces is considered; in kinetics is discussed the action of forces producing or changing motion. (Loney, 1904, p. 1)

The above definition is essentially the Newtonian conception of "dynamics," which finds elaboration in a variety of subfields of physics, for example:

> *aerodynamics:* the branch of physics that deals with the forces (resistance, pressure, etc.) exerted by air or other gases in motion
>
> *electrodynamics:* the branch of physics dealing with the phenomenon of electric currents and associated magnetic forces
>
> *thermodynamics:* the science that deals with the relationship of heat and mechanical energy and the conversion of one into the other (*Webster's New World Dictionary*, 1955)

Compare these definitions with Freud's characterization of psychoanalysis:

You can perceive from these examples [of parapraxes] what the aim of our psychology is. Our purpose is not merely to describe and classify the phenomena, but to conceive of them as brought about by the play of forces in the mind, as expressions of tendencies striving toward a goal, which work together or against one another. We are endeavoring to attain a *dynamic conception* of mental phenomena. In this conception, the trends we merely infer are more prominent than the phenomena we perceive. (Freud, 1917, p. 60)

Psychodynamics, then, is concerned with "the play of forces in the mind" (Freud, above), with their "interaction and counteraction" (Fenichel, 1945, p. 11).

We saw in Chapter 1 (pages 10–11) that such a dynamic viewpoint was inherent in Freud's earliest writings. Intensive notions that implied a direction (such as, drive, motive, will, and so forth) could be thought of in force-vector terms. Thus, a "cathexis" (*Besetzung*) is a quantity of directed psychic energy or excitation. (Note: The merely intensive aspect of mental phenomena, irrespective of direction or interaction, is termed the "economic" viewpoint in psychoanalysis. It is a "scalar" notion rather than a "vector" notion.)

The idea of *conflict* flows naturally from this framework; conflict is the result of forces working at cross-purposes.

Repression or *defense* is only a special variant of conflict (and, therefore, of psychodynamics). Gratification or consciousness of some emergent wish, impulse, memory, drive, or idea—note the admixture of motivational and cognitive terms—is opposed by a counterforce, repression:

Thus, the "dynamic unconscious" (in the strong sense) is the part of the unconscious that is excluded from consciousness by "living forces," that is, repression.

The question inevitably arises: Are we to understand that forces or energies literally exist in the mind, or are these importations from physics into psychology only representational expedients, or metaphors?

The question, which bears on the scientific status of the construct, is best approached by first raising another question: Is the concept of force taken literally in physics itself? To begin with, it should be noted that the concept of force underwent a significant elaboration in the nineteenth century as a result of Faraday's research on electromagnetic phenomena. The concept of force was replaced by the subtler notion of the "force field" (which Maxwell later formalized in his "field equations"). Faraday believed, though not without misgivings, in the literal existence or substantiality of force fields (Maxwell, less so), but there was already something decidedly strange about them. They no longer involved the force exerted by one particle or "body" upon another. Rather, the bodies themselves were part of the field, comprising the points of maximal density of the "force field lines" (that is, their points of convergence). Thus, the distinction between matter and field was abrogated in Faraday's theory; the field—whatever that is—became the ultimate reality and could be studied as a system in its own right, without reference to material bodies (Berkson, 1974; Capra, 1975; Davies, 1979; Einstein and Infeld, 1938; Hesse, 1961; Zukav, 1979). Gradually, the "reality" of the force field lost its literal connotation: "The mechanical models are no longer thought of as literal descriptions of entities existing in nature, but only as interpretations, in terms of mechanical devices, of phenomena that are described mathematically but whose ultimate nature cannot be regarded as crudely mechanical" (Hesse, 1961, p. 206).

Gestalt psychology (e.g., Wolfgang Köhler's [1940] *Dynamics in Psychology*) made an explicit attempt to apply Faraday's force field concept to perception and memory. In shifting from the simple force notion to the force field analog, Gestalt psychology revealed the full compatibility (and, perhaps, indistinguishability) of the dynamic viewpoint and cognitive psychology. The theoretical effort proved premature, however, and eventually foundered, in part because of the literalization of the force field metaphor. Attempts to demonstrate experimentally the literal existence of physiological force fields were, not surprisingly, unsuccessful.

In the meantime, the force field notion in physics had evolved into an even more recondite abstraction. Its synthesis with quantum mechanics gave rise to "quantum field theories":

The apparent contradiction between the particle and the wave picture [of light] was solved in a completely unexpected way which called in question the very foundation of the mechanistic world view—the concept of the reality of matter. At the subatomic level, matter does not exist with certainty at definite places, but rather shows "tendencies to exist." ... Quantum theory has thus demolished the classical concepts of solid object and the strictly deterministic laws of nature. At the subatomic level, the solid material objects of classical physics dissolve into wavelike patterns of probabilities, and these patterns, ultimately, do not represent probabilities of things, but rather probabilities of interconnections. . . ." (Capra, 1975, pp. 56–57)

> In . . . "quantum field theories," the classical contrast between the solid particles and the space surrounding them is completely overcome. The quantum field is seen as the fundamental physical entity: a continuous medium which is present everywhere in space. Particles are merely local condensations of the field, concentrations of energy which come and go, thereby losing their individual character and dissolving into the underlying field. (Capra, pp. 196–197)

By this point, it would be difficult to literalize the notion of force; the term, in fact, has by and large dropped out of use in modern physics.

> The concept of force is . . . no longer useful in subatomic physics. It is a classical concept which we associate (even if only subconsciously) with the Newtonian idea of a force being felt over a distance. In the subatomic world there are no such forces, but only interactions between particles, mediated through fields. . . . Hence physicists prefer to speak about interactions, rather than about forces. (Capra, p. 203)

There is some irony in the evolution of the force concept in physics, for it suggests that what we originally were inclined to think of as an importation into psychology from physics was, on the contrary, a psychological metaphor all the time (cf. R. S. Jones, 1982; Leary, 1983; Manuel, 1968):

> As Frank Manuel (1968) has pointed out, Newton originally thought of gravity or attraction as "sociability" (p. 68). The fact that masses of matter tend to move towards one another in the absence of any detectable mechanical force found its analog, in the development of Newton's thought, in the attraction of human persons toward one another.
> Later, of course, Newton referred to "gravity," not "sociability," on the assumption that the former was a more neutral term, despite its mechanistic connotations. Gravity was simply a word that stood for a mathematically describable phenomenon. (Leary, 1983, p. 11)

The reason that the term *force* drops out of quantum field theories is that the interactions that it deals with have no psychological counterpart, and consequently the term would be descriptively superfluous. The crucial aspect of field theories is that they describe in some mathematical formalism certain interactive aspects of events. This, of course, is also the basis of classical mechanics. The formula for gravitational force is valid in so far as it predicts certain types of physical interactions, irrespective of what we call these interactions. That it makes sense to label these interactions *forces* is a psychological artifact: The interactions that the formalism describes (unlike those of quantum field theories) happen to be *subjectively experienced* by the physicist.

Thus, force is ultimately a psychological concept. The literalization problem arises not when we employ the notion of force in psychology but when we extrapolate *physics' operationalizations* of force onto the psychological domain: "Force" in psychology is not *mass* times *acceleration; Fields of Force* (the title of a recent chess book on the Fischer-Spassky games) are not described by Maxwell's field equations, even though they may involve quite specific interactions and probabilities of interactions.

In sum, the most general meaning of *dynamics* in psychology, as in physics, is *interaction*. The specific metaphor system through which interactions of interest are articulated can vary (as in physics) from one problem area to the other, and even within a problem area, and need not be tied to the notion of force. The crucial feature of any psychodynamic theory, Freudian or non-Freudian, is the description of some interactive phenomenon. The interactions of interest may in fact have forcelike properties—as in the case of wishes, fears, resistances, conflicts—or they may be more fieldlike—as in context effects in perception and memory, retinal fields, synapse dynamics, and so forth (e.g., Glass, Holyoak, and Santa, 1979; Lindsay and Norman, 1972). Motivational concepts naturally lend themselves to force descriptions; cognitive phenomena often do not. There is, however, no hard and fast dividing line. Moreover, because the interactions of interest are often higher-order interactions (the interactions of interactions), it often makes sense to mix metaphor systems in describing them.

In semantic context effects, for example, we have a clear instance of the interaction of an event, ϵ, with its contextual surround, $[\epsilon]$. As we saw in Chapter 2, $\epsilon \neq \epsilon|[\epsilon]$. At the same time, we have noted that motives may cause the subject to process the contextual ecology in a biased fashion so as to achieve (or avoid) the extraction of a particular latent content (see pages 102–105). This biased processing of the contextual ecology may be conceptualized in terms of the "weights" the subject assigns to the contextual items. He might overemphasize the import of a particular contextual item or altogether ignore it (by assigning it a weight, $w_i = 0$; hence $w_i\epsilon_i = 0$). Thus, as suggested on pages 103–104, $\epsilon|[w_i\epsilon_i] \neq \epsilon|[w_i'\epsilon_i]$, where $[w_i]$ and $[w_i']$ represent different sets of weight factors. It goes without saying that the weights in question do not imply the literal operation of the force of gravity in biased semantic processing.

In conclusion, there is no fundamental distinction between psychodynamics and cognition, just as, ultimately, there is none in physics be-tween "matter" and "field." All cognition (all psychology) is dynamic —in the sense of being interactive—insofar as the units of analysis and observation are not artificially delimited for methodological con-venience (as they have typically been in psychology until recently). To the extent that the units of analysis are fieldlike in complexity, which they increasingly are (and which they always were in psychoanalysis, given its clinical background), the material is inevitably dynamic, that is, interactive. Thus, dynamics is hardly unique to psychoanalysis. Indeed, most modern cognitive psychology—with its emphases of context and field effects, control processes, selectivity and bias, schemas, cueing and spread of activation effects, motivational factors in decision theory, attention- and effort-allocation principles, and so forth—has become dynamic, though this transmutation has gone largely unrecognized, probably because of the lingering tendency to associate dynamics with the metaphor of force (but see Erdelyi and Goldberg, 1979; Kahneman, 1973).

Psychoanalysis is distinctive as a dynamic psychology (if, in fact, it can still be considered distinctive) only in its emphasis of certain classes of interactions, notably the interactions of motives and cognition; and even in this regard psychoanalysis is no longer unique, given the ad-vent of mathematical decision theory and its formal elaboration of the effects of "payoffs" (negative and positive) upon performance (e.g., Green and Swets, 1966; Swets, 1964; Swets, Tanner, and Birdsall, 1961). As suggested elsewhere by the author (Erdelyi, 1974; Erdelyi, 1985; Erdelyi and Goldberg, 1979), what are conceived of as merely *response* bias effects (β) in conventional decision theory applications (that is, simple psychophysical situations) can readily transmute into bona fide cognitive effects (d') in more complex ones.

By this juncture, the dynamic character of psychoanalysis and mod-ern cognitive psychology are fully compatible, and ripe for integration. The differences that can be observed are accidents of history and meta-phorical nuance, not any longer of theoretical necessity. Because of its roots in information theory, mathematical decision theory, and com-puter analogs, cognitive psychology has tended to be framed in terms of "ideal observers" and "information processing"; psychoanalysis, on the other hand, with its clinical background, in terms of *non*ideal ob-servers and tendentious information *mis*processing. However, this no longer constitutes a difference in theoretical orientations but in theo-retical focus. The computer analog does not *naturally* yield interest in the strange problems (from its standpoint) of a special class of comput-ing systems—humans—who are often motivated (by some wish or fear) *not* to compute, or not to compute correctly. (But the analog is fully capable of describing and even simulating such a system—e.g.,

Colby [1981].) The discovery and elaboration of this type of misprocessing—generally known as defense processes in psychoanalysis—is
one of the fundamental contributions of psychoanalysis to cognitive
psychology. We now turn to their consideration.

REPRESSION (DEFENSE PROCESSES)

Meaning and Evolution of the Repression/Defense Concept

Freud's use of the concept of defense (if not the term itself) antedates
psychoanalysis. We have seen in Chapter 1 (pages 10–11) that in his
report, "A Case of Successful Treatment by Hypnotism" (1892–1893),
Freud advanced a dynamic conception of hysteria, in which one side of
a conflict is intentionally barred—"suppressed," "excluded," "dissociated"—from consciousness: "The distressing antithetic idea, which
seems to be inhibited, is removed from association with the intention
and continues to exist as a disconnected idea, often unconsciously, to
the patient himself" (Freud, 1892–1893, p. 122).

This basic notion was developed over the next several years
through a bewildering profusion of more-or-less interchangeable
rubrics, including "repression," "suppression," "inhibition," "exclusion," "removal," "censorship," "defense," "resistance," "forcible re-
pudiation," "intentional forgetting," and "disavowal" (denial). Not
surprisingly, such terminological sprawl produced confusions in both
terminology and concept (cf. Brenner, 1957; Erdelyi and Goldberg, 1979;
Eriksen and Pierce, 1968; Holmes, 1974; MacKinnon and Dukes, 1964;
Madison, 1956; 1961; Sjöbäck, 1973; Wolitzky, Klein, and Dworkin,
1976).

After an initial burst of terminological experimentation, which
never altogether subsided and which for a brief period saw *defense*
emerge as a key term synonymous with repression, Freud settled upon
repression (*Verdrängung*) as the generic construct, though never with
complete consistency or generality. In his late writings (e.g., Freud,
1926), he sought to reverse himself and supplant repression with
defense; but he never managed to maintain consistency in this regard,
and so the terms *repression* and *defense* are to be regarded as synonymous (except in one sense, to be explained below). Although psychoanalysts today tend to favor the general term, *defense*, most of Freud's
important theoretical writings on the topic are formulated in terms of
repression. Thus, when he states that "repression is the foundation
stone on which the whole structure of psychoanalysis rests, the most essential part of it" (Freud, 1914b, p. 16), we are to understand that he is
speaking of defense processes in general.

The terminological problem is almost surely not one merely of carelessness but involves a subtle evolution of the concept itself, one that bears some parallels to the evolution of the force concept in physics. In Freud's earliest writings, *repression* referred to the (apparently) simple notion that some distressing wish, idea, or memory was forced out or kept out of consciousness. Thus: "*A hysterical subject seeks intentionally to forget an experience or forcibly repudiates, inhibits and suppresses an intention or idea*" (Freud, 1892/1940, p. 153); "it was a question of things which the patient wished to forget, and therefore intentionally repressed from his conscious thought and inhibited and suppressed" (Breuer and Freud, 1893, p. 10). In hysterics, his earliest patients, the effect of this repression was rather straightforward: It resulted in amnesia for the rejected material. However, it very soon became obvious that the process was often more subtle. As early as 1894, for example, Freud observed in connection with obsessive-compulsive patients, who as a rule do not exhibit amnesia for distressing events, that repression can take another form: What these patients repress are not the actual facts or details of a painful event but their emotional component. Thus, "[the] defense against the incompatible idea was effected by separating it from its affect; the idea itself remained in consciousness" (Freud, 1894, p. 58). This affective form of repression, which already resists expression in simple force-vector terms (requiring some kind of previous splitting or dissociation between cognition and affect) has come to be known in psychoanalysis as the defense mechanism of *isolation*. In Freud's terminology (at least until 1926) isolation was to be understood, simply, as a form of repression.

With the accumulation of additional clinical experience, it became clear that there were actually many ways in which distressing or "unbearable" mental contents could be excluded (or partially excluded) from consciousness. In just two published case histories, the "Rat Man" (1909) and the "Psychotic Dr. Schreber" (1911) Freud deals with more than a dozen of such specific devices (not always by actual name), including omission and ellipsis, symbolization, isolation, displacement, doubt, regression, reaction formation, undoing, rationalization, denial, and projection. These constructs are no longer synonyms of one another but are used to describe distinct mechanisms by which repression (defense) can be implemented.

With the progressive broadening of the repression concept, the problem eventually had to be faced: How was repression in this general sense (subsuming a multiplicity of specific techniques) to be distinguished from the original, simplistic notion of repression as the forcing out or keeping out of some specific mental content from consciousness? It is this problem that Freud sought to resolve in his monograph, *Inhibitions, Symptoms and Anxiety* (1926), where he proposed that the term *defense (Abwehr)* replace the by then overgrown construct of *repression,* and that the original term be reserved for the early, simple meaning, namely, motivated amnesia or forgetting. Although the suggestion is implemented by some later psychoanalysts (e.g., Fenichel, 1945; A. Freud, 1936), Freud himself did not pursue it with any consistency. *Repression* in Freud's later writings continues to be, on the whole, synonymous with *defense,* although from time to time Freud distinguishes the two senses of the term by speaking of "repression in the broadest sense" (defense) and "repression in the narrow sense" (motivated forgetting). We shall here follow Freud's general practice of equating repression with defense, qualifying the term on those occasions when it is intended narrowly.

Having touched on some of the terminological issues, let us now turn to the more substantive question of meaning. Nomenclature aside, what does the concept of repression (defense) signify? Since there are unresolved problems in this connection also, we decompose what might be regarded as the "standard" definition in contemporary psychoanalysis (e.g., Brenner, 1973) into its constituent elements, only the first two of which, in the author's judgment, are actually crucial.

Defense mechanisms constitute:

1. techniques for distorting or outrightly rejecting from consciousness some feature of reality (physical or psychological)
2. for the purpose of avoiding the unbearable psychological pain ("anxiety") which it would provoke in consciousness.
3. Defense mechanisms are often conceived of as ego devices which
4. are prototypically unconscious.

The first component of the definition is essentially a paraphrase of Freud's own statement in his article on the topic, "Repression" (Freud, 1915a): *"the essence of repression lies simply in the function of rejecting and keeping something out of consciousness"* (p. 105).

The second element of the definition incorporates Freud's statement in the same article and many of his other writings that the rejection from consciousness has a defensive purpose (hence *defense* mechanisms), that of "avoiding 'pain'" (p. 105). In *Inhibitions, Symptoms and Anxiety* (1926) the psychological pain motivating defense is reconceptualized as "anxiety," which Freud uses in the broadest possible sense to mean realistic fears ("reality anxiety"), irrational fears ("neurotic anxiety"), and guilt ("moral anxiety").

The third component of the definition makes sense in the framework of the structural model, but it is hardly crucial for the concept (note that the structural model was introduced in 1923, more than a quarter of a century after the concept of repression/defense). It would be possible to jettison the structural model without in the slightest degree undermining the viability of the theory of defense. Thus, the notion that defense mechanisms are *ego* mechanisms (Freud, 1923; 1933; A. Freud, 1936) is a subsidiary idea grafted onto the basic repression/defense concept.

As regards the last component of the definition, there is wide consensus among contemporary psychoanalysts that the defenses are unconscious. However, this feature is by no means basic to Freud's own stance. In his later writings (perhaps under the influence of Anna Freud), Freud does stipulate that defense processes are themselves unconscious. However, up to 1915 if not later (cf. Erdelyi and Goldberg, 1979), defense or repression was often treated as conscious, so much so, that at one juncture Freud felt compelled to remind the reader that defenses are not *necessarily* conscious (Freud, 1915a, p. 106). It is often suggested in textbooks that repression is the unconscious mechanism of which *suppression* is the conscious counterpart. This is not so. As Erdelyi and Goldberg (1979) have demonstrated, there is no real basis for such a distinction in the writings of Freud, who, from his earliest writings (e.g., Breuer and Freud, 1893) to his last (Freud, 1940), treated repression and suppression interchangeably.

Although clinical experience shows that defenses are often used unconsciously, there exists no theoretical necessity to foist a sharp distinction upon their conscious and unconscious deployment. Such a distinction would not only be artificial but theoretically pernicious as well. It would confuse the question of defense with the question of the unconscious, producing an error that is the obverse counterpart of the pre-Freudian philosophical fiat that unconscious processes are (by definition) not psychological. With such an imposed dissociation upon the continuity of mental life, no meaningful science of psychology is possible, as Freud emphasized (see Chap. 2, pages 51–55). To turn around now and exclude conscious activity from the continuity of mental life—to impose another gratuitous theoretical discontinuity—would be equally inappropriate and unpromising. If the question of unconsciousness should be at issue in a particular clinical or experimental context one need only qualify the defenses under consideration as conscious or unconscious—conscious versus unconscious repression, conscious versus unconscious displacement, and so forth.

Repression (in the Narrow Sense): Suppression, Censorship, Denial, and Isolation

In this section we deal with defense processes that are similar in postulated mechanisms, or which are in effect synonyms of one another. It has been already suggested that *repression* (in the narrow sense) and *suppression* are used interchangeably in Freud's writings (if not in the psychoanalytic literature). *Censorship,* discussed in some detail in Chapter 4, is included here because, except for the fact that it is the term of choice in Freud's discussions of dream life, it corresponds substantially to the repression-suppression notion.

Isolation is obviously a cognate notion. In a sense, it is a special form of censorship: It excludes affect from consciousness while allowing the "cold facts" to register.

Denial is a highly problematic term (see Sjöbäck, 1973, Chap. 8), sometimes distinguished from, sometimes equated with repression. One distinction, proposed as well as contradicted by Freud (see also A. Freud, 1936; Janis, Mahl, Kagan, and Holt, 1969) is that denial is a special type of repression, one involving external rather than internal events; in some sense, then, it is a failure of sight. The distinction, as usually applied, turns out to be artificial and ultimately misleading (see Sjöbäck). Denial will be treated here as a failure of sight, but only in a special sense—in the sense of "I see your point" versus "I see a point of light." It is a form of repression which excludes from consciousness not the manifest event(s), ϵ or $[\epsilon]$, but some latent content, $\epsilon|[\epsilon]$. Thus, it is not so much a failure of sight as a failure of insight. We shall return to this point later.

Theoretical Conceptualizations of Repression: Sociopolitical, Neobehavioristic, and Information-Processing

Given the central role of repression in Freud's system, there is surprisingly little formal treatment of the construct in his writings. His most ambitious effort (excluding his rejected *Project for a Scientific Psychology*) is Chapter VII of *The Interpretation of Dreams,* which we have examined in some detail in Chapter 3 of this book (pages 115–126). This approach, supplemented to some extent in his article,"The Unconscious" (1915b), is, as we have seen, essentially an information-processing scheme in search of its natural analog premise, the computer. Freud's most serviceable analog in the absence of the computer was censorship, which provided him with a sociopolitical model—a living-system simulation—of the clinical phenomena he was attempting to describe. The implicit sociopolitical model of individual psychological processes, adumbrated in *Totem and Taboo* (1913), was made explicit in *Group Psychology and the Analysis of the Ego* (1921) (for example, "The contrast between individual psychology and social or group psychology, which at first glance may seem to be full of significance, loses a great deal of its sharpness when it is examined more closely" [p. 69]).

Sociopolitical Model. Since sociopolitical systems are information-processing systems (among other things), this particular analog framework is actually a variant of the information-processing approach to defenses. Its drawback is that it is unwieldy; it cannot be manipulated for experimental purposes. The other side of this weakness is its strength: It cannot ever be dismissed as an artificial, post hoc simulation; it is a living, real-life model which embodies the complexities that information-processing models tend to eschew.

In Chapter 4 we have had occasion to examine a variety of real-life examples of censorship devices. We have seen that there is no single technique of censorship. Materials may be selectively expunged from the final product; the material may be toned down through hints, modifications, and allusions; or, in conjunction with the other techniques, it may be tendentiously elaborated; or, even more subtly, it may be distorted through misplacement of accent (emphasis).

We turn here to a few additional contemporary examples of censorship techniques to illustrate other facets of this complex family of processes.

Figure 5.1 is a political cartoon by Herblock dealing with former President Ford's active encouragement of amnesia for the traumatic events of Watergate. In a similar fashion, presumably, individuals encourage themselves to forget traumatic events in their own lives. Notice one interesting implication of this example, which may be taken either as a corrective or as a distortion (analog warp) of Freud's concept: A shredder does not merely render information inaccessible but permanently unavailable.

Figure 5.2 illustrates another variant of censorship, one in which what is "shredded" is not the offending material but the agency that is responsible for it. In this sample of behavior we see the psychological disturbance that sexual themes continue to provoke (see also Figure 5.3). Note the absence of any logical justification for the censorship; the motivation is purely psychological—it offends and is therefore labeled "abusive." Also we have here a real-life simulation of the Freudian economic model of repression (cf. Freud, 1915b): Repression/censorship is achieved through the withdrawal of necessary allocations (of moneys, attention-cathexes, and the like). (Such economic models of attention/effort allocation are increasingly appearing in modern information-processing theories [e.g., Kahneman, 1973]. The title of a recent experimental article gives a flavor of the approach: "Concurrent Automatic and Controlled Visual Search: Can Processing Occur without Resource Cost?" [Schneider and Fisk, 1982].) By eliminating not just the offending material but the offending organ or subsystem, the executive system prevents any future transgressions of the executive system's taboos. Had the blasphemous material been partially censored through hints, modifications, or allusions (as in, for example, Botero's painting, Figure 4.10), this more drastic form of censorship, superimposed from above, might have been avoided.

However, as was emphasized in Chapter 4, the amount of anxiety-

Figure 5.1 (From *Herblock On All Fronts*, New American Library, 1980.)

provoking material allowed expression is never a clear-cut matter, and depends on the occasion, place, and individuals involved. As the excerpt in Figure 5.4 demonstrates, considerable pressure exists for the censorship of materials that many individuals would consider quite acceptable.

The varied examples provided here and in the previous chapters serve to underscore the empirical reason why a simple articulation of repression, much less of defenses in general, is not possible. There is no single mechanism or technique. In real life, there are wide variations in the stratagems through which the basic defensive goal is put into effect.

A Halt to Funds For Paper Voted At City College

Move Follows Publication of Obscene Photographs

Students at the City College in New York voted late Tuesday night to cut off financing of The Observation Post, a campus newspaper, after the editors had published photographs of a woman dressed as a nun masturbating with a crucifix.

The 474-to-455 vote came after a month-long crusade by student organizations urging that the 32-year-old publication be suspended. The vote is being reviewed by City University lawyers after questions arose regarding the validity of 37 ballots.

After the photographs appeared in its May 4 issue, the newspaper drew condemnation from students and faculty members as well as from the Roman Catholic Archdiocese of New York, feminist organizations and some city officials. State Senator Frank Padavan, a Queens Republican, said he would seek action in Albany to deny the newspaper financial support.

Harold M. Jacobs, chairman of the Board of Higher Education, met Tuesday with representatives of District Attorney Robert M. Morgenthau to see whether the student editors of the newspaper could be prosecuted under state obscenity laws.

Prosecution Called Unlikely

In an interview yesterday, Mr. Jacobs said he was told it was unlikely that they could be prosecuted. However, saying that the university could not sit idly by, he said he would ask Robert J. Kibbee, Chancellor of the City University, to ascertain whether the students could be suspended.

A spokesman for Mr. Morgenthau declined to comment.

Dr. Kibbee ordered the establishment of two review panels to "forestall the recurrence of abuses typified in the recent incident." He also recommended revision of the Board of Higher Education's bylaws governing student newspapers, suggesting that the present regulations did not "provide adequate protection against abuse."

The Observation Post is one of three student newspapers at the City College school governed by a media board set up in 1974 to disburse student-activity funds among the publications.

Alex Coroneos, news editor of The Observation Post, said it had consulted a lawyer and would take the issue to court. "There is more at stake here than what O.P. printed," he said. "If any other campus newspaper printed anything against the grain, the same thing could happen again." He said at first he had thought the photographs were a "silly sophomoric stunt," but that he was glad the newspaper published them. "We did not act irresponsibly by printing what we saw fit," he added.

Figure 5.2. City College's censorship of campus newspaper (*The New York Times*, May 24, 1979, p. B3). (Copyright © 1979 by The New York Times Co.)

Pope: Marriage Is Good, but Virginity Is Better

John Paul: quotes St. Paul

VATICAN CITY (UPI)—Pope John Paul II, in an intricate personal analysis of scripture, said yesterday that virginity and celibacy are spiritually better than marriage, but those who marry do no wrong.

"Those who choose matrimony do well, and those who choose virginity or voluntary abstinence do better," he said during his weekly audience in St. Peter's Square.

The pope, who last year made a series of pronouncements on the themes of human sexuality and the human body, began a new theme of virginity and matrimony in his address.

JOHN PAUL QUOTED EXTENSIVELY from St. Paul's first letter to the Corinthians, which advised the unmarried and widowed to remain such and urged that persons should even strive for virginity within marriage.

" 'He who gives his virgin in marriage does well, and he who does not give her does better,' " the pope quoted from St. Paul's epistle.

"The author affirms that maintaining virginity is an advice given and not a commandment," the pontiff explained.

"At the same time he gives advice to persons already married, as well as to persons considering marriage and finally to those in the state of widowhood."

"HE [ST. PAUL] . . . EXPLAINS that the decision concerning abstinence, or concerning a life of virginity, must be voluntary and that only in such abstinence is it better than matrimony," the pope said.

John Paul explained that the distinction was "not one of good and bad but one of good and better."

However, a number of Christian theologians—including Roman Catholic theologians—have interpreted the same letter of St. Paul as saying there is no spiritual distinction between virginity and conjugal married life.

Some have gone as far as to say the epistle originally was intended to discourage celibacy for most Christians.

Figure 5.3. (*Philadelphia Daily News*, June 24, 1982. Photo reprinted by permission of United Press International.)

The excerpt in Figure 5.5 illustrates another point, one that bears on the issue of conscious versus unconscious defenses. We have here reference to the formula, of Watergate fame, the "cover-up of the cover-up." This is a real-life simulation of the notion (cf. Erdelyi and Goldberg, 1979) that if the act of repression should itself produce distress, then the act (of repression) itself can be repressed. Thus, conscious repression can give rise to unconscious repression through the simple process of iteration. (A conscious repression may itself be consciously repressed, which act may in turn be consciously repressed, and so on, so that the original act of conscious repression becomes unconscious.) The excerpt from *The New York Times* in Figure 5.5 provides further examples of the virtually limitless way in which censorship/repression can be achieved. The sociopolitical model helps put into perspective the danger of oversimplification in conceptualizing dynamic phenomena.

Repression, as was emphasized in our discussion of psychodynamics in this chapter, is a special case of conflict. Part of the system desires access to some information, another part opposes such access. The sociopolitical model lends weight to this notion; there is perpetual tension about how much may be made accessible, and how much should be withheld (e.g., Figures 5.6 and 5.7).

Neobehavioristic Conceptualization. In contrast to the unwieldy sociopolitical model, the neobehavioristic approach to repression is starkly simple. In this lies its attractiveness—as well as its weakness. It takes the extensively investigated behavior of laboratory animals, such as rats, dogs, cats, and pigeons, and treats them as analogs of human cognitive processes.

Perhaps the most brilliant, certainly the most influential version of this perspective, is that of Dollard and Miller (1950). Consciousness is treated as behaving like a frightened laboratory rat, which tries by every means possible to escape from the source of its fright. This conception dovetails nicely with Freud's frequently voiced formula (e.g., Freud, 1926, p. 153), that "repression . . . is, fundamentally, an attempt at flight."

To understand this perspective in concrete terms, we turn to the prototypic experimental situation to which Dollard and Miller's treatment is anchored. A rat is placed in a "Miller Box," which is a rectangular enclosure divided into two compartments by a partition in the middle. One compartment is all white, the other is all black. The floor of the white compartment consists of a metal grill through which electric shock may be administered to the rat. An interesting feature of the partition is that it contains a closed door which opens if the rat performs some specific action, such as turning a wheel or pressing a lever, allowing the rat to scurry from one compartment to the other.

At the beginning of the experiment the tame rat is not frightened of

228

Censorship Foes Stage A 'Read-Out' at Library

Mark Twain, Anne Frank, John Steinbeck, Ernest Hemingway, J. D. Salinger, Bernard Malamud, Kurt Vonnegut, Isaac Asimov, Eve Merriam and other authors, living and dead, had their day in the sun yesterday at a midtown rally against censorship.

Protesters gathered between two Sabrett hot-dog umbrellas in the street and the stone lions flanking the steps of the New York Public Library on Fifth Avenue at 41st Street. The authors had one thing in common: All have had their works banned or burned in schools and libraries by self-appointed censors around the country.

Summoned by the fanfare of a trumpeter, Robert Delfausse, a candidate for a master's degree in classical music at City College, a floating crowd of several thousand attended a "read-out" by writers and actors reciting passages from banned books.

David Garrison, who plays the police sergeant in "Pirates of Penzance," read a favorite passage from "Huckleberry Finn," which had been suppressed in some high schools by black parents who called it "racist" and white parents who said that "it did not reward good and punish bad." Calling the Twain passage a metaphor for freedom, Mr. Garrison read:

"We said there warn't no home like a raft, after all. Other places do seem so cramped up and smothery, but a raft don't. You feel mighty free and easy and comfortable on a raft."

Miss Merriam, whose "The Inner City Mother Goose" has been banned, updated her nursery rhymes by taking the occasion to have Simple Simon come out against "anti-ballistic missiles instead of decent jobs" and against government corruption: "There was a crooked man—and he did very well."

In addition to books, speakers pointed out that magazines were also subject to censorship. Joanne Edgar of Ms. Magazine said that many high school libraries banned the publication on flimsy grounds, saying that some of the language was offensive when "their real reason is that they are against what the feminist movement stands for."

Band of 'Frightened People'

The read-out was organized by the American Society of Journalists and Authors, a 600-member association of freelance nonfiction writers, and supported by a score of other concerned organizations—including church and civil-liberties groups and those connected with the book and magazine trades.

"We are deeply concerned to see books swept off the shelves by a small minority of frightened people," said Sally Wendkos Olds, president of the sponsoring writers society.

Representing People for the Ameri-

Figure 5.4. (*The New York Times,* February 4, 1982, p. B3. Copyright © 1982 by the New York Times Co. Don Hogan Charles/*NYT Pictures.*)

Isaac Asimov reading from one of his works at an anti-censorship rally outside the New York Public Library at Fifth Avenue and 41st Street.

can Way, Rosalyn Udow, its New York regional director, said: "Topics the textbook censors find unacceptable include the current women's movement, slavery and poverty in America, sex education and human anatomy, evolution and the labor movement. It is easy to see how critical mind control poses to our democracy."

NIXON PORTRAYED BY PROSECUTION AS CONSPIRATOR

Ben-Veniste Opens Case by Saying Ex-President Had a Crucial Role in 1973

TELLS OF 'SCENARIOS'

Asserts Meetings Were Held to Devise Procedure for 'Cover-Up of Cover-Up'

By LESLIE OELSNER

Special to The New York Times

WASHINGTON, Oct. 14—The special Watergate prosecution opened its case in the Watergate cover-up trial today with an account to the jury that portrayed former President Nixon as one of the central conspirators.

Mr. Nixon was described as having had a particularly crucial role in the spring of 1973, when the cover-up was coming apart and, according to the prosecution, the "cover-up of the cover-up" was under way.

...Richard Ben-Veniste, the assistant special prosecutor presenting the opening statement on behalf of the seven-member prosecution team, told the jury that Mr. Nixon held a "multitude of meetings" in April, 1973, with John D. Ehrlichman and H.R. Haldeman—then his chief aides and now two of the five defendants in the trial—to devise "scenarios" and "lines" for handling the situation.

In one conversation, Mr. Ben-Veniste said, quoting from a previously undisclosed White House tape recording, the group discussed a scenario that the prosecutor called "drawing wagons around the White House"—sacrificing some persons to the prosecution to save others.

He said that the possible sacrifices included John N. Mitchell, now a defendant in the case but formerly the Attorney General and Mr. Nixon's campaign manager.

"Give the investigators an hors d'oeuvre," Mr. Ben-Veniste quoted Mr. Nixon as saying. "Maybe they won't come back for the main course."

...Mr. Ben-Veniste spent nearly four hours outlining these charges to the jury and to the scores of other persons crowded into Judge John J. Sirica's second-floor courtroom at the United States Court House.

Essentially, the prosecution theory of the case goes thus: Several persons at the re-election committee, including Mr. Mitchell, had advance knowledge of the break-in plan; two of the Watergate burglars participated in an earlier, at that point still-secret break-in at the office of Dr. Daniel Ellsberg's psychiatrist; Mr. Nixon's re-election was coming up; disclosure of the facts surrounding the break-in might hurt his chances for re-election (and also the chances for some defendants to continue in Government work); it might also reveal other things, such as the Ellsberg break-in, that the White House did not want disclosed.

Figure 5.5. The cover-up of the cover-up (L. Oelsner. *The New York Times.* October 15, 1974, pp. 1, 30). (Copyright © 1974 by The New York Times Co.)

Much of what Mr. Ben-Veniste said was familiar, a repetition of findings or charges that were heard before the Senate Watergate committee in 1973 or before the House Judiciary Committee during the impeachment proceedings, or that were spelled out in the indictment.

$400,000 in Hush Money

But there were new allegations as well. Mr. Ben-Veniste said that more than $400,000 had been paid as hush money to the original Watergate defendants, and that some of this had come from funds held in Florida by Charles G. Rebozo, Mr. Nixon's close friend.

The prosecutor also told the jury that Mr. Mitchell had approved a political surveillance plan that led to the break-in. Jeb Stuart Magruder, a campaign aide who has already pleaded guilty to a role in the cover-up, testified to this effect before the Senate Watergate committee. Mr. Mitchell, however, in his own appearance before the committee denied it.

Mr. Ben-Veniste said too that Mr. Mitchell was among those who "received assurances designed to induce them not to tell all they know."

... In another Presidential discussion, the prosecutor recounted, Mr. Ehrlichman reported that Mr. Moore's memory had grown "feeble beyond measure" after being advised about possible liabilities he himself faced.

Subsequently, on April 28 by Mr. Ben-Veniste's account, Mr. Nixon told Mr. Haldeman he was "gratified" that Mr. Moore's memory had "dimmed."

---

either compartment. It is then placed in the shock compartment (the white side) and exposed to shock. The rat shows every sign of intense fright (it jumps around, urinates, defecates, and so forth). In this agitated state it eventually emits the crucial response of, say, pressing the lever (either by accident or through previous behavior "shaping"), whereupon the compartment door opens, and the rat scampers through it to safety. The procedure is repeated several times until the rat shows clear evidence of having learned the critical instrumental response (pressing the lever).

This part of the experiment demonstrates the phenomenon of instrumental (or Skinnerian) conditioning: The animal learns to respond to a stimulus, S_i (the lever), with a particular response, R_i (pressing), as a result of previous reinforcement, S_j (in this case negative reinforcement, namely, the cessation of shock). Schematically, the instrumental conditioning may be rendered as:

$$S_i \rightarrow R_i \rightarrow S_j$$

Now a second phase of the experiment begins. The rat is placed in the shock compartment but without any further shock being administered. Despite the absence of shock the rat dashes to the lever, presses it, and runs through to the safe compartment. Why does the rat escape in the absence of shock? Dollard and Miller (1950) explain it in terms of

HOUSE AND NIXON SEEM NEAR CLASH ON WITHHELD DATA

Evidence Denied Jaworski and Sought by Inquiry on Impeachment Is at Issue

---

WHITE HOUSE IS BALKING

Ziegler Hints at Reluctance to Give Material—Panel Shows Rising Irritation

---

By BILL KOVACH

Special to The New York Times

WASHINGTON, March 12—A major confrontation between Congress and the White House appeared today to be developing over information the White House is withholding from the House Judiciary Committee.

At issue is the request of the committee's impeachment inquiry for evidence covering the same ground as evidence the President refused to give to the special Watergate prosecutor, Leon Jaworski.

In a long briefing today, the White House press secretary, Ronald L. Ziegler, suggested that the Administration was unwilling to supply further materials to the impeachment inquiry.

... The White House attitude toward the committee's request seems to support the growing feeling on Capitol Hill that Mr. Nixon would sooner risk impeachment for defying the House committee than on the basis of any further evidence accumulated in the impeachment inquiry.

That feeling was supported by Vice President Ford when he told newsmen today that White House refusal to comply with a House subpoena, should one be issued, might be the catalyst that would bring about President Nixon's impeachment. He added, however, that he did not believe the White House would follow such a course.

Material Withheld

The material that both Mr. Jaworski and the impeachment inquiry have been unable to obtain from the White House covers Presidential conversations with five aides over a number of days both before and after the March 21 conversation in which the President contends he learned of the Watergate cover-up.

Figure 5.6. (*The New York Times,* March 13, 1974, p. 1. Copyright © 1974 by The New York Times Co.)

classical conditioning: The previously neutral white compartment (CS), through its association with electric shock (UCS), which produces intense fright (UCR), now also elicits fright (CR). Schematically (see pages 27–28), several trials of:

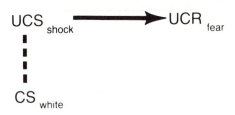

results in:

Thus, the rat's behavior in the second, no-shock phase of the experiment, is explained by a dual-factor theory of conditioning: (1) through *classical conditioning* the rat learns to associate fear with the white compartment; (2) through *instrumental conditioning* it learns to avoid the white compartment.

In humans, consciousness is assumed to behave like the conditioned laboratory rat: Memories previously associated with trauma are avoided (by consciousness). This is another way of saying that memories associated with trauma in the past are rejected or kept out of consciousness, even though, as in the case of the rat, the events in question—perhaps from childhood—are no longer realistically dangerous.

The following question often arises in connection with this rat analogy: The rat avoids the physical compartment that was associated with shock, but why should the human subject avoid thoughts or memories when these (as opposed to the physical events that gave rise to them) were never directly punished? For example, a child may have been severely punished for some misbehavior, and it is understandable that he might avoid emitting the punished *behavior*. But why should he avoid thoughts and feelings associated with the behavior, which are impossible for parents to punish (unless they read minds)?

The answer follows from another well-established conditioning phenomenon, that of generalization. In both instrumental and classical conditioning, it has been amply demonstrated (e.g., Dollard and Miller, 1950) that conditioned responses (R_i, CR) are emitted not just to the actual conditioned stimulus (S_i, CS) but also to stimuli that are *similar* to them. Dollard and Miller (1950) argue that in humans the conditioned

By 383 to 8, House Votes Bill to Strengthen Public's Access to Government Information and Records

By RICHARD L. MADDEN

Special to The New York Times

WASHINGTON, March 14—Despite opposition from the Nixon Administration, the House passed today legislation aimed at strengthening the public's access to Government information and records.

The bill, which was passed by a vote of 383 to 8, now goes to the Senate, where a judiciary subcommittee has approved a similar measure.

At the same time, the House Government Operations Committee, splitting 24 to 16, approved a separate bill that would let the Federal courts determine—except in an impeachment proceeding—whether a President could withhold information from Congress.

However, the bill now goes to the House Rules Committee, where it faces an uncertain fate, and the Administration officials have warned of a presidential veto.

Under the committee bill, a Congressional committee could get House or Senate approval to go into court whenever the President directed an agency to withhold information sought by the committee.

Several Democrats opposed the bill, which had the support of a number of Republicans. Representative Jack Brooks, Democrat of Texas, said it was "disastrous legislation" that would "inscribe into law the concept of executive privilege and give to every agency of the Government, as well as the President, the appearance of legitimacy in denying certain information to Congress.

The bill approved by the full House dealing with the public's access to records would make the first changes in the Freedom of Information Act of 1966 and would give Federal courts the option of privately examining any classified documents to determine if the documents had been properly withheld from the public.

The provision would reverse a recent United States Supreme Court decision, which said that the contents of documents withheld from the public, such as for national security reasons, were not reviewable by the courts.

The Supreme Court's ruling in January was on a suit brought under the Freedom of Information Act by Representative Patsy T. Mink, Democrat of Hawaii, and other members of Congress who had sought to force the disclosure of classified documents relating to an underground nuclear test.

"This bill offers a sensible and workable compromise between a Democratic government and the Government's need for national security," Representative Spark M. Matsunaga, Democrat of Hawaii, said during the relatively brief House debate....

The 1966 law sought to grant Americans the right of access to Federal

---

Figure 5.7. (*The New York Times*, March 15, 1974, p. 15. Copyright © 1974 by The New York Times Co.)

records and specified categories of information, such as that dealing with national security, trade secrets and intra-agency memos, which could be kept secret.

The bill passed today would, among other things, set various time limits for Federal agencies to respond to public requests for information and would require the agencies to make annual reports to Congress on how they had implemented the act.

Also, the courts would be permitted to award the cost of legal fees and court costs to a plaintiff seeking information if the court decision went against the Government agency.

In addition, the bill would expand the definition of Federal agencies covered by the 1966 law to include agencies within the executive branch, such as the Office of Management and Budget and the National Security Council and Government corporations, such as the Tennessee Valley Authority.

---

response of anxiety which motivates avoidance—"cognitive avoidance" (Eriksen and Pierce, 1968; Mischel, 1980)—generalizes to thoughts and impulses related to the punished behavior. Neal Miller has substantiated this hypothesis experimentally:

Human subjects were asked to read aloud a sequence of the letter T and the number 4 (to say "T," "four," "T," "four," and so forth). The saying of *one* of these (for example "T" but not "four") was followed by shock. In short order, the subjects learned (through classical conditioning) to be anxious whenever they pronounced the critical item. The conditioned anxiety was objectively indexed through the monitoring of the galvanic skin response (GSR), which showed selective deflections to T but not to 4. In the second phase of the study, the subjects were informed that no more shock would be administered for the remainder of the experiment. Further, they were told that a series of dots were going to be presented to them. On the appearance of the first dot, they were to *think* (not say) "4"; on the presentation of the second dot they were to think "T"; on the third presentation of the dot, to think "4"; and so forth. They were in every case to *think* of the appropriate stimulus but never to pronounce it aloud. The question of interest was whether the conditioned anxiety (CR) would generalize from the punished *behavior* (the *saying* of "T") to the *thinking* of the item (T). The results, as Figure 5.8 shows, were unequivocally positive. Subjects became anxious when *thinking* of the stimulus, even though they had been punished only for *saying* it aloud. Dollard and Miller concluded that thoughts (feelings, impulses, and so on) associated with punishment are themselves subject to conditioned avoidance, that is, exclusion from consciousness.

Dollard and Miller additionally suggest that in conjunction with conditioning, there may be a supplementary phylogenetic disposition to adopt a "freeze" or "possum" reaction in response to intense fright, involving cessation of motor activity, vocalization, and (one may assume) thinking.

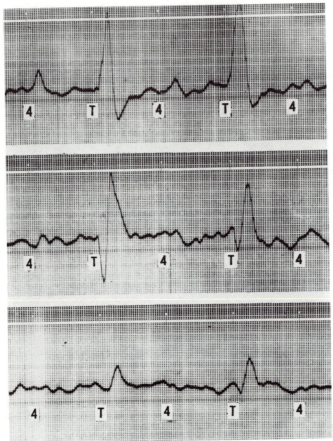

Figure 5.8. "The generalization of conditioned galvanic skin responses from words pronounced aloud to thoughts. The subject was presented with T followed by an electric shock and 4 not followed by shock in an unpredictable order. He named each symbol when he saw it. After a discrimination had been established, the subject was presented with a series of dots and instructed to think 4 when he saw the first dot, T when he saw the second, etc. These are his galvanic responses to presentations 1–5, 11–15, 21–25" (from Dollard & Miller, 1950, p. 206; figure from Miller, 1935, p. 65).

Dollard and Miller's theory is termed *neobehavioristic* because of its inclusion of a protocognitive description of the covert processes involved. The model is framed in stimulus-response terminology but incorporates, nevertheless, hypothesized events in the "black box" intervening between the observable stimulus, S, and the response, R. This model, which resembles in important respects Freud's linear compound-instrument model (Chapter 3, pages 116–126), provides some insights into the way in which conscious repression may become unconscious and how unconscious mentation may result in a shift away from secondary- to primary-process types of thinking.

The model is straightforward. It is assumed that the overt response, R, to the observed stimulus, S, is mediated by a sequence of internal stimulus-response events, which Dollard and Miller term, *cue-producing responses* (this terminology is meant to convey the notion that a mediating event in a sequential chain functions both as a response—to the previous event—and as a stimulus or cue—to the subsequent event.) Schematically:

$$S \rightarrow [\text{r-s-r-s-r-s-r-s} \ldots \text{r-s-r-s-r-s-r-s}] \rightarrow R$$

It is assumed by Dollard and Miller (like Freud) that regions close to the terminal response, R, are associated with consciousness. Specifically, to Dollard and Miller (following an isolated suggestion by Freud), this terminal region, prior to R, is associated with verbal-symbolic processes that are conscious. In terms of the scheme:

Region of
verbal/conscious
mediation

$$S \rightarrow [\text{r-s-r-s-r-s} \ldots \overbrace{\text{r-s-r-s-r-s-r-s}}] \rightarrow R$$

The notion that *behavioral* avoidance generalizes to *thought* may be alternately conceptualized as a form of backward temporal generalization—responses generalize not only to stimuli that are physically similar but also to stimuli that are temporally close. Such backward temporal generalization results in anticipatory response inhibition, that is, the inhibition of not just the behavior but of the thoughts that precede the behavior. If the human subject thinks as the rat behaves in the Miller Box, then it may be assumed that response inhibition (or avoidance) generalizes backward in the mediating chain. Hence, the subject may both avoid speaking of certain things—as well as thinking of certain things:

$$S \rightarrow \left[\text{r-s-r-s-r-s} \ldots \text{r-s-r-s-r-s-r-s-r-s}\right] \rightarrow R$$

behavior inhibition
conscious repression

Up to this point, the conscious, symbolic system is intact enough for the maintenance of consciousness of the fact that inhibition (repression/suppression) is taking place. Under more extreme circumstances, when potential anxiety is very intense, the anticipatory inhibition/avoidance extends further back (there being ample experimental evidence that under high motivation or drive, generalization increases), to the mediation regions prior to consciousness. In this case, the subject loses consciousness of both the material avoided and of the avoidance itself:

> We would expect the response of stopping thinking to tend to become anticipatory like any other strongly reinforced response. Therefore, the patient should stop thinking, or veer off onto a different line of thought before he reaches the memory of the traumatic incident. [Moreover] he should learn to avoid not only thoughts about the fear-provoking incident but also the associations leading to these thoughts. (Dollard and Miller, 1950, p. 202)

Schematically:

$$S \longrightarrow \left[\text{r-s-r-s-r-s} \ldots \text{r-s-r-s-r-s-r-s-r-s-r-s} \right] \longrightarrow R$$

behavior inhibition
conscious repression
unconscious repression

Although the process of anticipatory avoidance/inhibition is viewed as a "more-or-less" rather than "all-or-none" phenomenon (the greater the anxiety, the greater the backward temporal generalization), the consequence of engaging in conscious rather than unconscious inhibition is seen as critical. As long as basic verbal-symbolic functions are not inhibited, the subject may engage in higher-order discriminations and generalizations, that is, discriminations and generalizations based on symbolic versus physical differences and similarities; when inhibition extends further back, to a point prior to symbolic mediation, discriminations and generalizations are reduced to physical similarities or differences (for example, knife ≅ penis, mother ≅ wife, and so forth).

An excessive reliance on unconscious repression results in "neurotic stupidity." Not only are major areas of thought excluded from consciousness (in what might be thought of as functional ablations) but the generalizations and discriminations critical to intelligent thinking become dependent on primitive, concretistic (versus abstract) similarities and differences.

A major problem with this approach is the same as that encountered in Freud's linear model (Chapter 3, pages 115–126). There is no feedback built into the model, which tends to be crudely mechanical as a result. There is, for example, no place in it for subtle, symbolic analyses of the input prior to the decision whether it is to be avoided or permitted access to consciousness.

Information-Processing Approach. We take up here not a specific model but a general approach, one that emphasizes the processing (or misprocessing) of information. Broadly conceived, the two preceding conceptualizations are also "information-processing" in character: The sociopolitical model of censorship unquestionably deals with the transmission or nontransmission of information; the neobehavioristic model, though it is couched in stimulus-response terminology, nevertheless has as its focus the unfolding or inhibition of informational ("cue-producing") mediational sequences. Similarly, Freud's compound-instrument model (pages 115–126) and the implicit neurological notions that influenced it (Pribram and Gill, 1976; Sulloway, 1979), are likewise, as has been already emphasized, information-processing in nature.

In the most general sense—the sense that a model deals in some way with the processing or misprocessing of information—probably most models of psychological functioning are information-processing in character. What gives modern information-processing approaches their unique flavor is their espousal (unlike that of previous approaches) of the computer analog. Although this is in no sense an "ultimate" analog, it is nevertheless fundamental in its consequence, for it provides psychology a viable metaphor system for the higher mental processes that allows for "tailor-made" as opposed to "ready-made" models (see Chapter 3), much as mathematics does for physics. Thus, the crucial feature of computer-based information-processing conceptualizations is that they are theoretically malleable; the metaphor system allows, within broad limits, a flexible specification of precisely the type of description one desires to achieve and, also, the possibility of substantive adjustments at a later point. We have already seen this in Chapter 3 (pages 124–126; see especially Figures 3.9 and 3.11): Quite different models can be created within the same metaphor system. Actually, every sociopolitical censorship device illustrated in this and previous chapters, as well as Dollard and Miller's scheme, is capable of expression in precise information-processing terms and of computer simulation.

This last point brings us to another fundamental advantage of the computer metaphor system, its ability, like mathematics, to articulate theory with minute and unambiguous precision. The flowcharts that are the usual summaries of information-processing theories are short-hand for processes that in principle can be simulated through a full-fledged computer program. Flaws or hidden paradoxes (such as the analog warp in Freud's compound-instrument model—see pages 115–126) emerge unmistakably in such simulations and cannot be camouflaged with clever writing or rhetoric. Further, such simulations can prove, with mathematical precision, that notions that might be considered logically or "common-sensically" untenable may not in fact be so. It had been suggested, for example (cf. Erdelyi, 1974), that the phenomenon of "perceptual defense" (perceptual repression) was impossible, because in order to know that one had to defend against seeing something, one had first to see it. (Sartre [1943] raised similar objections to the notion of self-deception or repression.) Moreover, it was argued that such a process as perceptual defense was scientifically untenable because it implied the existence of a homunculus—a little man—in the head, responsible for making decisions about defense. The computer information-processing approach has shown such misgivings to be unfounded (Erdelyi, 1974), for computers easily simulate the processes that had been considered impossible (e.g., Figure 3.11).

Figure 3.11 conveys in flowchart terms the basic features of the model of censorship/repression (of both external and internal events) that Freud was attempting to articulate in Chapter VII of *The Interpretation of Dreams* (1900). In contemporary information-processing flowcharts the "censors" or "screens" (or "filters") in the model would be usually rendered as "decision nodes." In Figure 5.9 this simple model of repression/censorship is paraphrased in modern flowchart form with decision- and command-nodes supplanting the earlier censors. The first censor corresponds to the decision node (in first triangle), "Is anxiety level $x \geq \mu$?" (where "μ" is the current criterion of "unbearability"). Thus, if the level of anxiety that the information would provoke in consciousness matches or exceeds the unbearability criterion, the information-processing is aborted ("Stop processing/accessing information"), without it being transferred to Pcs. (a preconscious information buffer). Note that the value of μ may actually vary, so that when the individual feels in a particularly vulnerable state the criterion value, μ, may be set very low, whereas under more auspicious circumstances, it might be set much higher (allowing for the possibility of consciousness for the painful material that is excluded from consciousness in other circumstances). Also, any agent (such as hypnosis or sodium pentothal) that would lower the level of anxiety, x, associated with the information, would necessarily result in greater potential consciousness for the material.

If $x < \mu$ (that is, x is not $\geq \mu$), then the information is processed/transferred into the buffer Pcs. Here the material is subjected to another censorship (as in Figure 3.11), in the guise of a new decision test, "Is $x \geq v$?" where v is an anxiety criterion that is laxer than the

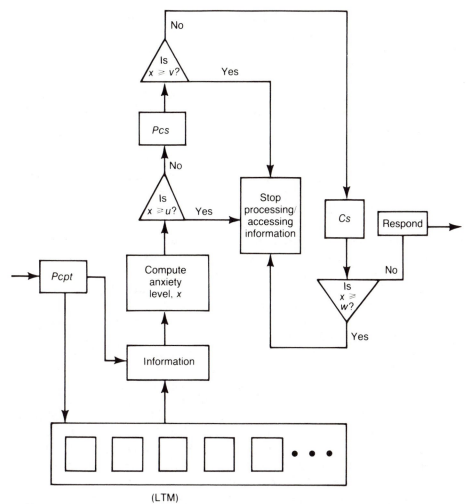

(LTM)

Figure 5.9. Freud's repression/censorship notion in modern information-processing terms.

former, μ. If the material is still too anxiety-provoking by this criterion ($x \geq v$) then, again, it fails to be processed, and is not made accessible to consciousness. (Freud's discussion of the preconscious would suggest that a subject might consciously alter, "through a decision of will," the criterion value of v so as to access, if necessary, material that may be fairly, but not unbearably, distressing; thus, material in the preconscious buffer may be rendered accessible with effort.)

In the flowchart, an additional decision node has been added, namely, "Is $x \geq w$?" which determines whether material in consciousness (which may be quite anxiety-provoking, even if $x < v$) is to be acted out or communicated (through free association, for example). In the experimental literature the subject's failure to *report* anxiety-provoking (perhaps embarrassing) conscious *thoughts* is termed *response suppression*. It is with this decision node, which concerns overt-response decisions, that mathematical decision theory has concerned itself (cf. Erdelyi, 1974; Green and Swets, 1966; Swets, 1964). As Erdelyi and Goldberg (1979) have argued, there is no theoretical reason why this extremely fruitful mathematical framework should not be conceptually generalized to earlier decision nodes, resulting in a grand unification within a highly formal theoretical system of dynamic phenomena. It is for this reason in part that the author argued earlier against the exclusion of conscious defenses from the domain of defense processes in general.

Although Freud did not specifically include this third "screen" in his Chapter VII model, it is implicit in his overall theory—and therapeutic experience. The withholding of embarrassing conscious ideas in psychoanalytic psychotherapy—the breaking of the "basic rule"—is standard fare. By including two censors in his Chapter VII model, Freud's intent was not to suggest that there were merely two such sites, but rather that there were more than one: "We shall do well . . . to assume that to every transition from one system to that immediately above it (that is, every advance to a higher stage of psychical organization) there corresponds a new censorship" (Freud, 1915b, p. 192).

The author (Erdelyi, 1974; Erdelyi and Goldberg, 1979) has shown how biased decisions are in fact ubiquitous at all levels, starting at the perceptual periphery (for example, "Shall I look?") extending to the response periphery ("Shall I report what I have seen/thought?"). Thus, "there is no single locus or set of loci at which tendentious processing (censoring, filtering, etc.) occurs; rather, *bias begins at the beginning and ends only at the very end of information processing*" (Erdelyi and Goldberg, 1979, p. 391).

Obviously, then, the flowchart in Figure 5.9 is a *very* schematic summary of the model. It oversimplifies in conceptual as well as in trivial ways. For example, as rendered here, without certain necessary subroutines there is no provision for clearing information from the various buffers once the information has been entered into them. At a more conceptual level, it is clear that variants of repression, such as isolation, would require another set of decision and command nodes. In the case of isolation, the nodes would have to bring about the dissociation between affect and factual information in order to allow the facts (minus the affect) to be experienced in consciousness (assuming that the affectless facts do not breach the decision criteria, μ and v). Because of the immense complexity of defense processes, probably any general model would be oversimple. Nevertheless, actual simulations of complex defensive maneuvers have been written and tested by Colby and his associates (e.g., Colby, 1981; Faught, Colby, and Parkinson, 1977). In their work, they report on a sophisticated self-deceiver, the paranoid PARRY (a program), which manages to pass Turing-like tests of indistinguishability vis-à-vis human paranoids (Colby, Hilf, Weber, and Kraemer, 1972). When PARRY is sufficiently threatened, its reality-testing routine (the INFERENCE process) is overridden by the reality-distorting PARANOID MODE, which defends it against unbearable mental distress, "shame." Thus: "If shame crosses a threshold for paranoia (SHAME equal to 10), the paranoid mode is activated. The first consequence of the paranoid mode is the rejection of the belief that led to the increase in shame by resetting the truth value of the belief.... Instead an alternate belief is inferred" (Faught, Colby, and Parkinson, 1977, pp. 175–176). It should be noted, moreover, that in the simulation, the paranoid intention is "activated outside the normal intention process on condition of extreme shame affect. Such a process is a clear example of unconscious processing, an intentional process that is not available to conscious inspection either during or after its performance" (p. 179).

Although the variety of specific ways in which distressing information can be rejected from consciousness is for all practical purposes limitless (the reader can no doubt generate his or her own flow diagrams for diverse possible repression tactics), a unifying theme—a grand strategy, if not the specific tactics—of repression (in the narrow *or* the general sense) is the biased or tendentious processing of information at decision nodes. Thus, repression/suppression/censorship can be conceptualized in the powerful framework of mathematical decision theory as the *biased* setting of decision criteria across the sequence of decision nodes through which information must pass. In signal-detection theory terms (the best known realization of mathematical decision theory in psychology), materials to be repressed/suppressed are subjected to overly stringent decision criteria, β, the consequence of which, given the fact that the input of later stages is the output of earlier stages, is a diminution of d' (accessibility) because β effects in sequence generate consequent d' effects (Erdelyi, 1974; 1985).

The mechanism of *denial*, conceived of here as tendentious failure of insight, can be readily formalized in these terms, as has already been suggested (pages 221–222). In the narrowest sense of repression, some manifest content, ϵ, is denied access into consciousness (conceived here as the result of biased β settings throughout the sequence of decision nodes). In denial, the biases involved are conceptualized as biased criterion settings for items in the contextual ecology to be included in the operative context, $[\epsilon]$. Another way of saying this (see

pages 103–104) is that each item in the limitless contextual ecology is assigned a biased weight, w_i, which results, in effect, in the tendentious
selection of certain contextual items (when $w_i > 0$) and not others
(when $w_i = 0$), which in turn results in a tendentious conception
(sight, insight, and so forth) of reality, that is, $\epsilon | [w_i \epsilon_i]$. Colby and his
associates' work is, in effect, a simulation of this basic idea.

The Empirical Evidence for Repression[1]

Clinical Evidence.   Excepting a transitory fascination with Jung's reac-
tion-time studies of word associations, Freud saw little need or value in
laboratory demonstrations of repression. (Jung himself was later to turn
against the experimental approach to complex mental processes:
"Whosoever wishes to know about the human mind will learn nothing,
or almost nothing, from experimental psychology [Jung, 1928, p. 246].")
The basic phenomenon, if not its varied manifestations, was too obvious in Freud's view, ubiquitously observed in the clinic and in everyday life. Responding in 1934 to reprints sent to him by Rosenzweig on
attempts to demonstrate repression experimentally, Freud stated
bluntly that he could not "put much value" on such confirmations
because repression was based on a "wealth of reliable observations"
that made it "independent of experimental verification," adding, with
little apparent confidence, that the exercise could at least "do no harm"
(cf. MacKinnon and Dukes, 1964). What types of observations was
Freud alluding to? These were essentially of a clinical nature, and we
now turn to their consideration under two organizing paradigms.

HYPERMNESIA PARADIGM.   Data subsumed under this heading involve
those not infrequent situations in which the subject (in therapy, hypnosis, or with just the passage of time) manages to remember some
heretofore inaccessible painful idea, including in many instances the
original resolve to reject the material from consciousness. This is a
direct form of what Freud sometimes referred to as "the return of the repressed" and, as such, constitutes the most straightforward proof of the
existence of repression. There are numerous instances of such hypermnesias (that is, lifting of amnesias) scattered across Freud's clinical
reports. In Freud's famous case, "The Wolfman" (Freud, 1918), the patient, after some premonitory dreams, suddenly recalled his sister's

[1]This section, based in part on a chapter by Erdelyi and Goldberg (1979), reviews the
empirical evidence, both clinical and experimental, for the existence of repression. The
review of laboratory research (pages 249–259) is somewhat detailed and may be side-
stepped by readers not concerned at this juncture with the technical status of the experimental literature.

seduction of him ("Let's show one another our bottoms," and so forth). In the case of Elizabeth von R. (Breuer and Freud, 1895), the patient experienced terrible physical pain whenever she began to broach the idea that she was eventually to retrieve into consciousness, the wish that her beloved sister should die so she might marry her brother-in-law. Even before the climactic hypermnesia, Elizabeth was aware that she had "carefully avoided" certain thoughts (such as, the possibility that her sister might die of her illness); after the hypermnesia, she felt excruciating guilt, the motive for "fending off" the idea. Getting at the painful psychological material was a "layer by layer" process, akin to "excavating a buried city (p. 139)," except that the patient fought the "work of recollection" at every step. We have already had occasion to consider Freud's observations on the retrieval of unbearable memories: Such memories are "stratified concentrically" about a traumatic "nucleus," the material becoming progessively more inaccessible as the subject gets closer to the traumatic kernel.

Such hypermnesia-based evidence for repression is not, of course, limited to Freud's observations. It is a virtually standard feature of any long-term clinical interaction, whether the therapist is psychoanalytically oriented (e.g., Deutsch, 1965; A. Freud, 1936; Lindner, 1955) or otherwise (e.g., Thigpen and Cleckley, 1957). In Thigpen and Cleckley's famous case, *The Three Faces of Eve,* the patient, with the initial help of hypnosis, manages to recover a variety of originally inaccessible aversive memories (such as, the terrifying experience of being forced by her mother to touch the face of her dead grandmother). Moreover, the patient was able to recall in some instances the hitherto unconscious undertaking of the repression itself, an effort experienced consciously as headaches (e.g., p. 29). Similarly, there exists an abundance of reports in the literature on traumatic neurosis of recoveries of unbearable memories through hypnosis, drugs, or dynamic therapies (e.g., Gillespie, 1942; Grinker and Spiegel, 1945a, 1945b; Janis, Mahl, Kagan, and Holt, 1969; Kardiner and Spiegel, 1947). Gillespie (1942), for example, reports the case of a man buried alive by an explosion. After his rescue, the man developed symptoms of cramps and bed wetting that could be neither cured nor explained until the patient recalled, under Evipan narcosis, the terrible leg cramps from which he had suffered while trapped in the debris and his desperate effort to avoid the shame of wetting his pants while thus trapped. Grinker and Spiegel (1945a) report the permanent cure of a patient's vomiting symptom after the patient was able to gain consciousness (under the influence of sodium pentothal) of hitherto unconscious resentment toward his superior officers (Case 30). Another patient (Case 43) was cured of his symptoms of depression, moodiness, and insomnia after gaining consciousness (again under sodium pentothal) of his unconscious resentments against his family, particularly his younger brother. Without hypnosis or drugs, another patient (Kardiner and Spiegel, 1947) was eventually able to recall, after several years of intermittent dynamic therapy, the actual details of the airplane crash he survived, of which he had been hitherto amnesic. Typically, patients experience great anxiety in recovering traumatic memories and struggle against the work of recollection.

The hypermnesias of traumatic materials achieved by combat neurotics have been construed by some experimentalists as constituting unambiguous corroboration of "the reality of repression" (Dollard and Miller, 1950, p. 201). Actually, experiences of this nature are by no means restricted to such special settings nor, for that matter, to the formal confines of the clinic. It appears that the vast majority of ordinary people can recollect the past use of one form of defense or another for the purpose of avoiding "psychic pain" (anxiety, guilt, shame, and so forth). In a recent survey of college students by the author, virtually every subject (85 of 86) reported having used "conscious repression" ("excluding painful memories or thoughts from consciousness for the purpose of avoiding psychological discomfort"). Moreover, a very high percentage of subjects were able to recall past use of unconscious defenses; that is, they were now conscious of previous unconscious use of defense techniques such as unconscious projection (72 percent), unconscious reaction formation (46 percent), unconscious displacement (86 percent), and unconscious rationalization (93 percent). Clearly, then, the direct hypermnesia paradigm of repression yields abundant support for repression: Most people, inside or outside formal clinical settings, can recall materials they had previously excluded from consciousness in order to avoid psychic pain and can, moreover, recall the specific techniques of defense by which the rejection from consciousness was achieved.

It remains only to ask whether such broad-based evidence allows any continuing doubt about the reality of repression. Actually, there are two methodological issues that must be confronted, both related to the problem of the shifting of *report criteria* with pressures to produce recoveries of memories (Egan, 1958; Erdelyi, 1970; 1972; Green and Swets, 1966). The first of these is, in the terminology of signal-detection theory, the problem of *false alarms,* or in Freud's system, the problem of *paramnesias* or "false recollections." It is possible that subjects purportedly recovering lost memories are in fact generating not memories of true events but fanciful guesses, fantasies, or plain confabulations. Such data would then constitute evidence not of repression but of imagination.

There can be little question that clinicians have seriously underestimated this problem, no doubt because subjects will frequently generate false recollections with every sign of believing in them (cf. Erdelyi,

1970; 1984; Orne, Soskis, Dinges, and Orne, 1984). Freud himself, as noted in Chapter 2, fell prey to this methodological trap when, being too credulous of his early patients' apparent hypermnesias of childhood seductions, he rushed into his "infantile seduction theory" of hysteria only to have to repudiate it in short order (Freud, 1906). Hypnotic hypermnesias are similarly suspect (Orne et al., 1984). It was shown in Chapter 2, for example, that under hypnosis subjects can be induced to recall "memories" from previous reincarnations as well as from the future. As Bernheim used to warn his students, "when a physician employs hypnosis with a patient it is wise always to be aware who may be hypnotizing whom" (cited in Thigpen and Cleckley, 1957, pp. 136–137).

The methodological solution to this problem is to obtain some independent verification of the accuracy of the hypermnesias produced by the subject. Unfortunately, this is not always possible; moreover, even when it is, clinicians have not as a rule made efforts to verify their patients' hypermnesias, partly because it is difficult, partly because clinicians are not sensitized to the methodological issue, and partly because it is, according to many, of little clinical import. Nevertheless the problem is not insurmountable. A careful search will turn up specific hypermnesias of painful materials that are consistent with already-known facts (as in the details of the air crash of which Kardiner and Spiegel's [1947] patient was amnesic) or which are independently confirmed by relatives and acquaintances (e.g., F. R. Schreiber, 1973; Thigpen and Cleckley, 1957).

Even if the recovered memories can be shown to be veridical (that is, to constitute "hits" rather than "false alarms"), there remains the residual methodological issue, underscored by signal-detection theory, of whether the subject is actually remembering more or merely reporting more (see Chapter 2, pages 71–72). For example, it is possible that Elizabeth von R. was from the beginning aware of her shameful wishes toward her sister and brother-in-law but could not initially bring herself to acknowledge them to her therapist. This brings us to the murky frontier between deception and self-deception (Sackeim and Gur, 1977), that is, report bias versus memory bias. Despite the impressive contribution of signal-detection theory (which might yet find profitable application in the clinic) the fact remains that no absolutely foolproof technique exists for resolving the problem—which is tantamount to saying that psychology has not yet devised a fully reliable technique for reading minds. In the interim we must remain content with a Bayesian approach, involving conditional probabilities rather than certainties. Fortunately, there are myriad clinical situations in which we are able, by virtue of our combined knowledge of the subject, the context of events, and the types of events involved, to dismiss with some confidence the possibility of the initial withholding of the eventually recovered materials. Laboratory data, moreover, with maximal controls over shifting report criteria (and total control over false-alarm effects) have confirmed the feasibility of achieving extensive hypermnesias of hitherto inaccessible materials (see Chapter 2).

DISSOCIATION PARADIGM. Evidence falling under this heading involves situations in which the subject is aware of an idea (wish, attitude, and so forth)—ϵ—yet, unbeknownst to himself, betrays by a multitude of minor but converging signs a quite different disposition—$\epsilon | [\epsilon]$—that is antithetical and repugnant to the conscious one. The subject, then, is emitting double messages while being aware of only one. Thus, a conscious belief (such as, ϵ: "I hate him") is, or gives the appearance of being, dissociated from an unconscious belief ($\epsilon | [\epsilon]$: "I love him").

The psychotic Dr. Schreber (Freud, 1911), for example, initially claimed to be grateful to his physician, but both the manner in which he stated his gratitude and the wider context of his case suggested a contrary disposition. He did not want to be homosexually assaulted by his physician or God (father?), but he gave every sign of desiring precisely that.

Though not everyone is likely to have had firsthand experience with such a dramatic delusional case, probably most readers can recall instances in their own lives or that of their acquaintances in which a conscious disposition was contradicted by a confluence of concurrent behaviors implying the contrary, but not necessarily conscious, disposition. (In normal people, troubled love relations are a particularly fecund source for the observation—or remembrance—of such motivated psychological dissociations, or repressions.) Despite the ubiquity of this type of occurrence in everyday life, experimental psychology has ignored it in its approach to the problem of repression. Perhaps the reason is that this type of evidence is indirect and, more seriously, based on *interpretation*. It could be argued that there exists no formal method by which the existence of latent dispositions can be logically proven. Thus, the attribution of unconscious homosexual desires to Schreber—never acknowledged by him—is really a matter of inference or interpretation, not of logical demonstration.

Yet all of us, regardless of theoretical predisposition, engage in psychological interpretation for *normal* communication; indeed, the overliteral communicator is aberrant (e.g., Kasanin, 1964). Thus, though there is no logical technique for proving that a sarcastic remark, such as "Brutus is an honorable man," actually means, "Brutus is *not* an honorable man," the real but latent meaning is obvious to all. Indeed, the understanding of a whole family of communication modalities, as we have seen in Chapter 4, is predicated on the ability to interpret latent meanings; thus, not "getting a joke" constitutes a failure of interpretation. To prove the existence of such latent meanings to a person who has a sense of humor is superfluous; it is obvious without laboratory demonstrations. But to prove such latent meanings to a person who operates at a purely literal level—an insight-blind person—is beyond the pale of any logic or methodology, as would be the proof of the existence of green grass to a sightless person. The problem of attempting to prove logically that a person who consciously detests homosexuality (ϵ) latently is attracted toward homosexuality ($\epsilon|[\epsilon]$) while avoiding awareness of the latent fact is the same.

Laboratory Evidence

THE JUNG-RIKLIN WORD-ASSOCIATION STUDIES. The earliest laboratory studies applied to the repression problem were those of Jung and Riklin (1904–1905; Jung, 1906), both then at the famed Burghölzli Clinic of Eugen Bleuler. Perhaps the best way to grasp the rationale of these studies is first to consider some of Jung's related work on lie detection (Jung, 1935), from which modern lie-detection systems are partly derived.

Jung and his colleagues found that a dissimulating criminal—or patient—could unwittingly give himself away through certain anomalous responses, such as changed pulse rates, depth of breathing, elevated galvanic skin responses, or a variety of abnormalities in word associations (unusually long reaction times to critical stimuli; superficial, repetitive, or clang associations; and the like). The emotionally toned topics about which the subject was deliberately (and consciously) trying to lie produced emotional reactions that these more subtle "indicators" gave away. For example, three nurses suspected of stealing some money from their hospital were individually administered word-association tests by Jung. One of the nurses gave unusually slow reactions to stimulus words related to the crime (such as, *money*), on which basis Jung accused her of the theft. Thereupon she broke down and confessed. The emotional ideation, despite the subject's attempt at dissimulation, was registered by the more sensitive indicator.

The question now arises: What if a person gives the appearance through these indicators of emotionality of lying but is not conscious of any attempt to lie or even of the subject about which he is presumably lying? One might infer, as Jung did, that the person was engaged in a private lie, that is, he was lying to himself. In this view, then, the person is treating his own consciousness as an outside agent from which some emotional facts are being hidden but that, as in the case of the public lie, more sensitive indicators register and reveal. It was such evidence of emotional reactivity in the absence of awareness that led Jung to construe his experiments as demonstrating the existence of "emotionally-toned ideational complexes" existing in dissociation from consciousness.

Though interesting, and certainly important for the field of lie detection, the research program cannot be said to shed much light on the problem of repression. A careful reading of this body of work reveals a plethora of methodological as well as conceptual flaws. For example, anomalous reactions such as delayed reaction-times need not indicate emotionality; other factors, such as familiarity or complexity, might yield similar effects, a problem for which Jung was criticized and for which he had no answer (Jung, 1935, p. 65). Then, even if the indicator correctly reveals emotionality as opposed to some other factor, it still does not follow that the subject was unconscious of the ideation triggering the emotion. Indeed, a careful reading of Jung's writings on the topic typically shows Jung unveiling a conscious rather than an unconscious secret (that is, a secret withheld from others rather than from the self). Moreover, for those cases in which the subject reports no awareness of the ideation producing emotional reactions, it is never clear what he is repressing, if anything. Jung often supplies some inferred complex, but one can never be certain whether the subject's lack of awareness of it reflects repression or faulty interpretation on the part of the therapist. Thus, it is by no means clear how—if at all—these experimental data extend the insights obtainable in straightforward clinical settings, especially if the demonstration must also ultimately hinge on clinical interpretation.

DISTURBED MEMORY FOR UNPLEASANT OR ANXIETY-PROVOKING EVENTS. Another early experimental approach to repression was the attempt to demonstrate that memory for unpleasant events is poorer than for pleasant events (e.g., Koch, 1930; Meltzer, 1930; Moore, 1935). Perhaps no other research effort in the area has been as universally criticized by opponents as well as proponents of psychoanalysis. Again, the problems are conceptual as well as methodological (for an in-depth review, see Rapaport, 1942). Perhaps the most obvious experimental issue is whether in fact it is true that memory for the unpleasant is inferior to that for the pleasant. Thus, Cason (1932) demonstrated that extremely pleasant and unpleasant experiences tend to be remembered equally, but both are remembered better than mildly pleasant or unpleasant experiences.

At the theoretical level, it has been claimed that such laboratory work rests on a basic misunderstanding of Freud's concept in that not all unpleasant, but only anxiety-provoking, materials tend to activate repression (Eriksen and Pierce, 1968; MacKinnon and Dukes, 1964; Sears, 1936; 1942). Wolitzky, Klein, and Dworkin (1976) have extended

the point by insisting that conflict must also be present. This line of criticism is probably unjustified. Not until 1926 (in *Inhibitions, Symptoms
and Anxiety*), near the end of his career, did Freud specifically formulate
his notion that anxiety instigates repression. Moreover, a broad conception of "anxiety" (including guilt and shame) is hard to disentangle
from the unpleasant, especially in the light of Freud's pleasure-
unpleasure principle, in which unpleasure is defined generally as tension (and pleasure as the reduction of tension).

The more serious theoretical problem with this research approach,
in the author's view, is the erroneous assumption that unpleasant
things in general are repressed. This certainly was never Freud's position. It does not follow that because things that *are* repressed are unpleasant (or lead to "unpleasure")—a position that Freud did hold—
unpleasant things therefore are necessarily repressed. Freud (1917),
actually, addresses this point:

> [Is it not] that which is painful which ... is hard to
> forget ... as for example the recollection of grievances or hu-
> miliations? This fact is quite correct, but the objection [with
> respect to the repression notion] is not sound. It is important
> to begin early to reckon with the fact that the mind is an arena,
> a sort of tumbling ground, for the struggles of antagonistic im-
> pulses; or to express it in non-dynamic terms, that the mind is
> made up of contradictions. ... (p. 68)

Here Freud is emphasizing that the psychological system is not
unitary, based solely on the pleasure-unpleasure principle. The reality
principle opposes the developmentally primitive pleasure-unpleasure
principle, and it is precisely with respect to the relatively innocuous
events experienced in the laboratory that contact with reality is likely to
prevail. Thus, the innocuous stimuli of the laboratory are the least likely
to activate defenses (and even if they were activated, a variety of defensive devices, such as isolation, would not necessarily yield a diminution
of episodic memory).

In an effort to come to grips with the problem of ineffective laboratory stimuli, researchers cast about for some experimental manipulation
that would be disturbing enough psychologically to trigger repression.
A major breakthrough (or so it was thought) was provided by what
MacKinnon and Dukes (1964) have aptly termed "Zeigarnik's uninten-
tional study of repression" (p. 675). Zeigarnik is best known for her
famous, if often disputed, Zeigarnik effect, the discovery that uncompleted tasks tend to be better remembered than completed tasks.
The relevance of this work for repression is Zeigarnik's (1927) discovery
of a systematic exception to the Zeigarnik effect: When the noncomple-
tion of a task was construed by the subject as a personal failure rather

than merely a consequence of insufficient time, that is, when the subject felt stupid, awkward, or inferior because of the failed task, then it was the uncompleted rather than the completed task that tended to be "extremely often forgotten." These tasks—Zeigarnik called them "repressed tasks"—were thought to produce an "ego-threat" of sufficient seriousness as to mobilize repression, accounting for the forgetting of failed tasks.

This approach was systematically explored and extended by subsequent researchers (e.g., Buss and Brock, 1963; Eriksen, 1952; Flavell, 1955; Glixman, 1949; Gould, 1942; Holmes, 1972; Holmes and Schallow, 1969; Lazarus and Longo, 1953; Rosenzweig, 1933; 1943; 1952; Rosenzweig and Mason, 1934; Zeller, 1950a; 1950b; 1951), though the emphasis soon shifted away from the interruption of tasks per se to direct manipulation of anxiety through the laboratory induction of feelings of failure or success, guilt, psychopathology, and so forth (for reviews, see Eriksen and Pierce, 1968; Holmes, 1974; MacKinnon and Dukes, 1964).

The performance decrement effects for anxiety-related materials are reasonably robust, particularly if individual differences in defense strategies are taken into account (cf. Eriksen, 1952; Lazarus and Longo, 1953). Nevertheless, the findings—or the conclusions derived from the findings—have been subjected to a variety of criticisms:

> that diminution in memory is in itself an insufficient demonstration of repression unless the return of the repressed, that is, hypermnesia for the forgotten, can be effected by the removal of the associated anxiety (Zeller, 1950a; 1950b; 1951)

> that performance decrements in themselves need not arise from repression but might result instead from other mechanisms, such as disturbed attention (Aborn, 1953), response "interference" or "competition" (Holmes, 1972; Holmes and Schallow, 1969; Russell, 1952), or the general effect of anxiety upon the performance of complex tasks (Truax, 1957)

> that since subjects have been found to ruminate about their anxiety-provoking experience before recall trials, the subsequent memory decrements cannot be a consequence of repression (D'Zurilla, 1965)

> that the memory decrement effect cannot involve repression since it appears to be subject to conscious control (Aborn, 1953)

> that the studies in question do not tap repression, since the threat manipulations produced in the laboratory are simply not powerful enough to mobilize repression (Kris, 1947) or at least not such gross defensive reactions as outright amnesias (Wolitzky, Klein, and Dworkin, 1976)

> and that—and here the author adds his own criticism—it has not been demonstrated that the obtained performance decre-

ments reflect true memory rather than merely report bias processes.

Although there is merit to some of these criticisms, many of them may also be shown to be flawed. Aborn's (1953) objection, for example, that repression must be a process beyond conscious control is not valid. As we have seen (Chapter 1), Freud's earliest nonhypnotic technique for recovering repressed memories was nothing other than conscious effort (Breuer and Freud, 1895). D'Zurilla's (1965) observation that subjects ruminate about their failures is interesting and in accord with clinical experience, as with the repetition-compulsion nightmares of war neurotics (Janis et al., 1969), but it does not follow that the resultant memory failures are therefore not a product of repression. Zeller's (1950a) critique has been very influential, yet is probably off the point, having more to do with the demonstration of *the repressed* than with the existence of *repression*. It is true, of course, that at least some repressed materials should be subject to recovery. This, after all, is the goal of psychoanalytic psychotherapy. However, the return of the repressed is not a necessary condition for the assumption of repression; psychoanalysis in fact maintains that most repressed materials are never recovered. A modern conception of memory, moreover, would specifically suggest that, contrary to Freud, some repressed materials will in fact be lost irretrievably. Thus, although materials rejected from long-term memory are likely to remain available for subsequent retrieval, rejection from other memory buffers, as, for example, iconic memory stores (Neisser, 1967), would result in permanent loss of the material—not because repression erases the memory trace, but because memory traces in buffers other than long-term memory tend to decay precipitously (Erdelyi, 1974).

The "response interference" or "disturbed attention" notions need not be viewed as criticisms of repression; they may be regarded as theoretical or, possibly, terminological recapitulations of repression. Freud's own concept of repression is an "interference" one (though he did not, of course, use behavioristic terminology), and Freud specifically viewed the withdrawal of attention ("attention cathexis") as one means by which repression is effected (Freud, 1915a). The important criticism behind Holmes' (1972) response-interference position, however, is the question of whether the interference is tendentious, that is, purposeful, as opposed to being merely a "non-defensive attentional process." This, Holmes is right to assert, has not been proven. His own research has shown, for example, that performance decrements can be obtained not only with ego-threat but with ego-boosting manipulations as well.

PERCEPTUAL DEFENSE: IS IT REPRESSION?   Probably no topic in the recent history of experimental psychology has led to as bitter and sustained a controversy as the issue of perceptual defense, the purported tendency of subjects to resist perceiving anxiety-provoking stimuli (Dixon, 1971; 1981; Erdelyi, 1974). (With certain identifiable subjects, at certain levels of stimulus emotionality, an opposite, sensitization phenomenon may be observed, termed *perceptual vigilance.*) The exceptional attention lavished on the topic by a generation of psychologists has produced what is perhaps the most profound and wide-ranging analysis of the issues confronting the study of repressionlike phenomena in the laboratory. Probably every question to have arisen in other laboratory literatures on repression has cropped up in the perceptual-defense area, where it is likely to have been subjected to deeper and more articulated analysis than elsewhere. The contested issues have ranged from the most technical methodological matters to questions of logic and philosophy.

For example, it was thought initially by some critics that the very notion of perceptual defense rested on a logical absurdity, for it seemed altogether paradoxical to conceive of a subject defensively *not perceiving* a stimulus without first *perceiving* the stimulus to be defended against. This issue, as Sackeim and Gur (1977) have pointed out, is analogous to certain philosophic objections (e.g., Sartre, 1943) to the general notion of repression and the unconscious.

Even a psychological version of Zeno's paradox arose, wherein it was argued that perceptual defense implied a censoring homunculus, which in turn had to imply a homunculus within the homunculus, and thus an infinite (and therefore impossible) regress of homunculi. Such arguments were a natural consequence of the now-abandoned behavioristic Weltanschauung of the experimental psychology of those days.

It is worth noting that these philosophic difficulties of perceptual defense were resolved neither by laboratory research nor by philosophy but, instead, by an analogy. As soon as the rat gave way to the computer as experimental psychology's central metaphor, the problems dissolved of their own weight, since it now became clear, indeed trivially obvious, that computers could selectively regulate their own input (and thus perceive at one level without perceiving at another level) through the operation of "control processes" that were neither mystical nor eternally regressive.

On the methodological side, there was a wide assortment of issues. The most fundamental of these was the question of whether the phenomenon was in fact *perceptual* in nature, a problem of little consequence for the issue of repression, particularly in those cases where critics maintained that the effect was not a *perceptual* but a *memory* or *cognitive* phenomenon, which is tantamount to saying that it is not *perceptual* defense but rather *memory* or *cognitive* defense—that is, standard repression.

The trivializing criticism in this family of criticisms was that the phenomenon constituted not a *perceptual* bias, but a *report* bias, resulting from the subject's embarrassment at having to report taboo items. The application of signal-detection techniques to this area, together with its theoretical reconceptualization in terms of modern nontachistoscopic work on selective attention (Erdelyi, 1974), have cast doubt on the latter criticism, so that after almost a decade of general disrepute, perceptual defense is regaining wide credibility (Nisbett and Wilson, 1977).

Has the laboratory literature on perceptual defense, then, finally accomplished the task of proving the existence of repression in the laboratory? Some issues remain to be answered. First, is it proper to view perceptual defense as a form of repression? Note, for example, that it does not pass Zeller's (1950a) criterion, since there is no evidence that the input defended against can be recovered. As already noted, however, Zeller's notion is not well taken. Though the "return of the repressed" might be a reasonable goal for clinicians, accustomed as they are to exploring long-term memory, an effect based on the "function of rejecting and keeping something out of consciousness" from a fleeting memory buffer will result in the permanent loss of that "something." It is felt, therefore, that perceptual defense conforms to Freud's fundamental definition of repression and may be properly regarded as a form of repression.

Another issue, however, is more problematic. It is essentially the same as that applied by Holmes to the memory studies of the previous section. Granted that perception and cognition may be disrupted in the processing of emotional stimuli, does it necessarily follow that the disruption is tendentious? That is, does lowered sensitivity necessarily imply a defensive intention not to see, as opposed to a general disruption of processing by emotionality? Thus, for example, in a perceptual experiment reminiscent of some of Holmes' work, Erdelyi and Appelbaum (1973) demonstrated that the perception, by religious Jews, of a neutral tachistoscopic display was as much disrupted by a contiguous swastika as by a contiguous Star of David. The subjects presumably were not "defending" against the stimulus items associated with the Star of David.

In the case of tachistoscopic stimuli, on which the vast bulk of the perceptual-defense literature rests, the methodological problem of proving intention is even more intractable than elsewhere; the disruption processes occur so rapidly that the perceiver would not even be in a position to give subjective reports of their cognitive activities or intentions during the disruption. Thus, though it is probably safe to conclude, despite the weight of past controversies, that brief emotional stimuli may yield disrupted perception, it does not necessarily follow that the disruption occurs because of a deliberate rejection of the emotional material.

Much more helpful in this regard is the large modern literature on selective attention (e.g., Broadbent, 1958; 1971; Moray, 1970; Norman, 1976), which, though never pursued with repression in view, has nevertheless demonstrated persuasively that the perceiver can intentionally reject selected perceptual inputs. Neisser and Becklen (1975), for example, extending the auditory shadowing paradigm to the visual modality, demonstrated a similarly remarkable selectivity in visual processing. Thus, subjects were shown capable of massively blanking out an unfolding visual scene at which they were actually staring in order to attend to another overlapping scene that had been superimposed on the same visual field.

Two separate facts, then, have been demonstrated in the laboratory, both critical to the repression concept. It has been experimentally shown that (a) emotional stimuli may yield impaired perception and (b) that the perceiver can intentionally and selectively reject perceptual inputs. What has *not* been demonstrated in the laboratory, however, is the conjoint fact that the perception of emotional stimuli is disrupted *because* of intentional rejection by the perceiver. It is highly plausible of course, that such may be the case; it would be unthinkable that such remarkable cognitive capability would not be put to instrumental use.

In this case, moreover, a demonstration of the conjoint fact is not beyond the reach of the experimental paradigm in question: It can probably be shown without much difficulty (especially if individual differences are taken into account at the outset) that a traumatic visual sequence superimposed over a neutral sequence will result, without any prompting from the experimenter, in an intentional rejection of the aversive material. This would be the cognitive counterpart of closing or averting one's eye in order not to see some unbearable scene.

HYPNOTIC AND NONHYPNOTIC STUDIES OF INTENTIONAL FORGETTING.   If the frequency with which Freud refers to Bernheim's work on hypnotically directed forgetting (which Freud personally witnessed during a brief visit to Bernheim's clinic in 1889) is any indication, research on intentional forgetting played a significant role in the development of the repression concept. In "astonishing experiments upon his hospital patients" (Freud, 1925b, p. 17), Bernheim would hypnotize a patient, subject him to a variety of experiences and posthypnotic suggestions, direct the patient *not* to recall the hypnotic experiences (but nevertheless to carry out the indicated posthypnotic behaviors), awaken him from the trance, and then question him about the to-be-forgotten, though just experienced, hypnotic events (cf. Freud, 1917, p. 245). The patient typically would recall little or nothing (posthypnotic amnesia), though Bernheim also showed that with persistent pressure the subject could be made gradually to recover the lost material (hypermnesia), a fact that Freud was later to turn to clinical account (Breuer and Freud, 1895).

Bernheim's informal hypnotic demonstrations have since been extensively replicated in the laboratory (for recent studies, see Kihlstrom and Evans, 1976; 1979; Kihlstrom, Evans, Orne, and Orne, 1980; Spanos and Ham, 1973). Further, a major experimental program on *non*hypnotic "directed forgetting" ("intentional forgetting," "voluntary forgetting," "selective amnesia," and so on) has arisen in the modern cognitive literature (e.g., Bjork, 1972; Bjork, LaBerge, and Legrand, 1968; Davis and Okada, 1971; Epstein, 1972; Geiselman, Bjork, and Fishman, 1983; MacLeod, 1975; Rakover, 1975; Roediger and Crowder, 1972; Shebliske and Epstein, 1973; Weiner, 1968), though with few exceptions (Geiselman et al., 1983; Roediger and Crowder, 1972; Weiner, 1968), the relationship of this work to either Bernheim's research or to the issue of repression has been ignored. Nevertheless, this contemporary work on intentional forgetting, like the modern research on selective attention and inattention, tends to confirm the basic repression mechanism—if not the defense—posited by Freud, that is, "the function of rejecting and keeping something out of consciousness."

There are, of course, a variety of methodological problems, the major one, once again, being the question of whether the effect is a report-bias ("response withholding") or memory-bias phenomenon. Especially in early efforts (Weiner, 1968), as in Bernheim's work, where subjects are first instructed to forget, then to remember, one needs to be concerned about the crosscurrent of implicit demands impinging on the subject and the problematic consequence of these conflictual demands upon what the subject is willing to say he does and does not remember.

In order to bypass these obvious problems, many of the recent studies have used indirect measures, such as, the reduction of interference by the (presumably) forgotten items on the remembering of other learned materials. The disadvantage of these more indirect approaches is that the conclusions that can be drawn are necessarily more indirect as well.

Fortunately, despite many unresolved problems, there can be no doubt of the existence of intentional forgetting in at least short-term memory tasks. The very nature of the demonstration of short-term memory (Brown, 1958; Peterson and Peterson, 1959)—namely that nonrehearsal of new inputs results in rapid memory loss—necessarily means that the subject can voluntarily effect selective forgetting through selective nonrehearsal. Archer and Margolin (1970) have confirmed this expectation experimentally.

Granted, then, that certain types of memories can be intentionally rejected and kept from consciousness, can these experimental demonstrations be construed as proofs of repression? Scholars in the field, as has been noted, have tended to sidestep this issue. They have proposed, however, various explanatory mechanisms for the effect which bear striking similarities in conception, and recently in actual wording, to Freud's own ideas. Thus, Epstein's (1972) "selective search" or selective "depth of search" hypothesis may be thought of as recapitulating Freud's (1915a) "attention cathexis" notion; similarly, Bjork's (1972) "differential grouping" hypothesis appears to be a variant of Freud's early (e.g., 1892–1893) "dissociation" theory; Rakover's (1975) "blocking" is reminiscent of Freud's (1900) "inhibition/censorship/suppression/repression." And recently, Geiselman, Bjork, and Fishman (1983) have reported uncovering a "missing mechanism" of intentional forgetting, namely, "retrieval inhibition" or "repression."

Has this line of research, then, finally come round to confirming in the laboratory Freud's clinically derived notion of repression?

The answer rests again on the considerations that confronted us in the case of selective inattention. The mechanisms—retrieval inhibition, repression, blocking, dissociation, and so on—clearly exist for the undertaking of defense. Also, aversive stimuli may be shown to disrupt memory (Erdelyi and Blumenthal, 1973; Loftus and Burns, 1981; Suedfeld, Erdelyi, and Corcoran, 1975). Yet, as before, the compound fact—that the available mechanisms are in fact deployed for defense against aversive stimuli—as plausible as it might appear, has not been demonstrated experimentally.

Conclusion on the Evidence for Repression with Some Observations on Methodology. What has been shown? The answer would seem to depend on whether one looks at the clinical or laboratory data, for the two approaches have had palpably different yields. Such differences, the author believes, reflect inherent differences in the two approaches, not some peculiar inconstancy of the phenomenon itself.

The strength of the clinical approach is its ability to reveal truly complex cognitive processes. It can uncover compound facts such as the conjoint occurrence of (a) tendentious rejection from awareness of (b) aversive materials (c) for the purpose of avoiding pain (d) often by unconscious means (though the latter fact is not essential for the proof of repression). From the clinical standpoint, the evidence for repression is overwhelming and obvious.

The weakness of the clinical approach, on the other hand, is its looseness of method. The most ubiquitous evidence is indirect, based on unregimented interpretation, which up to now has been more of an art form than a scientific instrument—though we should not forget that we use that "art" for everyday communication. The more direct evidence, namely hypermnesia effects, is methodologically more solid. Quite clearly, people at times forget traumatic events and then subsequently remember both the forgotten material and the defensive intent to forget. Even so, some features of these data cannot be fully verified. Report-bias effects have not been formally controlled. Moreover, as far as the paramnesia problem is concerned, one may verify the objective truth of an objective event (such as, "my father died") but not the objective truth of a subjective intent ("I wished not to face the fact that my father died"). Scientific psychology has yet to develop a methodology of purpose.

The strength of the laboratory/experimental approach, unlike the clinical, is its methodological rigor; its overriding weakness is its inability to deal with truly complex processes. Thus, none of the four critical facts in themselves are in any doubt within experimental psychology: (a) that there can be selective information rejection from awareness; (b) that aversive stimuli tend to be avoided; (c) that organisms strive to defend themselves against pain; and (d) that many psychological processes occur outside of awareness. All these facts, independently, are not in dispute; what is in dispute, and what has not been demonstrated experimentally, is the conjoint fact, that is, all the component facts integrated into a higher-order fact. In the absence of a clear-cut demonstration of the compound phenomenon, experimental psychologists have reflexively held the phenomenon accountable—not the method.

Displacement and Sublimation

We have already encountered displacement in the operation of the dream-work. In *displacement of accent*, as we have seen, there is a diversion of emphasis from the important to the trivial. More generally, displacement as a mechanism of defense refers to a family of techniques involving some kind of substitution. The drive (thought, feeling, and so forth) is diverted—transferred, retargeted, rechanneled, or the like—away from a taboo object onto another, more innocuous one. Displacements, then are "substitute formations" (Freud, 1917, p. 209). The therapeutic phenomenon of transference was viewed by Freud as a complex of displacements: Highly charged (often unconscious) emotions and attitudes applying to critical family members are displaced—transferred—onto the less anxiety-provoking figure of the therapist.

Sublimation is a special variant of displacement (for a summary of other conceptions of sublimation, see Madison, 1961; Sjöbäck, 1973). Sublimation is a form of displacement (rechanneling, diversion, substitution, transfer, and so on) in which the new object or drive is not merely less anxiety-provoking but actually positively valued socially.

Displacement is a mechanism that can be viewed fruitfully from the neobehavioristic learning vantage point. Consider the stimulus generalization function depicted in Figure 5.10. If the conditioned response to the conditioned stimulus (and other stimuli highly similar to it) produces intolerable distress, the response is inhibited. The conditioned response (in weaker form) will be emitted to less similar stimuli that fall outside the region of inhibition. Thus, "when the dominant response is prevented from occurring, the next strongest one will occur" (Dollard and Miller, 1950, p. 172).

Substitutive "displacement activities" (Lorenz, 1966) are seen in animals as well as humans. Ethologists such as Goodall (1971) and Lorenz (1966) have identified displacement behaviors in natural settings in species as diverse as fish, birds, and chimpanzees.

The "region of inhibition" is not as cut and dry as suggested in Figure 5.10. A more dynamic, articulated version of this approach to displacement has been provided by Dollard and Miller (1950) in their famous conflict model (Figure 5.11): An approach response tendency (which increases in strength the closer the goal) is opposed by an avoidance tendency (which also increases in strength the closer the goal, but at a faster rate). Both these are viewed as generalization functions. The point of strongest displacement, as Figure 5.11 suggests, is a stimulus of intermediary dissimilarity from the goal stimulus, corresponding to the maximal net strength of the resultant response tendency. Note that any change in the strength (height) of the approach or the avoidance tendency would shift the point of equilibrium and maximum net response strength. Thus, for example, a stronger approach drive—or a weaker avoidance drive—would result in the subject getting closer to the goal.

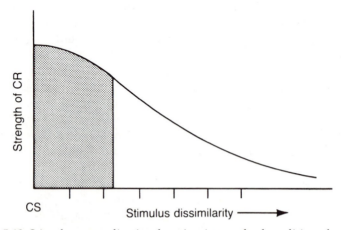

Figure 5.10. Stimulus generalization function (strength of conditioned response, CR, as a function of dissimilarity from the condition stimulus, CS). The shaded area respresents a region of inhibition.

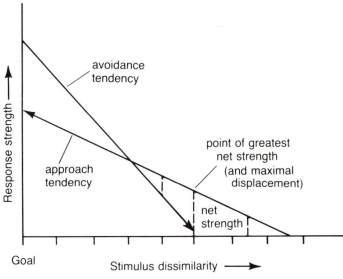

Figure 5.11. Dollard and Miller's (1950) model of displacement in terms of the generalization functions of approach and avoidance tendencies.

Dollard and Miller extend their analysis to include not only stimulus generalization but also *response* and *drive* generalization. Thus, if a particular response, R_i, is too anxiety-provoking, the organism may substitute another less anxiety-provoking response, R_i', to the same stimulus. Similarly, one drive may be substituted for another, unacceptable one (such as hunger for sexual arousal).

Despite the generality and heuristic fruitfulness of the Dollard and Miller approach, it is likely that it is oversimple as an all-purpose model of displacement. Thus, the "displacement activities" observed by ethologists often have no discernible stimulus (response, drive) similarity to the original—for example, a fight-versus-flight conflict may yield to a vigorous bout of self-grooming rather than either flight or fight. Also, the "substitutes" chosen by humans (a dog for a sister, as in the case of Deutsch's patient, pages 48–51, for example) are often not obviously similar. Thus, the stimulus-dissimilarity dimension of the Dollard and Miller model may not be psychologically valid.

It should be clear that the neobehavioristic approach is fully compatible with an information-processing conceptualization. It would be a trivial programming exercise to simulate the processes posited by Dollard and Miller. The basic component of one such simulation would be some kind of iterative routine which would examine the consequences of responding to a stimulus, S_i. If the response, R_i, to S_i were calculated to be overly anxiety-provoking, then another stimulus, S_i' (or another response, R_i') would be considered, until the calculated anxiety level undershot some preset anxiety threshold level.

Projection

Projection, the principal mechanism of paranoia, refers to the attribution of some unacceptable feeling or impulse of one's own to another person or outside agency.

Freud's monograph (1911) on the psychotic Dr. Schreber provides the classic psychoanalytic treatment of projection. The mechanism is viewed as a form of information misprocessing, one involving a particular type of propositional mistransformation (for a mathematical treatment, see Suppes and Warren, 1975): An unconscious proposition (of the form, subject-predicate-object) undergoes, in its representation in consciousness, a reversal of subject and object. Thus, for example, the unconscious proposition,

I love *him*

becomes, in consciousness,

He loves *me*.

The Schreber case is by no means atypical. Consider the paranoid subject, N., described by Erdelyi and Goldberg (1979, p. 372):

> This patient continually rails against homosexuals, whom he detests with a violent passion. After a brief, unsuccessful marriage, followed by impotence, he began to experience delusions of persecution, according to which the CIA and the FBI were continually observing him with the ultimate purpose of getting him to submit to the sexual advances of Richard Nixon. He gave up all attempts at heterosexual sex, because he "would not make love in public," i.e., in front of the lurking agents. He soon came to understand also that his impotence had been imposed on him, via laser rays, by Nixon's agents. Satellites specifically sent up for this purpose began to bombard him with homosexual messages. Finally he constructed a special protective hat fitted with a complex electrical jamming device. He wore this hat continually, at home and in public places, including restaurants and work (he was soon dismissed). Even so, the messages that he should submit to Nixon increased in intensity and began to "penetrate" at times. Around this period he took all his jackets to a tailor and had the tailor sew up the slits (or flaps) in the back of the jackets. He implored his male acquaintances to do likewise, lest they be taken for "slot-jacket ass panderers." He deplored tight dungarees because they

revealed buttocks too openly and therefore constituted a disgraceful invitation to sodomy. He complained that the CIA was spreading rumors that he was a homosexual; indeed they had contrived to find a "double" for himself and a friend and photographed them—the doubles—in "disgusting" homosexual acts, all for the purpose of blackmail, so that he might submit to the homosexual importunings of the "anarcho-communist sodomite" Gerald Ford, who, as he now came to realize, was really "behind" the conspiracy (Nixon, it now turned out, was just a "front"). Ford, he believed, succeeded in having his landlord evict him from his apartment, so that he would be forced to live in the local YMCA among "faggots." This was meant to be a "softening-up" tactic. Without any possible doubt, he consciously hated homosexuals; indeed the extent of his hatred was worrisome, for he began to speak of destroying them, seeing himself an innocent heterosexual victim of homosexual persecution. Yet all the contextual signs suggested that he in fact was homosexually inclined—though he would have met such a suggestion not only with vehemence but probably violence.

Real-life examples, such as the present case of N. or that of Dr. Schreber, suggest that the subject-object reversal is carried out through biased sampling of the contextual ecology. By inappropriately weighting "facts"—that N. was evicted from his apartment; that most men's jackets have slits in the back; that people did, in some literal sense, follow N. at times; that Gerald Ford had assumed the presidency around this period, and so on—led N. to the conclusion that he was the victim of homosexual persecution. Modern social-psychological research is providing experimental corroboration of the existence of "motivational attributional biases" that result in projection or other "defensive attributions" (cf. Burger, 1981; G. G. Sherwood, 1981). (For a critique of the evidence and for a comment on the critique see, respectively, Holmes, 1981; G. G. Sherwood, 1982.) Colby's simulation of the paranoid process (Colby, 1981; Faught, Colby, and Parkinson, 1977) provides, of course, an articulated information-processing treatment of this general approach to projection.

Reaction Formation

One ubiquitous fact to emerge from real-life examples is that defenses (like the dream-work processes) never operate in isolation but in organic combinations. Even the brief case report on N. illustrates this fact in several ways. N.'s paranoid features, for example, are heavily supplemented by reaction formation, another defense that can be viewed as constituting a propositional mistransformation (cf. Freud, 1911; Suppes and Warren, 1975).

In the case of reaction formation it is the propositional predicate that is reversed—into its opposite. Thus, the unacceptable proposition,

I *love* him

is transformed on its way to consciousness into,

I *hate* him.

In paranoid cases, the projections utilized tend to engender extensive reaction formations. If one sees himself as inexplicably persecuted by homosexuals, it is only natural to vent one's hatred upon the persecutors. In Freud's formula (1911, p. 63): "I do not *love* him—I *hate* him, because HE PERSECUTES ME."

In short, projection gives one a sustaining rationale for reaction formation.

Rationalization

The term *rationalization* was coined by Ernest Jones and adopted by Freud to refer to the biased selection or concoction of rationales. The biased deployment of rationales (reasons, causes, explanations, and so forth) can serve as an effective defense because disturbing or unacceptable feelings (thoughts, behaviors) can often be rendered acceptable if a proper reason can be found for them. We have here, then, one more case of attributional bias, that is, a bias concerning causes. It would be unacceptable to experience hatred toward a person or subgroup (Ford, homosexuals) unless one had good reasons to do so. N.'s eminently good reason—had the reason been true—was that they persecuted him. As Aesop showed long ago in his story of the fox and the grapes, rationalizations can also mitigate one's distress over personal failures. Thus, according to N., his abandonment of heterosexual relations was not a case of impotence (having perhaps to do with his underlying homosexuality) but a reasonable disinclination to "make love in public." As if this were not enough of a reason, N. adds his later insight that laser rays had been directed at him, at the behest of Nixon, to disrupt his sexual functioning.

Since the cause of one's behavior is never an easy matter to determine (cf. Nisbett and Wilson, 1977; Nisbett and Ross, 1980), it becomes an easy matter to select, among a variety of potential causal explanations, the one that results in the diminution of distress. Thus, rationalization, like other defense mechanisms, may be understood as a particular form of biased information-processing.

Symbolization

Symbolization, as we have seen in our discussion of the dream-work, can be used defensively and is often indistinguishable from censorship devices (hints and allusions, displacement of accent, and so forth). For no obvious reason, it is rarely referred to in the psychoanalytic literature as a defense mechanism in its own right, except in the special guise of "undoing" (Freud, 1909), which refers to a *symbolic act* of denial.

The paranoid subject, N., symbolically denies his latent homosexuality (more precisely, his anal eroticism) by sewing up the slits in the back of his jackets—as if to say, through "dramatization" or "plastic word representation," that that part of his body is closed. But symbolization is also used as a technique of repression/isolation/censorship (allusional reference), as for example in the use of "slot" instead of "slit"; N.'s representation of his backside in terms of the backside of his jacket; N.'s representation of his homosexual aspect in terms of his "double"; N.'s experience of "penetration" despite his defensive effort (his special "hat"); and so forth.

Conclusion

It should be clear that the distinctions among the defenses are rarely, perhaps never, a clear-cut matter. Denial can be effected through symbolization; symbolization can be viewed as a form of displacement (symbols, after all, are "substitute formations"); projection and reaction formation may in turn be understood as extreme forms of displacement; sublimation is a special variant of displacement; projection and reaction formation are also special forms of denial—special types of failures of insight ("*I* do not love him, *he* loves me;" "I do not *love* him, I *hate* him," and so on)—arising from tendentious sampling of the contextual ecology; denial is a special form of repression/suppression/censorship; and so forth.

It is for this reason that the attempt to distinguish between repression in the narrow sense and repression in the general sense (defense) is not likely to prove theoretically fruitful (Erdelyi and Goldberg, 1979). There is probably no standard or discrete list of defensive tactics, just as there are no finite number of sentences in the English language. The specific tactics are probably infinite, though the basic strategy is uniform: biased processing in the service of defense.

REFERENCES

♦

Most quotations from Freud are taken from the *Standard Edition of the Complete Psychological Works of Sigmund Freud* (Hogarth Press), edited by James Strachey. However, all references to Freud's *General Introduction to Psychoanalysis* (entitled *Introductory Lectures on Psychoanalysis* in the *Standard Edition*) are from Joan Riviere's translation (Liveright). In a few other cases, where translations from other than the *Standard Edition* are used, the fact is indicated in the text by the inclusion, following the original date of publication and a slash, of a second date, which indicates the publication date of the alternate translation used; the full reference to the alternate translation is provided here, along with that of the *Standard Edition.*

Aborn, M. 1953. The influence of experimentally induced failure on the retention of material acquired through set and incidental learning. *Journal of Experimental Psychology, 45,* 225–231.

Aldridge, A. (Editor.) 1980. *The Beatles Illustrated Lyrics.* New York: Dell.

Allers, R., and Teler, J. (1924.) On the utilization of unnoticed impressions in associations. Translated by J. Wolff, D. Rapaport, and S. Annin. *Psychological Issues, 3,* 1960, Monograph 7, 121–154.

Anderson, B. W. 1957. *Understanding the Old Testament.* Englewood Cliffs, N.J.: Prentice-Hall.

Apfelbaum, B. 1965. Ego psychology, psychic energy, and the hazards of quantitative explanation in psycho-analytic theory. *International Journal of Psycho-Analysis, 46,* 168–181.

Archer, B. U., and Margolin, R. R. 1970. Arousal effects in intentional recall and forgetting. *Journal of Experimental Psychology, 86,* 8–12.

Ariam, S., and Siller, J. 1982. Effects of subliminal oneness stimuli in Hebrew on academic performance of Israeli high school students: Further evidence on the adaptation-enhancing effects of symbiotic fantasies in another culture using another language. *Journal of Abnormal Psychology, 91,* 343–349.

Atkinson, R. C., and Shiffrin, R. M. 1968. Human memory: A proposed system and its control processes. In *The Psychology of Learning and Motivation,* edited by K. W. Spence and J. T. Spence. Vol. 2. New York: Academic Press.

Atwood, G. E. 1971. An experimental study of visual imagination and memory. *Cognitive Psychology, 2,* 290–299.

Averbach, E., and Coriell, A. S. 1961. Short-term memory in vision. *Bell Systems Technical Journal, 40,* 309–328.

Averbach, E., and Sperling, G. 1961. Short-term storage of information in vision. In *Symposium on Information Theory,* edited by C. Cherry. London: Butterworth.

Baddeley, A. D. 1976. *The Psychology of Memory.* New York: Basic Books.

Bakan, P. 1969. Hypnotizability, laterality of eye-movements, and functional brain asymmetry. *Perceptual and Motor Skills, 28,* 927–932.

Balota, D. A. 1983. Automatic semantic activation and episodic memory encoding. *Journal of Verbal Learning and Verbal Behavior, 22,* 88–104.

Bandura, A. 1969. *Principles of Behavior Modification.* New York: Holt, Rinehart & Winston.

———. 1971. *Social Learning Theory.* Morristown, N.J.: General Learning Press.

———. 1977. *Social Learning Theory.* Englewood Cliffs, New Jersey: Prentice-Hall.

Bandura, A., and Walters, R. H. 1963. *Social Learning and Personality Development.* New York: Holt, Rinehart & Winston.

Barber, T. X. 1969. *Hypnosis: A Scientific Approach.* New York: Van Nostrand Reinhold.

Barber, T. X., and Ham, M. W. 1974. *Hypnotic Phenomena.* Morristown, N.J.: General Learning Press.

Bartlett, F. C. 1932. *Remembering.* Cambridge: Cambridge University Press.

Bateson, C. 1972. *Steps to an Ecology of Mind.* New York: Ballantine.

Berkson, W. 1974. *Fields of Force.* New York: Wiley.

Bernstein, M. 1956. *The Search for Bridey Murphy.* New York: Lancer.

Bjork, R. A. 1972. Theoretical implications of directed forgetting. In *Coding Processes in Human Memory,* edited by A. W. Melton and E. Martin. Washington, D.C.: Winston.

Bjork, R. A., LaBerge, D., and Legrand, R. 1968. The modification of short-term memory through instructions to forget. *Psychonomic Science, 10,* 55–56.

Bogen, J. E. (1969.) The other side of the brain: An appositional mind. In *The Nature of Human Consciousness,* edited by R. E. Ornstein. San Francisco: W. H. Freeman and Company, 1973.

Bogen, J. E., Fisher, E. D., and Vogel, P. J. 1965. Cerebral commissurotomy: A second case report. *Journal of the American Medical Association, 194,* 1328–1329.

Boring, E. G. 1950. *A History of Experimental Psychology.* New York: Appleton-Century-Crofts.

Bower, G. H. 1970. Organizational factors in memory. *Cognitive Psychology, 1,* 18–46.

Bowers, K. S. 1976. *Hypnosis for the Seriously Curious.* Monterey, Calif.: Brooks/Cole.

Bransford, J. D., and Franks, J. J. 1971. The abstraction of linguistic ideas. *Cognitive Psychology, 2,* 331–350.

Bransford, J. D., and McCarrell, N. S. 1974. A sketch of a cognitive approach to comprehension: Some thoughts about understanding what it means to comprehend. In *Cognition and the Symbolic Processes,* edited by W. B. Weimer and D. S. Palermo. Hillsdale, N.J.: Erlbaum.

Bregman, A. S. 1977. Perception and behavior as compositions of ideals. *Cognitive Psychology, 9,* 250–292.

Brenner, C. 1957. The nature and development of the concept of repression in Freud's writings. *Psychoanalytic Study of the Child, 12,* 19–46.

———. 1973. *An Elementary Textbook of Psychoanalysis* (2nd ed.). Garden City, N.Y.: Doubleday.

Breuer, J., and Freud, S. (1893.) On the psychical mechanism of hysterical phenomena: Preliminary communication. Translated by A. Strachey and J. Strachey. In *The Standard Edition of the Complete Psychological Works of Sigmund Freud,* edited by J. Strachey. Vol. 2. London: Hogarth Press, 1955.

———. (1895.) *Studies on Hysteria.* Translated by A. Strachey and J. Strachey. In *The Standard Edition of the Complete Psychological Works of Sigmund Freud,* edited by J. Strachey. Vol. 2. London: Hogarth Press, 1955.

Broadbent, D. E. 1958. *Perception and Communication.* London: Pergamon Press.

———. 1971. *Decision and Stress.* New York: Academic Press.

Broca, P. 1861. Remarques sur le siège de la faculté du langage articulé, suivies d'une observation d'aphémie (partie de la parole). *Bulletin de la Societé Anatomique de Paris, 6,* 330–357.

Brody, N. 1972. *Personality: Research and Theory.* New York: Academic Press.

Brown, J. 1958. Some tests of the decay theory of immediate memory. *Quarterly Journal of Experimental Psychology, 10,* 12–21.

Buñuel, L., and Dali, S. (1929.) *Un Chien Andalou.* New York: Simon and Schuster, 1963. (Film originally shown, 1929.)

Burger, J. W. 1981. Motivational biases in the attribution of responsibility for an accident: A meta-analysis of the defensive-attribution hypothesis. *Psychological Bulletin, 90,* 496–512.

Buss, A. H., and Brock, T. C. 1963. Repression and guilt in relation to aggression. *Journal of Abnormal and Social Psychology, 66,* 345–350.

Butterfield, F. 1979. *The New York Times,* January 21, p. E3.

Calderón de la Barca, P. (1635.) *La vida es sueño.* Madrid: Espasa-Calpe, 1971.

Capra, F. 1975. *The Tao of Physics.* New York: Bantam.

Carroll, L. (1865.) *Alice in Wonderland.* New York: Washington Square Press, 1976.

Carus, C. G. (1846.) The Unconscious. Part 1 of *Psyche: On the Development of the Soul.* Translated by C. Drake. New York: Spring Publications, 1970.

Cason, H. 1932. The Pleasure-Pain Theory of Learning. *Psychological Review, 39,* 440–466.

Castaneda, C. 1974. *Tales of Power.* New York: Simon and Schuster.

———. 1977. *The Second Ring of Power.* New York: Simon and Schuster.

———. 1981. *The Eagle's Gift.* New York: Simon and Schuster.

Cermak, L. S. 1982. *Human Memory and Amnesia.* Hillsdale, N.J.: Erlbaum.

Clark, R. W. 1971. *Einstein: The Life and Times.* New York: Avon.

Clarke-Stewart, A. 1983. *Children: Development through Adolescence.* New York: Wiley.

Colby, K. M. 1981. Modeling a paranoid mind. *The Behavioral and Brain Sciences, 4,* 515–560.

Colby, K. M., Hilf, F. D., Weber, S., and Kraemer, H. C. 1972. Turing-like indistinguishability tests for the validation of a computer simulation of paranoid processes. *Artificial Intelligence, 3,* 199–221.

Condon, T. J., and Allen, G. J. 1980. Role of psychoanalytic merging fantasies in systematic desensitization: A rigorous methodological approach. *Journal of Abnormal Psychology, 89,* 437–443.

Craik, F. I. M., and Lockhart, R. S. 1972. Levels of processing: A framework for memory research. *Journal of Verbal Learning and Verbal Behavior, 11,* 671–684.

Crowder, J. E., and Thornton, D. W. 1970. Effects of systematic desensitization, programmed fantasy and bibliotherapy on a specific fear. *Behavior Research and Therapy, 8,* 35–41.

Crowder, R. G. 1976. *Principles of Learning and Memory.* Hillsdale, N.J.: Erlbaum.

d'Espagnat, B. 1979. The quantum theory of reality. *Scientific American, 241,* 158–179.

D'Zurilla, T. J. 1965. Recall efficiency and mediating cognitive events in "experimental repression." *Journal of Personality and Social Psychology, 3,* 253–256.

D'Zurilla, T. J., Wilson, G. T., and Nelson, R. A. 1973. Preliminary study of the effectiveness of graduated prolonged exposure in the treatment of irrational fear. *Behavior Therapy, 4,* 672–685.

Davies, P. C. W. 1979. *The Forces of Nature.* Cambridge: Cambridge University Press.

Davis, J. C., and Okada, R. 1973. Recognition and recall of positively forgotten items. *Journal of Experimental Psychology, 89,* 181–186.

Davison, G. C., and Wilson, G. T. 1973. Processes of fear reduction in systematic desensitization: Cognitive and social reinforcement factors in humans. *Behavior Therapy, 4,* 1–21.

Delgado, J. 1967. Social rank and radio-stimulated aggressiveness in monkeys. *Journal of Nervous and Mental Disease, 144,* 383–390.

Delgado, J. M. R., Roberts, W. W., and Miller, N. E. 1954. Learning motivated by electrical stimulation of the brain. *American Journal of Physiology, 179,* 587–593.

Deese, J. 1972. *Psychology as Science and Art.* New York: Harcourt Brace Jovanovich.

Dement, W. C. 1976. *Some Must Watch While Some Must Sleep.* San Francisco: W. H. Freeman and Company.

Deutsch, H. 1965. *Neuroses and Character Types.* New York: International Universities Press.

Dixon, N. F. 1971. *Subliminal Perception: The Nature of a Controversy.* London: McGraw-Hill.

————. 1981. *Preconscious Processing.* New York: Wiley.

Dollard, J., and Miller, N. 1950. *Personality and Psychotherapy.* New York: McGraw-Hill.

Dooling, D. J., and Lachman, R. 1971. Effects of comprehension on retention of prose. *Journal of Experimental Psychology, 88,* 216–222.

Dostoyevsky, F. (1864.) *Notes from Underground.* Translated by C. Garnett. New York: Dell, 1960.

Eagle, M., Wolitzky, D. L., and Klein, G. S. 1966. Imagery: Effect of a concealed figure in a stimulus. *Science, 151,* 837–839.

Ebbinghaus, H. (1885.) *Memory.* Translated by H. A. Ruger and C. E. Bussenius. New York: Dover, 1964.

Edelson, M. 1975. *Language and Interpretation in Psychoanalysis.* New Haven, Conn.: Yale University Press.

Edinger, D. (1963.) *Bertha Pappenheim, Freud's Anna O.* Highland Park, Ill.: Congregation Solel, 1968.

Egan, J. P. 1958. *Recognition Memory and the Operating Characteristic.* Bloomington, Ind.: Indiana University Hearing and Communication Laboratory Technical Note (Contract No. AF19(604)-1962, AFCRC-TN-58-51).

Einstein, A., and Infeld, L. 1938. *The Evolution of Physics.* New York: Simon and Schuster.

Ellenberger, H. F. 1970. *The Discovery of the Unconscious.* New York: Basic Books.

————. 1972. The story of "Anna O.": A critical review with new data. *Journal of the History of the Behavioral Sciences, 8,* 267–279.

Epstein, W. 1972. Mechanisms of directed forgetting. In *The Psychology of Learning and Motivation: Advances in Research and Theory,* edited by G. Bower. Vol. 6. New York: Academic Press.

Erdelyi, M. H. 1970. Recovery of unavailable perceptual input. *Cognitive Psychology, 1,* 99–113.

————. 1972. The role of fantasy in the Pötzl (Emergence) phenomenon. *Journal of Personality and Social Psychology, 24,* 186–190.

————. 1974. A new look at the New Look: Perceptual defense and vigilance. *Psychological Review, 81,* 1–25.

————. 1982. A note on the level of recall, level of processing, and imagery hypotheses of hypermnesia. *Journal of Verbal Learning and Verbal Behavior, 21,* 656–661.

————. 1984. The recovery of unconscious (inaccessible) memories: Laboratory studies of hypermnesia. In *The Psychology of Learning and Motivation: Advances in Research and Theory,* edited by G. Bower. Vol. 18. New York: Academic Press, pp. 95–127.

———. 1985. On the transmutation of base bias (β) into informational gold (d'). Manuscript in preparation.

Erdelyi, M. H., and Appelbaum, G. A. 1973. Cognitive masking: The disruptive effect of an emotional stimulus upon the perception of contiguous neutral items. *Bulletin of the Psychonomic Society, 1,* 59–61.

Erdelyi, M. H., and Becker, J. 1974. Hypermnesia for pictures: Incremental memory for pictures but not words in multiple recall trials. *Cognitive Psychology, 6,* 159-171.

Erdelyi, M. H., and Blumenthal, D. 1973. Cognitive masking in rapid sequential processing: The effect of an emotional picture on preceding and succeeding pictures. *Memory and Cognition, 1,* 201–204.

Erdelyi, M. H., Finkelstein, S., Herrell, N., Miller, B., and Thomas, J. 1976. Coding modality vs. input modality in hypermnesia: Is a rose a rose a rose? *Cognition, 4,* 311–319.

Erdelyi, M. H., and Goldberg, B. 1979. Let's not sweep repression under the rug: Toward a cognitive psychology of repression. In *Functional Disorders of Memory,* edited by J. F. Kihlstrom and F. J. Evans. Hillsdale, N.J.: Erlbaum.

Erdelyi, M. H., and Kleinbard, J. 1978. Has Ebbinghaus decayed with time?: The growth of recall (hypermnesia) over days. *Journal of Experimental Psychology: Human Learning and Memory, 4,* 275–289.

Erdelyi, M. H., and Stein, J. 1981. Recognition hypermnesia: The growth of recognition memory (d') over time with repeated testing. *Cognition, 9,* 23–33.

Eriksen, C. W. 1952. Individual differences in defensive forgetting. *Journal of Experimental Psychology, 44,* 442–447.

———. 1958. Unconscious processes. In *Nebraska Symposium on Motivation: 1958,* edited by M. R. Jones. Lincoln: University of Nebraska Press.

———. (Editor.) 1962. *Behavior and Awareness.* Durham, N.C.: Duke University Press.

Eriksen, C. W., and Pierce, J. 1968. Defense mechanisms. In *Handbook of Personality Theory and Research,* edited by E. Borgatta and W. Lambert. Chicago: Rand McNally.

Eysenck, H. J. 1960. Learning theory and behavior therapy. In *Behavior Therapy and the Neuroses: Readings in Modern Methods of Treatment Derived from Learning Theory,* edited by H. J. Eysenck. Oxford, England: Pergamon Press.

Faught, W. S., Colby, K. M., and Parkinson, R. C. 1977. Inferences, affects, and intentions in a model of paranoia. *Cognitive Psychology, 9,* 153–187.

Fehrer, E., and Raab, D. 1962. Reaction time to stimuli masked by metacontrast. *Journal of Experimental Psychology, 63,* 143–147.

Fenichel, O. 1945. *The Psychoanalytic Theory of Neurosis.* New York: Norton.

Fisher, C. 1954. Dreams and perception. *Journal of the American Psychoanalytic Association, 3,* 380–445.

———. 1956. Dreams, images, and perception: A study of unconscious-preconscious relationships. *Journal of the American Psychoanalytic Association, 4,* 5–48.

———. 1959. The effects of subliminal visual stimulation on images and dreams: A validation study. *Journal of the American Psychoanalytic Association, 7,* 35–83.

Fiss, H., Goldberg, F., and Klein, G. 1963. Effects of subliminal stimulation on imagery and discrimination. *Perceptual and Motor Skills, 17,* 31–44.

Flavell, J. H. 1955. Repression and the "return of the repressed." *Journal of Consulting Psychology, 19,* 441–443.

———. 1977. *Cognitive Development.* Englewood Cliffs, N.J.: Prentice-Hall.

Flor-Henry, P. 1977. Progress and problems in psychosurgery. In *Current Psychiatric Therapies,* edited by J. H. Maserman. New York: Grune & Stratton.

Foulkes, D. 1978. *A Grammar of Dreams*. New York: Basic Books.

Fowler, C. A., Wolford, G., Slade, R., and Tassinary, L. 1981. Lexical access with and without awareness. *Journal of Experimental Psychology: General, 110, 341–362.*

Franks, J. J. 1974. Toward understanding understanding. In *Cognition and the Symbolic Processes*, edited by W. B. Weimer and D. S. Palermo. Hillsdale, N.J.: Erlbaum.

Freeman, L. 1972. *The Story of Anna O.* New York: Walker.

Freud, A. (1936.) *The Ego and the Mechanism of Defense*. Translated by C. Baines. New York: International Universities Press, 1946.

Freud, S. (1892a.) Sketches for the "preliminary communication" of 1893: (A) Letter to Joseph Breuer. In *The Standard Edition of the Complete Psychological Works of Sigmund Freud,* edited and translated by J. Strachey. Vol. 1. London: Hogarth Press, 1966. (Written, June, 1892; originally published, 1941.)

————. (1892b.) Sketches for the "preliminary communication" of 1893: (C) On the theory of hysterical attacks. In *The Standard Edition of the Complete Psychological Works of Sigmund Freud,* edited and translated by J. Strachey. Vol. 1. London: Hogarth Press, 1966. (Written, possibly with J. Breuer, in November, 1892; originally published, 1940.)

————. (1892–1893.) A case of successful treatment by hypnotism: With some remarks on the origin of hysterical symptoms through "counter-will." In *The Standard Edition of the Complete Psychological Works of Sigmund Freud,* edited and translated by J. Strachey. Vol. 1. London: Hogarth Press, 1966.

————. (1893.) Charcot. Translated by J. Bernays. In *Freud: Early Psychoanalytic Writings,* edited by P. Rieff. New York: Collier, 1963. Also in *The Standard Edition of the Complete Psychological Works of Sigmund Freud,* edited by J. Strachey. Vol. 3. London: Hogarth Press, 1962.

————. (1894.) The neuro-psychoses of defense. Translated by J. Rickman. In *The Standard Edition of the Complete Psychological Works of Sigmund Freud,* edited by J. Strachey. Vol. 3. London: Hogarth Press, 1962.

————. (1895.) *Project For A Scientific Psychology*. In *The Standard Edition of the Complete Psychological Works of Sigmund Freud,* edited and translated by J. Strachey. Vol. 1. London: Hogarth Press, 1966. (Unpublished manuscript, originally entitled "Psychology for Neurologists," completed in 1895.)

————. (1896a.) Further remarks on the defense neuro-psychoses of defense. Translated by J. Rickman. In *The Standard Edition of the Complete Psychological Works of Sigmund Freud,* edited by J. Strachey. Vol. 3. London: Hogarth Press, 1962.

————. (1896b.) The aetiology of hysteria. Translated by C. M. Baines and J. Strachey. In *The Standard Edition of the Complete Psychological Works of Sigmund Freud,* edited by J. Strachey. Vol. 3. London: Hogarth Press, 1962.

————. (1900.) *The Interpretation of Dreams*. In *The Standard Edition of the Complete Psychological Works of Sigmund Freud,* edited by J. Strachey. Vols. 4 and 5. London: Hogarth Press, 1953.

————. (1901a.) *On Dreams*. In *The Standard Edition of the Complete Psychological Works of Sigmund Freud,* edited and translated by J. Strachey. Vol. 5. London: Hogarth Press, 1953.

————. (1901b.) *The Psychopathology of Everyday Life*. Translated by A. Tyson. In *The Standard Edition of the Complete Psychological Works of Sigmund Freud,* edited by J. Strachey. Vol. 6. London: Hogarth Press, 1960.

————. (1905a.) On psychotherapy. Translated by J. Bernays and J. Strachey. In *The Standard Edition of the Complete Psychological Works of Sigmund Freud,* edited by J.

Strachey. Vol. 7. London: Hogarth Press, 1953. (Delivered as a lecture, 1904; originally published 1905.)

———. (1905b.) *Jokes and Their Relation to the Unconscious.* In *The Standard Edition of the Complete Psychological Works of Sigmund Freud,* edited and translated by J. Strachey. Vol. 8. London: Hogarth Press, 1960.

———. (1905c.) *Three Essays on the Theory of Sexuality.* In *The Standard Edition of the Complete Psychological Works of Sigmund Freud,* edited and translated by J. Strachey. Vol. 7. London: Hogarth Press, 1953.

———. (1905d.) Fragment of an analysis of a case of hysteria. Translated by A. Strachey and J. Strachey. In *The Standard Edition of the Complete Psychological Works of Sigmund Freud,* edited by J. Strachey. Vol. 7. London: Hogarth Press, 1953.

———. (1906.) My views on the part played by sexuality in the aetiology of the neuroses. Translated by J. Bernays. In *The Standard Edition of the Complete Psychological Works of Sigmund Freud,* edited and translated by J. Strachey. Vol. 7. London: Hogarth Press, 1953.

———. (1907.) Creative writers and day-dreaming. Translated by I. F. Grant Duff and J. Strachey. In *The Standard Edition of the Complete Psychological Works of Sigmund Freud,* edited by J. Strachey. Vol. 9. London: Hogarth Press, 1959. Also: The relationship of the poet to day-dreaming. Translated by I. F. Grant Duff. In *Freud: Character and Culture,* edited by P. Rieff. New York: Collier, 1963.

———. (1909.) Notes upon a case of obsessional neurosis. Translated by A. Strachey and J. Strachey. In *The Standard Edition of the Complete Psychological Works of Sigmund Freud,* edited by J. Strachey. Vol. 10. London: Hogarth Press, 1955.

———. (1911.) Psychoanalytic notes upon an autobiographical account of a case of paranoia (dementia paranoides). Translated by A. Strachey and J. Strachey. In *The Standard Edition of the Complete Psychological Works of Sigmund Freud,* edited by J. Strachey. Vol. 12. London: Hogarth Press, 1958.

———. (1912a.) The dynamics of transference. Translated by J. Riviere. In *Freud: Therapy and Technique,* edited by P. Rieff. New York: Collier, 1963. Also in: *The Standard Edition of the Complete Psychological Works of Sigmund Freud,* edited and translated by J. Strachey. Vol. 12. London: Hogarth Press, 1958.

———. (1912b.) A note on the unconscious in psychoanalysis. In *The Standard Edition of the Complete Psychological Works of Sigmund Freud,* edited by J. Strachey. Vol. 12. London: Hogarth Press, 1958.

———. (1913.) *Totem and Taboo.* In *The Standard Edition of the Complete Psychological Works of Sigmund Freud,* edited and translated by J. Strachey. Vol. 13. London: Hogarth Press, 1953.

———. (1914a.) On narcissism: An introduction. Translated by C. M. Baines. In *The Standard Edition of the Complete Psychological Works of Sigmund Freud,* edited by J. Strachey. Vol. 14. London: Hogarth Press, 1957.

———. (1914b.) *The History of the Psychoanalytic Movement.* Translated by J. Riviere and J. Strachey. In *The Standard Edition of the Complete Psychological Works of Sigmund Freud,* edited by J. Strachey. Vol. 14. London: Hogarth Press, 1957.

———. (1914c.) Remembering, repeating, and working-through: Further recommendations in the technique of psychoanalysis, II. Translated by J. Riviere and J. Strachey. In *The Standard Edition of the Complete Psychological Works of Sigmund Freud,* edited by J. Strachey. Vol. 12. London: Hogarth Press, 1958.

———. (1915a.) Repression. Translated by C. M. Baines and J. Strachey. In *The Standard Edition of the Complete Psychological Works of Sigmund Freud,* edited by J. Strachey. Vol.

14. London: Hogarth Press, 1957. Also: translated by C. M. Baines in *Freud: General Psychological Theory*, edited by P. Rieff. New York: Collier, 1963.

———. (1915b.) The unconscious. Translated by C. M. Baines and J. Strachey. In *The Standard Edition of the Complete Psychological Works of Sigmund Freud*, edited by J. Strachey. Vol. 14. London: Hogarth Press, 1957. Also: translated by C. M. Baines in *Freud: General Psychological Theory*, edited by P. Rieff. New York: Collier, 1963.

———. (1917.) *A General Introduction to Psychoanalysis*. Translated by J. Riviere. New York: Liveright, 1963. Also: *Introductory Lectures on Psychoanalysis*. In *The Standard Edition of the Complete Psychological Works of Sigmund Freud*, edited and translated by J. Strachey. Vols. 15 and 16. London: Hogarth Press, 1961 and 1963.

———. (1918.) From the history of an infantile neurosis. Translated by A. Strachey and J. Strachey. In *The Standard Edition of the Complete Psychological Works of Sigmund Freud*, edited by J. Strachey. Vol. 17. London: Hogarth Press, 1955.

———. (1919.) Lines of advance in psychoanalytic therapy. Translated by J. Riviere and J. Strachey. In *The Standard Edition of the Complete Psychological Works of Sigmund Freud*, edited by J. Strachey. Vol. 17. London: Hogarth Press, 1955.

———. (1920a.) A note on the prehistory of the technique of analysis. In *The Standard Edition of the Complete Psychological Works of Sigmund Freud*, edited and translated by J. Strachey. Vol. 18. London: Hogarth Press, 1955.

———. (1920b.) *Beyond the Pleasure Principle*. In *The Standard Edition of the Complete Psychological Works of Sigmund Freud*, edited and translated by J. Strachey. Vol. 18. London: Hogarth Press, 1955.

———. (1921.) *Group Psychology and the Analysis of the Ego*. In *The Standard Edition of the Complete Psychological Works of Sigmund Freud*, edited and translated by J. Strachey. Vol. 18. London: Hogarth Press, 1955.

———. (1923.) *The Ego and the Id*. Translated by J. Riviere and J. Strachey. In *The Standard Edition of the Complete Psychological Works of Sigmund Freud*, edited by J. Strachey. Vol. 19. London: Hogarth Press, 1961.

———. (1924.) The dissolution of the Oedipus-complex. Translated by J. Riviere and J. Strachey. In *The Standard Edition of the Complete Psychological Works of Sigmund Freud*, edited by J. Strachey. Vol. 19. London: Hogarth Press, 1961.

———. (1925a.) A note upon the "mystic writing pad." In *The Standard Edition of the Complete Psychological Works of Sigmund Freud*, edited and translated by J. Strachey. Vol. 19. London: Hogarth Press, 1961.

———. (1925b.) *An Autobiographical Study*. In *The Standard Edition of the Complete Psychological Works of Sigmund Freud*, edited and translated by J. Strachey. Vol. 20. London: Hogarth Press, 1959.

———. (1926.) *Inhibitions, Symptoms and Anxiety*. Translated by A. Strachey and J. Strachey. In *The Standard Edition of the Complete Psychological Works of Sigmund Freud*, edited by J. Strachey. Vol. 20. London: Hogarth Press, 1959.

———. (1927a.) *The Future of an Illusion*. Translated by W. D. Robson-Scott and J. Strachey. In *The Standard Edition of the Complete Psychological Works of Sigmund Freud*, edited by J. Strachey. Vol. 21. London: Hogarth Press, 1961.

———. (1927b.) *Humour*. Translated by J. Riviere and J. Strachey. In *The Standard Edition of the Complete Psychological Works of Sigmund Freud*, edited by J. Strachey. Vol. 21. London: Hogarth Press, 1961.

———. (1930.) *Civilization and its Discontents*. Translated by J. Riviere and J. Strachey. In *The Standard Edition of the Complete Psychological Works of Sigmund Freud*, edited by J. Strachey. Vol. 21. London: Hogarth Press, 1961.

———. (1933.) *New Introductory Lectures on Psychoanalysis*. In *The Standard Edition of the Complete Psychological Works of Sigmund Freud*, edited and translated by J. Strachey. Vol. 20. London: Hogarth Press, 1964.

———. (1937.) Analysis terminable and interminable. Translated by J. Riviere and J. Strachey. In *The Standard Edition of the Complete Psychological Works of Sigmund Freud*, edited by J. Strachey. Vol. 23. London: Hogarth Press, 1964.

———. (1940.) *An Outline of Psycho-Analysis*. In *The Standard Edition of the Complete Psychological Works of Sigmund Freud*, edited and translated by J. Strachey. London: Hogarth Press, 1964.

Galin, D. 1974. Implications for psychiatry of left and right cerebral specialization: A neurobiological context for unconscious processes. *Archives of General Psychiatry, 31*, 572–583.

Galin, D., Diamond, R., and Braff, D. 1977. Lateralization of conversion symptoms: More frequent on the left. *American Journal of Psychiatry, 134*, 578–580.

Garcia, J., McGowan, B. K., Ervin, F. R, and Koelling, R. A. 1968. Cues: Their relative effectiveness as a function of the reinforcer. *Science, 160*, 794–795.

Gazzaniga, M. S. 1970. *The Bisected Brain*. New York: Appleton-Century-Crofts.

Geiselman, R. E., Bjork, R. A., and Fishman, D. L. 1983. Disrupted retrieval in directed forgetting: A link with posthypnotic amnesia. *Journal of Experimental Psychology: General, 112*, 58–72.

Gibson, E. J. 1969. *Principles of Perceptual Learning and Development*. New York: Appleton-Century-Crofts.

Gibson, J. J. 1950. *The Perception of the Visual World*. Boston: Houghton Mifflin.

Gill, M. M. 1976. Metapsychology is not psychology. In *Psychology Versus Metapsychology*, edited by M. M. Gill and P. S. Holzman. New York: International Universities Press.

Gill, M. M., and Holzman, P. S. (Editors.) 1976. *Psychology Versus Metapsychology*. New York: International Universities Press.

Gillespie, R. D. 1942. *Psychological Effects of War on Citizen and Soldier*. New York: Norton.

Glass, A. L., Holyoak, K. J., and Santa, J. L. 1979. *Cognition*. Reading, Mass.: Addison-Wesley.

Glixman, A. F. 1949. Recall of completed and incompleted activities under varying degrees of stress. *Journal of Experimental Psychology, 39*, 281–295.

Gödel, K. 1931. Über formal unentscheidbare Sätze der Principia Mathematica und verwandter System I. *Monatshefte für Mathematik und Physik, 38*, 173–198.

Goodall, J. 1971. *In the Shadow of Man*. Boston: Houghton Mifflin.

Gould, R. 1942. Repression experimentally analyzed. *Character and Personality, 10*, 259–288.

Graf, P., Squire, L. R., and Mandler, G. 1984. The information that amnesic patients do not forget. *Journal of Experimental Psychology: Learning, Memory, and Cognition, 10*, 164–178.

Gray, H. 1973. *Anatomy of the Human Body*. Philadelphia: Lea & Febiger.

Green, D. M., and Swets, J. A. 1966. *Signal Detection Theory and Psychophysics*. New York: Wiley.

Greenwald, A. G. 1980. The totalitarian ego: Fabrication and revision of personal history. *American Psychologist, 35*, 603–618.

Gregory, R. L. 1969. *Eye and Brain*. New York: McGraw-Hill.

Grinker, R. R., and Spiegel, J. P. 1945a. *Men Under Stress.* New York: Blakiston.

———. 1945b. *War Neurosis.* New York: Blakiston.

Guntrip, H. 1961. *Personality Structure and Human Interaction.* London: Hogarth Press.

Gur, R. E., and Gur, R. C. 1975. Defense mechanisms, psychosomatic symptomatology, and conjugate lateral eye movements. *Journal of Consulting and Clinical Psychology, 43,* 416–420.

Haber, R. N., (Editor.) 1968. *Contemporary Theory and Research in Visual Perception.* New York: Holt, Rinehart & Winston.

———. 1969. *Information-Processing Approaches to Visual Perception.* New York: Holt, Rinehart & Winston.

Haber, R. N., and Erdelyi, M. H. 1967. Emergence and recovery of initially unavailable perceptual material. *Journal of Verbal Learning and Verbal Behavior, 26,* 618–628.

Hall, M. M., Hall, G. C., and Lavoie, P. 1968. Ideation in patients with unilateral or bilateral midline brain lesions. *Journal of Abnormal Psychology, 73,* 526–531.

Harris, R. J., and Monaco, G. E. 1978. The psychology of pragmatic implication: Information processing between the lines. *Journal of Experimental Psychology: General, 107,* 1–22.

Hartmann, H. (1927.) Understanding and explanation. In *Essays on Ego Psychology.* New York: International Universities Press, 1964, pp. 369–403.

———. (1939.) *Ego Psychology and the Problem of Adaptation.* New York: International Universities Press, 1958.

Hartmann, H., Kris, E., and Loewenstein, R. M. (1945–1962.) Papers on psychoanalytic psychology. *Psychological Issues,* Monograph 14. New York: International Universities Press, 1964.

Haspel, K. C., and Harris, R. S. 1982. Effect of tachistoscopic stimulation of unconscious Oedipal wishes on competitive performance: A failure to replicate. *Journal of Abnormal Psychology, 91,* 437–443.

Heath, R. G., and Mickle, W. A. 1960. Evaluation of seven years' experience with depth electrode studies in human patients. In *Electrical Studies on the Unanesthetized Brain,* edited by E. R. Ramey and D. S. O'Doherty. New York: Hoeber.

Hecaen, H. 1964. Mental symptoms associated with tumors of the frontal lobe. In *The Frontal Granular Cortex and Behavior,* edited by J. M. Warren and K. Akert. New York: McGraw-Hill.

Heilbrun, K. S. 1980. Silverman's subliminal psychodynamic activation: A failure to replicate. *Journal of Abnormal Psychology, 89,* 560–566.

Heisenberg, W. 1971. *Physics and Beyond.* New York: Harper & Row.

Helmholtz, H. von. (1850.) *Physiological Optics.* Edited by J. P. C. Southall. Optical Society of America, 1925.

Hesse, M. B. 1961. *Forces and Fields.* New York: Thomas Nelson & Sons.

Hilgard, E. R. 1962. What becomes of the input from the stimulus? In *Behavior and Awareness,* edited by C. W. Eriksen. Durham, N.C.: Duke University Press.

———. 1965. *Hypnotic Susceptibility.* New York: Harcourt, Brace, and World.

———. 1973. A neodissociation interpretation of pain reduction in hypnosis. *Psychological Review, 80,* 396–411.

———. 1977. *Divided Consciousness: Multiple Controls in Human Thought and Action.* New York: Wiley.

Holmes, D. S. 1972. Repression or interference? A further investigation. *Journal of Personality and Social Psychology, 22,* 163–170.

————. 1974. Investigations of repression: Differential recall of material experimentally or naturally associated with ego threat. *Psychological Bulletin, 81,* 632–653.

————. 1981. Existence of classical projection and the stress-reducing function of attributive projection: A reply to Sherwood. *Psychological Bulletin, 90,* 460–466.

Holmes, D. S., and Schallow, J. R. 1969. Reduced recall after ego threat: Repression or response competition? *Journal of Personality and Social Psychology, 13,* 145–152.

Holt, R. R. 1965. A review of some of Freud's biological assumptions and their influence on his theories. In *Psychoanalysis and Current Biological Thought,* edited by N. S. Greenfield and W. C. Lewis. Madison: University of Wisconsin Press.

————. 1972. Freud's mechanistic and humanistic images of man. In *Psychoanalysis and Contemporary Science,* edited by R. R. Holt and E. Peterfreund. Vol. 1. New York: Macmillan.

————. 1976. Drive or wish? A reconsideration of the psychoanalytic theory of motivation. In *Psychology Versus Metapsychology,* edited by M. M. Gill and P. S. Holzman. New York: International Universities Press.

Holt, R. R., and Peterfreund, E. (Editors.) 1972. *Psychoanalysis and Contemporary Science.* New York: International Universities Press.

Holzman, P. S. 1976. Theoretical models and the treatment of the schizophrenias. In *Psychology Versus Metapsychology,* edited by M. M. Gill and P. S. Holzman. New York: International Universities Press.

Holzman, P. S., and Klein, G. S. 1954. Cognitive system-principles of leveling and sharpening: Individual differences in assimilation effects in visual time-error. *Journal of Psychology, 37,* 105–122.

Hook, S. (Editor.) 1959. *Psychoanalysis, Scientific Method, and Philosophy.* New York: New York University Press.

Hull, C. L. 1943. *Principles of Behavior.* New York: Appleton-Century-Crofts.

Jackson, J. H. (1874.) On the scientific and empirical investigation of epilepsies. In *Selected Writings of John Hughlings Jackson,* edited by J. Taylor. New York: Basic Books, 1958.

Jacobson, E. 1938. *Progressive Relaxation.* Chicago: Chicago University Press.

Jacoby, L. L., and Witherspoon, D. 1982. Remembering without awareness. *Canadian Journal of Psychology, 32,* 300–324.

James, W. 1890. *The Principles of Psychology.* Vol. 1. New York: Holt.

————. 1902. *The Varieties of Religious Experience: A Study in Human Nature.* New York: Longmans, Green & Co.

Janis, I., Mahl, G., Kagan, J., and Holt, R. 1969. *Personality: Dynamics, Development, and Assessment.* New York: Harcourt, Brace & World.

Jones, E. 1953. *The Life and Work of Sigmund Freud.* Vol. 1. New York: Basic Books.

Jones, R. S. 1982. *Physics and Beyond.* Minneapolis: University of Minnesota.

Joyce, J. (1916.) *A Portrait of the Artist as a Young Man.* New York: Modern Library, 1928.

Joyce, J. (1939.) *Finnegan's Wake.* New York: Viking, 1945.

Jung, C. G. (1906.) *Studies in Word-Association.* Translated by M. D. Eder. London: Heinemann, 1918.

————. (1928.) Two essays on analytical psychology. Translated by R. F. C. Hull. In *The Collected Works of C. G. Jung,* edited by H. Read, M. Fordham, and G. Adler. Princeton, N. J.: Princeton University Press, 1953.

————. (1935.) *Analytical Psychology: Its Theory and Practice.* New York: Pantheon, 1968. (Originally presented at the Tavistock Clinic, 1935.)

Jung, C. G., and Riklin, F. (1904–1905.) Experimentelle Untersuchung über Assoziationen Gesunder. *Journal für Psychologie und Neurologie, 3–4,* 55–83, 145–164, 193–214, 238–308, 24–67, 109–123.

Kafka, F. (1915.) The metamorphosis. In *Selected Short Stories of Franz Kafka,* translated by W. Muir and E. Muir. New York: Modern Library, 1952.

Kahneman, D. 1968. Method, findings, and theory in studies of visual masking. *Psychological Bulletin, 70,* 404–425.

———. 1973. *Attention and Effort.* Englewood Cliffs, N.J.: Prentice-Hall.

Kardiner, A., and Spiegel, H. 1947. *War Stress and Neurotic Illness.* New York: Hoeber.

Kasanin, J. S. (Editor.) 1964. *Language and Thought in Schizophrenia.* New York: Norton.

Kazdin, A. E., and Wilcoxon, L. A. 1976. Systematic desensitization and nonspecific treatment effects: A methodological evaluation. *Psychological Bulletin, 83,* 729–758.

Kelly, G. A. 1963. *A Theory of Personality: The Psychology of Personal Constructs.* New York: Norton.

Ketcham, H. 1974. Dennis the Menace. *New York Post,* June 15.

Kihlstrom, J. F., and Evans, F. J. 1976. Recovery of memory after posthypnotic amnesia. *Journal of Abnormal Psychology, 85,* 564–569.

———. 1979. Memory retrieval processes during posthypnotic amnesia. In *Functional Disorders of Memory,* edited by J. F. Kihlstrom and F. J. Evans. Hillsdale, N.J.: Erlbaum.

Kihlstrom, J. F., Evans, F. J., Orne, E. C., and Orne, M. T. 1980. Attempting to breach posthypnotic amnesia. *Journal of Abnormal Psychology, 89,* 603–616.

Klatzky, R. L. 1980. *Human Memory: Structures and Processes.* San Francisco: W. H. Freeman and Company.

Klein, D. B. 1977. *The Unconscious: Invention or Discovery?* Santa Monica, Calif.: Goodyear.

Klein, G. S. 1958. Cognitive control and motivation. In *Assessment of Human Motives,* edited by G. Lindzey. New York: Holt, Rinehart & Winston.

———. 1970. *Perception, Motives, and Personality.* New York: Knopf.

———. 1973. Is psychoanalysis relevant? In *Psychoanalysis and Contemporary Science,* edited by B. Rubinstein. Vol. 2. New York: Macmillan.

———. 1975. *Psychoanalytic Theory: An Explanation of Essentials.* New York: International Universities Press.

Klein, G. S., and Schlesinger, H. J. 1949. Where is the perceiver in perceptual theory? *Journal of Personality, 18,* 32–47.

Klein, M. 1932. *The Psychoanalysis of Children.* London: Hogarth Press and Institute of Psychoanalysis.

Kline, M. V. 1958. The dynamics of hypnotically induced anti-social behavior. *Journal of Psychology, 45,* 239–245.

Klüver, H., and Bucy, P. C. 1939. Preliminary analysis of functions of the temporal lobes in monkeys. *Archives of Neurology and Psychiatry, 42,* 979–1000.

Koch, H. I. 1930. The influence of some affective factors upon recall. *Journal of Genetic Psychology, 4,* 171–190.

Koestler, A. 1964. *The Act of Creation.* New York: Dell.

———. 1967. *The Ghost in the Machine.* Chicago: Henry Regnery.

———. 1972. *The Roots of Coincidence.* New York: Vintage.

Kohlberg, L. 1981. *The Philosophy of Moral Development.* New York: Harper & Row.

Köhler, W. 1940. *Dynamics in Psychology.* New York: Liveright.

Kovach, B. 1974. House and Nixon seem near clash on withheld data. *The New York Times*, March 13, p. 1.

Kris, E. (1947.) The nature of psychoanalytic propositions and their validation. In *Psychological Theory: Contemporary Readings*, edited by M. H. Marx. New York: Macmillan, 1951.

———. (1932–1952.) *Psychoanalytic Explorations in Art*. New York: International Universities Press, 1952.

Kuhn, T. S. 1962. *The Structure of Scientific Revolutions*. Chicago: University of Chicago Press.

Kunst-Wilson, W. R., and Zajonc, R. B. 1980. Affective discrimination of stimuli that cannot be recognized. *Science, 207*, 557–558.

Lazarus, R. S., and Longo, N. 1953. The consistency of psychological defense against threat. *Journal of Abnormal and Social Psychology, 48*, 495–499.

Leary, D. 1983. Psyche's Muse: The role of metaphor in psychology. Paper presented at the Annual Meeting of the Western Psychological Association, San Francisco, April, 29.

Levy, J. 1969. Possible basis for the evolution of lateral specialization of the human brain. *Nature, 224*, 614–625.

Levy, J., Trevarthen, C., and Sperry, R. W. 1972. Perception of bilateral chimeric figures following hemispheric disconnection. *Brain, 95*, 61–78.

Lindner, R. 1955. *The Fifty-Minute Hour*. New York: Holt, Rinehart & Winston.

Lindsay, P. H., and Norman, D. A. 1972. *Human Information Processing*. New York: Academic Press.

Loftus, E. F., and Burns, T. E. 1981. Mental shock. Paper presented at the Annual Meeting of the Psychonomic Society, Philadelphia, November.

Loftus, E. F., and Loftus, G. R. 1980. On the permanence of stored information in the human brain. *American Psychologist, 35*, 409–420.

Loftus, E. F., and Zanni, G. 1975. Eyewitness testimony: The influence of the wording of a question. *Bulletin of the Psychonomic Society, 5*, 86–88.

Loney, A. M. 1904. *A Treatise on Elementary Dynamics*. Cambridge: At the University Press.

Lorenz, K. 1966. *On Aggression*. New York: Harcourt Brace Jovanovich.

Luborsky, L. 1984. *Principles of Psychoanalytic Psychotherapy*. New York: Basic Books.

Luria, A. R., and Homskaya, E. D. 1970. Frontal lobe and the regulation of arousal processes. In *Attention: Contemporary Theory and Research*, edited by D. Mostofsky. New York: Appleton-Century-Crofts.

McCauley, C., Parmelee, C. M., Sperber, R. D., and Carr, T. H. 1980. Early extraction of meaning from pictures and its relation to conscious identification. *Journal of Experimental Psychology: Human Perception and Performance, 6*, 265–276.

McGinnies, E. 1949. Emotionality and perceptual defense. *Psychological Review, 56*, 244–251.

MacIntyre, A. C. 1958. *The Unconscious*. London: Routledge & Kegan Paul.

MacKinnon, D., and Dukes, W. 1964. Repression. In *Psychology in the Making*, edited by L. Postman. New York: Knopf.

MacLean, P. D. 1949. Psychosomatic disease and the "visceral brain": Recent developments bearing on the Papez theory of emotion. *Psychosomatic Medicine, 11*, 338–353.

———. 1958. Contrasting functions of limbic and neocortical systems of the brain and their relevance to psycho-physiological aspects of medicine. *American Journal of Medicine, 25*, 611–626.

MacLeod, C. M. 1975. Long-term recognition and recall following directed forgetting. *Journal of Experimental Psychology: Human Learning and Memory, 104,* 271–279.

Madden, R. L. 1974. By 383 to 8, House votes bill to strengthen public's access to government information and records. *The New York Times,* March 15, p. 15.

Madison, P. 1956. Freud's repression concept. *International Journal of Psychoanalysis, 37,* 75–81.

———. 1961. *Freud's Concept of Repression and Defense, It's Theoretical and Observational Language.* Minneapolis: University of Minnesota Press.

Mahl, G. F. 1969. *Psychological Conflict and Defense.* New York: Harcourt Brace Jovanovich.

Mandler, G., and Shebo, B. J. 1981. The Kunst-Wilson and Zajonc experiment: Failures to replicate. Unpublished paper.

Manuel, F. E. 1968. *A Portrait of Isaac Newton.* Cambridge: Cambridge University Press.

Marcel, A. J. 1980. Conscious and preconscious recognition of polysemous words: Locating the selective effects of prior verbal context. In *Attention and Performance VIII,* edited by R. Nickerson. Hillsdale, N.J.: Erlbaum.

———. 1983a. Conscious and unconscious perception: Experiments on visual masking and word recognition. *Cognitive Psychology, 15,* 197–237.

———. 1983b. Conscious and unconscious perception: An approach to the relations between phenomenal experience and perceptual processes. *Cognitive Psychology, 15,* 238–300.

Marcel, A. J., and Patterson, K. E. 1978. Word recognition and production: Reciprocity in clinical and normal studies. In *Attention and Performance VII,* edited by J. Requin. Hillsdale, N.J.: Erlbaum.

Martin, E. 1975. Generation-recognition theory and the encoding specificity principle. *Psychological Review, 82,* 150–153.

Melton, A. W. 1963. Implication of short-term memory for a general theory of memory. *Journal of Verbal Learning and Verbal Behavior, 2,* 1–21.

Meltzer, H. 1930. Individual differences in forgetting pleasant and unpleasant experiences. *Journal of Educational Psychology, 21,* 399–409.

Merikle, P. M. 1982. Unconscious perception revisited. *Perception & Psychophysics, 31,* 298–301.

Miller, G. A. 1956. The magical number seven, plus or minus two: Some limits on our capacity for processing information. *Psychological Review, 63,* 81–97.

Miller, G. A., Galanter, E., and Pribram, K. H. 1960. *Plans and the Structure of Behavior.* New York: Holt, Rinehart & Winston.

Miller, J. G. 1942. *Unconsciousness.* New York: Wiley.

Miller, N. E. 1935. The influence of past experience upon the transfer of subsequent training, Ph. D. dissertation, Yale University.

———. 1950. Learnable drives and rewards. In *Handbook of Experimental Psychology,* edited by S. Stevens. New York: Wiley.

Milner, P. M. 1970. *Physiological Psychology.* New York: Holt, Rinehart & Winston.

Mischel, W. 1976. *Introduction to Personality.* 2d ed. New York: Holt, Rinehart & Winston.

Monaco, G. E., and Harris, R. J. 1978. Theoretical issues in the psychology of implication: A reply to Keenan. *Journal of Experimental Psychology: General, 107,* 28–31.

Moore, E. H. 1935. A note on the recall of the pleasant vs. the unpleasant. *Psychological Review, 42,* 214–215.

Moray, N. 1970. *Attention: Selective Processes in Vision and Hearing.* New York: Academic Press.

Moscovitch, M. 1982. Multiple dissociations of function in amnesia. In *Human Memory and Amnesia,* edited by L. S. Cermak. Hillsdale, N.J.: Erlbaum.

Nagel, E., and Newman, J. R. 1973. *Gödel's Proof.* New York: New York University Press.

Neisser, U. 1967. *Cognitive Psychology.* New York: Appleton-Century-Crofts.

———. 1976. *Cognition and Reality.* San Francisco: W H. Freeman and Company.

———. 1981. John Dean's memory. *Cognition, 9,* 1–22.

———. 1982. *Memory Observed.* San Francisco: W. H. Freeman and Company.

Neisser, U., and Becklen, R. 1975. Selective looking: Attending to visually specified events. *Cognitive Psychology, 7,* 480–494.

The New York Times. 1974. December 15, p. 1.

———. 1974. Court limits F.B.I. on criminal files. April 24.

———. 1977. Vantage is solving a lot of my problems. June 14, p. C9.

———. 1979. November 3, p. 24.

———. 1979. A halt to funds for paper voted at City College. May 24, p. B3.

———. 1980. Four in Iran executed by stoning. July 4, p. 1.

———. 1981. Pakistan's grim Islamic law is not just a threat. September, 17, p. A2.

———. 1982. Censorship foes stage a "read-out" at library. February 4, p. B3.

Niederland, W. G. 1959. Schreber: Father and son. *Psychoanalytic Quarterly, 28,* 151–169.

———. 1974. *The Schreber Case.* New York: Quadrangle.

Nisbett, R. E., and Ross, L. 1980. *Human Inference: Strategies and Shortcomings of Social Judgment.* Englewood Cliffs, N.J.: Prentice-Hall.

Nisbett, R. E., and Wilson, T. D. 1977. Telling more than we can know: Verbal reports on mental processes. *Psychological Review, 84,* 231–259.

Norman, D. A. 1973. Discussion: Section 1. In *Contemporary Issues in Cognitive Psychology: The Loyola Symposium,* edited by R. L. Solso. Washington, D.C.: Winston.

———. 1976. *Memory and Attention.* 2d ed. New York: Wiley.

Oelsner, L. 1974. Nixon portrayed by prosecution as conspirator. *The New York Times,* October 15, pp. 1 and 30.

Olds, J. 1956. Pleasure centers in the brain. *Scientific American, 195,* 105–116.

———. 1958. Self-stimulation of the brain. *Science, 127,* 315–324.

Olds, J., and Milner, P. M. 1954. Positive reinforcement produced by electrical stimulation of septal area and other regions of the rat brain. *Journal of Comparative and Physiological Psychology, 47,* 419–427.

Orne, M. T., Soskis, D. A., Dinges, D. F., and Orne, E. C. 1984. Hypnotically-induced testimony and the criminal justice system. In *Eyewitness Testimony,* edited by G. L. Wells and E. F. Loftus. New York: Cambridge University Press.

Ortnoy, A. (Editor.) 1979. *Metaphor and Thought.* New York: Cambridge University Press.

Paivio, A. 1971. *Imagery and Verbal Processes.* New York: Holt, Rinehart & Winston.

Pap, A. 1959. On the empirical interpretation of psychoanalytic concepts. In *Psychoanalysis, Scientific Method, and Philosophy,* edited by S. Hook. New York: New York University Press.

Papez, J. W. 1937. A proposed mechanism of emotion. *Archives of Neurology and Psychiatry, 38,* 725–743.

Penfield, W. 1969. Consciousness, memory, and man's conditioned reflexes. In *On the Biology of Learning,* edited by K. Pribram. New York: Harcourt, Brace & World.

Penfield, W., and Perot, P. 1963. The brain's record of auditory and visual experience. *Brain, 86,* 595–596.

Penfield, W., and Roberts, L. 1959. *Speech and Brain Mechanisms.* Princeton, N.J.: Princeton University Press.

Peterfreund, E., and Schwartz, J. 1971. Information, systems and psychoanalysis. In *Psychological Issues,* edited by G. S. Klein. Vol. 7. New York: International Universities Press.

Peters, R. S. 1958. *The Concept of Motivation.* New York: Humanities Press.

Peterson, L. R., and Peterson, M. J. 1959. Short-term retention of individual verbal items. *Journal of Experimental Psychology, 58,* 193–198.

Philadelphia Daily News. 1982. Pope: Marriage is good, but virginity is better. June 24, p. 5.

Piaget, J. (1932.) *The Moral Judgment of the Child.* Translated by M. Gabain. New York: Free Press, 1960.

Plato. *The Republic.* Translated by B. Jowett. Book IX, pp. 280, 281. Oxford: Clarendon Press, 1888.

Plato. *The Timaeus.* In *The Dialogues of Plato,* translated by B. Jowett. Vol. 3. p. 514. London: Oxford University Press, 1892.

Polanyi, M. 1966. *The Tacit Dimension.* Garden City, N.Y.: Doubleday.

Posner, M. I., and Warren, R. E. 1972. Traces, concepts, and conscious constructions. In *Coding Processes in Human Memory,* edited by A. W. Melton and E. Martin. Washington, D.C.: Winston.

Pötzl, O. (1917.) The relationship between experimentally induced dream images and indirect vision. Translated by J. Wolff, D. Rapaport, and S. Annin. *Psychological Issues,* 1960, *3,* Monograph 7, 41–120.

Pribram, K. H., and Gill, M. M. 1976. *Freud's "Project" Reassessed.* New York: Basic Books.

Purcell, D. G., Stewart, A. L., and Stanovich, K. E. 1983. Another look at semantic priming without awareness. *Perception & Psychophysics, 34,* 65–67.

Raab, D. H. 1963. Backward masking. *Psychological Bulletin, 60,* 118–129.

Rakover, S. S. 1975. Voluntary forgetting before and after learning has been accomplished. *Memory and Cognition, 3,* 24–28.

Rapaport, D. (1942.) *Emotions and Memory.* New York: International Universities Press, 1971.

Ricoeur, P. 1970. *Freud and Philosophy: An Essay on Interpretation.* New Haven, Conn.: Yale University Press.

Rieff, P. (Editor.) 1963. *Freud: General Psychological Theory.* New York: Collier.

Robbins, H. 1981. *Goodbye Janette.* New York: Pocket Books.

Roediger, H. L. 1982. Hypermnesia: The importance of recall time and asymptotic level of recall. *Journal of Verbal Learning and Verbal Behavior, 21,* 662–665.

Roediger, H. L., and Crowder, R. G. 1972. Instructed forgetting: Rehearsal control or retrieval inhibition (repression)? *Cognitive Psychology, 3,* 255–267.

Roediger, H. L., Payne, D. G., Gillespie, G. L., and Lean, D. S. 1982. Hypermnesia as determined by level of recall. *Journal of Verbal Learning and Verbal Behavior, 21,* 635–655.

Rosenzweig, S. 1933. The recall of finished and unfinished tasks as affected by the purpose with which they were performed. *Psychological Bulletin, 30,* 698.

———. 1943. An experimental study of "repression" with special reference to need-persistive and ego-defensive reactions to frustrations. *Journal of Experimental Psychology, 32,* 64–74.

————. 1952. The investigation of repression as an instance of experimental idio-dynamics. *Psychological Review, 59*, 339–345.

Rosenzweig, S., and Mason, G. 1934. An experimental study of memory in relation to the theory of repression. *British Journal of Psychology, 24*, 247–265.

Rosvold, H. E., Mirsky, A. F., and Pribram, K. H. 1954. Influence of amygdalectomy on social behavior in monkeys. *Journal of Comparative and Physiological Psychology, 47*, 173–178.

Rubenstein, R., and Newman, R. 1954. The living out of "future" experiences under hypnosis. *Science, 119*, 472–473.

Rubinstein, B. B. 1973. On the logic of explanation in psychoanalysis. In *Psychoanalysis and Contemporary Science*, edited by B. B. Rubinstein. Vol. 2. New York: Macmillan.

————. 1975. On the clinical psychoanalytic theory and its role in the inference and con-firmation of particular clinical hypotheses. In *Psychoanalysis and Contemporary Science*, edited by D. P. Spence. Vol. 4. New York: International Universities Press.

————. 1976. On the possibility of a strictly clinical psychoanalytic theory: An essay in the philosophy of psychoanalysis. In *Psychology Versus Metapsychology*, edited by M. M. Gill and P. S. Holzman. New York: International Universities Press.

Russell, W. 1952. Retention of verbal material as a function of motivating instructions and experimentally induced failure. *Journal of Experimental Psychology, 43*, 207–216.

Sackeim, H. A., and Gur, R. C. 1977. Self-deception, self-confrontation and con-sciousness. In *Consciousness and Self-Regulation: Advances in Research*, edited by G. E. Schwartz and D. Shapiro. New York: Plenum.

Sackeim, H. A., Gur, R. C., and Saucy, M. C. 1978. Emotions are expressed more in-tensely on the left side of the face. *Science, 202*, 434–436.

Salmon, W. C. (1959.) *Psychoanalytic Theory and Evidence*. In *Philosophers on Freud*, edited by R. Wollheim. New York: Jason Aronson, 1977.

Sartre, J. P. (1943.) *Being and Nothingness: An Essay on Phenomenological Ontology*. Translated by H. M. Barnes. London: Methuen, 1958.

Saxon, W. 1979. Liu Shao-Chi's death reported by Peking. *The New York Times*, January 29, p. A9.

Schafer, R. 1976. *A New Language for Psychoanalysis*. New Haven, Conn: Yale University Press.

Schatzman, M. 1963. *Paranoia or Persecution: The Case of Schreber*. In *The Experience of Anxiety*, edited by M. J. Goldstein and J. D. Palmer. New York: Oxford University Press.

————. 1973. *Soul Murder: Persecution in the Family*. New York: Random House.

Schmeck, H. M. 1982. Mysterious thymus gland may hold the key to aging. *The New York Times*, January 26, pp. C1–C2.

Schneider, W., and Fisk, A. D. 1982. Concurrent automatic and controlled visual search: Can processing occur without resource cost? *Journal of Experimental Psychology: Learn-ing, Memory, and Cognition, 8*, 261–278.

Schrafstein, Ben-Ami. 1975. In *The Sound of the One Hand*, translated by Y. Hoffman. New York: Bantam.

Schreber, D. P. (1903.) *Memoirs of My Nervous Illness*. Edited and translated by I. Macal-pine and R. A. Hunter. London: Dawson, 1955.

Schreiber, F. R. 1973. *Sybil*. New York: Warner Books.

Schwartz, G. E., Davidson, R. J., and Maer, F. 1975. Right hemisphere lateralization for emotion in the human brain: Interactions with cognition. *Science, 190*, 286–288.

Sears, R. R.   1936. Functional abnormalities of memory with special reference to amnesia. *Psychological Bulletin, 33*, 229–274.

———.   1942. *Survey of Objective Studies of Psychoanalytic Concepts.* New York: Social Research Council.

Seligman, M. E. P.   1971. Phobias and preparedness. *Behavior Therapy, 2*, 307–320.

Sem-Jacobsen, C. W., and Torkildsen, A.   1960. Depth recording and electrical stimulation in the human brain. In *Electrical Studies on the Unanesthetized Brain,* edited by E. R. Ramey and D. S. O'Doherty. New York: Hoeber.

Shapiro, S., and Erdelyi, M. H.   1974. Hypermnesia for pictures but not words. *Journal of Experimental Psychology, 103,* 1218–1219.

Shebliske, W., and Epstein, W.   1973. Effects of forget instructions with and without the conditions of selective search. *Memory and Cognition, 1,* 261–267.

Sherwood, G. G.   1981. Self-serving biases in person perception: A reexamination of projection as a mechanism of defense. *Psychological Bulletin, 90,* 445–459.

———.   1982. Consciousness and stress reduction in defensive projection: A reply to Holmes. *Psychological Bulletin, 91,* 372–375.

Sherwood, M.   1969. *The Logic of Explanation in Psychoanalysis.* New York: Academic Press.

Shevrin, H., and Luborsky, L.   1958. The measurement of preconscious perception in dreams and images: An investigation of the Poetzl phenomenon. *Journal of Abnormal and Social Psychology, 56,* 285–294.

Shiffrin, R. M., and Atkinson, R. C.   1969. Storage and retrieval processes in long-term memory. *Psychological Review, 76,* 179–193.

Shope, R. K.   1973. Freud's concept of meaning. In *Psychoanalysis and Contemporary Science,* edited by B. B Rubinstein. Vol. 2. New York: Macmillan.

Shor, R. E., and Orne, M. T. (Editors.)   1965. *The Nature of Hypnosis.* New York: Holt, Rinehart & Winston.

Silverman, L. H.   1983. The subliminal psychodynamic activation method: Overview and comprehensive listing of studies. In *Empirical Studies of Psychoanalytic Theories,* edited by J. Masling. Vol. 1. Hillsdale, N.J.: Erlbaum.

Sjöbäck, H.   1973. *The Psychoanalytic Theory of Defensive Processes.* New York: Wiley.

Skinner, B. F.   1953. *Science and Human Behavior.* New York: Macmillan.

Slobin, D. I.   1971. *Psycholinguistics.* Glenville, Ill.: Scott, Foresman.

Smokler, I. A., and Shevrin, I.   1979. Cerebral lateralization and personality style. *Archives of General Psychiatry, 36,* 949–954.

Spanos, N. P., and Ham, M. L.   1973. Cognitive activity in response to hypnotic suggestion: Goal directed fantasy and selective amnesia. *The American Journal of Clinical Hypnosis, 15,* 191–198.

Spelt, D. K.   1948. The conditioning of the human fetus in utero. *Journal of Experimental Psychology, 38,* 375–376.

Spence, D. P.   1982. *Narrative Truth and Historical Truth: Meaning and Interpretation in Psychoanalysis.* New York: Norton.

Sperling, G.   1960. The information available in brief visual presentations. *Psychological Monographs, 74,* 11, Whole No. 498.

———.   1967. Successive approximations to a model of short term memory. *Acta Psychologica, 27,* 285–292.

Sperry, R. W.   1968. Hemisphere deconnection and unity in conscious awareness. *American Psychologist, 23,* 723–733.

Springer, S. P., and Deutsch, G. 1981. *Left Brain, Right Brain.* San Francisco: W. H. Freeman and Company.

Stern, D. B. 1977. Handedness and the lateral distribution of conversion reactions. *Journal of Nervous and Mental Disease, 164,* 122–128.

Stone, L. J., Smith, H. T., and Murphy, L. B. 1973. *The Competent Infant.* New York: Basic Books.

Suedfeld, P., Erdelyi, M. H., and Corcoran, C. R. 1975. Rejection of input in the processing of an emotional film. *Bulletin of the Psychonomic Society, 5,* 30–32.

Sulloway, F. J. 1979. *Freud: Biologist of the Mind.* New York: Basic Books.

Suppes, P., and Warren, H. 1975. On the generation and classification of defense mechanisms. *International Journal of Psychoanalysis, 56,* 405–414.

Suzuki, D. T. 1949. *Essays in Zen Buddhism.* New York: Grove Press.

Swets, J. A. (Editor.) 1964. *Signal Detection and Recognition by Human Observers.* New York: Wiley.

Swets, J. A., Tanner, W. P., and Birdsall, T. G. 1961. Decision processes in perception. *Psychological Review, 68,* 301–340.

Tao Tĕ-Ching. Translated by R. B. Blakney, New York: Mentor, 1955.

Thigpen, C. H., and Cleckley, H. M. 1957. *The Three Faces of Eve.* New York: McGraw-Hill.

Thompson, R. F. 1967. *Foundations of Physiological Psychology.* New York: Harper & Row.

Titchener, E. B. 1917. *A Textbook of Psychology.* New York: Macmillan.

Truax, C. B. 1957. The repression response to implied failure as a function of the hysteria-psychoasthenia index. *Journal of Abnormal and Social Psychology, 55,* 188–193.

Tucker, D. M. 1981. Lateral brain function, emotion, and conceptualization. *Psychological Bulletin, 89,* 19–46.

Tulving, E. 1972. Episodic and semantic memory. In *Organization and Memory,* edited by E. Tulving and W. Donaldson. New York: Academic Press.

Tulving, E., and Pearlstone, Z. 1966. Availability versus accessibility of information in memory for words. *Journal of Verbal Learning and Verbal Behavior, 5,* 381–391.

Tulving, E., and Thomson, D. M. 1973. Encoding specificity and retrieval processes in episodic memory. *Journal of Experimental Psychology, 80,* 352–373.

Tulving, E., Schachter, D. L., and Stark, H. A. 1982. Priming effects in word-fragment completion are independent of recognition memory. *Journal of Experimental Psychology: Learning, Memory, and Cognition, 8,* 336–343.

Turvey, M. T. 1973. On peripheral and central processes in vision: Inferences from an information-processing analysis of masking with patterned stimuli. *Psychological Review, 80,* 1–52.

Van de Castle, R. L. 1971. *The Psychology of Dreaming.* Morristown, N.J.: General Learning Press.

von Bertalanffy, L. 1968. *General Systems Theory.* New York: George Braziller.

Wachtel, P. 1977. *Psychoanalysis and Behavior Therapy.* New York: Basic Books.

Watson, J. B. 1924. *Behaviorism.* New York: Norton.

Watson, J. B., and Rayner, R. 1920. Conditioned emotional reactions. *Journal of Experimental Psychology, 3,* 1–14.

Watts, A. 1957. *The Way of Zen.* New York: Pantheon.

Webster's New World Dictionary. 1955. Springfield, Mass.: Merriam.

Wechsler, A. F. 1973. The effect of organic brain disease on recall of emotionally charged versus neutral narrative text. *Neurology, 23,* 130–135.

Wechsler, I. S. 1929. *The Neuroses*. Philadelphia: Saunders.

Weiner, B. 1968. Motivated forgetting and the study of repression. *Journal of Personality, 36*, 213–234.

Weisstein, N. 1966. Backward masking and models of perceptual processing. *Journal of Experimental Psychology, 72*, 232–240.

Werner, H. 1948. *Comparative Psychology of Mental Development*. New York: International Universities Press.

Wernicke, C. 1874. *Der Aphasische Symptomencomplex*. Breslau: Cohn & Weigert.

Whyte, L. L. 1960. *The Unconscious Before Freud*. New York: Basic Books.

Wilkins, W. 1971. Desensitization: Social and cognitive factors underlying the effectiveness of Wolpe's procedure. *Psychological Bulletin, 76*, 311–317.

Witcover, J. 1974. Memo shows Nixon taking 'culpability.' *The Washington Post*, June 18, pp. 1 and 7.

Wittgenstein, L. (1930–1933.)Wittgenstein's lectures in 1930–33. In *Philosophical Papers*, edited by G. E. Moore. London: Allen & Unwin, 1959. (Lectures originally delivered in 1930–1933.)

———. (1942, 1943, and 1946.) Conversations on Freud. In *Philosophers on Freud*, edited by R. Wollheim. New York: Jason Aronson, 1977. (Notes originally taken by R. Rhees in 1942, 1943, and 1946.)

———. (1946–1949.) *Philosophical Investigations*, 3d ed. Translated by G. E. M. Anscombe. New York: Macmillan, 1958. (Originally written between 1946–1949.)

Wolitzky, D. L., Klein, G. S., and Dworkin, S. F. 1976. An experimental approach to the study of repression: Effects of a hypnotically induced fantasy. In *Psychoanalysis and Contemporary Science*, edited by D. P. Spence. Vol. 4. New York: International Universities Press.

Wolpe, J. 1958. *Psychotherapy by Reciprocal Inhibition*. Stanford: Stanford University Press.

———. 1961. The systematic desensitization treatment of neuroses. *Journal of Nervous and Mental Disorders, 132*, 189–203.

———. 1973. *The Practice of Behavior Therapy*, 2d ed. New York: Pergamon Press.

Zeigarnik, B. 1927. Über das Behalten von erledigten und underledigten Handlungen. *Psychologische Forschungen, 9*, 1–85.

Zeller, A. 1950a. An experimental analogue of repression: I. Historical summary. *Psychological Bulletin, 47*, 39–51.

———. 1950b. An experimental analogue of repression: II. The effect of individual failure and success on memory measured by relearning. *Journal of Experimental Psychology, 40*, 411–422.

———. 1951. An experimental analogue of repression: III. The effect of induced failure and success on memory measured by recall. *Journal of Experimental Psychology, 42*, 32–38.

Zukav, G. 1979. *The Dancing Wu Li Masters*. New York: Bantam.

NAME INDEX

♦

SUBJECT INDEX

♦